POLITICS IN

Oxford in India Readings
in Sociology and Social Anthropology

GENERAL EDITOR
T. N. MADAN

POLITICS IN INDIA

Edited by
SUDIPTA KAVIRAJ

DELHI
OXFORD UNIVERSITY PRESS
CALCUTTA CHENNAI MUMBAI
1999

Oxford University Press, Great Clarendon Street, Oxford OX2 6DP

Oxford New York
Athens Auckland Bangkok Calcutta
Cape Town Chennai Dar es Salaam Delhi
Florence Hong Kong Istanbul Karachi
Kuala Lumpur Madrid Melbourne Mexico City
Mumbai Nairobi Paris Singapore
Taipei Tokyo Toronto

and associates in

Berlin Ibadan

© *Oxford University Press 1997*
First published 1997
Oxford India Paperbacks 1999

ISBN 0 19 564873 0

Typeset by Print Line, New Delhi 110048
Printed at A.P. Offset, Delhi 110032
and published by Manzar Khan, Oxford University Press
YMCA Library Building, Jai Singh Road, New Delhi 110001

Oxford in India Readings in Sociology and Social Anthropology

Other books available in the series :

Religion in India
T. N. Madan (ed.)

Social Ecology
Ramachandra Guha (ed.)

Family, Kinship and Marriage in India
Patricia Uberoi (ed.)

Social Stratification
Dipankar Gupta (ed.)

The Sociology of Formal Organizations
Abha Chaturvedi and Anil Chaturvedi (eds.)

Social Conflict
N. Jayaram and Satish Saberwal (eds.)

Forthcoming titles in the series include the following :
Social Demography
Methodology
Sociology of Law
Sociology of Education
Urban Society
Rural India

Contents

Contents

Introduction

SUDIPTA KAVIRAJ

The study of political facts can have two initial forms: its purpose can be either to describe or to explain. It can either simply content itself by asking *what* happened, or go on to enquire about *why* what happened did actually happen in that manner. But there can be various different styles of going down the explanatory path. It is well known that a discipline like politics uses both types of clarifications known to science: explanation by making a reference to causality, adapting that of course to the special complexities of the historical world, and understanding social actions by seeking their intentional horizons or reasons. Political explanations are normally mixed, in the sense that they must try to combine the logic of both types of puzzle solving procedures.[1] To identify a political act, to understand correctly exactly what kind of action it was, it is essential to refer to the world of intentions. First, it is necessary to understand what the actor intended his act to be. To use a well known example, it is an elementary but entirely unavoidable part of political analysis to determine whether the raising of a hand by an individual is a matter of simply involuntary physical action or an act of voting.[2] Or when we try to disentangle the possibility that someone simply has nervous tic which closes his eye, or he deliberately winked to convey a certain meaning.[3] Now, in both these simple cases, of winking and voting, the actor must refer to some generally accepted and implicitly shared ideas and social practices. The

identification of intention is thus not merely a matter of understanding individual psychological facts, but grasping conceptual
structures which are public, socially created and given.[4]

When we seek to understand the causes behind a political
fact, or event, or ask why did it happen, we can either take a
simple chronological line, and refer one state of affairs to a previous
one. For example, if we wish to understand why the Nehru government decided to follow a particular policy, we can refer to the
state of things existing in the previous regime. There is however
another, equally common way of finding out why something
happened: that is to refer political events to non-political phenomena of different kinds — like the state of the economy, or the
structure of the caste system or the cultural preferences of a particular group. Political sociology seeks to understand systematically the underlying social forces that determine the shape and
lines of movement of political life.

Political sociology represents the discipline which seeks an understanding of the political world through the sociological bases
of political action. Politics of all societies need to be looked at
that way, if we have to make any explanatory sense at all; if we
are not merely content with asking what happened in politics,
but why it happened that way, or why what happened did instead
of something else which was also possible. But, precisely because
it assumes an explanatory dimension some forms of political sociology can also easily fall into insupportibly large claims. It can,
for instance, contend that large and deterministic explanatory
claims of Marxian political economy are false, only to place its
own equally general substitutes on the ground from which Marxists have been freshly evicted. Unfortunately, much of the debate
about caste and class in Indian politics has sometimes been conducted in that spirit of unyielding dogmatism.

THE RELATION BETWEEN POLITICS AND SOCIOLOGY

Puzzlements about the relation between politics and other types
of practice[5] which together constitute a society must be the starting
point of a political sociology. There are various ways of seeing
society. One popular picture presents it as a complex whole which
is designed in layers. This picture which conceives of society like
a layered cake, or an architectural structure, is often accompanied

by a sense that there is some kind of a causal hierarchy among these levels or layers. Marxist scholarship has particularly accustomed us to thinking in terms of a dichotomy between surface and deep structures. The lower, and more underlying the level the more causally effective it is. The metaphor of underlyingness has an additional connotation. Since what lies under also often escapes notice, it can be implied that the most fundamental processes are not only causally most efficient but also unamenable to immediate knowledge of individuals living in society. This seems to create the picture of social 'nature' processes which affect and determine people's lives fundamentally, but which they do not understand and therefore cannot control. The most common form of this kind of thinking is again the Marxist idea that, of these various levels, the productive enjoys a kind of causal supremacy, the substance of the tangled debate about primacy of the economic or productive practices in a society's arrangement.[6]

Another fairly common and influential image is that of a floral model of social organization in which each petal stands for one type of substructure, forming by their interaction the global structure of society. The difference from the earlier picture is that it sees all petals as being necessary for the flower as a whole. It resists, intrinsically, a reductionist view of society, though it still can accommodate a sense of centrality if not determination. Different observers can choose to put one or the other practice at the centre of this arrangement. Putting a practice at the centre of this picture may have two different implications. It might suggest an epistemic strategy:since we study politics, it is at the centre of our cognitive field (like a visual field); for others, other things or processes may be similarly put at the centre of vision. A stronger view would claim an ontological priority for some practices, like the economic or the political. They would claim, in that case, not just that politics is at the centre of our attention, because of our contingent cognitive interest about this matter, but it is, in the nature of things, at the centre of the historical process. In this case, it is not very different from the deterministic thesis discussed earlier.

Whatever form and methodology it may take, political sociology must seek to elucidate the relation between politics and society, and must use tools from both these disciplines.

POLITICAL SOCIOLOGY IN INDIA

The discipline of political sociology in India is a relatively recent development. As academic disciplines, both politics and sociology existed in relative indifference towards each other till the sixties, although much that was excellent in social and political analysis was of course spontaneously interdisciplinary. Sociological interest in politics and political scientists' seeking help from sociological theories began through an appreciation of inadequacy in conventional studies of political facts. Political science emerged as a discipline in Indian universities in the late thirties. Initially, however, its methodological procedures were practically indistinguishable from constitutional law. The emphasis on constitutionalism is of course easily understandable in a new nation, quite apart from the influence of conventional study of political institutions in the West.[7] New states which got independence from colonial rule generally imitated constitutional forms of metropolitan states; and it was generally assumed that the constitutional form itself would provide the consequences in the shape of political stability, democratic rule, accountability of government, the features remarkable in the politics of western states. Political analysis in India in the early years after independence demonstrated an understandable naivete: a vaulting legal optimism that a wholly new and altogether better society would be constructed by the careful fashioning of clauses and subclauses by lawyers completely devoted to national unity and ideals of moderate social reform. Questions that were accorded great significance in political debates as well as academic discussions tended to be constitutional questions: to take two most important issues, the limits to the enjoyment of the right to property, which was involved in the abolition of zamindari; and the relations between centre and state governments, and the related issue of the discretionary powers of governors. It was only afterwards, as it appeared that actual politics diverged often quite significantly from constitutional legal rules, and understanding this required a different mode of analysis, that political scientists moved towards a more sociologically orientated questioning of their field: not only asking how many voted for a particular party, but why.

With the greater explanatory ambitions of political scientists, encouraged partly by the vogue for similar studies in the US at the time, a movement in sociology coincided. Social anthropologists, given conventionally to a blithe pretence of immutability of the structures they studied, confessed that these structures showed a perplexing capacity of altering themselves, although these had reportedly stayed unchanged for centuries.[8] Although such changes in structures of traditional social practice could be rather unhelpfully attributed to a vague and abstract logic of modernization, it called for more specific attribution of causality. It was felt that although economic reorganization of society through capitalist industrialization surely altered social structures, customary practices and identities changed with remarkable rapidity in response to direct inducements from parliamentary politics. Structures like caste, which showed a remarkable ability to withstand impact of economic reorganization, tended to respond with paradoxical flexibility to the invitations and opportunities of democratic electoral procedures. Not surprisingly, this kind of reflection went with a questioning of the conventional concept of tradition. Sociological theory had earlier defined tradition as a set of relatively static, unchanging practices, resistant to proposals for historical change. It seemed preferable to define tradition as a set of rules of social practice which adapted to historically altered conditions through a surreptitious adaptability, so that although they changed, they also typically tried to conceal the evidence, by an ideological rhetoric of immutability. If this latter conception of tradition was valid, then traditional structures of Indian society like caste or religious self-identifications would not be expected to melt away with the advent of modernity, but to adapt to the demands of new institutions.[9]

To understand politics, it is essential, therefore, to look at some of the enduring forms of social organization in India. Two of these durable modes of identity are religion and caste. Obviously, there is a certain oddity to speaking of them separately, as caste is a special mode of organization internal to Hinduism; but recent research has shown that the case is hardly so clear cut.[10] Other religions could not exist for centuries with close transactive relations with Hinduism without being affected by its central social processes. In India, Islam and Christianity, not as religious doctrines, but as social communities, show considerable influence of caste practices. If Nirmal Kumar Bose's seminal work is to be trusted in this matter of historical anthropology,[11] this was less due to revision of theological principles out of doctrinal transactions (which did happen in the case of Sufism), or a sort of practical memory of pre-conversion social practices (which might have initially played a part), than to the more insidious, tangible and overwhelming necessity of finding a place in the ongoing arrangement of production in a stable, firmly structured agrarian community. Other groups were slowly brought to submission by its logic of distribution of productive resources and roles in terms of caste. Both groups belonging to other religions, like Islam or Christianity, and to reform religions like Vaishnavism, may declare their hostility to the ideology of the caste system, but the productive roles of agricultural society were so firmly embedded in caste practices, that before the development of a substantial non-agrarian economy, it was impossible to break free of its economic logic. Bose's work is so startling because it shows an instance of an even stronger case of conversion of non-caste tribal communities into the Hindu caste system.[12] It is not wholly surprising that social groups which had recently converted themselves to Islam, would still have to continue with caste markers of their identity, as a sort of historical-practical memory. His work shows however that tribal groups who lived in more communitarian and equal social organizations before their amalgamation into Hindu society, had to use some technical productive skill to prise their way into Brahminical Hindu communities at times of crisis, and could do so only at the expense of accepting a caste identity. It appears that a similar logic of inclusion into the larger structure of the ongoing practices of the caste-based economy also holds for those who became Muslims and Christians. But in these cases, there is of course the added factor of their simply continuing with their earlier productive placement in society. Many Muslim or Christian groups therefore were treated as quasi-castes by Hindu society. And since they were involved in all manner of transactive networks, these social groups, irrespective of the doctrinal contradiction with their religious beliefs, had to respond to the Hindu segments of the society perhaps as quasi-castes.

Paradoxically, the caste system had been seen as the best illustration of the strange and peculiar immutability of the Indian social order.[13] It lay at the basis of all rumours of invincibility of the 'village community', since castes obviously existed at the time of the *Vedas* as indubitably as at the time of independence.

Yet it was also indubitably changing and restructuring itself under the pressure of electoral politics.[14] New caste categories were being introduced into the language of politics: the Scheduled Castes, a constitutional innovation and suggestion, which was initially a caste for others, gradually came to constitute a caste for themselves, a self-described and self-conscious agent of modern political action.[15]

There are two general questions which need to be asked about caste: first, whether caste is really as unchanging as its formal ideology makes it out to be. It seems misleading to state that traditional societies differ from modern ones in that the former are 'cold', and latter are 'hot', that they do not have history/change, and modern ones do. Undoubtedly, the nature and pace of change differ. But more significantly, traditional and modern societies seem to have different attitudes towards historical change. In traditional social formations, change operates within a governing rhetoric of continuity. Historical change is accomplished surreptitiously, without declaration or trace, often shamefacedly, with something like a sense of guilt. Even when these societies have changed, they try their best to pretend they have not. In modern societies, on the contrary, life is governed by a distinctive rhetoric of newness, so that even insignificant changes are celebrated as remarkable. In Indian society, there is plentiful trace of such historical changes in the caste structure. Most often, political power could alter the internal values of the caste system to some degree. Since the general rule was that the Kshatriyas would wield political authority, it was easy to convert this rule into its obverse in a historical universe of uncertainty in dynastic destinies and governments. Upstart rulers, often coming from the lower strata of caste or even outside settled Hindu society, usually found obliging Brahmins willing to read the doctrine the other way round, and enunciate that those who wielded political power must be treated as virtual Kshatriyas, and anoint them into a dubious but functional title to kingship. At this price, however, the system bought reprieve from destruction at the hands of those who came to acquire political power. Secondly, small-scale changes in caste status were possible, provided families and individuals moved long distances away from their former habitation. They appear to have been able to renegotiate their position in a different caste hierarchy of a separate region. Often this was rendered possible because of the great regional diversity of the caste hierarchy, that strictly equivalent castes were not always to be found in a different region to the one that one had left behind. Entrant or upwardly mobile groups would then undertake the cultural processes of what has been called Sanskritization.[16]

The second major question about caste relates to contemporary politics. Observers of Indian society and political policy makers expected at the time of independence that institutions of democratic government would éxert a destructive influence on the structures of caste. This argument was certainly not implausible. Two powerful and complementary forces were expected to work, inside the logic of modernity, against the segmentation constitutive of the caste order. Emergence of a modern economy of industrialized production, pursued in different ways by both the state and the private sector, would create pressures towards the formation of labour markets, ensuring relatively free movement of labour through the entire economy. This economically driven process of social individuation[17] was to be reinforced, it was believed, by the processes of electoral representative government. The powerful discourse of modern citizenship, which also created a stark relation between the individual and the state, breaking down all intermediate affiliations of identity and loyalty, was expected to reinforce this trend. The logic of industrial development and the logic of democratic citizenship were both to work as a combined logic of individuation, dissolving primordial identities like caste and religion. What actually happened with the introduction of democratic political processes was a surprising deviation from this entirely plausible picture.[18] Since elections required aggregation of perceived interests, and the format of perception of identity was deeply traditional, appeals to caste or occasionally religious identities were more effective in the short term. Politicians naturally wished to win elections before they modernized their country. Representative political process therefore came to operate at two distinct levels with a guilty, shamefaced, disingenuous relation between them. Formally, parties and groups spoke of citizens of a modern universalist democracy; in fact, politicians manipulated the existence of traditional identities in actual electoral practice. Such appeals to traditional belongingness like caste and religion could hardly contribute to their speedy disappearance. Thus the logic of electoral politics, instead of cutting at the identity and memory of caste practice, tended to remind people of them. Though electoral democracy served to underline caste identity, this too had its internal complexity. Two consequences of electoral appeals to caste are easy to identify. First, appeals to caste loyalties by setting up candidates from dominant caste groups in a constituency in fact yielded little electoral mileage. Since it was easy for all parties to pick candidates from the same caste, so that the actual electoral advantage from this move was effectively neutralized. Indeed, this is precisely what has tended to happen in large parts of India. Yet, since most parties invoked caste identity, it was that identity which got reinforced to the exclusion of other, some more modern ones. Some effects of caste politics have been more interestingly complicated. Clearly, representative politics has given rise to affiliations which are obviously caste-related, but by no means part of the traditional repertoire of caste practice. The political identity of the Scheduled Castes was a legal creation of the Indian constitution; but its effects are tangible. While earlier each community of untouchables might have suffered in separation, now they can resist together. The constitution conferred on them a new possibility of identity-making, which they seized with enthusiasm. The modern identity of the Scheduled Castes has, as it has grown and matured, sought to create a separate iconography for itself through a long but rather haphazard tradition from the Buddha to Guru Ravidas to Ambedkar. It has also given rise to a trend which seeks to transfer its grievance from a caste language to a class language, highlighting the idea of exploitation associated with social indignity, and to confer on themselves a self-description as *dalit* groups. A common identity of the Scheduled Castes/untouchables/dalits is therefore a constructed, modern identity, but no less effective despite its lack of impressive genealogy; indeed, this new coalescence of untouchables appears historically irreversible. But clearly this makes it rather difficult to answer the old question: does this show a weakening of the force of caste practice or its renewed vigour?

A very similar trend can be seen in case of the politics of the intermediate castes, an identity not produced through constitutional law, but by the latent demands for majority-yielding coalitions in electoral politics. According to the logic of the traditional caste system, individual castes like Ahirs and Gujjars were quite distinct social categories, who would not have considered each other as identical; it is the requirement of electoral politics,and perhaps the dramatic example of the effectiveness of the modern identity of the Scheduled Castes which pushed them into a new form of self-description: as intermediate or 'backward' castes. Again, the basic element of this identity is undoubtedly caste; yet, equally certainly, it is not an identity that could have been part of the traditional logic of caste segmentation. Politics of the modern democratic state has produced a logic of anti-segmental aggregation. Once these aggregations have taken place, it appears unlikely that these would disappear, to dissipate into more traditional, segmented caste identities of former times. Caste has thus become both stronger and weaker. It has grown stronger in terms of the effect it has on everyday electoral politics. In terms of the historical long term, it must have become weaker, and the more it is made to do ungrammatical jobs in the service of politics, its entrenchment in the social practices of tradition must become more diluted. Thus Indian politics may have become more casteist, and Indian society less caste-ridden.

HISTORICITY OF STRUCTURES

If the difference between tradition and modernity is not between history and the lack of it, but between surreptitious and declared history, or history seen through two rather different rhetorics, we must take into account the historicity of structures themselves, particularly of those specially wicked ones which encourage us to forget they had a history. This does not deny those characteristics of structures that structuralist theory formerly emphasized: these are public; these are above individual agency, which they shape, mould and constrain in various ways; they provide as it were a horizon of historical possibilities, a most serious form of determination over individual acts. Yet these are not invulnerable to pressures, small, infinitesimal shifts caused by individual improvisation in face of historical or situational necessity. These structures in other words, without losing their structure-like qualities, have their history.

Although this history becomes the most explicit in the period after British colonial authority is securely established, there are earlier traditions of state formation which either remain effective through British initiatives themselves, or are embedded in lower levels of social activity and practice. Historians of early political formations have pointed out the inappropriateness of an absent-minded use of concepts borrowed from western history and assuming that these would yield useful descriptions of the historical evolution of the Indian state. A concept which lies as an unstated premise under the very language of modern western political theory is the idea of sovereignty. A language of the sovereign state, or rather a language which is practised in the description of the destiny of sovereign states is inappropriate for the political formations which existed in traditional India.[19]

The political formation of colonial India should not be theorised around a state, at least in the first period of its establishment, because British power spread in India in a primarily mercantile form. The process did require frequent military conflict with Indian and European rivals for influence over various regions, but it also involved deft negotiation of terms between the mercantile and economic power of the Company and the formal political authority of local kings, such that, over the long term, these kingships became mere hollow shells. Recent historical research suggests that the British traders were not the only group who rejoiced at this drain of effective authority from traditional imperial rulers. Wealthy Indian merchants and ambitious and commercially inclined subordinate political elites found it to their interest, and assisted it through collaboration with the British.[20] When British power established itself firmly, it obviously made preparations for a long stay; and it brought into the Indian colony the entire apparatus of state-building currently available in the West. Given the current vogue of utilitarian beliefs in the malleability of social forms, European institutions of procedural legality, state accounting, taxation systems, census operations were all brought in and deployed in India. The colonial administration, probably without a clear intent, began to create a state of an unprecedentedly new type: a state of great reach, like the European institutions of the nineteenth century. But its efforts were always marked by an inescapable externality. European state forms, absolutist, constitutionalist, and finally liberal-democratic, emerged from and were shaped directly by the historical sense of necessity of these societies, and the institutions were therefore commensurate with some practical popular understanding of their internal structure and functions.[21] In India, these remained external impositions or

suggestions, and therefore resisted effectively either by mis-
comprehension of their nature and functions, or sometimes a more
serious resistance because they constituted a threat to traditional
ways of organizing rural existence.[22] External motions of submission to the processes of colonial governance did not always mean
a real transformation of political structures. Some modern historians have made a fairly persuasive case about the colonial
state being rather thin,[23] and in a *long duree,* Braudelian history
of Indian society and its ability to restructure social and economic
formations should not be exaggerated. In any case, the scholarly
picture of precolonial India has come round to be one of considerable internal layering and complexity. Despite the incontestable power of the economy to cause long term changes, or
the equally undeniable ability of the state to extract shorter-term
exaction, differing layers of the totality of society change at different rates, and to different degrees. The nature of colonialism
has been a subject of persistent controversy in the historical literature, and its impact on traditional Indian society has been seen
in two rather different ways. Nationalist historiography tended
to see colonial power as a process which invaded every little
atom of the traditional structure of society, and forced them to
change in the direction of a forcible, distorted modernity. Those
critical of this standard nationalist argument have often tended
to minimize the significance of colonialism by suggesting that
the *long duree* rhythms of Indian society were too deeply
entrenched to be entirely transformed by a relatively thin colonial
control which lasted at most two centuries, in fact, in most parts
of India, for a much shorter period. To claim that it altered the
structure of the whole society is to attribute mystical powers to
the colonial mechanism.

But the two options need not be entirely exclusive, as the ideological contest on the question of colonialism implies. Colonialism
might not have had either the force or the time to restructure
Indian society entirely according to its own plan and image. Yet
that does not mean that it could not have a decisive and irreversible
influence on Indian history. What colonialism changes is probably
less the whole structures of Indian productive life, more the
dominating and governing mechanisms and most emphatically
the *imaginaire,* the way Indians conceived of the social world and
its possibilities of organization.[24] While it appears most likely

that both colonialists and nationalists exaggerated the transformative powers of the colonial regime, for their own special ideological interests, its consequences were really historically decisive. Colonialists claimed that they had counted and mapped the Indian society under their control; which was certainly not true. Peasant societies demonstrate unsuspected reserves of cunning to fend off well intended invasion of their traditional practices, a cunning of unreason, so to speak. Their ceremonial prostration before colonial authority was sometimes taken by colonial rulers as the mark of their success in changing the traditional Indian society into a modern civilization. Legal transformations like the Permanent Settlement were not insignificant institutions in economic terms; yet they were not able to turn around the fundamental cycle of agricultural practices, and the distribution of productive responsibilities and rewards. There were real limits to the power of the modern state and its mechanisms of modern discipline. Still, the coming of colonialism brought about Indian society's contact with modernity which, through its many complex turns, has in fact restructured the trajectory of Indian history. Indeed, one of the most intriguing things about modern Indian political history is to differentiate between trends which are ascribable to modernity, and to colonial subjection.

Although the paradoxical idea of a promised but perpetually deferred 'self-government' was part of the ideological discourse of late colonialism, it came to Indian politics in a serious form only after independence. Earlier, colonial administrations, especially in the latter part of colonial rule, professed to grant self-government to Indians by prudent degrees, according to their slow acquisition of the rational powers such intricate operations required. Besides, Indians had to be protected from themselves; from their own primordial loyalties which could tear the society apart if government was devolved to them in unwisely large measure. Democracy however came to constitute a central part of the political *imaginaire* of the Indian political elite. Though the idea of democracy came through the colonial contact with Britain, the presence of British power delayed the institution of genuine democracy in the eyes of most nationalists. The state in India after independence therefore created a constitution based on universal suffrage.

Universal suffrage was not an isolated innovation. It formed a part of a large, internally consistent plan for the modernization of India. Representative democracy was only the political aspect of the process of creating modernity, of which development planning, secularization, elimination of caste practices in favour of a common modern citizenship, were the other, equally necessary elements.[25] An essential part of this theory of historical change was the belief that each of these elements would support and strengthen the others.[26] Capitalist growth would foster democracy. These in turn would reinforce secularization and the conversion of identities based on the primacy of communities to those based on the primacy of individuals. Although this symmetrical view of growth of bourgeois democracy appears a little worn out now, it was a highly plausible one in the fifties. Besides, it was also the dominant view all over the world: both bourgeois and communist ideological partisans believed in the functional reciprocity of these constituents of modernity, though communists believed that they had a better model to offer on the question of economic and political construction.

For the first twenty years after independence political events seemed to follow obediently the lines laid down by this theory of history. Since late sixties however some disquieting divergences from this historical script became increasingly evident. To use a distinction from de Tocqueville, in the first two decades after independence, India seemed to operate a democratic *government* in the absence of a democratic *society*.[27] A democratic society, for de Tocqueville, is one in which the deference for the cultural and social habits of the traditional upper classes has broken down, where ordinary people, despite poverty and cultural deprivation, do not hesitate to act politically on their own ideas. As long as popular pressure on politics did not break the mould of a highly formal, restrained, 'civilised' elite politics, as long as the ordinary and the poor were content to address their grievances through the format of the system rather than alter that format itself, democratic civilities were maintained with impeccable form: elections were punctual, peaceable, orderly. Parliamentary procedures, despite their legal arcaneness, were understood and maintained. Courts ruled meticulously on the basis of British and American constitutional legal precedents. Ministers resigned assuming responsibility for mistakes committed by their bureaucracies. Most significantly of all, the world of Indian politics looked and sounded exactly like a copy of the politics of West European democracies, with some modifications to suit the exotic circumstances. Political conflict centred on ideological issues, and recognised divisions between right, centre and left depended on the question of how the social constitution of India should be arranged.[28] Broadly, Congress enjoyed power at the Centre and most of the state legislatures, though with a large but undramatic majority.[29]

This familiar and placid world of standardly modern politics began to change seriously after Nehru's death, and the passing away of the leadership of the national movement. By 1967, after the fourth general election, which Congress lost in most northern states, even the electoral picture began to change in a rather unfamiliar direction. The division among the communists in 1964 led to a decline in the presence of the left, and this had a serious consequence for the manner in which language and rhetoric was used in the political world. As the left had been the most stridently ideological in its politics, it had been able to impose a certain ideological quality on the entire universe of serious political discussion; and this was of course assisted by Nehru's own highly ideological understanding of what political activity was about. Both these factors disappeared rather suddenly from Indian politics in the mid-sixties. Nehru was succeeded by a group of leaders whose view of the substance of politics was quite different. The communist movement split twice between 1964 and 1968, and their political conversation turned inwards, each segment of the movement questioning the credentials of others, rather than setting questions for the government party to answer. Electorally, the relative weakness of each of the divided parties now made them dependent on electoral support from other political forces, which would not come if they did not curb their style of ideological rhetoric considerably. This led to a situation in which the left ceased to speak in a single, and therefore more serious voice; rather, out of their weakness, they began to modify their discourse and provide justifications for different types of electoral combinations. The one-party-dominant system had, from the start, made ideological opposition unnecessary to some extent, as interests of both leftist and rightist politics could be articulated through groups inside the Congress itself.[30] The decline of the serious right-wing politics of the Swantantra party, and the temporary decline of the communists after their split, made for a less ideological type of political struggle. Ideology was however brought in a new, fraudulent way, by the populist appeals of Indira Gandhi's temporary 'socialism', but its 'ideology' was so disingenuous that it never contributed to a renewal of .the old type of political discourse.[31] Further unfamiliar changes followed. Despite her unprecedented majority in the elections of 1971, Mrs Gandhi's government was so besieged by the end of 1974, that she brought in the first spell of serious authoritarianism, calling into question two widespread theories about the politics of underdevelopment. The first was the educative theory of 'civic culture' which asserted that experience of a democratic civic form of government would train people politically so that authoritarianism would cease to be feasible. The second idea was that democracy could be put in jeopardy through the incomprehension and unrestricted passions of the uneducated masses, not through the ambition and lust for power of political elites.[32]

CASTE, CLASS AND ELECTORAL POLITICS

Besides these changes at the level of political incidents, other worrisome occurrences began to appear. Effects of government policies in the historic long term were often quite different from what were expected of them. Half-hearted attempts at land reform created a new landed agricultural class who benefited from the ruin of the traditional landed aristocracy, the emergence of a more integrated market for agricultural goods and the processes of the green revolution.[33] Increased prosperity of such groups of course translated easily into political power, first somewhat less than proportionally, later more equally to their assets, but their entry into politics did not follow the expected line of development. They brought into politics with themselves a new language whose relation with modernity was very complex, indeed an older language in some ways. They revitalized in surprising ways political forces and patterns of behaviour which should have disappeared according to the modernist historical plan: castes, religious identities, an increased sense of regional loyalty.[34] It inflamed the latent conflict between the political users of English and the vernaculars. This entire transformation of the real world of politics can not be explained by formal institutional political study:

constitutional law debates, discussions about the formal structures of federalism and fundamental rights etc. To analyse these things at all, political study must enter into political sociology, and in doing so, it must look at the present as history.

Serious investigation of this historical sociology of the present is however distributed unevenly over various academic disciplines, particularly political science and sociology, and to a lesser extent economics.[35] Now the myth of caste being an unchanging, immutable social form in Indian history has been permanently destroyed. If caste, despite its rhetoric of immutability, changed during earlier periods, its change in the colonial period and after 1947 is more explicit.[36] But social structures always find ways of giving the slip to collective designs and intentions. Just as caste structures changed slipperily even when collective designs probably tried to keep it unchanged, the modernist projects of colonial and nationalist transformation met with ironic success. Government policies aimed at caste affiliations changed them, often dramatically, but not in the direction intended. Electoral politics, as we saw earlier, instead of contributing to a fading away of castes, led to a reinforcement of identities in a startlingly nontraditional way.

Class formation in India has been equally refractory, if seen in terms of conventional theory. On the question of caste and class, there was for long a wholly wasteful ideological conflict in Indian political sociology, the line between Marxist and liberal scholarship being drawn between the advocacy of caste and class as central categories of analysis. Marxist analysts often made the daring pretence of discovering a code for simple translation of caste differences into class distinctions, most often simply shifting onto the Indian rural society the entire structure of Mao Ze Dong's celebrated analysis of rural classes in Chinese society without much adaptive modification.[37] This did not enter into the significant and interesting question raised by Marx's own argument that all societies do not give equal significance to the economic; and therefore, we cannot, in a society like India where capitalism is struggling to emerge and transform a very different kind of pre-existing social order, simply take the existence of classes for granted. It is necessary even for a more cautious Marxist approach to ask to what extent classes have been formed, the question of class formation in the more literal sense. In much of rural India politics is obviously not dominated by class interests or affiliation, except in the sense in which Marx speaks of objective class.[38] Additionally, the transition from caste to class is not a simple, linear, symmetrical transformation, so that the upper layers of caste society move simply into the corresponding upper layers of a modern class order. Since criteria of caste and class are quite different, it gives rise to great, unsuspected complexity which varies considerably between regions.

Interestingly, the historical refigurations that have occurred in caste identity have both nullified and confirmed earlier expectations in a manner of speaking. Radical commentators on Indian politics hoped that the regional differentiation and segmentation of the caste system, which prevented large collective actions in the political field on the basis of common economic interests, would gradually decline in the face of the spreading labour market, and result in large horizontal integration of classes. It would be hasty to say that this historical expectation has been entirely falsified. Large lateral integration on the basis of common interests have appeared; but two of its features have confounded earlier theories. The commonality of interests have been seen and pursued as being *political*, arising out of the necessity of getting things from the electoral system of the state, rather than economic — a solidarity that it both produced and directed at the industrial organization of the economy. Secondly, its form has been a reinforcement of caste rather than its dilution. Historically, therefore, there has been a sort of class-effect of caste, without caste being whittled down. Caste has taken over some of the political functions of class.

The politics of caste is related on two other sides with the longer term logic of the reservation system, through which not only caste groups but also other groups, like religious minorities, have sought to gain advantage from the huge resources of the state directed economic system. Nothing else can explain the stampede of various groups to get themselves declared as minorities and disadvantaged communities. Political changes in caste society have been caused obviously by deliberate and unintended results of state policies, especially policies related to economic growth and redistribution. The land reform proposals, through various levels of hesitation and conflict, undoubtedly failed if their objective is seen to be maximal, that is, the redistribution of land assets from the landlords to the landless or poor peasantry. Actually, the intermediate and rich peasantry, whose title to land was not tied to colonial *zamindari* rights, intercepted this redistribution. Over the long term, therefore, land reform did not produce the changes it intended; but the ones it did came to have enormous significance for politics. Peasant organizations have acted as strong pressure groups in politics in every part of India; yet they seem to recognize strange regional frontiers of their interests. No national articulation of peasantry has ever been attempted by any of those parties, though a transition from a regional to national organization of the peasantry would have turned them, unlike the working class, into a practically irresistible force, both in electoral arithmetic and economic bargaining.

RELIGION AND ELECTORAL POLITICS

Historical changes in religious identities have often taken an equally unexpected direction. At the time of independence, British India was partitioned into two states which offered a significant contrast; but this contrast could be seen in different ways. The British, who made the partition, saw this as a division between states with two religious majorities. But the Nehruvian section of the Indian leadership strenuously contested this reading of the event and saw in it a distinction between two ways of organizing political life, between a theocratic and a secular state. In the generally exultant atmosphere of the early fifties, when the process of decolonization meant an historic opportunity to recreate the social form of western modernity in the former colonies which had been denied by imperialism, the implicit westernism of this choice seemed quite unanswerably right. Controversies centred around the quickest means, the path, the trajectory, the spread, but not the historical feasibility of the end. At least, in the Indian subcontinent, the connection between nationalism and modernity appeared self-evident. Even a leader of the stature of Gandhi, without whom the success of Indian nationalism would have been inconceivable, offered criticisms which were mostly ignored rather than seriously answered. Gandhi's doubts about the feasibility and the actual consequences of introducing a westernised modernity were not seen as a set of valid, or serious, historical questions, but as personal fads to be indulged and ignored at the same time.[39]

This is not to suggest that Gandhi's ideas were historically feasible in a direct fashion. It seems now more appropriate to take them as utopian, in the sense that these suggested some fundamental problems about the positive construction of modernity through the admittedly unfeasible idea of recovering a past society based on small village communities. Utopian constructions of politics have two components: first, they point to some basic flaws in the structure of present social reality; second, they also suggest an alternative way of reconstituting it. Simply because the second part is unconvincing we cannot conclude that the first has nothing significant to teach. Most utopian doctrines are more instructive in their critical parts than the constructive; and this seems to be true of Gandhi's critique of modernity as well.[40] It seriously questioned the hierarchy of values that western modernity proposed for universal acceptance. It doubted the material and spiritual consequences of an unrestricted growth of desires so characteristic of the ideal of good life that modernity placed before mankind. It also called into question, very significantly, modernity's constructivist conceit — the idea, underlying practically all constitutions of newly independent countries, that their societies could be remodelled like lumps of clay by elegantly drafted constitutional documents, and the equally scientific recipes of economic planning. In an ironic way, therefore, although Gandhi was not known for advancing arguments of historical sociology, his doubts about both the desirability and feasibility of the structures of modern life could be given a very persuasive historical-sociological form. Suitably modified, his anxieties could be rendered into the following argument. Societies evolve over long historical sequences what can be called a grammar of politics and social power, a kind of effective underlying structure which gives form and sets limits to transactions between groups and individuals. Modernity seeks to impose a grammar of politics fundamentally different from the traditional one with which Indian society had been familiar. This underlying grammar is to an extent invulnerable to the hasty initiatives of reforming elites. Besides, the choice between the grammars of politics should be made with great care. Simply because a political form, built around the modern nation-state, has been successful in establishing its dominance in the modern world, it does not follow that it is preferable, nor the fact that it is more recently invented. Gandhi would have given a negative answer to both the questions implicit in this rendering of his critique of modernity. He would have considered the social form of modern individuality, materialist consumerism, state control by a centralized authority — all worse than traditional forms: of collective existence, restraint on desires, and a distant and marginal state leaving room for rural self-governance. But apart from the question of preference, he also implicitly pointed to the more intractable problem of feasibility. Modernists might easily dismiss his preferences, but cannot with equal ease ignore his judgement that western forms óf politics would not work successfully, because those would go against the grammar of social power.

Although it seemed in the two early decades that Indian politics was making admirable progress towards democratic maturity, the late sixties began an era of unexpected and unprecedented change. Initially, it appeared that the troubles were merely electoral, reflected in the deepening inability of the Congress party to hold on to its monopoly of power over the entire country. And it seemed perverse to suggest that a crisis of the Congress might indicate a crisis of the entire polity. Gradually, through a series of populist electoral manoeuvres by different actors in the political realm, seeking desperately to bring under control a political world which was speedily getting out of their grasp and terms of familiarity, Indian politics entered a phase of what is generally recognised as a form of structural crisis.[41] One major feature of this crisis was the increasing strain on the secular form of the state and its formal constitution.[42] Academic and journalistic writing had complained for a long time that under the general rules of equality before law, minorities were treated unequally in the actual operation of governmental machinery. The treatment of the minorities was indeed paradoxical in the extreme. For, on the one hand, the constitutional system seemed to accord them some 'privileges', precisely because their cultures could be more easily threatened. On the other hand, in actual state practice, there were frequent complaints about effective discrimination against minority groups. In fact, it could be argued from the point of view of minority groups that this combination was particularly invidious, because it allowed discrimination to be practised while blocking off their avenues of complaint by apparent solicitousness about their well-being in formal terms. Indeed, the constitutional provisions for protective discrimination for the minorities in certain areas were used by the state, nervous about its inability to control such discrimination, to.silence a section of the minority elite by privileges, and symbolic sinecures. Yet the historical result of this was not a gradual creation of a liberal-individualist civil society of equal citizens, but a contra-citizenship process. Muslims, for instance, could justifiably claim that they were underprivileged and systematically discriminated against; while resentful Hindus could also point out relative advantages that the state accorded to minority elites. The idea that being a minority was advantageous was so widespread that reform sects like the Rama Krishna Mission formally applied for recognition of their minority status. Since the intent behind and consequence of the introduction of a secular state diverged so dramatically, this gave rise, unsurprisingly, to serious critical reflection about the feasibility of the secular state, and the historical relation between the principles of secularism and democracy.[43]

Undoubtedly, the entire arrangement of social-political construction adopted by the independent governing elite in India depended on a specific reading of the history of European modernity, and the processes and interdependencies through which the modern secular, democratic, bourgeois state had emerged there. Since secularism, constitutionalism, democracy, capitalism all existed in a relation of seeming functional interdependence in the developed stage of western modernity, there was a natural tendency on the part of the nationalist elites to believe that these were always functionally related to each other: that one logically supported the other, and created each others' condition for existence. Constitutionalism, secularism, democracy, capitalist individualism were thus seen to stand or fall together; and India was given the best of all possible constitutions which incorporated all these modernist features at once. Evidently, both this institutional structure and the supporting historical thinking behind it are coming in for serious questioning.

There are however several possible explanatory hypotheses. It has been argued quite forcefully that perhaps western political models are unintelligible to ordinary Indian people,[44] and the more they take an active part in decision-making, these models would be abandoned. Secularism, on this view, comes under serious strain because it postulates that religion should not play a part in public decision making. Ordinary Indian electors are deeply religious, and it is part of a religious cast of mind that it is precisely those issues which are of wide and general significance which they would want to be submitted to the ordination of religious principles. To a religious person, therefore, to say that an issue is of vital significance and that it should be kept out of religious judgement is a contradiction. For him, the secular demand is incoherent from the point of view of his premises: precisely because an issue involves a vast number of people, and not just individual destinies or simple individual acts, it requires to be enacted according to the religious principles of rightness.

This indicates a complex practical difficulty, but not an insuperable theoretical argument showing secularism to be unfeasible. It can be argued for instance that seventeenth century European politics was plagued by precisely similar rigidities of religious beliefs.[45] When social life extended in scale and made intense interactions between social groups unavoidable, the first impulse on the part of rulers of European absolutist states was to order their polities according to the principles of the faith they happened to hold. As ordering social life according to the principles of the religion held by the majority or by those who held political power proved impossibly troubleprone, and threatened constant civil war, European societies gradually experimented their way out of such chaos by establishing secular regimes of power. Since the situation in India threatens to be quite similar, the advantages of secular organisation of the state presumably should appear similarly obvious to the Indian electorate. This might mean a substitution of the basis of secularism, from an elite preference to an electoral and popular consensus. It has been argued, with plausibility, that a secular state is a product of a secular society, and since Indian society is not secularised, a secular constitution is inherently unworkable. If the foregoing argument is right, then just the opposite of this is true: the impartiality of the state in political matters is a special requirement of a society in which religious identity remains strong, but the state comprises of different communities and therefore faces the prospect of unending conflict if it is identified with a particular creed.

A more interesting problem arises with regard to the argument that secularism is rejected by Indian electors primarily because it is a western idea unfamiliar to them in terms of their traditional identification of social values. Though certainly plausible, this runs into difficulties because the idea of democracy, of political equality of individuals, was an equally unfamiliar, untraditional, and in the same sense an alien, western idea. Yet the idea of democracy is in no danger of being similarly rejected; though it can certainly be argued that its meanings have often been bent out of recognizable shape.

What appears to be undeniable is the somewhat ironic combination of two processes relating to religion in modern Indian society. There is no doubt that religion as a political force, and a basis of collective action, is being reactivated, through the assertions of Hindu and Muslim militant identities. Yet it is hard to call this an intensification of religious practices in the traditional sense, as a certain process of slow but unrelenting desacralization of life continues to go on, not merely in society generally, but even in the actual life practices of those engaged in communal politics. Intensification of communal politics is thus accompanied by a depletion of the sacred, and a weakening of the strong religious injunctions about the time, space, materials in which the sacred was to be given representation and shown reverence. In myriad ways the contamination of modernity undermines the sacred; and the paradox is that this is true when they act together or at cross purposes. Thus active and energetic secularism of the state undermines traditional religiosity as much as the successful use ↑f communal politics in electoral and democratic institutions. Besides the political field, traditional religiosity is being diluted in social practices, sometimes in and through processes which wish to reinforce religious ideas. The filming of myths makes the sacred stories tangible, but also humanizes them in a modernist fashion. The images of ubiquitous cheap calender art does something quite fundamental to the symbolic and imagic perception of the divine. Demands of modern daily life displaces and abbreviates sacred time: other functions are not governed by the time of worship, worship has to find a place in a timetable governed by more insistent mundane pursuits. Thus the religion that is causing intense problems in the realm of politics is, on the other hand, in its social sphere, a religion constantly reduced, thinned down, diminished, depleted. It can indeed be argued that it is only with a religion that has been adapted to the one-sidedness of modernity that people can cause the type of trouble they do in the arena of democratic politics. It appears essential therefore to reflect more systematically on the relation between secularism as an institutional idea and secularization as a historical process: because, in some subtle ways, the political defiance against a secularist programme could itself be an episode in a slower, subtler, surer process of Weberian 'disenchantment'. Doing modern things with religion does nothing to legitimize religion, because religion's legitimacy comes from other sources; it confers greater legitimacy on modernity, and creates an historical possibility of decline of religious politics if it is found that those purposes can be better pursued by means other than the religious.

MODERNITY AND IDENTITIES

All sociological discussions about politics lead to a common concern with the problem of historical formation of identities.[46] In Indian politics, the major problem appears to be the connection between modernity as a proposal for arranging social life, and what its essential, ineradicable pressures do to the configuration of identities. Modernity changes fundamentally what people are, what they think they are, and more fundamentally and elusively, their way of being what they are. Hindus and Muslims, of course, existed earlier as well; but they are Hindus and Muslims now in quite a different way, and there is a new way of being a Hindu or a Muslim. Some identities, like the nation, or the collective identity of citizens of a modern sovereign state, are clearly made possible by modernity. Some others, like religion, caste, in some cases linguistically based regional identities, certainly existed earlier, but with modernity, even these are fundamentally redefined. As the simplistic dichotomy between modernity and tradition obstructed even a clear posing of the problem, political reflection has not achieved great clarity about what is involved in this change. Essentially, to carry on with the same phraseology, the main problem seems to be to what extent people can be what they think they are.

One major new area of interest in recent political sociology, not surprisingly, is the historical formation of identities. This evidently has two sides to it: first there is the historical process through which a particular identity comes into being, and becomes available for people for self description. Two cases of modern identities are nation and class. Despite the normal pretence of nationalist writers that they are struggling to free a nation already formed, and slowly evolving for a very long time, it is undeniable that the nation is a modern organization of the social imaginary.[47] Although a general cultural sense of Bharatavarsha, Hindustan or an unnamed but deeply felt cultural identity had existed for a long time, it is incontestable that that could not be called a nation. Indeed, the analysis of peoples' language itself shows some important aspects of this question. The term used for the nation in some languages, in Bengali for example, is *jati*, a term which can stand for two meanings. First, it has a generic etymological meaning of a logical class; but it also carries obviously the meaning of being a caste in the traditional Hindu social order. In ordinary language in traditional society, *jati* obviously means the relevant social group to which one belongs, which can differ from one occasion to another, and from one historical period to another. In modern Bengali, for instance, this does not create any confusion, because which particular meaning of the term is implied can be clearly deduced from the context of statements: the *brahman jati* will indicate the caste, while *bharatiya jati* would refer to the Indian nation.

Besides this, there is the significant process by which individuals and social groups choose one or another amongst the various possible self-descriptions available to them. Choosing to foreground one identity rarely annihilates the others; they are simply put into the more obscure background of social consciousness, to be taken out for strategic deployment when the situation changes. Evidently, a majority of the inhabitants of Eastern Bengal decided in the late forties that their Islamic identity was more significant than the linguistic one; but they, or their successors allowed their Bengaliness in the late sixties, to overrule their identity in Islam. Or are these continuities simply problems of language, creating counterfeit continuities where it does not really exist, because these were two distinct groups of people?

Clearly, this must constitute a central concern of political sociology in India, and perhaps more generally in the Third World. While the stabler politics of the West makes it reasonable to ask the question: why do people act in politics the way they do? A more significant question in India and the Third World seems to be to ask why people choose to be who they are? Why did people in Telengana believe they were primarily poor peasants in the late fifties, and primarily residents of Telengana twenty years later? Why did considerable sections of the Bihar peasantry see themselves as primarily peasants, and thirty years later primarily as people belonging to their respective castes? Even if these are, in some cases, redescriptions of essentially the same people, without altering the lines of conflict, this is not so in all cases. In most, such redefinitions of the collective self involve a drawing of the lines of enmity and alliance in politics on very different points of the social world.

Historically, it is quite evident that modernity does something quite fundamental to the logic of identities, to the ways in which people fashion self descriptions.[48] First of all, practically all identities go through a process of enumeration through the inevitable accompaniment of European colonization — the factual countings of the census, of maps, of the emergence of a fundamentally different world of counted and mapped identities.[49] It appears possible after all to alter the nature of traditional patriotism into forms of familiar modern nationalisms.[50] But it is not only the nation that is counted and readied for political action; all other identities are as well, at the same time. If people become dissatisfied with modern nation states, they immediately have available to them a whole range of other types of identities. In India, the identities on offer are both traditional and modern. Democracy is seen as a logic of self-determination; but the earlier, classical literature of self-determination assumed, now it seems too simplistically, that the putative subjects for this right were only nations, or proto-national communities. In situations like modern India, a whole range of other identities might wish to assert complex rights of self-determination. I call these complex, because all of them do not really aspire towards a substitution of the national state, or to have a national state of their own. Some of these clearly wish for a renegotiation of the internal structure of identities that a national state renders possible: for a kind of restructuring of rights. There is a large and impressive philosophical literature which argues that the advent of modernity brings in with itself a new notion of a self[51] that is prior to all its possible attributes, a sort of paradoxically non-existent hook on which these attributes are hung. And one complicating feature of this process is the autonomy of the individual to decide what he would like to be regarded as, to choose his identity in certain cases. Identities which were formerly mandatory, seem to become optional, matters of choice. A major question for the political sociology of India and the Third World seems to be whether modernity creates a similar 'economy' of identities from which collectivities choose. It goes without saying however that choosing to have a different identity means that the lines of division would run along different spaces or areas, and people who were earlier part of 'us' would now become parts of 'them', with the attendant process of readjustment of relations, substituting friendship with enmity and conceptual nearness with distance. There is also the question of determining whether all identities, traditional and modern, follow the same logic of formation and disarticulation, or do they follow different ones?

CRISIS OF THE STATE

Finally, much of the literature on political sociology of India converge on a sense of crisis of the state. But this is in many ways a most misleading convergence. For the estimation of the nature and the depth of crisis vary a great deal between different authors, schools, methodologies, political positions. They see the crisis as stemming from different sources, and therefore would expect its solution from radically different expedients. The idea of a crisis is thus not at all a mark of emerging consensus, except in a purely negative sense.

Broadly, crisis arguments can be classified into several types. One distinctive argument states that the difficulties of the modern Indian state stem from its alien provenance, the unintelligibility of some of its essential forms and procedures to the common people of India; and the solution of the crisis must lie in. the direction of some more understandable, traditional, or indigenist forms of political construction.[52] A second line of argument would see the crisis as stemming from the excessive narrowness of the lines of participation, and would see the western structure of political parties as inherently productive of hierarchies and stifling participation.[53] As a corollary, some of these observers would expect the solution to come from political processes which are less formalised, the non-party political process.[54] Marxist observers have persistently linked the present crisis to the logic of capitalist development in India which destroys earlier structures without providing the advantages of a mature capitalism, and see the contradictions of capitalist economy seeking expression through political conflicts in modern Indian society.[55] It is also possible to work out an attractive Tocquevillian perspective about the crisis of democracy, in which the arrival of a democratic society is making the functioning of democratic government more problematic.[56] Any explanation with any claim to adequacy must combine strands from many of these; but that immediately raises questions of internal coherence of the argument and the compatibility of the logic of different explanatory paradigms.

The selection of essays presented in this collection does not make any claim to exhaustiveness. It is neither exhaustive in terms of the possible themes of India's political sociology, nor in terms of the varying approaches adopted to address them. It simply tries to present a wide selection of representative ways of analysing the major problems. Some of the major premises behind this selection should perhaps be stated explicitly; because, if we adopted other principles, it would have yielded quite a different selection of explanatory projects. The first controlling idea behind the selection is that social structures, though immutable in the short term, and resistant to manipulation by individuals and collectivities in the present, do have histories. While their constraining 'structural' qualities should not be denied, their histories should not be erased either; indeed, in India, it is essential to understand their historical form of immutability. Thus politics is seen in terms of fundamental social structures, especially caste. But the tribulations of modern politics arise from the meeting of two histories: the historical processes of surreptitious, shamefaced, subterranean change of traditional Indian society, and the dramatic, overt changes brought in by modernity. Colonial modernity, the entire apparatus of the colonial economy, its structure of power, its cultural processes, despite their rhetoric of domination, control, reform, change etc. probably dramatically exaggerated the extent to which it succeeded in restructuring basic processes of Indian social life. It was probably a rather thin system, making unfoundedly large claims about its own powers of dominance and transformation. Yet, a thin state could have introduced, and triggered off processes of fundamental transformation which would eventually prove quite decisive. Several essays thus deal with the colonial period and the impact on Indian society that its structures and policies had, both directly and through unintended consequences. There are two sections dealing with the transformation of the two basic traditional identities, caste and religion, and their unpredictable transformations through modernity, especially modern politics rather than the modern industrial or capitalist economy. Some papers deal with the political sociology of identities, without any one of them really going into the more general question of identity and modernity. There is finally a section in which various approaches to the crisis of the state are presented. No implicit claim is made to the effect that these papers are the only ones that deserve notice, or indeed, they represent the most cogently argued case in their methodological genre. The collection simply seeks to present faithfully the enormous variety of methodological and theoretical currents in academic writing and reflection on Indian political sociology.

NOTES AND REFERENCES

1. It is essential to understand the connection between the general disputes about philosophy of social sciences and the problems of approaching political facts. However, this is not the place to discuss these questions in detail. Some of the major positions can be seen presented with force and lucidity in the collections: Ryan, Alan (ed.), *Philosophy of Social Explanations*, Oxford University Press, Oxford, and Gardiner, Patrick (ed.), *Philosophy of History*, Oxford University Press Oxford, 1974.

2. Taylor, Charles, 'Interpretation in the Sciences of Man', in *Philosophical Papers*, Cambridge University Press, 1988. vol. II, 15-57.

3. Ryle, Gilbert, 'The Thinking of Thoughts', in *Collected Papers*, Thoemmes, Bristol, 1990, 480-496. Volume II, and the application of this idea of 'thick description' to anthropological facts in Geertz, Clifford, *Interpretation of Cultures*, Hutchinson, London, 1975, 3-30. Chapter 1.

4. For an illuminating discussion of the nature of social facts, Bhargava, R., *Individualism in Social Science*, Oxford Clarendon Press, 1991.

5. For a discussion of what constitutes a social practice, see Macintyre, Alasdair, *After Virtue*, Duckworth, 1981, but more clearly, Bhargava, *Individualism in Social Science*.

6. The economic and the productive need not be used interchangeably;

and thus, the primacy of the economic and of the productive may have somewhat different implications.

7. Indian political scientists drew their training in the description and study of politics from such classic texts as A.V. Dicey and Ivor Jennings.

8. Both the disciplines involved in the study of social organization, history and social anthropology, tended to agree about an unchanging village society, a picture reinforced by a paradoxical latent consensus among imperialist history, academic sociology and ethnography and the political ideology of nationalism.

9. For the first attempts at a critique of the hard dichotomy between tradition and modernity, see Rudolph and Rudolph, *The Modernity of Tradition*, Chicago University Press, Chicago, 1968.

10. Ahmad, Imtiaz, (ed.), *Caste and Social Stratification Among Muslims*, Delhi, Mahohar, 1973.

11. Bose, N.K., *The Structure of Hindu Society*, (trans. André Béteille), Sangam Books, 1975.

12. Ibid, chapter 3.

13. For an example of the earlier type of caste study, Hutton J., *Caste in India*: Oxford University Press, Bombay, 1963.

14. The changeability of the caste system was underscored by the influential work of two scholars; social-anthropologist M.N. Srinivas emphasized the fact that caste also had a history; its structures changed through deliberate strategies of mobility. Rajni Kothari pointed out the paradoxical and at the same time puzzling fact that electoral politics instead of diluting caste seemed to reinforce it: electoral practices changed the caste system just as the caste system altered the functioning of the democratic system, a most interesting form of the adaptability of tradition to modernity. Also Rudoph and Rudolph, *The Modernity of Tradition*.

15. Galanter, Marc, *Competing Equalities*, California University Press, Berkeley, 1984.

16. Sanskritization has entered the language of Indian sociology quite firmly through the work of M.N. Srinivas.

17. The process of individuation, the historical process through which persons see themselves as individuals bearing certain social characteristics by their own choosing rather than by a passive belongingness to their primordial communities, has not been a subject of careful study in India. In contrast to the spate of research on industrialization and parliamentary democracy, the individuation process, so crucial to both in European modernity, has been deeply neglected. Yet interesting questions can be raised in connection with this: is individuation essential for the growth of a modern capitalist economy? Evidence from Japan and some East Asian economies would suggest that this is more contigent than was once believed.

18. Cf. Hawthorn, Geoffrey, 'Caste and Politics in India since 1947', in McGilvray, D.B., (ed.) *Caste Ideology and Interaction*, Cambridge University Press Cambridge, 1982, 204-220.

19. One of the most influential presentations of this view is by Stein, Burton, *Peasant State and Society in Medieval South India*, Oxford University Press, Delhi, 1980 Cf. also, Chattopadhyay, B., 'Political Processes and structure of polity in early medieval India: problems of perspective', *Social Scientist*.

20. Cf. Bayly, C.A., *Indian Society and the Making of the British Empire*, Cambridge University Press, Cambridge, 1988.

21. For an interesting analysis of the stages in which the European nation-states were formed see Hont, Istvan, 'The permanent crisis of a divided mankind', in Dunn, John, (ed.) *Crisis of the Nation-State?* Blackwell, Oxford, 1995.

22. However, I think the argument about 'externality' of modernity, though an essential argument, must be handled with some care. Social groups and individual actors in Indian society improvised in the face of these institutions, and related to them or rejected them according to their interest. Some aspects of modernity, like democracy, were welcomed and owned by some groups, and thus, when they understood what these things implied, ceased to be external. Other institutions, like property rules, evoked a divided response. New middle classes embraced them, and owned these rules, but others, both traditional elites and poorer groups, found them inconvenient and morally illegitimate. Actually what happens in much of Indian social life is a combination of externality, 'owning' and innovation.

23. Cf. Bayly, C.A., *Indian Society and the Making of the Biritish Empire*.

24. In the sense in which Castoriadis uses this term, see Castoriadis, C., *The Imaginary Institution of Society*, Cambridge, Polity Press, 1987.

25. For discussion of the constitution making process in India, Austin, Granville, *The Indian Constitution: Cornerstone of a Nation*, Clarendon Press, Oxford, 1966. Austin analyses the debates which took place in the Constituent Assembly, and is less interested in the historical theory that informed the entire political construction.

26. It is important to recognize that a theoretical understanding of the emergence of European modernity played a crucial role in the whole planning for modernity in India. Schematically, its premise was that the different constituents of modernity — capitalist industrialization, secularism, constitutional government and democracy etc — all mutually supported each other throughout the history of modern society. If this view is right, then of course, to strive simultaneously for all these elements is right, and it makes the achievement of modernity more likely. However, if it is not a correct picture of their historical conjunction, then the situation becomes considerably more complex.

Some recent research encourage a view that the relation between capitalism and democracy, that is the economic and political organizations, is contradictory. Capitalism could develop in its early stages precisely because of the absence of anything like universal suffrage politics. If this historical view is right, then the simultaneous pursuit of the goals of modernity might make its attainment more difficult.

27. The locus classicus for this is of course his *Democracy in America*, a text which seems to me crucial for an understanding of the travails of Indian democracy; but it has hardly ever been used. Political theorists in the middle of the nineteenth century were troubled by the emergence of democracy and its possible consequences for bourgeois society. Modern democracy was quite different from the Athenian model, because in modern societies, once universal suffrage was achieved, even the economically poorest and culturally most backward groups were not excluded from exercising a vital influence on policy-making. By contrast Athenian democracy was more socially homogenenous. The major threat emerging from democracy was outlined with the greatest clarity in the works of de Tocqueville and John Stuart Mill. Democracy inevitably brought in pressures for levelling, for greater political and social equality amongst classes. But this equality could go in two opposite directions. The happy possibility was the one in which the lower orders force their way into the cultural refinements which were earlier the preserve of the aristocratic orders in society. But there was also the disturbing possibility of the lower orders destroying the culture of the higher groups and imposing their own low culture on the society as a whole. If the poorest and least informed and literate people control decision making, how can society protect itself from an increasing irrationality of decisions, and an attack on cultural refinements which would be seen as preserves of aristocratic culture. How can a democratic society defend itself from its own democratic process? Mill's views on this question can be read most clearly in his review of Tocqueville, in Mill, J.S., *On Politics and Society*, (ed. G.L. Williams) Fontana, Glasgow, 1985, Chapter 9.

28. On how the language of Indian politics has changed, Manor, J., 'Anomie in Indian Politics', *Economic and Political Weekly*, Annual Number, vol XVIII, nos 19-21, 1983, 725-34.

29. I have discussed the change in the nature of the electoral process, and the emergence of negative majorities in 'Indira Gandhi and Indian Politics', *Economic and Political Weekly*, vol. XXI, no. 38, 39, 1986, 261-67.

30. Cf, for the celebrated account of the one-party dominant system, Kothari, Rajni, 'The Congress "System" in India', *Asian Survey*, vol. IV, no. 12, December, 1964, 1161-73.

31. For the view that Indira Gandhi's politics was more ideological than Nehru's, Frankel, Francine, *India's Political Economy*; for the directly opposed view that populism of the Indira Gandhi variety is less ideological, Kothari, R., *'State Against Democracy*; Kaviraj S., 'Indira Gandhi and Indian Politics', Nandy, Ashis, *At the Edge of Psychology*.

32. Both these possibilities were anticipated in the political thought of the nineteenth century; the first by de Tocqueville and Mill, and the second by Marx and Engels. Cf. Engels's 1895 introduction to Marx's *Class Struggles in France*.

33. For an excellent account of Congress policies on this question, Frankel, Francine, *India's Political Economy*; Herring, R., *Land to the Tiller*, Yale University Press, New Haven, 1983 and for a discussion of these developments concisely in terms of their effects on the coalition of classes governing Indian society, Pranab Bardhan, *The Political Economy of Development in India*, Oxford University Press, Delhi, 1984.

34. For a discussion of their entry into Indian politics, with a certain focus on north India, see Paul Brass.

35. Economists have been generally rather unwilling to build sociological categories into their work. This has had two rather unfortunate consequences: first, this has often made economic analysis of rural society itself unrealistic, because of its narrow rationalistic bias. Indeed, the debate about the mode of production in Indian agriculture is marked by this kind of rationalist conception of social behaviour and formation of group interest. Secondly, this has made it more difficult to arrange transacations between economic analyses and political sociology. There are however interesting and eminent exceptions. Cf, Bhaduri, Amit, 'On studying agriculural performance in India: What the sociologists could do for the economist', *Contributions to Indian Sociology*, vol. 14, no. 2, July-Dec. 1980, 261-67.

36. Cf. Srinivas, M.N., *Caste in Modern India*.

37. Mao Ze Dong, 'The Analysis of Classes in Chinese Society', *Selected Works*, London: Lawrence and Wiehart, vol I, 13-20, 1954.

38. The difficulties of applying the Marxist concept of class to the peasantry have been noted for long: for an interesting and complex discussion, Shanin, T., *The Awkward Class*, Clarendon Press, Oxford, 1972, also, Shanin T., and Alavi, H., (eds.) *Introduction to the Sociology of Developing Societies*, Macmillan, Basingstoke, 1982.

39. For discussions on Gandhi, see Parekh, Bhikhu, *Colonialism, Tradition and Modernity*, Sage, Delhi, 1988; Brown, Judith, *Gandhi*, Yale University Press, New Haven, 1989.

40. Some of the most interesting lines of thought in current Indian debates, which have used Gandhi, have taken this kind of direction. Cf., the highly suggestive work of Ashis Nandy.

41. There is a great variety of crisis arguments in the literature on Indian

politics: crisis of capitalist development, crisis of liberal politics, crisis of governability, crisis of democratic participation, and of course mixed modes.

42. See, especially, Madan, T.N., 'Secularism in its Place', *Journal of Asian Studies*, November, 1989; and Nandy, A., The Politics of Secularism and the Recovery of Religious Tolerance' in Das Veena, (ed.), *Mirrors of Violence*, Oxford University Press, Delhi, 1991.

43. Madan T.N., 'Secularism in its place', Nandy, A., 'Politics of Secularism and the recovery of religious tolerance'.

44. Madan T.N., 'Secularism in Its Place'.

45. This case has been made most persuasively in Koselleck, Reinhart, *Critique and Crisis*, Berg Publishers, Oxford, 1981.

46. For an excellent discussion of what it means to have an identity see Bhargava, R., 'Religious and Secular Identities', in Baxi, U., and Patrick, B., (eds.), *Crisis and Change in Contemporary India*, Sage, New Delhi, 1995, 317-49.

47. I have analysed the historical function of this pretence, most clearly seen in Nehru's wonderful narrative symbolism of the *Discovery* in 'The Imaginary Institution of India', in Chatterjee P., and Pandey, G., (eds.), *Subaltern Studies, VII*, Delhi: Oxford University Press, 1992, 1-29.

48. For general discussions, based on western experience, see Taylor, Charles, *The Sources of the Self*, Cambridge University Press, 1989; Giddens, Anthony, *Modernity and Self-Identity*, Cambridge: Polity Press, 1991.

49. Cohn, B., 'The census, social structure and objectification in South Asia' in *An Anthropologist among the Historians and Other Essays*, Oxford University Press, Delhi, 1987. Kaviraj, S., 'Imaginary institution of India'. For a more general discussion, Anderson, B., *Imagined Communities*, Verso, London, 1981.

50. But the society goes through various traumatic processes of integration, discussed with an appropriate scepticism about nationalist ideology in Gellner, Ernest, *Nations and Nationalism*, Blackwell, Oxford, 1981.

51. An influential phrasing of this has come from Sandel, Michael, 'The Procedural Republic and an the Unencumbered Self', *Political Theory*, vol. 12, 1984, 81-96. It might be better to call this curious notion of the self, an attributeless self.

52. Madan, T.N., 'Secalarism in its place'.

53. Kothari, R., *State Against Demōcracy*, Ajanta, Delhi, 1988, chs. 3 and 4.

54. The non-party political process has given rise to quite a debate in India. While those supporting the cause of a non-communist radicalism (Kothari) have enthusiastically supported them, leftist politicians have

generally condemned them as distractions or straightforward external conspiracies. It can however be argued that there is a latent complementarity between radical parties and the radical, smallscale voluntary agencies: these have grown where left parties had not existed, and vice versa. With a more imaginative vision, these two lines of radicalism could perhaps be seen as reciprocally supplementing each other.

55. Vanaik, Achin, *The Painful Transition*, Verso, London, 1990.
56. Kaviraj, S., 'On state, society and discourse in India', in Manor J., (ed.) *Rethinking Third World Politics*, Longman, London, 1991, 72-99.

I

Politics and Social Structure

Political institutions stand in a dual relation to societies. Institutions of the modern state always have the purpose of ordering, controlling and giving form to the behaviour of people who live inside them. At the same time, the society itself works on the basis of generally recognized and well-understood rules which its inhabitant follow. Rules of governance issuing from political institutions therefore shape social behaviour, and are influenced in turn by rules of common social behaviour. Those who thought in dichotomous terms, saw the state as 'modern' and the Indian society as 'traditional'. This led to the great historical question of modern Indian politics: would the state succeed in altering the practices of society, or succumb to their pressure?

The state which emerged from the Independence movement inherited two rather contradictory legacies. It was, in a way, the direct successor to the colonial state. Some of its institutions were shaped by the needs of colonial rule, and governed by principles formulated by the demands of colonial power. The structures of the army, bureaucracy, the police, the administrative rules through which government worked, and its larger relation of repressive aloofness from the ordinary people, were obviously consequences of this legacy. At the same time, the national state was also the product of a national movement, committed, at least formally, to the transformation of some of these structures in the interests of greater popular control.

It appears incontrovertibly true, in retrospect, that this state came to be driven by a highly rationalistic, modernist ideology because of Nehru's partly fortuitous domination of the state institutions. It was part of this ideology to assume that rationalistic procedures of the modern state were inherently more powerful than the disorganized, inexplicit, 'irrational' practices of traditional society, and that these would gradually be undermined as modern, 'rationalist' modes of behaviour took root in the economy and politics. In certain cases, the state also took energetic action to interfere with traditional structures of social practice and to alter them, e.g., in the formal abolition of untouchability, an inextricable part of the Hindu caste system. Historical thinking on which these ideas were premised used an explicit dichotomy between tradition and modernity, and at least for the modernists, there was a high correlation between modern and 'rational' behaviour. The state was seen as the paradigmatic and the most effective agency which modernity used to break down the often superstitious, uncomprehending resistance and inertia of traditional practice.

The actual historical process turned out to be much more complex. First, the concept of tradition implied in that model was too static and plainly misleading. It assumed that traditional practices attained their astonishing durability by means of an obstinate refusal to change. A more reasonable hypothesis about tradition would be that these practices changed surreptitiously, always attempting to erase traces of change and being governed by a dominant rhetoric of immutability. But simply because the ideological texts of a practice say it has never changed, we should not believe it really has not. On the contrary, traditions of religious practice, in Hinduism, Islam or Christianity show evidence of historical adaptation over the long term. So, the secret of the longevity of traditions might lie in their peculiar combination of actual adaptive flexibility and a rhetoric of unchangingness. In India, this kind of rhetoric of immutability (e.g., *sanatana dharma*) was assisted by the absence of written records of the kind available in the West since late medieval times.

A second point of possible debate is on the power of the modern state. Undoubtedly, the techniques of assembling, creating and disbursing power that the modern state has developed were not available to pre-modern political structures. Yet, some have argued that the power of the state can be overestimated. The decline in the practice of untouchability, for instance, could be seen as a consequence of previous social reform movements; the state then simply ratifies a change which it has not enunciated.[1] Thus, what appears to be a significant victory of the state may in fact be something quite different. It could be argued that the state has, since Independence, evidently struggled to give the economy a more rationalistic cast, to force economic activities into forms and channels which make them amenable to its cognitive and practical control. Yet, the meagreness of the tax revenue of the state and the existence of a flourishing shadow economy shows the limits of its powers of transformation of conventional economic practice.

One of the central problems of this kind of theory of modernization related to the conflict between state and society in terms of their basic organizing principles. Institutions of parliamentary democracy are premised on the existence of a highly individuated society, on the assumption that when people act in the political world, they would see their interests as 'individualistic'; and group interests would be merely the transient combinations of such individual interests. Evidently, ordinary people in actual Indian society lived according to social principles fundamentally opposed to individuation In relevant contexts, they are apt to act according to their membership of groups like castes, religious communities or linguistic blocs. It was logical to believe, in accordance with that theory, that either the logic of modern politics would disaggregate those social communities; or the strength of the logic of communal existence would disrupt the functioning of modern democracy. Political sociologists like Rajni Kothari were the first to show scepticism about this simple dichotomous historical model, and much of the early work on caste, meant to show that neither of these simple lines of possibility was being enacted in Indian political life, was gathered together in Kothari's early collection on the disobedience of caste practices in the face of such expectations. Like other forms of traditional practice, caste responded to the constraints and opportunities offered by modern electoral politics with characteristic suppleness and opportunism — giving rise to unexpected forms of caste mobilization. These forms often rejected the traditional segmentation of caste identities, and adapted themselves to the numerical logic of parliamentary electoral institutions. These new forms and the political skills which fashioned them could not be called, without obvious inappropriateness, either traditional or modern. The clearest example of such fusion of traditional principles with modern practices to produce unexpected results has been the politics of the formerly untouchable groups. Traditional caste system recognized individual, segmented castes which were treated as untouchables by higher groups in the caste hierarchy. Although untouchability may have been their common fate under the Hindu order, this did not implant in them a sense of common political agency. The Constitution used the term, Scheduled Castes, simply for a legal, textual exigency. The list of castes regarded untouchable was put into a Schedule of the Constitution. Rules of common treatment however created a perception of common interest, and quite soon, political parties started treating these groups as a single bloc of Scheduled Castes. And though this was a coinage out of legal exigency, the term has slowly entered the common everyday language of social description in contemporary India.

There is of course a certain simplification in treating caste alone as the ordering principle of Indian society. But this is done for two reasons. If modern social anthropology is to be trusted, then caste-like forms exist among non-Hindu segments of Indian society as well. But, more significantly, caste is chosen here not as the only principle of ordering in Indian society, but one of the most striking ones; and the picture of Indian society is sought to be made more complex as we go along to later sections.

The collection in this part starts, with this simplifying assumption, with Louis Dumont's treatment of the fundamental features of caste society and the place of territorially organized political power within that arrangement. Dumont subscribes to the view that the caste order limited the power of political authority severely, making it impossible to equate those structures of pre-modern government with the modern state, and accepts the idea that what is constant in the caste order is the principle of hierarchy (see however Dirks' contribution in Part II). But some types of modern research have maintained that the view is flawed in at least two respects. First, despite the undeniable rhetoric of immutability and the associated ideological bias against change, the actual historical record is considerably more mixed. Caste structure is not immune to historical shifts, though it has its own peculiar way of dealing with the problem of historical change and its ideological representation. Second, some scholars have suggested that there is strong evidence to show that the order of castes was heavily dependent on political power, and that the picture of an immutable caste system is partly at least produced by cognitive conventions associated with colonial practice.[2] The work of M.N. Srinivas began to study the ways in which traditional caste practices adapted to parliamentary forms of political behaviour. Kothari's essay approaches it from the other side, analysing how rules of electoral politics have encouraged mobilization of caste allegiance on non-traditional lines. André Béteille's essay gives a far more textured and detailed account of how the adaptation of caste to democracy has happened in the case of Tamilnadu, which has a caste order quite specific to the region. Finally, Partha Chatterjee's analysis of the history of a low-caste religion shows in what innovative ways subaltern groups fashioned a mode of resistance to Brahmanical dominance, but within the logic of the caste system itself.

NOTES AND REFERENCES

1. Chatterjee, P., 'Secularism and Toleration', *Economic and Political Weekly*, 9 July, 1994.
2. The reference is to Dirks, N., *The Hollow Crown*, 1993, University of Michigan Press, from which the excerpt in Section II is taken.

Power and Territory

LOUIS DUMONT

INTRODUCTION

We shall proceed as if we had finished with the ideology of caste; so, in conformity with our method, we shall now begin to set out what is actually encountered in caste society while not figuring directly in the ideology....

Confining ourselves provisionally to social organization, what is really at issue? One can already reply *a priori*, from the viewpoint of our own society, that we have to look for everything the ideology seems to have neglected. This corresponds fairly well, as a first approximation, to what we call the politico-economic domain, as opposed to the domain of religion. The ideology has led us to describe certain aspects of the society and in this description we have already met certain features, elements or factors which are extraneous to the ideology itself. The ideology does not take cognizance of these as they are in themselves, but merely cloaks them, so to speak, in its all-embracing language.

Actual caste systems, in contrast to the theoretical model, were organized within a fixed territorial area, were so to speak contained within a spatial framework. We often encountered this feature again in what followed, in connection with segmentation

Excerpted from Louis Dumont, 'Power and Territory', *Homo Hierarchicus*, The University of Chicago Press, Chicago, 1970, Paladin (Chicago) edn 196-211.

and hierarchy and with the *jajmāni* system, which functions within each village as a unit. So far as *jajmāni* is concerned, the orientation of the division of labour towards the whole is seen as a fundamental fact, a fact which in the last analysis is religious in nature; but at the same time we have stated both that this interdependence combined non-religious as well as religious aspects, and that the pivot around which it is organized — the dominant caste — was implicit rather than clearly recognized. Finally, studying hierarchy in the strict sense and leaving aside the question of command or authority on account of the component of power it contains ... limiting ourselves, that is, to status ranking *in concreto*, we have seen that power, devalued to the advantage of status at the overall level, surreptitiously makes itself the equal of status at the interstitial levels. It is true that this fact corresponds to the relationship established between priest and king in the theory of the *varnas*, but the latter definitely remains implicit in the ideology of caste as isolated here. From this point of view, we have, thus, already acknowledged that power exists and that it is located in a framework of ideas and values, confined within the limits of this framework but distorting it to some extent.

Territory, power, village dominance, result from the possession of the land. This we have already been compelled to recognize, and we must now deal directly with it. Having so far followed in Bouglé's[1] footsteps, we shall now take much more advantage of recent research, for these are the questions to which it has given preference and on which there is a notable consensus of opinion among specialists. Consequently one can be very brief, the major concern being to restore this partial domain to its place in the whole. The change of level raises a problem of terminology. We must above all define what we mean by 'power'. It is exclusively political power that is in question, the political domain being defined as 'the monopoly of legitimate force within a given territory'. Power is thus legitimate force. Today the definition may seem very limited. It has the advantage of corresponding quite well to Indian notions: power is roughly the Vedic *kṣatra*, the principle of the *kshatriya varna* (literally 'the people of empire'); it is force made legitimate by being subordinated hierarchically to the *brahman* and the Brahmans. So we shall deal successively with the territorial framework, the rights in land, the village with its dominant castes, and conclude with some remarks on the economic approach.

THE TERRITORIAL FRAMEWORK: THE 'LITTLE KINGDOM'

Contemporary anthropological literature frequently stresses the fact that actual caste systems are — or rather were — contained within a territorial setting of rather small scale. Here social anthropologists found what they were at the same time mistakenly seeking at the level of the village: a social whole of limited extent, established within a definite territory, and self-sufficient; a small society not too unlike the tribe, the usual object of their study, and which did not belie the territorial conceptions which are bred in us by the existence of nations. Authors readily dilate on the necessity for a caste system to have a limited spatial extent, and on the consequences of this fact. Once the common ideology on which all these actual systems rest has been recognized, as it has been here, the fact of territorial fragmentation is doubtless important. It should be noticed that this fact is closely linked to the ideology. In effect: (i) the ideology ignores territory as such; (2) an ideology which had a place for territory, which valued it, would obviously promote territorial, and hence political, unification; (3) caste ideology, as has sometimes been said, assumes and upholds political divisiveness....

Even reduced to the simplified notion that each 'little kingdom' had a caste system more or less different in actual fact from the neighbouring one, the matter has many aspects. The fact has been stressed that the 'local hierarchies' of castes differ from one another. And indeed each chiefdom has its own population and history, from which arise differences which may be very marked not only in the number, name and function of the castes (or subcastes) present, but even in the development of different ranking criteria. In particular, much must have depended on the Brahmanic settlement, on the variety or varieties of Brahmans present — and earlier on the extent of the popularity attained by Jainism and Buddhism. Similarly it must be thought that in the 'little kingdom' the king or chief would have been able to enjoy considerable power, patronage and influence as against the Brahmans. This can help to explain how the features of the royal way of life (meat diet, polygyny), although devalued

in relation to the Brahmanical model, have been able to survive
and set an example to some castes for so long. By contrast, the
disappearance of the king from vast regions under the Muslim
domination must, as various authors have supposed, have increased the Brahman's influence, which then would have lacked
any counter-balancing opposition....

British domination caused the disappearance of the traditional
compartments or, as Srinivas puts it, 'let the djinn out of the
bottle',[2] allowing among other things each sufficiently widespread
caste to unite on a much broader territorial basis, in associations
of which there are nowadays many examples. It is beyond doubt
that many castes or subcastes have taken advantage of the new
circumstances to extend well beyond their former confines. Thus
in Uttar Pradesh the Brahman castes cover a very wide area
and often many of them co-exist in a given district; but if one
pays close attention to the quantitative aspect of population,
one finds in each case that by far the greater part of the group
is concentrated in a few districts central to its present distribution,
and that the areas thus defined no longer overlap. It is just as
if each group had spread like a drop of oil, mingling peripherally
with its neighbours. Although there is not necessarily a political
unit in the strict sense in each case, this fact confirms the hypothesis that the composition of the settlements has recently become
more complicated compared with a previous period of regional
compartmentalization.

To conclude, there is one reservation to be made: The compartmentalization of the little kingdom must have been at its
height at periods of instability and political disintegration, although there was always some movement of warriors. But in
India, such periods have been interspersed with times of political
unification into large states, of spatial mobility at least for certain
castes of government officials or merchants. The case of Kerala
State is exceptional, and the neighbouring Tamil country, although much less a place of passage than the Gangetic plain,
demonstrates by its political history and the composition of its
present population that the isolation of small units was often
disturbed. One must think rather of a tendency for regions to
close in on themselves, a tendency sufficient to differentiate the
regional systems, but not sufficient to shelter them from external
influences and upheavals (one should think also of famines and

repopulation). The history of this topic alone would require a whole book, and we can only hope to piece together some fragments of it.

RIGHTS, ROYAL AND OTHER, OVER THE LAND

The question of the appropriation of the land, in the widest sense of the term naturally arises in the present consideration of power and territory. Land is the most important possession, the only recognized wealth, and is also closely linked with power over men. At least this was the case until recently, and it generally is so in complex traditional societies.

It so happens that the question of rights over the land, while amply discussed in the nineteenth and twentieth centuries, has scarcely ever been related to the caste system. As certain aspects of the question have been mentioned elsewhere, and as it will be encountered again in the following section, we shall be very brief Many questions have been discussed which are not independent of one another: in Hindu India, was the king the owner of the land? Was he, in ancient times, a god or a servant? Was there collective ownership, a kind of communism, in the 'village communities'? The concept of the king as a functionary appointed for public order is a rationalization resulting from the secularization of the royal function and the political domain, a secularization made much of in ancient literature. As far as the 'communities' go, to the extent that they existed they represented joint possession by the dominant caste or lineage. To look for 'ownership' of the land is a false problem, since everything shows a complementarity between different rights bearing on the same project, for example, those of the 'community' and those of the king. Moreover it is remarkable that the majority of British administrators tackled this question in terms of the more or less philosophical general concepts of the West and not with the special concepts of English law, which would have been closer to the actual state of affairs in India.

Just as the distribution of grain on the threshing floor show a series of rights of very different origins being actually exercised over the harvest, so the sometimes lengthy chain of 'intermediaries' between the king and the farmer shows a superimposition of rights, which are not only independent but even susceptible of variation in detail. Only if the king were to give up his own right and to take care that all rights were united in the same hands, as was the case with certain religious donations, would something like ownership be created. But even in this case, alienation of rights was probably impossible in principle.

In short, far from a given piece of land being exclusively related to one person, individual or corporate, each piece of land was the object of different rights relating to different functions, expressed in the right to a share of the product or to some due from the cultivator. The king's share in particular, far from representing a kind of salary for the maintenance of order, expressed an overall right over all land, but limited to this levy in each case. The interdependence of the castes is expressed here by the existence of complementary rights, where that of the king and that of the cultivator are only the main links in a chain which was something complex.

In short the caste system is strongly contrasted to what we call landownership and ownership. What takes place in this domain could almost have been deduced a **priori** from the general characteristics of the system. Given an object, the land, which in complex traditional societies in general is of the greatest importance and intimately linked with political power, one could have foreseen that the caste system would not relate it exclusively to an individual or a function, but rather to the whole set of functions comprised in the system. If something like customary rights are defined in practice, these will be fragmentary rights and mutually complementary; no doubt there will be an eminent right, but this will be a right subordinated to values and therefore subjudged to its function. Moreover, the system does not take cognizance of force, except when subjected to it: it is defenceless on this quarter, this is its Achilles heel. Not only royal favour, but violent interference can at any moment change the titulars, introduce new rights, modify what seemed to be stable rights (without so much as touching the principle of interdependence). The history of India must often have seen the dominant caste reduced to the state of tenants, tenants to dependence. This is how the caste system, by the fragmentation of 'rights' and by their insecurity, diminishes the importance that we are ready to accord to the appropriation of the land. A kind of collectivism is involved, but of a more subtle form than our predecessors imagined.

THE VILLAGE

The notion of dominance, or rather of the dominant caste, represents the most solid and useful acquisition of the studies of social anthropology in India. To appreciate it fully, the history of ideas about the Indian village must be briefly recalled.

The 'village community'

People have spoken for a long time of the 'village community', and the expression has taken on somewhat different meanings since the beginning of the nineteenth century. The first stage is that of the now famous descriptions by English administrators in the first thirty years of the century.... They described the village as a 'little republic', self-sufficient, having its own functionaries, and surviving the ruin of empires. The stress is above all on political autonomy; India tends to appear as a worm whose segments are the villages. There are regional peculiarities in these descriptions...there are real general characteristics (*jajmānī*), and there is also a certain amount of idealization. This was the romantic period and the great administrators of this time, rather paternalist as we would say nowadays, wanted to defend the indigenous institutions against the claims of bureaucrats and utilitarians who urged reform. The idealization can be seen from the fact that the village's link with the central power (levy on the harvests by the king and his representatives, nature of the official village chiefdom where it exists) is minimized; and it can be seen even more clearly from the fact that the inegalitarian aspect goes unmentioned, perhaps because at that time it still seemed normal. In any case, the 'community' continued its career under the banner of equality.

In the Victorian period, 'village community' took on another meaning related to the supposed communism of primitive peoples or of Indo-European prehistory. Marx shifted the stress from political autonomy to economic autarchy. While he finally attributed ownership of the land to the king, so that only possession in common remained to the communities, he considered them as 'units of production' which were consequently subject to division of labour *sui generis*. Maine stops short at the search for vestiges of the Indo-European commune. It is remarkable that these two authors, relying on the same source, missed its most important feature. Indeed Marx quoted Campbell, and it was from him that Maine drew the essential part of his data before setting out for India. Now Campbell stated clearly that joint ownership was found among the dominant castes and was accompanied by the subjection of the other inhabitants.[3] Marx overlooked this and Maine rejected it because he did not make use of his stay in the country to improve his ideas on this point. Here as elsewhere, European scholarship has been ill-fated. Where joint possession existed, it was related to two facts: kinship, or rather the lineage organization in the dominant group on the one hand, and on the other the structural unity of this group as against others who could have disputed or gradually eroded its position.

Finally, in the third period, Indian nationalists, relying on the descriptions and scruples of the British of the first period, constructed for themselves an idyllic picture of the village community as a secular and democratic institution — did it not have the assembly, the famous village panchayat? — which only the British domination ruined irremediably.

We shall encounter the question of the panchayat again in the next chapter. What lessons can be learnt from these various incarnations of the 'community'? In the first place, the elements of truth must be restored to their place in the setting of dominance, and the role of force and conquest, sources of instability, must be recognized. Further, the situation in the village is not independent of regional political circumstances: 'despotism' is often reflected to some degree in the village chiefdom, which not only represents local interests *vis-à-vis* the political power, but also the reverse. Finally, while recognizing that the 'village community' springs from a Western point of view which is inapplicable to India as a whole, because hierarchy and dominance are omnipresent, and the relation to the land less fundamental than has been supposed, one must also recognize considerable regional developments of communal solidarity (as among the *Jāt*), village exogamy (in the north), and village councils found for example in Tamil country in the Chola period.

The Dominant Caste

At the beginning of intensive studies in social anthropology, certain authors seem to have been attracted towards the 'village community': the village was considered at least as isolable, if not independent of environment, and the emphasis was placed on general characteristics rather than specific ones, on the territorial basis rather than the ideology of caste. It is scarcely too much to say that the introduction of the notion of 'dominant caste' had the chief merit of once again putting caste in the forefront and giving a more precise content to the vague idea of village 'solidarity', of, in short, extricating the Indian village from the sociological limbo in which it was still slumbering. Its second merit is to have isolated in the village the non-ideological aspect with which we are concerned here. We cannot observe a kingdom, but we have in the village a reduced version of it: the principle of the royal function. The word 'dominance' is well chosen in its opposition to 'status' — at least in the sense of those terms we have chosen here. Let us look closer. The term, borrowed from African anthropology ('dominant lineage' in a territorial group), was introduced by Srinivas. In an article on a village in Mysore, published in 1955, he defined the dominant caste as follows:

A caste may be said to be 'dominant' when it preponderates numerically over the other castes, and when it also wields preponderant economic and political power. A large and powerful caste group can more easily be dominant if its position in the local caste hierarchy is not too low.[4]

A rather vague definition, which must be discussed and made more precise. It is a fact that in the Indian village one (or more than one) caste had even recently the superior right over the land or the larger part of it. 'Superior right' is to be understood here in relation to the other villagers, for the king's right, itself higher than this one, lies above the level of the village. For example, the distinction has often been pointed out between occupants with full rights, those who possess the village land (whether originally or by conquest or allocation) and inferior or 'foreign' occupants, tolerated by the former.... We have noted before that the joint possession which, for Maine for example, gave the greatest strength to the 'village community' was in reality the joint possession by occupants of superior right, joint possession within the dominant caste or lineage. As Campbell emphasized, the 'village community' is dependent on this group. The numerical criterion introduced by Srinivas is somewhat surprising. Is it necessary for the caste which is dominant so far as the land goes also to be the most numerous in order to 'dominate' in general? One fact to be stated is that usually, when sufficient data are available, it can be seen that the most numerous castes in a village are, first, the dominant caste, and secondly the caste which provides the greatest part of the labour force and is usually untouchable, rather as if the castes in the closest relation to the land, both in theory and practice, had the greatest possibility of increasing in number. However, this would not be enough to introduce number as one of the criteria of dominance. Srinivas justifies it in an article on the dominant caste in the same village, in which he explains that the real status of one and the same caste in different villages can depend on the number of men it can put into the battle line, and that even Brahmans feel insecure where their numbers are rather small. This emergence of brute force does not cause much surprise. But it does not show that it is necessary for the caste which is powerful in land to be itself numerous, for such a caste easily attracts a following. Numbers also have a bearing in modern times, i.e. in elections, but here again the numbers can be made up by members of a following more surely than by the members of the dominant caste, among whom there would probably be rivalries or 'factions' once they are numerous. In the same article the author introduces a new criterion of dominance, the level of education: this arises from modern conditions and one might just as well introduce external relations, especially with the town, not to speak of entrepreneurship

There comes a point when we shall no longer follow this author, for he seems not only to contradict himself, but also to throw overboard everything worthwhile in the concept. This is when he speaks of 'ritual dominance' in connection with the Brahmans who are neither numerous nor rich in land. One naturally thinks of symmetrical uses of the word 'status' by authors who, not content to speak of the status they call ritual, add 'secular status' to designate in fact dominance, power, etc. At this point there would no longer be any essential difference between 'status' and 'dominance', for these would designate two different aspects of the same thing. We prefer to maintain a fundamental distinction between the two, a distinction which, as we have seen, is built into the theory of the varnas itself, if not into that of the castes.

Mayer[5] has enlarged the concept of dominance by considering in addition to the village two other levels, that of the little region and that of the little kingdom, where the dominant castes are not always the same, although there are certain links between them, at least in his example. A rather obvious proposition emerges from his analysis, as from those by Cohn,[6] namely that there is a homology between the function of dominance at village level and the royal function at the level of a larger territory: the dominant caste reproduces the royal function at village level. Let us list its main characteristics: (1) relatively eminent right over the land; (2) as a result, power to grant land and to employ members of other castes either in agricultural capacities or as specialists, to build up a large clientele, not to say an armed force; (3) power of justice also: the notables of the dominant caste are often entrusted with the arbitration of differences in other castes or between different castes, and they can exact penalties for unimportant offences; (4) generally speaking, monopoly of authority: if the village headman chosen by the state is not one of the dominant notables he can only be the pawn, unless he has unrivalled personal qualities; (5) the homology extends so far that the dominant caste is often a royal caste, a caste allied to royal castes (Mayer), or a caste with similar characteristics (meat diet, polygyny, etc.) The relationship between the Brahman and the dominant caste is the same as that between the Brahman and the king. It is understood that the Brahmans can be dominant just as they can be kings; in this case they lose their caste characteristic with respect to other Brahmans who serve them as priests....

'Factions'

A word must be said on a phenomenon which accompanies dominance and which, like it, is a question of fact and not at all of theory. Very commonly the Indian village is divided into 'factions'. People have long recognized the importance of quarrels, rivalries and legal wranglings in the Indian village.... The village is divided into more or less permanent rival groups of which the more powerful at least include a fraction of the dominant caste and at the same time a following recruited from dependent castes. The important point is obviously the fission of the dominant caste or lineage into two or more fragments which do not necessarily always follow lineal cleavages. The factions use every occasion of friction and litigation to insult each other; even if they do not instigate them it is probable that they considerably aggravate them. Lewis has given a very precise account of the membership and relations of these factions, which do not have only hostile relations but also those of sympathy and neutrality. One may wonder whether he has not somewhat reified the relations and made them rigid, when in reality they may be more fluctuating and often more ambiguous. Also, most importantly perhaps, his example, in which there are objective cleavages (the factions smoke separately), does not constitute a limiting case, as the Jāt peasantry in many ways represents a deviant type with respect to India in general. However, even if, as one is inclined to believe, things are in general more fluid and unstable, Lewis certainly put his finger on an important fact. The fact is confirmed by other works using the same concept, in particular that by Dhillon: after participating in the research just mentioned he studied a village in the Deccan in a similar way and brought out interesting differences (role of affinal kinship in the south). The overall fact is that within the village and within the dominant caste itself there is fission into units which spring from no traditional principle, and in which each man's adherence is mainly or to a large extent governed by his interests. In short we have here an important *empirical* addition to the groupings and divisions which spring from caste, lineal kinship, and local association. All kinds of questions arise. In particular, is this phenomenon bound up with the traditional organization in some way still not clear, or is it, as most authors are doubtless inclined to think, a modern fact, linked to recent changes brought about by the insertion of the village into a political and economic whole which has strongly affected it? It is clear that contemporary changes have multiplied the causes of friction, but this does not mean that the phenomenon itself is recent. Let us be content with one remark by way of transition to the following chapter. From the formal point of view, the fact seems to be linked to a characteristic of authority: as we shall see, in this system a man can only have uncontested authority with respect to people of dominated or inferior caste. Within a group of a given status, authority is more often plural than singular. It is a well-known fact that, apart from official functions, one rarely encounters a single chief or leader, authority and influence being more often shared among two or more elders.

THE PROBLEM OF ECONOMICS

Can we go further, and, as a sequel to the political implications of the caste system, study its economic implications? I would like here to raise the question of the applicability to traditional India of the very category of economics, and the connected question of the place of wealth in goods, and chattels, money and commerce in Indian society. To raise the question is not to answer it, but it does arouse doubts and also indicates some topics for study.

First of all, one must remember the elementary but too often forgotten fact that, even in our society, it was only at the end of the eighteenth century that economics appeared as a distinct category, independent of politics. So far as India is concerned, a further fact, many of whose aspects are known and studied but which is often overlooked in itself, in its full generality and fundamental character, is that the British domination emancipated wealth in goods and chattels by substituting for a political regime of the traditional type a modern type of regime, one of whose fundamental tasks was to guarantee the security of property, a regime which, compared to the previous one, abdicated part of its power in favour of wealth. The transformation of land into a marketable commodity is only a part of this change. No doubt there is in India today a distinct sphere of activity which may properly be called economic, but it was the British government which made this possible. However, there are many authors who do not hesitate to speak of the economy in traditional India, without always saying how they define it. We have already encountered the difficulty in connection with the *jajmāni* system, but it is not confined to this. Certain authors seem aware of the difficulty, for they do not separate politics from economics; unfortunately, what for them defines the 'politico-economic' domain is 'power' in the vaguest sense. Now 'power' is a notion which, while playing a central role in contemporary political science, is so obscure that it has scarcely justified this role. However, this procedure has one advantage, namely that we can find something in the Indian tradition which corresponds with the politico-economic domain, namely the domain of *artha*. In fact, throughout this chapter where we have said 'politics' we have assumed it to contain something like an implicit economic component. This is the case with dominance which consists in 'wealth', possession of landed interests, as well as political power. But the main characteristic of this society, like many other traditional societies, is that the two aspects are bound together in the same phenomenon, no distinction being made between them. One can say that just as religion in a way encompasses politics, so politics encompasses economics within itself. The difference is that the politico-economic domain is separated, named, in a subordinate position as against religion, while economics remains undifferentiated within politics. Indeed, one can study kingship in the Hindu texts, even if it receives less careful treatment than priesthood. But if we go one step further and raise the question of the merchant, the normative texts are silent. Thus we are reduced to putting a question of pure fact: to what extent was the merchant's wealth guaranteed by royal power, or, on the contrary, at its mercy? Various periods in history must then be explored to try to see what happened in this respect. The task is difficult. From a rapid inquiry, it seems to be the case that the situation varied greatly from one period or region to another. It was only in periods of political unification and large and fairly well-policed kingdoms that the king was able to concern himself with the kingdom's prosperity and promote trade for his own interests. Such fluctuations are to be expected, since the ideology is silent on the question....

NOTES

1. Bouglé, Celestin, *Essais sur le regime des castes*, Paris, 1908. *Dumont's work discusses his own position in relation to the scholarship which had gone earlier.*
2. Srinivas, M.N., *Caste in Modern India and Other Essays*, Bombay: Asia Publishing House, 1962, p. 15.
3. Campbell, George, *Modern India: A Sketch of the System of Civil Government*, London, 1852, p. 85.
4. Srinivas, M.N., 'The Social System of a Mysore Village' in McKim Mariott (ed.) *Village India: Studies in the Little Community*, Chicago: Chicago University Press, 1955, p. 18.

5. Mayer, Adrian, *Caste and Kinship Central India: A Village and Its Region*, London: Routledge, 1965.
6. Cohn, Bernard S., 'Law and Change', *Economic Development and Cultural Change*, 1959, vol. VIII, no. 1, pp. 79-93.

Caste and Modern Politics

RAJNI KOTHARI

The prevailing dichotomy between tradition and modernity has created a curious cognitive hiatus — in ideological thinking as well as in much of social science theorizing — between society on the one hand and polity on the other. The former is conceived, as if by definition, as 'traditional'; the latter, as modern and 'developmental'. In reality, however, this is a false approach to the phenomenon of modernization; it is especially misleading when the phenomenon takes place in the context of democratic politics. Political and developmental institutions do not anywhere function in a vacuum. They tend, of necessity, to find bases in society either through existing organization forms or by invoking new structures that cut across these forms. Moreover, a society that cares for legitimacy on a wide basis — and a democratic society is pre-eminently such a society — can proceed only by a conversation between the old and the new, a fusion of elements, and a readiness on the part of both the moderns and the ancients to be flexible and accommodative. In the process, no doubt, elements that prove dysfunctional to the realization of social purpose and the growth of a national consensus may need to be subdued; and this is the function of a determined leadership. The grounds for these, however, are not a priori but pragmatic and developmental.

Excerpted from Rajni Kothari (ed.), *Caste in Indian Politics*, Orient Longman, New Delhi, 1970, introduction, 8-23.

...Not until the institutional changes introduced in a particular society become part of the working relationships of that society, can they hope to gain stability and legitimacy. A 'modernizing' society is neither modern nor traditional. It simply moves from one threshold of integration and performance to another, in the process transforming both the indigenous structures and attitudes and the newly introduced institutions and ideas. This is a point that needs to be emphasized. The doctrinaire orientation of much recent thinking on development in India and in the West has produced an unhelpful dichotomy in conceptualization that stands in the way of a realistic appraisal of the development process. Fortunately, however, the processes of social change transcend the inhibitions of intellectuals and social scientists. This is especially true in an open and competitive polity. India was perhaps particularly fortunate in starting with a social system that had traditionally been flexible and capable of absorbing large shifts in the balance of social and political arrangements. It was further fortunate in having adopted a political framework which, among other things involved a free expression of interests, made competition the great medium of change through adaptation and integration, and thus avoided sharp discontinuities and disruption in the process of political modernization.

Everyone recognizes that the traditional social system in India was organized around caste structures and caste identities. In dealing with the relationship between caste and politics, however, the doctrinaire modernizer suffers from a serious xenophobia. He begins with the question: is caste disappearing? Now, surely, no social system disappears like that. A more useful point of departure would be: what form is caste taking under the impact of modern politics, and what form is politics taking in a caste-oriented society? Those in India who complain of 'casteism in politics' are really looking for a sort of politics which has no basis in society. They also probably lack any clear conception of either the nature of politics or the nature of the caste system.... Politics is a competitive enterprise, its purpose is the acquisition of power for the realization of certain goals, and its process is one of identifying and manipulating existing and emerging allegiances in order to mobilize and consolidate positions. The important thing is organization and articulation of support, and where politics is mass-based the point is to articulate support through the organizations in which the masses are to be found. It follows that where the caste structure provides one of the principal organizational clusters along which the bulk of the population is found to live, politics must strive to organize through such a structure. The alleged casteism in politics is thus no more and no less than politicization of caste. It is something in which both the forms of caste and the forms of politics are brought nearer each other, in the process changing both.... Politicians mobilize caste groupings and identities in order to organize their power. They find in it an extremely well articulated and flexible basis for organization, something that may have been structured in terms of a status hierarchy, but something that is also available for political manipulation — and one that has a basis in consciousness. Where there are other types of groups and other bases of association, politicians approach them as well. And as they everywhere change the form of such organizations, they change the form of caste as well....

There are still others who, while they do not suffer from such ·a reductionist compulsion and on the whole show a realistic understanding of the changes taking place in contemporary Indian society, have not been fully able to get rid of their professional rigidities into which their training seems to have pushed them. There are among these the 'progressive' economists who seem committed to brand anything to do with caste as reactionary, and conceive change as essentially change from caste to class relationships. There are, on the other extreme, those 'experts' on caste who consider it their duty to protect caste from any pollution of politics. In order to do this they resort to neat logical arguments regarding the 'essence' of the caste system and then proceed to define away all other aspects as not properly belonging to the operation of the caste system. Most of the latter are indologists and cultural anthropologists.... There are, finally, the political scientists who, fascinated as they are by the importance of the caste system in politics, cannot, however, escape the compulsion to reduce the interactions between caste and politics to a neat model. Although they have given up the traditional political scientist's aversion to caste, and have also mercifully given up the erstwhile dichotomy between voluntary and political forms as belonging to the 'modern' secular order and caste forms as belonging to the 'traditional' order, they fall in the same trap again by imagining a total transformation of the caste system through their involvement in politics, 'the democratic incarnation of caste' as an American author Lloyd Rudolph calls it. In the process such analysis tend to go over to the other extreme and to rarefy caste as the political force in contemporary India. Their approach once again is essentially one of explaining empirical phenomena in terms of a unified conceptual model that enables neat generalizations to be imposed on a complex reality.

All these approaches are basically dichotomous, oriented towards an ideal type 'contradiction' between caste and politics, and representing different variants of professional rigidity. What they all fail to see is that there never was a complete polarisation between the caste system and the political system, and that what is involved in the contemporary processes of change is neither a game of vested interests nor a total shift from one system to another but really a change in the context and level of political operation, a shift in social priorities, and a somewhat different picking and choosing between the variety of elements that in any case, at all times, have entered into the functioning of the social and political system in India. Thus a relative decline in the importance of pollution as a factor in determining caste hierarchy, and the diminishing emphasis on the summation of roles as involved in the *jajmani* system, do not by themselves involve any basic destruction of the caste system, but only a shift in the critical criteria of social awareness and the structural differentiations through which such an awareness is mobilized and organized. It is the virtue of a sophisticated social system such as that found in India that a reorientation of this kind is possible without damaging the overall stability of the system and without giving rise to a widespread feeling of alienation and dissonance. The caste-politics problem in India is not a problem of definition but clearly one of empirical understanding of a competitive and mobile system which could give us a reasonable model of social dynamics.

In what follows, we examine the relationship between caste and politics as basically a relationship for the specific purpose of organizing public activity....

Keeping in mind the focus of our inquiry, namely the organization of public activity and politics in a society articulated along caste lines, three aspects of the caste system call for special attention. The first is what may be called the secular aspect. In emphasizing caste as a stratification system in which distances are rigidly maintained through endogamy, pollution and the legitimacy of rituals, caste as a system of conflict and interaction has received sparse attention. Yet the fact is that factionalism and caste cleavages, patterns of alignment and realignment among the various strata, and a continuous striving for social mobility have always been prominent features of the caste system. At any rate, they are highly relevant from the point of view of secular development.

Traditionally there were two aspects to the secular organization of caste — the governmental aspect (caste councils, village arbitration procedures, and so on) and the political aspect (within caste and inter-caste authority and status alignments and cleavages). These were buttressed or dissipated by the authority relationships of local elites with the central political system or systems. Religion, occupation and territory provided the bases for secular mobility. These are still relevant for the generalised process of secularization that characterizes the major changes coming over caste society; only the emphases and proportions have changed. Instead of allegiance to a monarch or the justification of a new monarchy through the rise of a new sect or the elevation of certain caste or territorial groupings, and instead of management of the civil aspects of society at a variety of levels, we now have more participatory and aggregative modes of mobility and a greater co-ordination between levels through the agency of electoral and party politics. What has changed is the context, because of the rise of the nation-state and political democracy and the organizational structure inherent in these. But the change is not as radical as it appears at first sight; it is incremental and continuous as found in the gradual involvement and co-optation of more and more strata in the political decision-making processes....

Second, there is the integration aspect. The caste system not only determines the individual's social station on the basis of the group to which he is born but also differentiates and assigns occupational and economic roles. It thus gives a place to every individual from the highest to the lowest and makes for a high degree of identification and integration. At the same time it is an integration structure of a specific type, namely one that is more intense in its small group orientation and particularistic loyalties, and where wider loyalties operate only when they are structured through the prevailing differentiations. This aspect is important in understanding the structural impact of democratic nation-building. For the competitive style of democratic politics involves not only distributive and conflictual aspects but also aspects of group action and cohesion: democratic politics is as much a process of fusion and aggregation as of fission and segmentation. Similarly, the traditional emphasis in studies of the caste system on differentiation and affirmed segmentation has neglected the 'agglomerative' dimension. The political age, however, emphasises both, sharpens the aggregative aspect, and at the same time widens the conflict potential of aggregative processes on to a broader context. Differentiation has all along been an essential ingredient in the Indian approach to aggregation, and it has now become an important variable in the development of democratic politics.

It has been rightly pointed out that in actual operation caste affiliations take not the vertical homogeneous class and status form of *varna* but the horizontal heterogeneous and segmental form of *jāti*. And yet a system that has survived for so long creates a powerful symbolism, rationale and mythology of its own. The *varna* referent represents a 'scale of values' which provides both a spur to integrative behavioural patterns and a symbol of competition that enables the aspiring and mobile groups to lay claim to high status still affirming widely prevalent values. It 'furnishes an all-India frame into which myriad *jātis* in any single linguistic area can be fitted'. Furthermore, certain *varnas* also provide symbols of high status and at the same time symbols of 'opposition', as for example, the Kshatriyas against the Brahmins; 'disputes as to relative status are an essential feature of the caste system'. It thus enables the low-placed castes to affirm widely prevalent values in Indian society at the same time as laying claim to high status. Thus *varna* and *jati* are intimately connected in the Indian system which has made for a high degree of integration and containment of structural and psychological strains inherent in the process of technological and political change.

Third, there is the aspect of consciousness. Again, in their concern with stratification, sociologists have generally neglected the ideational underpinning that is inevitably associated with any social system. Thus the context for positions between various *jatis* often follows some variation of *varna*, either by approximating to the reality as in the case of Brahmins or by invoking a label as in the case of the claim of certain castes to be Kshatriyas. Indeed the very fluidity and nebulousness of the concept of Kshatriya, and yet its historically compelling symbolism for social mobility, has been an important lever in the secular struggles that have from time to time ensued in the various regions, following real shifts in the social and economic positions of different groups. The same holds true though in a lesser degree for the Brahminic symbol as well as the symbol of certain middle range castes. While *varna* has all the appearance of a neat and logical structure, *jàti* on the other hand is characteristically ambiguous. It has several meanings, refers to *varna* at one level and to other meanings of segmentation at other levels. By shifting from one referent to another, it demonstrates the basic continuity between the various referents — doctrinal, territorial, economic and occupational, ritual, and associational-federal (political). It also shows the difficulty of describing caste by any single set of attributes. Indeed by being different things at different points in social interactions, it provides for immense flexibility, continuity and tension management capabilities. It thus enables people to draw themselves and others at different orders of existence; and in different contexts as the situation demands. It follows that the system can also withstand the decline of certain features (considered 'essential' by some) such as the *Jajmani* system of role differentiation and summation; the importance of pollution as a system of hierarchical determination. Both functions can now be performed by other elements in the secularised setting of interrelationships....

Altogether, then, the secular, integrative and ideological aspects of caste have provided a sophisticated and differentiated cultural background for receiving the modernist impacts and responding to them without either great disruption or great withdrawal or hostility.

On such a society came the impact of 'westernization' and democratic secularism. Of interest here is the slow pace with which these influences penetrated Indian society and the positive manner in which it has on the whole responded to these changes....

Democratic politics of necessity led to...an involvement of the traditional structure and its leadership. Two results followed. The caste system made available to the leadership structural and ideological bases for political mobilization, providing it with both a segmental organization and an identification system on which support could be crystallized. Second, the leadership was forced to make concessions to local opinion, take its cue from the consensus that existed as regards claims to power, articulate political competition on traditional lines and, in turn, organize castes for economic and political purposes. With this came into being a new species of political organization, articulated around particularistic divisions, yet giving to these a secular and associational orientation. Politics and society began moving nearer and a new infra-structure started to come into being.

The actual process of interaction between caste and modern institutions was necessarily selective: it impinged on certain aspects of caste more than on others. The first to be drawn into the modernization stream was the power structure of the caste system. The second was the distribution of economic benefits. These two were closely related: the distribution of divisible benefits was interlinked with the nature of the power system that operated. A third factor that tied in with these was what may be called caste consciousness and perceptions. All of these were traditional components of the caste system that got drawn into the new processes of change.

Three stages can be noted in this process. The struggle for power and for benefits was at first limited to the entrenched castes in the social hierarchy. Leadership and access to governmental patronage came from a limited group of individuals who were the first to respond to new educational opportunities and were also traditionally endowed with pedagogic and sophistic skills that mattered most in the days of limited politics. This group, consisting of individuals from certain 'higher' castes, was not yet based on any militant caste consciousness, and was united more by a common social and intellectual endowment and idiom than through any organizational or political mobilization. However, whenever this took place mainly on the basis of one higher caste (or sub-caste), it soon gave rise to a feeling of deprivation and antagonism in other high castes, especially among those that had earlier enjoyed social or economic power, and resulted in the emergence of another political group, still drawn largely from the higher castes. The domination of an *entrenched* caste (when it took a caste form) thus produced a new response in the form of an *ascendant* caste, one that was not satisfied to simply function in the context of inter-dependence and complementarity in the social sphere that characterized the social and economic system for so long. The caste structure thus got polarized in its first encounter with the new secularism and gave rise to a bilateral structure of caste politics, very often between two castes or sub-castes, one entrenched, the other ascendant, but sometimes the latter including more than one caste or sub-caste. Such a polarization was avoided either where the one entrenched caste was greatly separated in social power and ritual status from all others or where the different 'higher' castes were entrenched at different power points, either regional or institutional, thus involving them in a legitimised coalitional pattern.

This bilateralism was followed by a second stage in which power strivings and demands for benefits exceeded the availability of resources, competing groups had to develop more numerous bases of support, and there started a process of competition *within* the entrenched and more articulate sections of society. This may be termed as the stage of caste fragmentation or of 'factionalism'. Inter-caste competition — between the entrenched caste and the ascendant caste — was now supplemented by *intra-caste* competition and the process of politicization....

The process was one of expanding the support base of rival leaders from the entrenched sections either by the simple process of co-opting leaders from hitherto dormant sections of society by providing them with junior positions and a part of the divisible benefits in return for electoral support; or, where it was not possible to tackle the problem on the basis of simple co-optation, by entering into a more organized process of mobilization through coalitions of sub-caste groups, alignment with a large number of leaders, bargaining with 'link men', appeals to wider identities and animosities, and on these bases, a secure basis of support. Where the simple co-optation device worked, the task was of including critical leaders into the power elite and not worrying about the backward 'masses'; where it did not work and the masses were more enlightened, they had to be themselves organized into the new schemes of mobilization. In the latter case, it was also likely that in course of time the new entrants to politics may themselves be able to forge a coalition strong enough to pose a challenge to the leaders from the 'entrenched castes'. This would depend upon their numerical strength, degree of economic independence and the nature of leadership. It would also depend on the extent to which the consciousness of caste in these sections took on the form of a *political class*, self-assertive and indignant against 'exploitation' from the upper castes, and eager to taste political power themselves....

We enter a third stage of development when the weakening of older identities and the introduction of politicized values coincide with other changes taking place in society through the impact of education, technology, changing status symbols, and urbanization. New and more expanded networks of relationship come into being, new criteria of self-fulfilment are created, the craving for material benefits becomes all-pervasive and family and migration systems undergo drastic changes. With these, the structure of particularistic loyalties gets overlaid by a more sophisticated system of social and political participation, with cross-cutting allegiances, a greater awareness of individual self-interest, and forms of involvement and alienation that are pre-eminently the products of modern education and the modern system of social communications. An essential feature of modernization is the development of new and sharp differentiations. Political, economic, educational and communicational functions, traditionally performed by the same social structure, are now differentiated and get established in terms of their own purposes, structures, and dynamics.

Politics, of course, is still a big enough influence but it is better understood as an active partner in the modernization process, more as providing schemes of integration and division to the developing social system than as either destroying or replacing caste as a secular social entity. What does take place is a widening base of institutional organization in which, on the one hand, caste identities themselves take to new forms of articulation thus changing the very ethics of the social system and diminishing the importance of its ritualistic and ascriptive bases; and, on the other hand, more diverse forms of organization and interest identification enter the political system and give rise to a highly mobile and cross-cutting loyalty structure in politics.

Caste on one side ceases to be an exclusive political support base and on the other side lends itself to increasing political articulation, both of which contribute to its participation in a broader network of relationships and a shift of its emphasis from a static system of stratification to a dynamic base of competition and integration. In its traditional form, the caste system integrated society through ordering primary identities along a legitimised hierarchy of status positions and occupational roles, including the 'political' roles of arbitration and adjudication. By participating in the modern political system, it is at first exposed to divisive influence and later to a new form of integration resulting from a new scheme of universalist-particularist relationships. This is, however, as already noted, no simple replacement of one system by another. In the transition, caste provides to politics on the one hand an ongoing structure of divisions and accommodations and on the other hand a cohesive element which absorbs tensions and frustrations through its intimate, particularistic, channels. Such an interactional scheme of change, while it does not suppress strata differences and individual interests, and gives rise to relatively abrupt shifts in power relations, also provides a system of containment of conflicts and angularities that facilitates the process of transition to a modern society....

It is an extremely involved process of adjustment that we have tried to describe here. The process gets crystallized in three distinct but related forms. First, there emerges what can be called a *dominant elite*, which is drawn from different groups but shares a common outlook and a secular orientation, which is structured into a diffuse network of relationships that stretches across social boundaries but yet continues to induct leaders from each important segment, which is homogeneous in terms of some of the values and rules of the game but is at the same time divided into many special groups and various elite and sub-elite positions. Such an elite structure articulates special interests and meaningfully represents the more organized segments of society, while at the same time allowing the mass of society to have its own pace of change and make its own adjustments with the modern world.

Second, castes take on an openly secular form for the new organizational purposes. There are several such forms such as

(a) 'associations' of caste members ranging from simple hostels and recreational bodies to reform clubs and pressure groups (b) caste 'institutions' or 'conferences' that are more broad-based and cover districts or even States, and (c) caste 'federations' composed of not one but several castes which may sometimes be socially homogeneous but which may at other times simply have some specific interest or political objective in common. It is this specificity of purpose that distinguishes these new organizational forms — caste associations and caste federations — from the more inclusive and ascriptive bodies traditionally known as caste. Generally speaking, they are oriented to the securing of economic benefits, jobs or special concessions, or for the more clearly political purpose of uniting to fight the hegemony of the 'upper castes' or the 'ruling castes', or for bargaining with a political party or the government, but in all cases for one or more specific purposes. The interesting thing about the caste federation is that, once formed on the basis of caste identities, it goes on to acquire non-caste functions, becomes more flexible in organization as time passes, even begins to accept members and leaders from castes other than those with which it started, stretches out to new regions, and also makes common cause with other voluntary organizations, interest groups and political parties. In course of time, the federation becomes a distinctly political group, wielding considerable bargaining strength and numerical power, but still able to appeal to caste sentiments and consciousness by adopting a common label (such as 'non-Brahmin' or 'Kshatriya'), claiming high status in the past and fostering a sense of deprivation in the present, and out of all this forging a strong and cohesive political group. It has gone far beyond the earlier caste associations in articulating group interests through political channels. The 'dominant elite' talked of above either includes leaders drawn from such organizations or is in close touch with them.

Third, alongside these new organizations, there has developed a vertical structure of factions along which the elite groups and their various support bases have been politically organized and through which channels of communication have been established between social and political forms. We have seen that such a factional structure is either fashioned along ongoing interrelationships that characterise areas dominated by peasant castes, or evolved through the operation of the political and electoral systems on the antecedent social structure thus resulting in a new polarization of solidarities and alignments. The resulting system of factions is such that it divides not only political groups but also social groups, both the traditional caste forms and the newly formed caste associations and other interest group organizations. It thus facilitates the process of cross-cutting identifications and provides an expanding network of political support for a leadership that is engaged in a competitive structure of power relationships. Factions thus provide common media of participation for both the traditional and the modernist sectors and make for their mutual accommodation and ultimate fusion....

Politics, on the other hand, is intrinsically a system of division and conflict and seeks material for the same. But at the same time it too is an integrative system based upon its own logic and mode of organization. When these two systems interact, what develops through various stages is a new mode of integration as well as a new mode of division. The process can be described as secularization of the social system and it is this process that holds the key to the tremendous shift that politics has brought about in Indian society. Whereas Sanskritization brought submerged caste groups out into the mainstream of society, and westernization drew the Sanskritized castes into the framework of modernization, it is secularization of both kinds of groups through their political involvement that is leading to a breakup of the old order and is gradually forging a *reintegration* on secular-associational grounds. During the transition, such a reintegrative process inevitably highlights parochial symbolism as providing reference points of identity and cohesion. But the same process also builds up new mixes of universalist-particularist orientations, renders the primordial basis of secular ties inefficient in itself and often prejudicial to individual and group interests, initiates the formally untutored masses into a slow awareness of the political community, and develops in them a stake in the latter.

On the other hand, for any political system to get stabilized it is necessary that its procedures and symbols are both internalized and *traditionalized*; they should not be accepted just for their utility but should be valued as such, as intrinsically meritorious and valuable, endowed with inherent goodness: in other words, the new procedures and values must themselves be turned into 'tradition', something that must be nurtured with care, developed further and made strong. No society lives without traditions and the essential challenge of modernity is not the destruction of tradition but the traditionalization of modernity itself. In the context of caste and politics, this means two things. First, those elements in the caste system that have a secular and integrational potential should get strengthened at the expense of the more obscurantist and dysfunctional elements. This, we have seen, is already happening. Second, the new dimensions that secular democratic politics has provided to the social system must themselves become enduring parts of India's traditions. This has yet to take place. The essential test of India's strategy of social change lies in this criterion of traditionalization of modernity....

NOTES

1. The term 'entrenched caste' is to be distinguished from 'dominant caste' as used by M.N. Srinivas. According to Srinivas's criteria, a dominant caste not only exercises preponderant influence economically and politically but is also 'numerically the strongest in the village or local area'. ('The Dominant Caste in Rampura', *American Anthropologist*, February, 1959). The entrenched caste, on the other hand, while it fulfils the chief criterion of economic and political power and is usually ritually 'high', it may be numerically quite small, and usually is small. On the other hand, in regions where large peasant castes are found in 'entrenched' positions at different power points as indicated later in the same para, there may be considerable overlap between 'dominant' and 'entrenched' castes, though all of Srinivas's criteria may not yet be fulfilled.

Caste and Political Group Formation in Tamilnad

ANDRÉ BÉTEILLE

It is a truism that the nature and content of politics undergo transformation from one territory to another. What is less obvious is that the caste system also evinces several levels of differentiation. These levels require to be specified before a proper understanding can be achieved of the transformations in the relations between caste and politics from one level of organization to another. Firstly, these relations are more immediate at certain levels than at others. A failure to recognize this is likely to lead to hasty and unsound generalizations. It is also likely to divert attention from the fact that the relations between caste and politics are not static but change continuously over time. Secondly, there are many alignments other than those based on caste which play an important part in the political process....

I shall begin with a consideration of how the problems of distribution and process relate to caste politics.

Excerpted from André Béteille, 'Caste and Political Group Formation in Tamilnad' in Rajni Kothari (ed.) *Caste in Indian Politics*, Delhi: Orient Longman, 1970, pp 259-98.

PROBLEMS OF DISTRIBUTION

Every society has its typical structures of power. One important feature of contemporary India lies in qualitative and quantitative changes in the traditional structures of power. New structures such as parties, *panchayats* and machines have proliferated since Independence and penetrated into the rural areas. The two main factors behind this are the adoption of adult franchise and the institution of Panchayati Raj.

These structures have also become more differentiated. In the past at the local level the dominant caste was often the principal locus of power. Today there are differentiated political structures of various kinds such as parties, *panchayats* and machines. Such differentiated structures are generally more easy to identify since they have often a formal organization. But it has to be remembered that particularly at the local level real power may be vested in an informal body such as a group of lineage elders rather than in a formal structure such as the statutory *panchayat*....

Two kinds of change seem to be taking place in the relation between caste and politics in Tamilnad, as well as in other parts of the country. In the first kind, power shifts from one dominant caste to another. This happened when Kallas and a few other castes wrested control over village politics from Brahmins in Sripuram.* It happened on a wider scale in Tamilnad as a whole when Brahmins were displaced by non-Brahmins in important political bodies.

The second kind of change is perhaps more radical than the first. Here the locus of power shifts from the caste system itself to differentiated structures of power. As indicated earlier, a vast body of new structures of power have emerged in India since Independence. Today traditional bodies such as groups of caste elders (which are functionally diffuse) have to compete increasingly with functionally specific structures of power such parties and statutory *panchayats*. Often there are mechanisms which bring about the interpenetration of the two sets of bodies.

---

* *Sripuram is the fictitious name of a village in which the author carried out his anthropological study.* Editor

PROBLEMS OF PROCESS

Structures of power exist within a framework of events and activities. This flow of events and activities creates changes in personnel and, over longer periods of time, changes in the structures themselves.

This implies that it is necessary for incumbents of political office to maintain support, in order both to acquire such office and to act effectively within it. In societies having representative government, such as contemporary India, there are specific institutional arrangements through which support is given, withdrawn or manipulated.

This support may be given in return for material benefits. But material benefits cannot be granted directly or immediately in exchange for every kind of support. For this reason the mobilization of support requires appeal to loyalties of various kinds which do not always have a tangible material basis.

It is in this sense that 'primordial loyalty' to caste provides powerful bases for political support in India. Other things being equal people are expected to support members of their own caste or kin group. To the extent that traditional values persist, loyalty and obligation to caste and community are considered 'good'. It is natural that they should be carried over to the field of institutional politics....

Caste may enter into the political process in a number of ways. Firstly, appeals may be made to caste loyalties in a general way as when Vanniyas are exhorted to vote for Vanniya candidates. The force of this kind of appeal is made evident in Tamilnad where rival parties often match caste with caste in the selection of candidates for electoral office. Secondly, networks of interpersonal relations are activized both during elections and at other times for mobilizing support along caste lines. Since kinship, marriage and commensality often stop short at the boundaries of caste, intra-caste relations are very important. Thirdly, caste associations such as the Vanniyakkula Kshatriya Sangam may seek to articulate caste interests in an organized manner.

I now turn to a brief consideration of the nature of caste. The caste system in Tamilnad is both elaborate and deeply segmented.

Segments of different orders assume importance at different levels of the political system. It seems that the political process itself plays some part in bringing about changes in the nature of segmentation in the caste system. Organized politics often necessitates the fusion of adjacent segments and this political fusion is likely in the long run to affect other aspects of inter-caste relations, such as commensality or intermarriage.

Again, the caste system is characterized by several levels of differentiations: the larger units are divided into smaller ones and these are subdivided on the basis of fairly enduring cleavages. The divisions and subdivisions either merge with one another or are placed in opposition, depending upon their context. In a given context, a unit of a lower order may lose its identity through merger with an adjacent unit, in another it may reappear as an independent entity. Thus the system as a whole retains a degree of continuity over time.

The segments themselves are differentiated according to styles of life. Each segment — whether subcaste, caste or caste group — is characterized on the one hand by certain *diacritical* distinctions and on the other by a set of *syncretic* values. The diacritical distinctions 'define the unity of the segment in terms of differentiation from other segments', whereas syncretic values 'define the unity of the segment in terms of internal solidarity'.[2] One caste differs from another in matters of dress, diet and other habits, while within the caste there is a consciousness of community. It is this which facilitates the mobilization of support on the basis of caste as opposed to other social categories such as class.

These diacritical differences are elaborate in Tamilnad. Further, some of the reinforcements they have had in the past still persist. Food habits, types of habitation, styles of dress and many other customs varied from one caste to another. The higher castes jealously preserved their traditional styles of life, even to the extent of cooking of serving food in a particular manner. The lower castes could imitate these ways to some extent, but ritual and other sanctions prevented such imitation proceeding beyond a certain point. In Tamilnad such sanctions were employed with considerable force even thirty years ago.

The unity which a caste derives from its diacritical distinctions is more in evidence at higher than at lower levels of segmentation.

Members of a broad division such as the Brahmins share only a few diacritical elements in common, whereas those of a subdivision of the Smartha Brahmins, for instance, share many. Similarly, internal solidarity is likely to be more intense within a sub-caste than within a group of related castes. The highest order of segmentation in the caste system is represented by a small endogamous unit whose members are the bearers of a homogeneous cultural tradition and are in fact related to each other by ties of kinship and affinity. At the other extreme are the primary segments (viz. Brahmins, non-Brahmins and Harijans) whose members share a few common customs and are bound together by a broad feeling of community.

We can present here only a brief account of the caste structure of Tamilnad. The population of Tamilnad can be broadly divided into three groups, the Brahmins, the non-Brahmins and the Harijans (or Adi-Dravidas). In the villages the three groups are generally segregated in different residential areas. The Brahmins live in brick and tile houses in a separate part of the village known as the *agraharam* and are marked off from the others by distinctive patterns of speech, dress and diet; within the *agraharam* there is a fairly intense community life from many areas of which non-Brahmins and Harijans are excluded. The Harijans in their turn live in their own streets known as *cheris* which have a unity no less distinctive than that of the *agraharam*. The non-Brahmins represent a broader spectrum of cultural variations and appear to be on the whole less cohesive than the two other primary segments.

Each primary segment, which appears as a unit in relation to the others, is internally subdivided. The Brahmins in Tamilnad are subdivided into Smartha, Shri Vaishnava, etc. Each of these evinces a greater measure of unity (both diacritical and syncretic) than the Brahmins taken as a whole. The Smartha Brahmins in their turn are similarly sub-divided into Vadama, Brihacharanam, Astasahashram and Vattiman. The Vadama Brahmins are subdivided into Vadadesha Vadama and Chozhadesha Vadama. Segmentation among the non-Brahmins is more complex and the Harijans as a unit appear to be less segmented than the Brahmins. But everywhere the pattern is broadly similar.

At which level of segmentation does caste enter into the political process? When we seek to analyse the role of caste in politics, which should be our unit of investigation, a broad grouping such as the Brahmins or a small subdivision such as the Vadadesha Vadama or the Pramalai Kalla?

Some have been inclined to argue that castes can successfully enter politics only when they combine into fairly large aggregates; too much segmentation, in their view, tends to reduce the viability of castes in the competition for power. There can be little doubt that organized politics at the State level has tended to bring about a certain aggregation of adjacent segments within the caste system....

The unity one encounters in the caste system is in a very real sense relative. Although a minor segment of a caste may be too small to act as an independent unit in State politics, it may be a viable unit in the village. Again, the fact that a group of subcastes unites against a like group over a certain issue does not mean that they cannot be divided over a different issue. Conversely, the fact that two subcastes contend for power in a particular arena does not mean that they cannot unite against a different caste in a wider arena. In fact, such fissions and fusions are an important feature of caste politics in Tamilnad. Further, since caste is a highly structured system, they are inclined to follow clearly-defined patterns.

Many have observed that the unity provided by caste has different degrees of inclusiveness. Srinivas tries to account for this in a way which appears to be characteristic.

The point which needs to be emphasised here is that for purposes of sociological analysis a distinction has to be made between caste at the political level and caste at the social and ritual level. The latter is a much smaller unit than the former.[3]

The distinction is drawn at the wrong place. What is important here is to distinguish not between political and social levels, but between different levels of organization in a 'merging series': State, district and village, or caste-group, caste and subcaste. Srinivas's conclusion derives from his preoccupation with the role of caste in State politics. But caste may also play a part in village politics and there the effective unit of organization may be fairly small. Nor is it correct to maintain that larger aggregates have no social or ritual unity. Such broad groupings as the Brahmins and the Harijans (and to a much lesser extent the non-

Brahmins) do have a measure of diacritical and syncretic unity and it is this fact which largely accounts for their persistence at every level of political organization.

Srinivas also appears to suggest that the larger aggregates are somehow new to the Indian scene. Even this position cannot be well sustained. Brother groupings such as Brahmins, Shudras and Panchamas were relevant to a wide variety of contexts even in traditional society.[4]

We conclude that caste may be significant to the political process at every level of segmentation, although organized politics at State and district levels has often led to a quasi-permanent aggregation of segments. Further, there seems to exist some broad relationship between the arena of politics and the level of segmentation at which caste enters into it. At the state (or even district) level, minor segments merge with one another so as to be able to operate as viable units. But this kind of merger easily comes about precisely because basis for it already existed in the traditional structure. At the village level a major segment may subdivide and its component units may be opposed to one another, again because the cleavage was present in the past.

The principle of segmentation operates even *within* the subcaste, viewed as the smallest unit of endogamy. In such cases the units which stand in opposition to each other are generally lineages.... When a subcaste is larger, culturally homogeneous and decisively dominant, the cleavages within the lineage system often assume great importance. Thus for certain purposes lineage, subcaste, caste and caste-group may be viewed as constituting a single series.

Although both the territorial system and the caste system show a similar pattern of division and subdivision, it would be wrong to assume a high degree of correspondence between levels of segmentation in the two. Even a broad grouping within the caste system such as the Brahmins may be relevant to village as well as State politics. Much depends upon the caste composition of the village or other territorial unit in question. A village which has a few castes of which one is decisively dominant will show a different kind of alignment from one where there are many castes and none enjoys decisive dominance. Everywhere, however, the caste system provides *one* set of cleavages along which units tend to merge or subdivide. Whether they do merge or subdivide

depends upon a variety of other factors, some of which are extraneous to the structure of caste. It cannot be too strongly emphasised that political alliances (at every level) often cut across
caste and are frequently based upon affiliations which have little
direct connection with caste.

The threefold division of society into Brahmin, non-Brahmin
and Harijan provides perhaps the broadest basis for 'communal'
politics in Tamilnad.... This division provides the basic framework
for the analysis of problems of both distribution and process,
and influences of political organization at all levels....

To what extent are we justified in treating such broad divisions
as castes? I have shown that a certain measure of unity is associated
with each category, and Brahmins and Harijans at least are certainly viewed as castes in a variety of contexts by the Tamil-
speaking people. The non-Brahmins admittedly are a more
heterogeneous division and sometimes (though not generally) they
are so broadly defined as to include even the Harijans. Even so
the non-Brahmin movement gave them a certain coherence and
unity, which seem to have outlived the movement itself. For that
reason it becomes necessary to analyse their role in Tamilnad
politics even though they constitute a kind of residual category....

Perhaps the most important consequence of the non-Brahmin
movement (about which more later) was the introduction of a
'communal' or caste idiom into South Indian politics. The composition of political bodies was changed by it, sometimes artificially, through reserved seats, and everywhere communal loyalties
became important in giving or withdrawing support. It is doubtful
whether the movement even attempted to organize politically
the entire body of non-Brahmins. But it certainly did succeed in
creating a lasting impression that in virtually every political context it was important whether a person was a Brahmin or a non-
Brahmin.

We can start our discussion with the Brahmins. As a social
stratum they were the first to be politicized and up to the 1920s
they enjoyed a dominant position in the former Madras Presidency. Their representation in most of the political bodies was far
in excess of their proportion in the population as a whole. The
changes in their political fortunes over the last fifty years bring
into focus not only the role of caste in politics but certain major
shifts in the bases of power in Tamil society. Certainly no section

of Tamil society of comparable size has for so long occupied the
storm centre of political debate and it is doubtful whether any
other section has undergone a more radical change in its relation
to the distribution of power.

To what do the Brahmins owe their unique position in Tamil
society? I have already commented on the diacritical differences
between the Brahmins and the others. These are certainly sharper
in Tamilnad (and in South India as a whole) than in North India.
Two of them may be considered to begin with: the real difference
in linguistic usage and the imputed difference in racial origins.
These distinctions, in part real and in part imaginary, have combined to create a popular and widespread belief that the Brahmins
represent an 'Aryan' element superimposed on an indigenous
'Dravidian' substratum. This belief has had far-reaching consequences for the development of political attitudes in Tamilnad.

The opposition to Brahmins has been expressed in economic
as well as ethnic terms. On the whole Tamil Brahmins enjoyed
a favourable position in the traditional economic system. A considerable section of them owned land, though there was a large
class of landowners — both big and small — among the non-
Brahmins. But Brahmin land-owners, whatever be the size of their
land holdings and whatever be their location, have been related
to the productive organization in a significantly different way
from the non-Brahmins. They are debarred by scriptural injunction
from the actual work of tillage.... Thus the contrast between Brahmin and non-Brahmin landowners, arises from difference not so
much in size of holdings as in styles of life. This has played a
most important part in the development of the non-Brahmin movement.

The initial consequences of British rule were probably to increase the structural distance between Brahmins and the rest of
Tamil society. Brahmins were the first to take to Western education
and Western-educated Brahmins entered the professions and services in large numbers. Those who entered the Government and
other services used the ties of kinship and affinity to recruit more
Brahmins. It is difficult to form an accurate estimate of their representation in professional, administrative and managerial positions, but there is little doubt that during the first quarter of the
present century it was extremely high. This was projected as a
major issue by the 'Justice Party which emerged in 1917 as a

champion of non-Brahmin interests and demanded more equitable representation for them in the educational system, in local bodies and in the services.

In this initial phase (which may arbitrarily be considered as ending with the formation of the Justice Party in 1917) the cleavage between Brahmins and non-Brahmins was widened in two important ways. As Brahmins entered the institutions of higher learning, the professions and the services, everywhere they formed cliques from which non-Brahmins were excluded. Between 1892 and 1904, out of 16 successful candidates for the ICS, 15 were Brahmins; in 1913 , 93 out of 128 permanent district *munsifs* were Brahmins; in 1914, 452 out of the 650 registered graduates of the University were Brahmins. In a system which was ostensibly competitive but in which the scales must have seemed heavily weighted against non-Brahmins, the latter inevitably developed deep feelings of resentment.

There was another important consequence of Westernization. As its pace mounted, Brahmins began increasingly to look outwards to the towns and cities. They left the *agraharams* in large numbers — at first temporarily but with an increasing measure of permanence — and joined schools, colleges and offices in the urban centres. They had at no time had the same intimate relations with the land as the non-Brahmins and Harijans, and Westernization loosened considerably such bonds as they did have with tenants and labourers in their ancestral villages. But although they began to turn outwards, they did not dispose of their land to any great extent, at least not in the initial period. Rather, they became rentiers and absentee landowners, returning to the village from time to time and even while there, keeping one eye on a job as a clerk or school teacher in a neighbouring town. It is evident that even within the village, relations between Brahmin landowners and non-Brahmin tenants were weakened as a general consequence of the Brahmins' Westernization. This is certainly true of other districts as well, although the changes in some districts seem to have been far less marked.

This, then, is the social background out of which the non-Brahmin movement emerged. The Brahmins were politically isolated first because they constituted a separate ethnic entity and then because they occupied privileged positions in the economy, both as landowners and as professionals and administrators. In addition, they formed a very small minority, only about 3 per cent of the total population of the old Madras Presidency....

Once non-Brahmin opposition was organized, it did not take long to dislodge the Brahmins from their privileged positions....

Political developments over the last fifty years have created among Tamil Brahmins a strong sense of identity as a minority. I have heard Brahmins with a flair for metaphor describe themselves as the Jews of South India. A strong feeling has taken root among them that they were made victims of every kind of discrimination. But they have not sought escape from organized politics. On the contrary, because of their feeling of political isolation and also because of the high rates of literacy and education among them, they are perhaps the most highly politicized section of Tamil society.

There is ample indication that the Brahmins are rapidly growing alive to the fact that if they are to survive politically they must come to terms with the non-Brahmins.... The non-Brahmin movement in its turn seems to have spent itself, having achieved its principal objectives....

It may now be useful to take a close-up view of the Brahmins at the district and village levels. I shall consider here only one district, Tanjore....

Tanjore district has been the classic stronghold of Brahmin *mirasdars*.... The Tanjore Brahmins are also highly educated and show a high degree of political consciousness. For all this, they are not very highly represented either in the organs of local government or in the local organization of the ruling party....

Till the mid-fifties the Tanjore Brahmins appear to have been solidly behind the Congress. This support was based as much on their traditional association with the Congress as on their opposition to the Communists and the DK who were then the two principal antagonists of the Congress. Things began to change rapidly after the mid-fifties. The veteran Brahmin leader, C. Rajagopalachari, was replaced by the non-Brahmin Kamaraj as Chief Minister and the Dravida Kazhagam, known and feared for its militant anti-Brahminism, switched its support to the Congress. The Congress enacted a series of laws curtailing the rights of landowners and many of the Brahmin *mirasdars* in Tanjore viewed these as being specifically directed against themselves. Finally in 1959 the Swatantra Party was formed under the leader-

ship of Rajagopalachari and many of the Brahmins of Tanjore
turned avidly towards the new party. In each of the half-a-dozen
Brahmin villages I visited in 1961-2, the Swatantra Party had a
solid core of supporters in the *agraharam*. In Tanjore district the
Swatantra Party soon came to be known as the Brahmin Party,
although many of its members were in fact non-Brahmins.

....Since the late fifties their political attitudes appear to have
been defined primarily in terms of opposition to the party then
in power....

As indicated earlier, the Brahmins in Tanjore have developed
a strong sense of unity in response to their political decline. Formerly there was active rivalry between the Smartha Brahmins and
the Shri Vaishnavas and between the two sections of the Shri
Vaishnava Brahmins. These are now largely forgotten. There is
a conscious effort on their part today to foster a sense of oneness.
The Brahmins today define their identity in terms of their distinctions from the non-Brahmins and not on the basis of subcastes.
In this regard they differ somewhat from the non-Brahmins.

Although the Brahmins constitute a very small minority in
the district, their position is different in each of the three villages
studied in detail. This is because these are all *agraharam* villages,
i.e. villages with large concentrations of Brahmins, unlike the
majority of Tanjore villages where there are no *agraharams* and
at best only a few families of priestly Brahmins.... At the beginning
of the present century Sripuram was a flourishing *agraharam* village, well known throughout Tanjore district for its large and
prosperous community of Brahmins. The *agraharam* at Sripuram
is rather unusual in the sense that it contains Brahmins belonging
to a number of different castes and subcastes. Fifty years ago the
Brahmins of Sripuram enjoyed decisive dominance. However,
the internal cleavages between the Smarthas and the Shri Vaishnavas, and among the latter between the Thengalai and Vadagalai
sections, were reflected in the competition for power relating to
the control of the village temple and other local institutions. Today
the power of the Brahmins has declined considerably, the old
disputes between the Smarthas and the Shri Vaishnavas have
been largely (though not entirely) forgotten and the Brahmins
try to face the challenge of the emerging non-Brahmin leadership
with a measure of unity.

Sripuram is, in Dahl's terminology, being transformed from a 'system of cumulative inequalities' to one of 'dispersed inequalities'.[5] In the past the Brahmins enjoyed the highest positions in the hierarchies of status, class and power. Today they continue to enjoy ritual and economic dominance but political power has shifted to the non-Brahmins. The shift in political power has been hastened by the introduction of *Panchayati Raj*.

Till the mid-forties the Brahmins dominated the village *panchayat*.... Everything changed after Independence. Now the *panchayat* is completely dominated by the non-Brahmins.... Symbolic of the transfer of power from the Brahmins to the non-Brahmins has been the shift in the location of the *panchayat*-hall from the *agraharam* to the non-Brahmin streets. In fact this shift is of more than symbolic significance. In an *agraharam*-village Brahmins and non-Brahmins live more or less segregated in their different residential areas and Brahmins do not formally go to the non-Brahmin streets unless specifically invited. Now that the *panchayat*-hall is the venue of important political gatherings in the village, many of the Brahmin residents find themselves automatically excluded from such gatherings....

These changes in Sripuram reflect changes in the bases of power in the wider system. In the traditional system power was derived largely from landownership and high ritual status. The introduction of new political structures and specialised political organs have helped non-Brahmin leaders of Sripuram (who command the support of numerically preponderant groups and have access to leaders and party bosses outside the village) to edge out of the *panchayat* the Brahmin landowners....

The non-Brahmin movement was formally launched with the issue of a Manifesto in December 1916.... The Justice Party captured the polls in the election of 1920, no doubt partly because of the withdrawal of the Congress. The three Indian Ministers placed in charge of 'transferred subjects' were all non-Brahmins and Justicites. The same pattern was repeated in the succeeding Legislature constituted in 1923. In 1926 the Justice Party was defeated by the Swarajists, but the latter refused to form a Ministry and an independent Ministry was formed under the non-Brahmin leader, P. Subbaroyan. The Justice Party rode into power again in 1930 and, though defeated in the elections of 1934, was not finally dislodged till 1937 when the Congress formed a Ministry under the leadership of C. Rajagopalachari.

After their success in the 1920 elections the leaders of the Justice Party settled down to the task of improving the position of non-Brahmins through legislative and executive action....

One of the first movements of the Council was to recommend the appointment in every district of a Protector of non-Brahmin subordinates in Public Services. Reservations for non-Brahmins were introduced in increasing proportion in the services, in local bodies and in the institutions of higher learning. With the Justice Party acting as the watchdog of non-Brahmin interests, changes began to come about in the distribution of power between castes....

However, although the Justice Party opposed the Brahmins and claimed to speak on behalf of the 40 million non-Brahmins of the Madras Presidency, it would be a mistake to identify it with the interests of the non-Brahmins as a whole. First of all, the 40 million non-Brahmins on whose behalf the Party claimed to speak included Muslims as well as Harijans, and people belonging to three language groups, Tamil, Telugu and Malayalam. While it is true that in its broadest definition the non-Brahmins included all who were not Brahmins, in practice the Depressed Classes and the Muslims were generally considered separate. Even without these two communities, non-Brahmins were a very heterogeneous group. Moreover, those who led and organizationally controlled the non-Brahmin movement in its first phase were drawn from a very narrow social base. The Justice Party actually was an elite party dominated by urban, Western-educated, landowning and professional people. It contained a formidable array of Rajas, *zamindars*, industrialists, lawyers and doctors. It was by no means a mass party and it is doubtful whether any serious effort was made to draw peasants and workers into its organization....

Though markedly elitist in character, the leadership of the Justice Party was heterogeneous in some ways. It was not a 'middle class' party for, besides professional people, there were in it landed and capitalist elements. It also included a fairly wide range of castes although most of the prominent people belonged to the upper crust of non-Brahmin castes....

Two broad conclusions emerge from a consideration of the non-Brahmin movement. Firstly, it created alliances which cut across linguistic and cultural divisions. The significance of this in a society in which 'linguism' and 'regionalism' played such an important part only a short while later can hardly be over-emphasized. Secondly, the political arena in which Brahmins and non-Brahmins stood poised against each other was a very restricted one: the participants were drawn almost wholly from the urban, Western-educated, landowning, business and professional classes.

It seems that little change took place in the distribution of power in the districts except in the towns. Non-Brahmin dominance in the organs of state and Municipal government began with the success of the Justice Party in the elections of 1920. Yet in the villages things appear to have remained unchanged for many more years.... It was only after the introduction of adult franchise and particularly of Panchayati Raj that the tables were turned on the Brahmins. By this time the Justice Party had been almost forgotten and the non-Brahmin movement had acquired an entirely different character....

The non-Brahmin ascendancy reached its peak in the mid-fifties. In recent years, with the consolidation of non-Brahmin power, internal cleavages have developed within it. These, an inherent feature of the caste structure, were partly overshadowed by a wider unity during the initial phase of the non-Brahmin movement. With the introduction of Panchayati Raj rifts amongst sub-castes probably widened, particularly at the village and Block levels.

Today the category of non-Brahmins has therefore become too broad to remain analytically useful and it is now necessary to employ the concept of dominant caste.... Dominant castes have come to play an important part in every sphere of Tamil politics and today every dominant caste of any significance is non-Brahmin. Each of these castes enjoys a greater measure of unity than the non-Brahmins as a whole although most of the major ones are themselves subdivided.

The major peasant castes are not evenly distributed throughout the State but have areas of concentration within it. Although there is no exact correspondence between these areas of concentration and the division of the State into districts, certain castes can be said to be dominant only in certain districts....

Geographical concentration may itself be seen as a criterion of dominance. Artisan castes are almost never dominant because they are territorially dispersed. A peasant caste may be dominant, although small in size, provided it is concentrated within a limited area. A caste tends to enjoy a higher position in a village within the area of its dominance than outside....

The relationships between non-Brahmin dominant castes are important at every level of contemporary Tamil politics but particularly in villages. Where the non-Brahmins operate as a single unit, they do so generally in opposition to the Brahmins (and today, increasingly, to the Harijans). In the vast majority of Tamil villages there are either no Brahmins or only a few families of priestly Brahmins who are politically insignificant. In non-*agraharam* villages (which constitute the overwhelming majority of villages in Tamilnad), the primary cleavages are often between two non-Brahmin castes or between two subcastes of a single non-Brahmin caste. (The relationship between non-Brahmins and Harijans in such villages will be considered later.)

Fairly powerful associations began to emerge among certain non-Brahmin castes from the end of the last century. These associations addressed themselves to social reform within the caste and sought to secure a better position for the caste in the wider society. A good example is the Nadar Sangam in the southern districts which agitated successfully for the rights of temple entry for the Nadars. Such associations have occasionally provided useful bases for the mobilization of political support....

The dominant caste operates in the political process not only through networks of interpersonal relations but also through an idiom which has come to be accepted by almost every section of Tamil society. A feeling has grown among people that members of non-dominant castes cannot compete successfully with those of the dominant caste. Political parties act on the basis of this feeling and are often unprepared to take the risk of setting up candidates from the non-dominant castes. Out of this has emerged the familiar electoral pattern of matching caste with caste. Even in the absence of statistical data, there is little doubt that the feature is a very general one....

In what way is caste utilized for the mobilization of political support? At the village level, leaders of the dominant caste have direct ties of kinship and affinity with their caste-fellows. Such ties may also play an important part at the level of the Assembly constituency. But electioneering at that level also involves a more general appeal to caste sentiments....

So far I have not considered the Harijans as an entity distinct from the non-Brahmins. As indicated earlier, a good deal of ambiguity is attached to the term 'non-Brahmin'....

The Manifesto of 1916 used the term non-Brahmin in its most inclusive sense, to cover not only Muslims and Christians but also the Depressed Classes....

For all this, the separateness of the Depressed Classes remained a persistent feature of social and political life in Madras. They had hardly any representation in the leadership of the Justice Party — not very surprising in view of the limited social base of the Party.... Further, the separateness of the Depressed Classes was given implicit recognition in the Constitution of 1919 in which 5 seats were reserved for them, to be filled through nomination by the Governor.

It is difficult to say how far the policy of separate representation for the Depressed Classes adopted by the British fostered a sense of isolation among them as Gandhi had feared it would. But it seems clear that in the cleavage-ridden Tamil society and in the atmosphere of 'communal' politics, the Harijans could hardly fail to emphasize the special character of their social and political needs. But their political demands were to remain unorganized for a long time. During the first three decades of the present century organized politics was largely the prerogative of the Western-educated urban middle class and the representation of the Harijans in this class was negligible.

In Maharashtra the Harijans had found in Ambedkar a leader who within a short time could inculcate in them a degree of political consciousness. In Tamilnad this was on the whole absent. Though the British gave some protection to Harijan interests for a variety of reasons and in Madras there were also a few Western-educated Harijan leaders, the group had to await the extension of the franchise after Independence before their impact as a significant political force in Tamilnad could be felt.

The issue of the civic rights has played a major part in the politicization of the Harijans in Tamilnad. Among the non-Brahmins politicization was spearheaded by a Western-educated urban middle class. Such a class did not exist among the Harijans in Tamilnad and perhaps does not exist even today. In their case it was more the ferment caused by the introduction (largely from outside) of liberal social values which contradicted the traditional interests of the dominant castes, thus creating the basis for organized political action. Traditionally Harijans had accepted their disabilities as a matter of course. As these disabilities came to be removed by law and as the Harijans sought to translate the new laws into practice, they came increasingly into conflict with the organized opposition of the dominant castes.

The disabilities which the Depressed Classes suffered with regard to the use of amenities such as wells, roads and temples or status symbols such as dress and ornaments, were generally more severe in Madras Presidency than elsewhere. Under the liberating influences of British rule and Gandhism the Harijans made attempts to do away with some of these disabilities. These attempts often met with reprisal from the dominant castes. In Tamilnad, Ramnad district has been a major arena of such conflict; conflict has particularly been a pervasive feature of the relations between non-Brahmins and Harijans throughout the state.... In Tanjore district and elsewhere young Harijans acquired a taste for organized politics in the fifties when their support was mobilised by the Communists and DK against the Brahmin landowners. Independence and...elections have now made them sensitive to their political rights and today they are no longer in a mood to have their houses burnt or their property destroyed without retaliation.

Adult franchise has changed their political situation more radically than in the case of any other comparable section of Tamil society. Although fewer in number than the non-Brahmins, they account for no less than 18 per cent of the population of Tamilnad. Their situation in relation to the non-Brahmins is, therefore, rather different from that of the Brahmins who constitute only about 3 per cent of the total population. There are *talukas* in Tamilnad where Harijans are matched fairly evenly with non-Brahmins and quite a few villages in which they outnumber them.

The Harijans also evince a high degree of unity. There are still many diacritical differences between them and the non-Brahmins and their internal solidarity in relation to the latter is often very strong....

Perhaps because of the physical isolation of the Harijans, traditional caste organizations seem to have survived to a greater extent among them than among other castes. At least in those areas of Tanjore district which I came to know directly, the traditional *kuttam* of the Pallas and their leaders, the *nattanmaikkarans,* still exercise a measure of authority, whereas similar institutions which once existed among some of the non-Brahmins are now no longer to be found. The existence of these traditional institutions often facilitates the mobilization of support by Harijan leaders from their caste.

Along with numerical strength and organization, the Harijans are also able to carry a certain measure of violence into political life. The role of organized violence in politics, particularly local politics, has not been sufficiently stressed in studies made in India so far. Yet the support of people with a reputation for violence is an important factor in village politics in contemporary India. In Tamilnad the Brahmins find the odds heavily against them in this regard. Nothing is more repugnant to the Western-educated Brahmin than to be engaged in a village brawl with members of the lower castes. Such considerations of self-esteem do not deter the Harijan from confronting the non-Brahmins.

However, although the Harijans constitute important reservoirs of political power, there are many factors which stand in the way of this power being actualized. Their economic position is in general very weak and this weakness is frequently used against them by the non-Brahmins. A long tradition of servility often prevents them from asserting their rights, although young Harijans are rapidly developing a spirit of challenge. Finally, lack of education and contact with the outside world stands in the way of their developing some of the skills which are essential for organized politics.

When this spirit of challenge confronts the entrenched interests of the dominant castes, the result is often some sort of violence....

Certain sections of the non-Brahmins are becoming resentful of the militant attitudes of the Harijans which, in their view, are fostered by the ruling party and the Government. For the poor and the landless non-Brahmins, the concessions to which the Harijans are entitled by law are a thorn in the flesh. For the landowners of the dominant caste, the rising demands of Harijan tenants and labourers are threats to their social and economic position. Clearly the dominant castes in the villages are not reconciled to the ideals of equality and social justice set by State and

Central legislatures. These conflicts are likely to persist irrespective of change in the party in power. Party leaders in their turn cannot afford to ignore the demands of the Harijans who constitute such an important reservoir of votes.

Old conflicts between the Harijans and the non-Brahmins are sometimes expressed in the new idiom of party politics....

The politicization of the Harijans has, in a sense, helped to sharpen their identity in relation to the upper castes. But it has also drawn them into new relationships which cut across the barriers of caste. Harijan and non-Brahmin leaders have learned to depend upon each other for support and patronage. New forms of association such as parties and *panchayats* are developing which are based on loyalties other than those of caste. It is true that such associations often mirror the cleavages of the wider society, but this is by no means always the case.

I have described above the part played by social entities such as subcastes, castes or caste-groups in Tamilnad politics. Although there are enormous differences between a subcaste such as the Vadama Smarthas and a broad aggregate such as the non-Brahmins, they are similar in one important respect: they are both based on particularistic criteria and as such are to be distinguished from universalistic groupings of the kind which democratic parties and governments are in principle supposed to be. In a traditional system, it would be unreal to expect the democratic process to operate without taking any account of them. But are such particularistic identities the only ones which are relevant to politics in India today? And does not the political process itself create new identities which cut across those of sub-caste, caste or caste-group?

Although most scholars would agree that caste and politics are closely related in certain parts of contemporary India, their assessment of the significance of this is likely to vary. Some like Srinivas argue that the political process tends to strengthen the loyalties of caste at least in the short run: 'One of the short-term effects of universal adult franchise is to strengthen caste'.[7] Others like Gough believe that politics in the modern sense tends to be disruptive of caste.[8]

Before turning to these questions it is well to remember that there are everywhere in India today forces external to the political system which tend to erode the loyalties of caste. I shall consider briefly some of the factors which, on the one hand, weaken the diacritical and syncretic unity of caste, and, on the other, create interests based on income, occupation, education, etc. which tend increasingly to become dissociated from the structure of caste.

As status groups, castes are differentiated from one another by their tradition of distinctive styles of life. Over the last hundred years new criteria of social differentiation have been introduced — Western education, occupation in non-traditional sectors and so on. To the extent that the new forms of differentiation run along traditional grooves, caste loyalties tend to be reinforced. We saw how the introduction of Western education at first served to increase the social differentiation between Brahmins and non-Brahmins, leading to political conflict between them. However, when these differentiations cut across traditional ones, castes become more and more heterogeneous in terms of income, occupation and education and new status groups based on these criteria are likely to compete with caste for people's loyalties....

It is also probable that caste plays a less important part in urban than in rural politics. A recent study of trade union politics in Coimbatore tends to confirm the view that caste enters into the political process there in only a marginal way. Among textile workers in Coimbatore, income, occupation and personal loyalties tend to play a far more important part in the determination of political attitudes than caste. The factory system tends to break down the homogeneity of caste and to replace it by unities of a different kind.

The political process seems to have a dual effect on caste. To the extent that the loyalties of caste or subcaste are consistently exploited, the traditional structure tends to become frozen. Thus there can be little doubt that the non-Brahmin movement arrested to some extent the attenuation of caste identities. But the political process does not operate by mobilizing only the loyalties of caste. To the extent that it leads to new associations and alliances cutting across caste, it loosens the traditional structure....

There are various ways in which participation in organized politics tends to alter the structure of caste. The processes by which this comes about are now beginning to be investigated. Rudolph and Rudolph have drawn attention to an important change which accompanies the emergence of caste associations. A caste association is no longer a 'birth status' group in which membership is automatically ascribed at birth: membership in a caste association has to be acquired, although the base of recruitment may be restricted to a single caste or a group of castes. Party programmes also may (and increasingly do) lead to splits within a caste and to alliances across castes.

Political alliances between castes and between castes and political parties tend to be rather unstable. Traditional groups which are in the same camp today may find themselves in opposite camps tomorrow. It is perhaps becoming less and less common for the same caste or subcaste to identify itself persistently with a particular political party or movement over any significant length of time. And to the extent that a caste does not identify itself persistently with any particular party but tends to divide and subdivide and to enter into multifarious alliances across its boundaries, its very contours ultimately become blurred....

The disruptive effect on caste of flexible and changing political arrangements must not be exaggerated. It is true that political parties tend to cut across caste, but so do factions and, as Brass has rightly pointed out, factions are a feature of the traditional order. Caste loyalties have persisted in spite of decades of factional politics and it is unlikely that party politics by itself will lead to their immediate dissolution. They are relatively persistent elements in the cultural idiom of Indian society in general and Tamil society in particular.

Parties, to the extent that they are responsible for the aggregation of interests, increasingly cut through the organization of caste. Everywhere leaders of the dominant caste try to capture the major political parties and this is rarely if ever done on a basis of planned, mutual understanding. Parties in their turn try to create an appeal for every major group and not merely a single group....

Today the political system is not unrelated to caste and class nor will it be so in the near future. But as it becomes more and more differentiated, new loci of power are developing and these are acquiring a weight of their own. In the past — at least at the local level — dominant caste and faction were probably the only significant loci of power, and the faction itself was largely structured by caste. This is no longer the case. Now it is possible for a man to acquire a certain measure of power by virtue of his position in the party hierarchy, irrespective of his caste or class. No doubt membership of the dominant caste helps a great deal,

but other factors are also becoming important. A fuller understanding of politics in Tamilnad can be achieved only by considering the changing relations among the major sources of power,
traditional and modern.

NOTES

1. See Béteille, André, *Caste, Class and Power: Changing Patterns of Stratification in a Tanjore Village*, Berkeley, University of California Press,
   1965.
2. Nadel, S.F., 'Dual descent in the Nuba Hills', in Radcliffe Brown
   and Forde (eds.), *African Systems of Kinship and Marriage*, London,
   1950, 337.
3. Srinivas, M.N., *Caste in Modern India and Other Essays*, 1962, p. 5.
4. Béteille, André, *Caste, Class and Power*, ch. 3.
5. Dahl, Robert, *Who Governs?*, New Haven, Yale University Press, 1961.
6. G.O. No. 114, dated 3.3.1921.
7. Srinivas, M.N. ibid., p. 75.
8. Gough, Kathleen, 'Caste in a Tanjore Village', in Edmund Leach (ed.)
   Aspects of Caste in South India, Ceylon, and North-West Pakistan, Cambridge,
   Cambridge University Press, 1960, 58-9.

The Nation and its Outcasts

PARTHA CHATTERJEE

THE SYNTHETIC THEORY OF CASTE

If there was one social institution that, to the colonial mind, centrally and essentially characterized Indian society as radically different from western society, it was the institution of caste. All arguments about the rule of colonial difference, and hence about the inherent incapacity of Indian society to acquire the virtues of modernity and nationhood, tended to converge upon this supposedly unique Indian institution.

In responding to this charge, Indian nationalists have adopted, broadly speaking, one of two strategies. The first is to deny the suggestion that caste is essential to the characterization of Indian society. This position has been especially favoured by the nationalist left as well as by Marxists. Caste, according to this argument, is a feature of the superstructure of Indian society; its existence and efficacy are to be understood as the ideological products of the specific precapitalist social formations that have their appearance in Indian history. With the supersession of these precapitalist formations, caste too would disappear. One implication of this argument is that by its refusal to ascribe to caste any fundamental significance, it is able to uphold without

Excerpted from Partha Chatterjee, *The Nation and its Fragments: Colonial and Post-Colonial Histories*, Princeton, Princeton University Press, 1993, pp. 173-99.

qualification the legal-political principles of the modern state, to dispute the rule of colonial difference in the public sphere, and to boldly advocate the cultural project of modernity.

Its difficulty as a nationalist argument, however, is that by whole-heartedly embracing all of the claims made on behalf of Western modernity and advocating them for modern India, it leaves little room for disputing on empirical grounds the colonialist criticism of India as a degenerate, caste-ridden society. By explaining the innumerable instances of caste practices as ideological manifestations of a premodern social formation, it seems to condemn virtually the entire corpus of traditional cultural institutions in India, both elite and popular. Such undifferentiated advocacy of the modern does not sit too well on claims about the identity of the 'national'. The case is made worse by a growing evidence that the spread of capitalist economic activities or of modern education does not necessarily bring about an end to caste practice....

The second strategy seeks to avoid these difficulties by retaining caste as an essential element of Indian society. The presence of a caste system, the assertion goes, makes Indian society essentially different from the Western. What is denied, however, in this nationalist argument is the charge that caste is necessarily contradictory to, and incompatible with, a modern and just society. This is achieved by distinguishing between the empirical-historical reality of caste and its ideality. Ideally, the caste system seeks to harmonize within the whole of a social system the mutual distinctness of its parts. This is a requirement for any stable and harmonious social order; the caste system is the way this is achieved in India.

This enormously influential nationalist argument has been addressed at different levels. Gandhi used to argue that the empirical reality of caste discrimination and even its sanction in the religious texts had 'nothing to do with religion'.[1] The ideal fourfold *varṇa* scheme was meant to be a non-competitive functional division of labour and did not imply a hierarchy of privilege. This idealism found a metaphysical exposition in Sarvepalli Radhakrishnan, who asserted that the *varṇa* scheme was a universal form of the organic solidarity of the individual and the social order.[2] Since then, successive generations of Indian sociologists, working with increasingly detailed and sophisticated ethnographic

materials, have propounded the idea that there is a systematic
form to the institutionalized practices of caste; that this system
is in some sense fundamental to a characterization of Indian
society, and that it represents a way of reconciling differences
within a harmonious unity of the social order.

Of the two strategies, each contains a critique of the other.
Both, however, accept the premise of modernity, the former
espousing it to condemn caste as an oppressive and antiquated
institution inconsistent with a modern society, the latter asserting
that caste in its ideal form is not oppressive and not inconsistent
with the aspirations of individuality within the harmony of a
unified social order. The former could be said to represent the
pure theory of universal modernity; the latter, its genealogy run-
ning deep into the traditions of Orientalist scholarship, upholds
a theory of Oriental exceptionalism. As nationalist arguments,
both adopt the externally given standpoint of bourgeois equality
to criticize the empirical reality of caste practices and to advocate
modernist reform. As for their overall framing devices, the former
argument, of course , has available to it the entire western discourse on modernity; the latter, on the other hand, has to construct
a special theory, in this case the synthetic theory of caste, which
however has the same form as any synthetic theory of 'the unity
of Indian society.'

REQUIREMENTS OF AN IMMANENT CRITIQUE OF CASTE

I wish to state here the requirements for a critique of the synthetic
theory of caste that does not rely on an external standpoint.
These, in other words, will be the requirements for an immanent
critique of caste. By implication, these will also give us the general
form for an immanent critique of all synthetic theories about
'the unity of Indian society'.

The starting point is the immediate reality of caste, namely
the diversity of particular *jātis* with specific characteristics. Each
jāti can be shown to have its particular quality: on the one hand,
a definition-by-self that is the positive characteristic which identifies the *jātis* as itself, and on the other a definition-for-another
by which other *jātis* are distinguished from it. Any particular
qualitative criterion that is supposed to identify a *jāti* will imply
both the positive and the negative definitions. Thus, if the Chamar

is identified as a caste that disposes of dead cattle, this definition-by-self immediately implies a definition-for-another, namely that other castes (at least, some other castes) do not have this occupation. It is thus that distinctions and classifications by quality can be made among *jātis*.

Now, these distinctive qualities of particular castes are finite and hence alterable. We have innumerable examples of the qualitative marks of particular *jātis* varying both regionally and over time. We also know that there is multiplicity of qualitative criteria which can serve to distinguish *jāti* from *jāti*. The finiteness of quality is negated by a definition-for-self of caste that shows the diverse individual castes to be many particular forms, distinguished by quantity, of one universal measure of caste. To give an example from another scientific field, particular commodities are immediately distinguishable from one another by a variety of finite qualities, but a definition-for-self of commodity, namely value, enables us to order by quantity, that is, exchange value, the entire range of particular commodities. Similarly, we can make determinate distinctions by quantity between all castes if we have a similar definition-for-self of caste. The most powerful candidate in sociological literature for this definition of 'casteness' is hierarchy. According to this argument, hierarchy fixes a universal measure of 'casteness' so that, at any given time and place, the immediate qualitative diversity of *jātis* can be ordered as a quantitative ranking in a scale of hierarchy. The universal measure appears for each particular caste as a determinate position, quantitatively fixed (higher/lower) and hence comparable, in the hierarchy of all castes. Thus the move is made from the unintelligibility of immediate diversity to an identification of the being-for-self of caste. Now it is possible to identify determinate castes, here and now, as an ordered set, unambiguous and non-contradictory, at least in principle.... This is precisely what Louis Dumont tells us in Chapter 2 of *Homo Hierarchicus*: he uses the substantive material of caste ethnology to fix the determinate being of castes.[3]

Dumont does something more, which also happens to be the next step in our immanent critique of caste. The being-for-self of caste, namely hierarchy, can be shown to imply a contradictory essence. As soon as we try to arrange the determinate, here-and-now evidence of the ethnological material in a sequence of change, we will discover in place of the immediacy of being the reflected or mediated self-identity of caste on the one hand and a self-repulsion or difference on the other. Dumont identifies from within the immediacy of caste practices a contradictory essence, mediated by ideology (or religion), namely, the opposition between purity and pollution. While the need to maintain purity implies that the castes must be kept separate (thus, Brahmans cannot engage in the polluting occupations of menial castes), it also necessarily brings the castes together (since Brahmans cannot do without the menial castes if their economic services are to be provided). The unity of identity and difference — in this case, *vide* Dumont, the unity of purity and pollution — gives us the ground of caste as a totality or system. The being of caste is here shown as mediated; its existence is now relative in terms of its interconnections with other existents within the totality of the ground. Dumont devotes the greater part of his book to defending his case that the unity of the opposites — purity and pollution — provides adequate ground for defining the totality of caste relations as a system.

Once grounded, the immediate relation in the system of castes will appear as the relation between the whole and the parts. Only the parts have independent being, but the relations between the parts themselves are the result of the contradictory unity of identity and difference. The parts can be held together only if they are mediated into self-relation within the whole of the system by force. In Dumont's treatment, the force that holds together the different castes within the whole of the caste system is *the ideological force of dharma*. The construct of *dharma* assigns to each *jāti* its place within the system and defines the relations between *jātis* as the simultaneous unity of mutual separateness and mutual dependence.

The movement of force must make apparent the process of uniting the essence of a system with its existence. Here, Dumont's claim is categorical. The central argument of his work is that the ideological force of *dharma* does in fact unite the mediated being of caste with its ideality. Thus the ideal construct of *dharma* is actualized in the immediacy of social institutions and practices. The claim is central not merely in Dumont; it must in fact be central to all synthetic constructions of the theory of caste, for all such theories must claim that the conflicting relations between the differentiated parts of the system (namely, *jātis*) are effectively united by the force of *dharma* so that the caste system as a whole can continue to reproduce itself. I have chosen to use Dumont's book as the most influential and theoretically sophisticated construction of the synthetic theory of caste.

In order to make a critique of the ideology of caste, then, we must show that this process of actualization necessarily contains a contradiction. We must show, in other words, that the unification of the essence of caste with its existence through the movement of the force of *dharma* is inadequate and one-sided; it is a resolution that reveals its falsity by concealing the contradiction within it. This is the crucial step in the critique of caste. By locating our critique at this level, where the claim that the mediated being of caste (that is to say, its ideality) has been actualized in immediate social reality is brought under critical examination, we look at caste neither as base nor as superstructure but precisely as the level of social reality that claims to unite the two. If this claim can be shown to be false, that is, if the data of caste can be shown to be *necessarily* at variance with its actuality, we will have the elementary means for an immanent critique of caste.

Dumont traverses the first two stages of this dialectic without attempting to move to the third. It is at the third stage that this critique of Dumont must be grounded. There may of course be several inaccuracies or incorrect statements in Dumont's delineation of the movement in the first two stages. To point these out is undoubtedly justified, and many commentators in the last two decades have done so, but these do not amount to a critique of Dumont, for it is theoretically possible to modify the actual contents of *Homo Hierarchicus* to yield a more correctly constituted Dumont-type construction. The critique must consist in showing the inherent plausibility and justification of the transition from the second to the third stage — and that move will destroy the central claim of Dumont (or of any synthetic construction of that type) that ideality lies united with actuality in the immediate reality of caste.

Interestingly, Dumont seems to be aware of this line of attack, and in his 1979 preface has attempted to fortify his position against it by declaring that the anthropologist's construction of a global ideology can never hope to 'cover without contradiction the entire field of its application' and must, at every stage, leave

a certain irreducible residue in the observed object. The demand
for an ideology that is 'identical in its breadth and content to
the reality as lived' is the demand of idealism, 'and it is surprising
to see it formulated by the same critics who have reproached
us in the name of empiricism for granting too much importance
to ideas and values'. He then states his own position, now suitably
modified: 'At the most general level, what our conclusion means
is that hierarchical ideology, like egalitarian ideology, is not perfectly realized in actuality, or, in other terms does not allow
direct consciousness of all that it implies.'[4] One could, of course,
say to Dumont that he cannot have it both ways. But let us
refrain from raising this obvious objection and point out instead
that the matter is not simply one of the empirical residue of
unexplained observations. Our objection will be that any Dumont-
like construction of the ideology of caste will be necessarily at
variance with its actuality because the unification is contested
within the 'observed object,' that is to say, within the immediate
system of castes.

We may also note here that Dumont himself acknowledges
that he has confined himself to the first two stages of the movement I have delineated above: his object, he says, is to 'understand' the caste system, not to criticize it. Speaking — necessarily
— from within the system of castes, I cannot, unfortunately,
afford this anthropologist's luxury, notwithstanding the fact that
many Indian anthropologists, in the mistaken belief that this is
the only proper scientific attitude to culture, have presumed to
share the same observational position with their European
teachers. Dumont further says that his is a study of 'structure,'
not of 'dialectic'. The oppositions within his structure do not
'produce' anything; they are static and not surpassed through
a 'development'; the global setting of the structure is given once
and for all. I am, of course, looking for contradictions that the
dialectical, where oppositions are surpassed through negation,
produces a developed unity and, once again, a new set of contradictions. I do not, however, agree with Dumont that the dialectical method is necessarily 'synthetic'. It is rather the
Dumont-type method of 'structure', where the whole is a
'structural' rather than a 'dialectical' whole, which, when applied
to immediate phenomena bearing the unexamined content of history, becomes profoundly 'synthetic' in its assertion that all

oppositions are necessarily contained within a global unity 'given once and for all'.

DUMONT DISINTERRED

It would be redundant here to attempt a review of the contents of such a well-known work as *Homo Hierarchicus*. I propose instead to rearrange the materials of a criticism of Dumont by Dipankar Gupta in terms of the framework outlined above and then assess what remains to be done for an adequate critique to emerge.[5]

Gupta's central criticism of Dumont consists in questioning the latter's claim that the essence of caste lies in a continuous hierarchy along which castes can be ordered in terms of relative purity. Gupta's counterargument is that the essence of caste lies in differentiation into separate and discrete endogamous *jātis*; the attribute of hierarchy is a property that does not belong to the essence of caste, and in any case, where hierarchy exists it is not purity/pollution that is the necessary criterion.

....Put in this form, the criticism cannot be sustained. The discreteness of separate endogamous *jātis* is of course the most obvious aspect of the immediate phenomenon of caste. When this separateness is seen as based on qualitative differences, we necessarily have for each *jāti* its being-by-self and being-for-another, involving, in this case, the ascription of the natural differences of biological species on an order of cultural differentiation. Every recognized qualitative attribute of a *jāti* serves to establish its natural difference from other *jātis*, and this difference is upheld above all in the rule of endogamy, which lays down that the natural order of species must not be disturbed. Kane notes the agreement of all medieval *dharmaśāstra* texts on this point and cites the *Sūtasaṃhitā*, which states explicitly that the 'several castes are like the species of animals and that caste attaches to the body and not to the soul'.[6] The point, however, is that as soon as these discrete *jātis* are recognized as particular forms belonging to the same class of entities, that is to say, they are all recognized as castes, the finiteness of discrete qualities will be negated by a being-for-self of caste embodying the universal measure of 'casteness.' Dumont identifies this universal measure as one of having a place in the hierarchy of castes. In relation to this being-for-self, particular castes can only be distinguished from one another by quantity, namely their relative place in that hierarchy. An ordering among determinate castes will then be necessarily implied. (Continuity is not, strictly speaking, necessary, even in Dumont's scheme: an unambiguous and transitive ranking by quantity is all that is required.) Gupta's criticism here is misplaced, for the critique of Dumont's method cannot be sustained at the level of the determinate being of caste.

Gupta, however, makes another set of criticisms that is far more promising. There is not one caste ideology, he says, but several, sharing some principles in common but articulated at variance and even in opposition to one another. Now, this criticism is leveled at the essence of caste as identified by Dumont. We have seen already that Dumont locates the essence of caste on the religious ground defined by the opposition of purity/pollution and claims that the force of *dharma* unites the determinate parts (the separate *jātis*) into a whole. To establish this claim, however, Dumont has first to dispose of a rather serious problem that arises in establishing the unity of the actuality of the institutions and practices of caste with its ideality. This problem has to do with the fact that the actual rankings of caste take variable forms in space (regional caste systems) and in time (caste mobility) and, further, that these specific orderings are not necessarily consistent with an ideal ordering in terms of purity/pollution. Dumont attempts to solve this problem, first, by positing an absolute separation between *dharma* and *artha*, and then asserting the absolute superiority of the former, the domain of ideology, to the latter, the domain of power. This enables him to allow power (economic, political) to play a residual role in the actual ranking of castes; specifically, the quantitative criterion of hierarchical ordering becomes a weighted numeraire where purity/pollution is the only variable allowed to fix the two extreme poles of the scale of ranking, while power variables are allowed to affect the ordering in the middle.

There is something inelegant in this solution offered by Dumont, and a large number of his critics have produced both textual and practical evidence to show that his assertion here is doubtful. But Gupta's criticism, that there is not one caste ideology (*dharma*) but several, has the potential, if adequately theorized, for a more serious critique of Dumont. If substantiated, it would amount to the assertion that the very universality of *dharma* as the ideality of caste is not generally acknowledged by every part of the system of castes. This criticism would hold even if Dumont's specific characterization of *dharma* is modified to take care of the factual inaccuracies; in other words, the criticism would hold for any synthetic theory of caste.

To develop these criticisms into a theoretical critique of Dumont one would need to show: (1) that the immediate reality of castes represents the appearance not of one universal ideality of caste, but of several which are not only at variance but often in opposition; (2) that the universal *dharma* which claims to be the force binding the parts of the system into a whole is a one-sided construction; (3) that this one-sided ideality succeeds in its assertion of universality not because of the self-conscious unity of subject and object in each individual part but because of the effectiveness of a relation of domination and subordination; and (4) that the fragmented and contradictory consciousness represent an actuality that can be unified only by negating the one-sided ideality of the dominant construction of *dharma*.

.... There is in popular beliefs and practices of caste an implicit critique which questions the claim of the dominant *dharma* to unify the particular *jātis* into a harmonious whole and which puts forward contrary claims. Second, just as the effectiveness of the claims of the one *dharma* is contingent upon the conditions of power, so also are the possibilities and forms of the contrary claims conditioned by those relations of power. Third, in their deviance from the dominant *dharma*, the popular beliefs draw upon the ideological resources of given cultural traditions, selecting, transforming, and developing them to cope with new conditions of subordination, but remaining limited by those conditions. Finally, the negativity of these contrary claims is an index of their failure to construct an alternative universal to the dominant *dharma* and is thus the mark of subalternity; the object of our project must be to develop, make explicit, and unify these fragmented oppositions in order to construct a critique of Indian tradition that is at the same time a critique of bourgeois equality.

.... Whereas Dumont treats the series of oppositions — life in the world/life of the renouncer, group religion/disciplines of salvation, caste/individual — as having been unified within the 'whole' of Hinduism by integration at the level of doctrinal Brahmanism and by toleration at the level of the sects, I will offer a different interpretation that treats these oppositions as fundamentally unresolved — unified, if at all, not at the level of the self-consciousness of 'the Hindu' but only within the historical contingencies of the social relations of power....

The question of identity or difference, one *dharma* or many, then ceases to be so much a matter of judging the inherent strength of the synthetic unification proclaimed by a dominant religion. Any universalist religion will bear in its essence the contradictory marks of identity and difference, the parts being held together in a whole by an ideological force that proclaims, with varying degrees of effectiveness, its unity. The question, rather, becomes a historical one of identifying the determinants that make this unity a matter of contingency.

It will be apparent from the histories of the minor sects that the varying intensities of their affiliation with the larger unity, the degree of 'eclecticism' the varying measures and subtleties of emphasizing their difference and their self-identity reveal not so much the desire to create a new universalist system but rather varying strategies of survival, and of self-assertion. The Bāuls openly proclaim their unconventionality and rejection of scriptural injunctions, both Brahmanical and Islamic, but live as mendicants outside society. They talk of love and the divine power that resides in all men and women and thus engage philosophically in the discourses both of Vaisnavism and Sufism, yet are marked out as unorthodox and deviant, not a proper part of the congregation. They enthrall their audiences by singing, with much lyricism, subtlety, and wit, of the 'man of the heart' and the 'unknown bird' that flies in and out of the cage which is the human body, but practice their own disciplines of *sādhan* and worship in secret, under the guidance of the *murshid*. Of sects that live on among a lay following of ordinary householders, most do not display any distinct sect-marks on the person of the devotee, so that in their daily lives the sectarians are largely indistinguishable from others. What they offer to their followers, as in the case of the Kartābhaja or the Sāhebdhanī, is a congregational space defined outside the boundaries of the dominant religious life, outside caste society or the injunctions of the *shari'ah*, but a space brought into active existence only periodically, at thinly attended weekly meetings with the *mahāśay* or the *fakir* and at the three or four large annual festivals where sectarians perform the prescribed duties of allegiance to their preceptor and their faith, while numerous others come just as they would to any religious fair — to eat and drink, listen to the music, pick up a few magic cures for illnesses and disabilities, and generally to collect the share of virtue that is supposed to accrue to one from such visits. The sect leaders preach, often in language that conceals under its surface imagery an esoteric meaning open only to initiates, doctrines that talk of their rejection of the Vedas and caste, of idolatry and *sastric* or *shariati* ritual, but the greater their sect's reach across the caste hierarchy, the less strident is their critical tone and the more vapid their sentiments about the sameness of all faiths. The Kartābhajā, for instance, originated in the eighteenth century from a founder who was probably Muslim, but the sect was organized in its present from in the early nineteenth century by a prosperous Sadgop family. It has retained its following among the middle and lower castes, and in particular draws a very large number of women, especially widows, to its festivals, but a fair number of upper-caste people have also been initiated into the faith. Not surprisingly, a distinction has been innovated between the *vyavahārik*, the practical social aspect of the life of the devotee, and the *pāramārthik*, the supreme spiritual aspect; the former virtually becoming marked as a ground of inevitable compromise and surrender to the dominant norms of society and the latter the secret preserve of autonomy and self-assertion.

All of these, then, are strategies devised within a relationship of dominance and subordination, and they take on doctrinal or ritual attributes and acquire different values according to the changing contingencies of power. But in all their determinate manifestations in particular historical circumstances, they are shaped by the condition of subalternity. I now propose to discuss the case of a minor sect whose historical effectiveness in propagating a deviant religion for the lowest castes seems to have been particularly unsuccessful: let us see if even this rather extreme case of 'failure' tells us something about the strategies of resistance and assertion.

A Teacher Among the Hāḍi

Along with the Ḍom, the Hāḍi is an archetypal *antaja* caste of Bengal. It is not particularly numerous in Nadia district, where in 1931 it constituted only about 0.02 percent of all untouchables castes and was considerably fewer in number than the Bāgdi, Muchi, Namaśūdra, or Mālo, which comprised the bulk of the 30 per cent or so of the Hindu population of that district which was classifiable as untouchable. But it stands as a cultural stereo-type of the lowest among the low; thus, for instance, when a Chittagong saying ridicules the proclivity among low castes to assert mutual superiority in ranking, it illustrates the fact precise-ly by picking out the Hāḍi and the Ḍom: 'The Ḍom thinks he is purer than the Hāḍi, the Hāḍi thinks he is purer than the Ḍom'. Risley classifies the Hāḍi as 'menial and scavenger class of Bengal Proper,' with whom no one will eat and from whom no one will accept water.[7] The Hāḍis have priests of their own and are forbidden from entering the courtyards of the great land owners as occupancy or nonoccupancy *raiyats*, but were mostly day labourers in agriculture, their traditional occupations being the tapping of date-palm trees, making bamboo implements, play-ing musical instruments at weddings and festivals, carrying palanquins, serving as syces, and scavenging. The removal of nightsoil was confined exclusively to the Methar subcaste. Risley reports that the Hāḍis also preferred infant marriage and per-mitted both divorce and the remarriage of widows, although the synonymous caste of Bhuinmāli in Dacca did not at that time allow the latter....

Balarām Hāḍi, founder of the Balarāmī sect, was born in Meherpur in Nadia sometime around 1780. In his youth he was employed as a watchman at the house of the Malliks, the Vaidya zamindars of Meherpur.[8] It is said that among the employees of the Malliks, a number of Bhojpuri Brahmans worked as guards and servants, with whom Balaram spent a lot of his time, listening to recitations from Tulsidas's *Rāmāyaṇa* and other devotional compositions. At this time there occurred one night a theft of some valuable jewelry with which the family deity of the Malliks was adorned. Balaram was suspected to have been involved in the crime and, by the order of his employer, was tied to a tree and severely beaten. Mortified by this, Balaram left Meherpur and did not return to his village for the next twenty years or more. He is said to have wandered about in the company of religious men, and when he came back to Meherpur to found his sect, he was fifty years old and a mendicant....

Balaram emerged as a religious leader sometime in the 1830s. Writing in the 1890s, some three decades after Balaram's death, Jogendra Nath Bhattacharya reported that the sect had a following of about twenty thousand people.[9] Collective memory within the sect has it that at some point in his life as a preacher, Balaram was invited by one of his disciples to Nischintapur in the Tehatta area of Nadia (not far from the infamous fields of Plassey), where they set up another centre of activity. Sudhir Chakrabarti gives a list of twelve of his direct disciples, all of whom were low-caste (Muchi, Namaśūdra, Jugi, Hādi, Māhiṣya, and Muslim), and three were women described as 'earning their livelihood by begging'.[10] Balaram also had a female companion, described variously as his wife or his *sevikā* (attendant), who later came to be known as Brahmamātā. She was Mālo by caste and ran the Meherpur centre after Balaram's death, while the Nischintapur centre was run by a Māhiṣya disciple called Tinu Mandal. Unlike the Sahajiyā Vaiṣṇava sects, the Balarāmīs do not have a *guru*-disciple structure in their order: the various centres are run by leaders called *sarkār*, but the post is not necessarily hereditary. Until a few decades ago, there were about a dozen active centres in various villages in Nadia. At present, most are in a decrepit state, although a few centres survive in Burdwan, Bankura, and Purulia, where two or three large festivals are held every year.

Like many other religious leaders who have been invested with the attributes of divinity, Balaram too has been the subject of myths that give to the story of his birth an aura of extraordinariness. It is said that at the time of his father's wedding the astrologers had predicted the son born of his marriage would be the last in the lineage. When the wife became pregnant she concealed the fact from everyone else. One afternoon a small child with a full growth of hair and beard suddenly dropped from the ceiling and, miraculously, the woman found her womb empty. She wrapped the child in a piece of cloth and quietly left it in the jungle. But she had a sister who lived in a next village. Balaram visited her in her dream. The next morning she came to the jungle and found the child lying under a tree, protected by two tigers. She took him away with herself. The foster mother found work in the house of a landlord, and when Balaram grew up to be a young boy, he was employed to tend the landlord's cattle.

The birth was miraculous, and the story has a certain resemblance with that of the cowherd Kṛṣṇa, brought up by his aunt in Vrindavan. One day the landlord Jiban Mukherjee was visited by his family *guru* and the boy Balaram was asked to accompany him to the river Bhairav, where the *guru* was to bathe. It was here that the aforementioned conversation between Balaram and the Brahmans supposedly took place, and the story goes on to assert that Balaram did in fact perform the miracle of sending the river water to a distant field. Greatly impressed by his feat, the Brahman *guru* came back and reprimanded his landlord disciple for employing a person with such miraculous powers as a mere servant. Balaram then asked that he be allowed to go back to the jungle from where he had come. Jiban Mukherjee donated a small piece of forest land to Balaram, and it was there that he set up his *ākhḍā*.

Not all Brahmans, however, were quite so generous in acknowledging Balaram's spiritual merits. The Brahman landlord of Nischintapur, for instance, greatly resented Balaram's growing influence over his tenants. One afternoon, while Balaram was away, the landlord arranged to set fire to the Nischintapur *ākhḍā*. When Balaram was told of this he remarked, 'He who sets fire to my house destroys his own'. Saying this, he left Nischintapur and in three long steps was ten miles away in Meherpur. Apparently, it began to rain from that moment, and it did not let up for the next nine days. Huge cracks appeared on the land surrounding the zamindar's barnhouse, and by the time the rain stopped, the entire barn had been swallowed by an enormous crater. The place is now called the 'barnhouse lake'.

Balaram's teachings, not surprisingly, were directed against the Vedas, the ritual injunctions of the *śāstra*, and the practices of caste. J.N. Bhattacharya, in his brief account of Balaram's sect, makes the remark: 'The most important feature of his cult was the hatred that he taught his followers to entertain towards Brahmans'.[11] He also forbade them to display any distinctive marks of their sect or, significantly, to utter the name of any deity when asking for alms. The mantras they were asked to chant were in plain Bengali, devoid even of the ornamental semblance of an *oṃ* or a Tantric *hrīṃ klīṃ ślīṃ*, and without the hint of an esoteric subtext. When Balaram died, his body was neither cremated nor buried nor thrown in the water; on his instructions, it was simply left in the forest to be fed to other living creatures. For a few generations after Balaram, the sect leaders were buried after death or their bodies thrown into the river, but now the *śāstric* procedure of cremation is generally followed.

The sectarian ideology of the Balāhāḍis pitted itself not only against the dominant Brahmanical religion, it also demarcated itself from the religion of the Vaiṣṇavas. Their songs refer with much derision to the practices of the Sahajiyā — their fondness for food, drink, sex, and intoxicants, their obsession with counting the rosary, indeed their very existence as vagabonds without habitation or kin. They laugh at the Gauḍīya dogma of complete servility of the devotee and retort: 'Why should I stoop so low when Hāḍirām is within me?' Ridiculing the concept of Caitanya as the dual incarnation of Kṛṣṇa and Rādhā, they ask, 'If Caitanya is Kṛṣṇa, then why does he cry for him? If it is the Rādhā in him that cries, then Caitanya is only half a being. Who is the complete being? Hāḍirām, of course. It is for him that Caitanya cries, for Caitanya can never find him. The perfect being appeared not in Nabadwip but in Meherpur.'[12]

The songs of the Balarāmī breathe the air of sectarianism. Boastful, aggressive, often vain, they produce the impression of an open battle waged on many fronts. There is little that is secretive about the ways of the sect. Although its following consisted overwhelmingly of low-caste and poor labouring people, there are none of the esoteric practices associated with the Sahajiyā cults. Perhaps the absence of prosperous house-holders among them made it unnecessary for the Balarāmīs to conceal their defiance of the dominant norms — after all, who cared what a few Hāḍis or Mālos proclaimed in their own little circles? As far as 'respectable' people were concerned, these untouchables were not particularly good religionists anyway — indeed, in a certain sense, incapable of good religion. It was their very marginality that may have taken the sting out of their revolt against subordination, and by asserting the unrelenting negativity and exclusiveness of their rebellious faith, they condemned themselves to eternal marginality.

THE GENEALOGY OF INSUBORDINATION

But the defiance was not without conceit. It would be worth our

while to delve into some of the mythic material with which the
Balarāmīs constructed their faith in order to address the question
raised before: How do the contingencies of power determine the
form and the outcome of rebellions against the dominance of a
dharma that proclaims its universality?

Among the myths is a very curious and distinctive account
of the origin of the species, which the Balarāmīs call their *jātitattva*.
It seems that in the earliest age, the *ādiyug*, there was nothing:
this was, so to speak, time before creation. In the next, the *anādi
yug*, were created plants. In the third age, the *divya yug*, there
was only Hāḍirām — and no one else. From his *hāi* (yawn) was
created Haimabatī, the first female, and from her the first gods,
Brahmā, Viṣṇu, and Siva, who would direct the course of the
sacred and profane histories in the *satya, tretā, dvāpar*, and *kali*
ages spoken of in the Purāṇas. The historical time of the four
ages is described in the Balarāmī songs as a trap, a vicious
snare that binds people to Vedic and Puranic injunctions. The
quest for Hāḍirām is to find in one's mortal life the path of
escape into that mythic time before history when the Hāḍi was
noble, pure, and worthy of respect.

The form of this creation myth is the same as that which
occurs in most of the popular cult literature of Bengal, the archetypal form of which is to be found in the *Sūnyapurāṇa*. There
too we find an age before all ages, when there was nothing and
the supreme lord moved about in a vacuum. The lord then creates
out of his compassion another personality called Nirajǎna, out
of whose yawn is born the bird Uluka. From the lord's sweat
is born Ādyāśakti, primordial energy in the form of a woman.
From Ādyāṣakti are born the three gods Brahmā, Viṣṇu, and
Śiva. In the Balarāmī cosmogony, not only does Hāḍirām take
the place of Nirajǎna, but he seems to usurp the powers of the
supreme lord as well.

Specifically, however, there is the story of Haimabati's birth,
a more direct and yet curiously unacknowledged element of borrowing. The literature of the Nāth cults of northern and eastern
Bengal tells the legend of how at the time of creation Śiva came
out of the mouth of the primordial lord, while out of the lord's
hāḍ, or bone, was born Haḍipā. When Śiva decided to take Gaurī,
the mother of the earth, as his wife and come down to earth,
Hāḍipā, along with the other *siddha* Mīnanāth, accompanied them

as their attendants. Hāḍipā, however, expressed his willingness to accept even the occupation of a sweeper if he could have as wife a woman as beautiful as Gaurī, and Śiva ordained that he live on earth as a Hāḍi in the company of the queen Maynāmatī. Hāḍipā was later to be celebrated in the Nāth literature as the preceptor of the great *siddha* Gopīcandra.

The similarity between this creation myth, hallowed in a much more well-known tradition in Bengal's folk literature, and the one held by that Balarāmīs, strongly suggest that Balarām in fact picked it up in order to assert a sacred origin of the Hāḍi. It is not surprising that a further transposition should be introduced into the Nāth legend in order to give Hāḍirām himself the status of the originator of the human species. What is remarkable, however, is that this source of the myth in a fairly well-established strand of popular religious tradition is entirely unacknowledged. There is nothing in the Balarāmī beliefs that claims any affiliation with the Nāth religion or with any other tradition of Śaiva religious thought.

All that is conceded is a somewhat desultory recognition that of the three sons of Haimabatī, Śiva went a little farther than his brothers Brahmā and Viṣṇu along the path of worship that led to Hāḍirām: he counted all of the 108 bones created by the latter and still wanders about, wearing a necklace of bones around his neck and singing the praises of Hāḍirām. Of the other two sons of Haimabatī, we get, in the third generation in the line of Brahmā's eldest daughter Ghāmkācanī, two brothers called Ājir Methar and Bhusi Ghoṣ, the Methar being a subcaste of the Hāḍi but the most degraded among them, while Ghoṣ is probably the Goālā caste, which is a 'touchable' Śudra caste, higher in status than both the Methar and the Hāḍi. Viṣṇu's section is more colourful, for in the line of his second daughter, Muchundarī Kālī, we get Hāoyā and Ādam, of whom are born two sons, Hābel and Kābel. Undoubtedly, we have here the Old Testament story of the genesis as related in the Koran — that is, Haw'wa (Eve) and Adam and their sons Habil (Abel) and Qabil (Cain) — slotted in the fourth and fifth generations of the human species. In Hābel's line, we then get four *jātis* — Sheikh, Saiyad, Mughal, and Pathan, the four traditional classificatory groups among Indian Muslims — and in Kābel's line we get Nikiri, Jolā (low-status Muslim fishermen and weaver castes), and, believe it or not,

Rajput. Of Visnu's third child, Musuk Kāli, are born three sons. The eldest, Parāśar, is a sage and he fathers eleven children, namely the goat, tiger, snake, vulture, mouse, mosquito, elephant, horse, cat, camel, and monkey! The youngest son, Rṣabh, is also a *muni* (sage) and from his grandsons originate thirteen Brahman groups, whose names are Dobe, Cobe, Pāṭhak Pāṇḍe, Teoyāri, Mi śir, and so forth — the most recognizable names here are those of Bihar and Uttar Pradesh Brahmans, and none is a Bengali name. (Perhaps we ought to recall Balarām's early assocaiton with Bhojpuri Brahmans in the house of his landlord employer.) The Bengali Brahmans originate in a particularly degraded section, for Pāthak had two children, Vṛṣa (bull) and Meṣa (sheep), one born of an untouchable Bede woman and the other of an untouchable Bāgdi woman. From them originate all of the Brahman lineages of Bengal, such as Bhāṭije, Bāḍije, Mukhuje, Gagāl, Ghuṣāl, Bāgji, Lahaḍī, Bhādariyā, and so forth.

There is much more in this extraordinary genealogical tree whose meanings are not transparent to the uninitiated; even the present-day leaders of the cult cannot explain many of the references. The ramifications of Balarām's *jātitattva*, inasmuch as it attempts to define a new set of relations between various social groups, are for the most part unclear. What is clear, however, is first that the scheme continues to undertake the classification of social groups in terms of the natural division into species, and it does this to a great extent by transforming the relations between elements within a popularly inherited mythic code; and second that by overturning the hierarchical order of the Puranic creation myths, it pushes the very ideality of the dominant scheme of caste to a limit where it merges with its opposite. Balarām's *jātitattva* does not assert that there are no *jātis* or differences between social groups akin to the differences between natural species. Rather, by raising the Hāḍi to the position of the purest of the pure, the self-determining originator of differentiations within the genus, and by reducing the Brahman to a particularly impure and degenerate lineage, it subverts the very claim of the dominant *dharma* that the actual social relations of caste are in perfect conformity with its universal ideality.

It does so without, of course, asserting a new universal. That mark is imprinted on the consciousness of the yet unsurpassed limit of the condition of subalternity. The conceit shown in the construction of Balarām's *jātitattva* is a sign of conscious insubordination. But there is no trace in it of a self-conscious context for an alternate social order.

Or are we being too hasty in our judgement?

THE BODY AS THE SITE OF APPROPRIATION

Caste attaches to the body, not to the soul. It is the biological reproduction of the human species through procreation within endogamous caste groups that ensures the permanence of ascribed marks of caste purity or pollution. It is also the physical contact of the body with defiling substances or defiled bodies that mark it with the temporary conditions of pollution, which can be removed by observing the prescribed procedures of physical cleansing. Further, if we have grasped the essence of caste, the necessity to protect the purity of his body is what forbids the Brahman from engaging in acts of labor that involve contact with polluting material and, reciprocally, requires the unclean castes to perform those services for the Brahman. The essence of caste, we may then say, requires that the laboring bodies of the impure castes be reproduced in order that they can be subordinated to the need to maintain the bodies of the pure castes in their state of purity. All the injunctions of *dharma* must work to this end.

When popular religious cults deviate from the dogma of the dominant religion, when they announce the rejection of the Vedas, the *śāstric* rituals or caste, they declare a revolt of the spirit. But the conditions of power which make such revolts possible are not necessarily the same as those that would permit a practical insubordination of labouring bodies. To question the ideality of caste is not directly to defy its immediate reality.

It is not as though this other battle has not been waged. Let us leave aside those high points of popular protest which take the explicit political forms of insurgency: these have received a fair amount of attention from historians, their general features have been examined, and their historical limits broadly delineated. We are also not considering here those particular or individual instances of disobedience, whether demonstrative or covert, which undoubtedly occur in the daily life of every village in India. Instead, let us turn our eyes to the practical aspects of the religious life of the deviant cults we have been talking about. All of these are fundamentally concerned with the body. The Sahajiyā cults practice the forms of bodily worship that do not respect the dictums of either the *śāstra* or the *shari'ah*. But they can be conducted only in secret, under the guidance of the guru, and their principles can be propagated only in the language of enigma. Where they seek an open congregation, it takes the antistructural form of the *communitas* of periodic and momentary religious festivals. And yet there is, underlying it all, the attempts to define a claim of proprietorship over one's own body, to negate the daily submission of one's body and its labour to the demands made by the dominant *dharma* and to assert a domain of bodily activity where it can, with the full force of ethical conviction, disregard those demands. Notice, therefore, the repeated depiction of the body in the songs of *dehatattva* not simply as a material entity but as an artefact — not a natural being at all but a physical construct. The body is a house, or a boat, or a cart, or a weaver's loom, or a potter's wheel, or any of countless other instruments or products of labour that remain at the disposal and use of one who possesses them. But the very secretiveness of those cult practices, the fact that they can be engaged in only, as it were, outside the boundaries of the social structure, sets the limit to the practical effectiveness of the claim of possession; nor surprisingly, it draws upon itself the charge of licentiousness.

The practical religion of the Balāhāḍis takes a different form. Their sectarianism is not, as we have seen, secretive, nor is it primarily conceived as a set of practices engaged in beyond the margins of social life. Rather, their forms of worship involve a self-disciplining of the body in the course of one's daily social living. Here too the body is an artefact, but it can be used by its owner with skill and wisdom or wasted and destroyed by profligacy....

...There are unmistakable signs here of a consciousness alienated from the dominant *dharma* but apparently bound to nothing else than its spirit of resolute negativity. Its practical defeat too is borne out by the facts of social history. Yet, is there not here an implicit, barely stated, search for a recognition whose signs lie not outside but within one's own self? Can one see here the trace of an identity that is defined not by others but by oneself? Perhaps we have allowed ourselves to be taken in too easily by the general presence of an abstract negativity in the autonomous domain of subaltern beliefs and practices and have missed those marks, faint as they are, of an immanent process of criticism and learning, of selective appropriation, of making sense of and using on one's own terms the elements of a more powerful cultural order. We must, after all, remind ourselves that subaltern consciousness is not merely structure, characterized solely by negativity; it is also history, shaped and developed through a changing process of interaction between the dominant and the subordinate. Surely it would be wholly contrary to our project to go about as though only the dominant culture has a life in history and subaltern consciousness is eternally frozen in its structure of negation.

THE IMPLICIT AND THE EXPLICIT

We must, however, be careful to avoid the easy, mechanical transposition of the specifics of European history. The specific forms of immanent development necessarily work with a definite cultural content. It seems quite far-fetched to identify in the criticisms of caste among the deviant religions the embryo of a Protestant ethic or an incipient urge for bourgeois freedom. What we have is a desire for a structure of community in which the opposite tendencies of mutual separateness and mutual dependence are united by a force that has a greater universal moral actuality than the given forms of the dominant *dharma*. For want of a more concrete concept of praxis, we may call this desire, in an admittedly abstract and undifferentiated sense, a desire for *democratization*, where rights and the application of the norms of justice are open to a broader basis of consultation, disputation, and resolution.

Every social form of the community, in the formal sense, must achieve the unity of mutual separateness and mutual dependence of its parts. The system of castes, we have seen, makes this claim, but its actuality is necessarily in disjunction with its ideality. The external critique of caste, drawn from the liberal ideology of Europe, suggests that a legal framework of bourgeois freedom and equality provides an alternative and, in principle, more democratic basis for this unification. This has been the formal basis of the constitutional structure of the post-colonial state in India. And yet the practical construction of this new edifice out of the given cultural material has been forced into an abandonment of its principles from the very start — notice, for instance, the provisions of special reservations on grounds of caste. The new political processes have, it would seem, managed to effect a displacement of the unifying force of *dharma* but have replaced it with the unifying concept of 'nation' as concretely embodied in the state. What has resulted is not the actualization of bourgeois equality at all but rather the conflicting claims of caste groups (to confine ourselves to this particular domain of social conflict), not on the religious basis of *dharma* but on the purely secular demands of claims upon the state. The force of *dharma*, it appears, has been ousted from its position of superiority, to be replaced with a vengeance by the pursuit of *artha*, but, pace Dumont, on the basis again of caste divisions. On the one hand, we have the establishment of capitalist relations in agricultural production in which the new forms of wage labour fit snugly into the old grid of caste divisions. On the other hand, we have the supremely paradoxical phenomenon of low-caste groups asserting their very backwardness in the caste hierarchy to claim discriminatory privileges from the state, and upper-caste groups proclaiming the sanctity of bourgeois equality and freedom (the criterion of equal opportunity mediated by skill and merit) in order to beat back the threat to their existing privileges. This was evidenced most blatantly in the violent demonstrations over the adoption of so-called Mandal Commission recommendations by the government of India in 1990. What are we to make of these conflicting desires for democratization?

There is no alternative for us but to undertake a search, both theoretical and practical, for the concrete forms of democratic community that are based neither on the principle of hierarchy nor on those of bourgeois equality. Dumont's posing of the principles of *homo hierarchicus* against those of *homo equalis* is a false, essentialist, positing of an unresolvable antinomy. We must assert that there is a more developed universal form of the unity of separateness and dependence that subsumes hierarchy and equality as lower historical moments.

The point is to explicate the principles and to construct the concrete forms of this universal. In Indian politics the problem of unifying the opposed requirements of separateness and dependence has been concretely addressed only at the level of the structure of federalism, a level where the problem is seen as permitting a territorial resolution. The attempt has had dubious success. In other domains, of which caste is a prime example, politics has drifted from one contentious principle to another (bourgeois equality, caste-class correlation, discriminatory privileges for low castes through state intervention, etc.) without finding adequate ground on which it can be superseded by a new universal form of community.

But, ...there does not exist a level of social life where labouring people in their practical activity have constantly sought, in their 'common sense', the forms, mediated by culture, of such community. The problem of politics is to develop and make explicit what is only implicit in popular activity, to give to its process of mediation the conditions of sufficiency. The point, in other words, is to undertake a criticism of 'common sense' on the basis of 'common sense'; not to inject into popular life a 'scientific' form of thought springing from somewhere else, but to develop and make critical an activity that already exists in popular life.

NOTES AND REFERENCES

1. Gandhi, M.K., 'Dr Ambedkar's Indictment II', in *Collected Works*, Publications Division, Delhi, 1976, vol. I, p. 53.
2. Radhakrishnan, S., *Eastern Religions and Western Thought*, Oxford University Press, New York, 1959.
3. Dumont, Louis, *Homo Hierarchicus*, ch. 2.
4. *ibid.*, revised ed. Delhi, Oxford University Press.
5. Gupta, Dipankar, 'Continuous Hierarchies and Discrete Castes', *Economic and Political Weekly*, vol. XIX, nos. 46-8, 1984.
6. Kane, P.V., *History of Dharmashastra*, vol. 2, pt. 1, Bhandarkar Oriental Research Institute, Poona, 1974, 52.
7. Risley, H.H., *The Tribes and Castes of Bengal*, Firma K. L. Mukherjee, Calcutta, 1981, vol. 1, 314-16.
8. The account relies on Chakrabarti, Sudhir, *Balahadi Sampraday ar Tader Gan*, Pustak Bipani, Calcutta, 1986.
9. Bhattacharya, J.N., *Hindu Castes and Sects*, Editions Indian, Calcutta, 1973, 388-9.
10. Chakrabarti, S., ibid. 27-8.
11. Bhattacharya, J.N., ibid., 389.
12. Chakrabarti, S., ibid., 44-5.

FURTHER READINGS

Bose, Nirmal Kumar, *The Structure of Hindu Society*, translated by André
    Béteille, Sangam Books, Orient Longman, New Delhi, 1975.
A concise, and subtle treatment of caste, this provides an excellent account
of both the structure of the caste order, and its historical logic of expansion.
It is particularly notable for its deft use of anthropological technique for
the construction of a historical argument. This book is also remarkable
for its refusal to divide the ideological and material-productive aspects
of the caste system.

Dutta, Bhupendra Nath, *Studies in Hindu Social Polity*, Purabi Publications,
    Calcutta, 1948.
This represents one of the first systematic attempts to understand the
caste order from the orthodox Marxist point of view, and shows both
its strengths and limitations.

Ghurye, G.S., *Caste and Class in India*, Popular Prakashan, Bombay, 1950.
An excellent discussion of the historical sociology of caste, starting from
the ancient period, discussing the historical changes in caste structure
in the medieval and colonial period in considerable detail.

Hutton, J.L., *Caste in India*, Oxford University Press, Bombay, 1963.
A detailed descriptive analysis of the structure and practices of the caste
system, which is attentive to regional variations and specificities.

Dumont, Louis, *Homo Hierarchicus: The Caste System and Its Implications*,
    Weidenfeld and Nicolson, London, 1970.
Among modern texts, Dumont's work has exerted enormous influence,
due to the clarity and persistence with which its central theses are developed.
Despite serious criticisms, this survives as a standard presentation of
what the caste system is about. Another useful feature of Dumont's treatment is his constant intercultural frame of reference.

Béteille, André, *Caste, Class and Power*, University of California Press,
    Berkeley, 1965.
Among the most lucid and complex analyses of the interaction between
caste structures and the institutional logic of modernity, this work draws
its arguments from a scrupulously detailed case-study of a Tamil village.

II

Historical Refigurations of Power

If we follow the argument sketched in Part I, we have to abandon the simple and indolent dichotomy of an unchanging tradition and fast-changing modern period. The idea of a 'tradition' remains a serviceable concept only if it is invested with some historical content, and we conclude that tradition is not ahistorical, but has a history which is different in rhythm and character from the history of modernity, and also a history which, for various reasons, is more difficult to reconstruct. One of the major problems in Indian history is to analyse the historical relation between the social and productive arrangement of caste and the power of political authority. But sociological histories of power are absent, and difficult to reconstruct. Social historians like D.D. Kosambi had given some attention to such transformations and their historical logic in the ancient and medieval periods, but the historical sociology of power in pre-modern India is still a relatively undeveloped subject.

Although the modern state in India, since at least colonial times, is a single entity, it does not follow that the historical antecedents of that state would be anything like so singular. Certainly, a historiographic convention grew up during the colonial times which sought to give this state a single history by forming a historical narrative of empires which seemed to form the natural 'history' of this colonial, and subsequently national state. This would trace a political history of a singular, unproblematic India from the great ancient empires, through the Sultanat of Delhi, the Mughals to the colonial rule of the British. But the actual political past was far more diverse, particularly beyond the state of colonial India when such an idea of territorial *political* unity had not formed. First, the times in which imperial orders existed were a segment of the entire history; and there were much longer periods when political life was not dominated by such large, spectacular imperial formations. Secondly, the different regions of India had separate pasts, with their specific political organizations and distinctive traditions of rulership. Satish Saberwal's wide-ranging exploration of the various ruling styles prevalent in pre-colonial India does a great deal to restore to us the sense of diversity of these pasts and bring them into some explanatory connection with the modern state that grew up during the colonial and the nationalist period. The great diversity of land settlement arrangements that the British installed in various parts of India showed that they had a practical awareness of these diverse traditions of rule and were seeking to find a modern institutional form which would suit local histories.

The imperial bias in telling the story of the state generally assumed that there was a cyclical movement in the organization of power in Indian society. When empires arose, society was brought under proper administration and authority; when they collapsed, society slipped into disorder. One ideological implication of this view was to see the establishment of British power as an event that rescued Indian society from the anarchy resulting from the collapse of Mughal order. Recent historical research has tended to question this equation of order with imperial formations, and particularly the assessment of the eighteenth century. Several works point to the eighteenth century as a period of great commercial and state-building energy, precisely because the large overarching imperial order, which sought to impose a relatively uniform regime of laws, declined, and allowed opportunity and space for improvisation. In any case, it seems hasty to equate order with imperial states; it seems more reasonable now to assume that both imperial and more local authority produced different kinds of power arrangements and ordering regimes, rather than a dichotomy of order and anarchy. This surely had something to do with the fact that modern histories were produced as either genealogies of the colonial or the national state; and ironically, it was ideologically beneficial for both of these to appropriate the imperial sequence as their 'proper' past.

Modern historians have also pointed out that if sovereignty, the power to take ultimate decision, is assumed in the definition of the state (as it usually is), it would be difficult to call many of such forms of political authority 'states' at all. They do not seem to have the vertical order of power normally associated with modern state forms, and the authority of the political ruler is severely constrained in many significant fields. Some historians have thus suggested a concept of a 'segmentary' state instead of simply the unmodified noun, which creates a misleading equation between those structures and the new kind of political power which emerged with colonialism. It has been suggested by some modern historical research that even before the British entered the political organization of Indian society, some endogenous beginnings of modernity are discernible. The Mughals, as their empire expanded and acquired stability, experimented with forms of administration which evolved towards bureaucratic forms. Though, this would appear doubtful if the Weberian concept of bureaucracy is applied more strictly; since, for Weber, what matters is not the size or reach of the organization, but its main principles, like abstract rules, anonymity, bureaucratic impersonality, service careers etc. Secondly, historians have at times drawn attention to the striking expansion of commercial activity in post-Mughal times, and implied that the British domination of India became possible not because it went against the logic of internal evolution, but in its favour. The British sided with the spirit of commercial expansion within India, and thus there was an elective affinity between British colonial moves and indigenous trends towards 'capitalist development'. On this question too there can be serious disagreements. While the expansive power of commerce is undeniable, it could be doubted if, on a more stringent definition of capitalism, this commercial expansion could be seriously termed a rise of capitalism, which was, ironically, blocked by the rise of British colonial power.

But whatever our view of the state of political things before the arrival of British power, the most serious and wide-ranging transformations took place with the coming of a colonial modernity in India. The British administration in India was armed with some techniques unprecedented in Indian history. It had control over not only far superior military technology, but also social techniques of organization associated with European rationalist reconstruction of society. Two of these were most significant. The first was the introduction of a systematic logic of bureaucratization of political power, which refers not only to the apparatus of a bureaucracy, but also to a certain way of producing and structuring rules. Compared to the modern states of nineteenth century Europe, colonial power in India lacked reach, control, penetration etc. But it was a far more ambitious and effective state than anything that had gone before. Since the British were foreign rulers acquiring the control over a land they saw as fundamentally different from their own societies, they engaged first in enormous cognitive enterprises of mapping and counting its features. Some of these rationalist processes may have led, ironically, to a freezing of elements which were allowed to act in more fluid ways in the premodern era, and colonialism may have played a part in artificially 'traditionalising' Indian society.

To sort out the modern from the colonial is essential, though difficult at times. Certainly, modern forms of political rule came into India with colonial power. The process of enumeration of identities, although imported into India by colonial administrative processes, is not intrinsically connected to colonialism; i.e., it would not disappear with colonial power. If we believe that the political world has a hierarchy of layers inside it, some of which change slowly over very long periods, others relatively faster, it is essential to enquire about the different pasts that the Indian state contains within itself, and has to contend with. It is of course possible to have a strongly one-sided belief in the state's power to restructure society and remain insulated from its influences. Some extreme forms of modern constitutionalism would encourage that kind of thinking. Constitutions are great foundational acts, which pretend to write new and appropriate rules on the relevant society, which must be supposed to be emptied of all its regulative contents. But this obviously puts excessive faith in the state. Even if the state could insulate itself completely from societal influence, ordinary people would respond and react to the new state according to rules of experience generated from their dealings with earlier forms of power. In this indirect and insidiously interactive way, the new state, which denied the existence of the past, may have to contend with its vestigial remains. History, or the weight of the past, might exist not as obstinate, ineradicable structures of institutional behaviour but as more elusive forms of political experience. It is better therefore, to bring the past into our discussion, than to pretend it does not exist. Satish Saberwal's essay serves to show the multiplicity of these histories which converge on the modern Indian state. Nicholas Dirks' contribution, excerpted from the introduction of his interesting ethno-history of a small South Indian kingdom suggests, against the Dumontian view of caste, that the social order of caste depended heavily on the power of the state. My paper deals with the specific problems of the form and function of colonial power.

On the Diversity of Ruling Traditions

SATISH SABERWAL

PRELIMINARIES

Very generally, we may see Indian society, over the past century or two, as a segmentalized, cellular society getting restructured for megasocietal space. This megasocietal space is subcontinental in scale, and recent decades have added to it a substantial international dimension with several components: not only the general global village aspect with its multinational corporations, mass media, and air travel and pools of symbols and technologies, but also, for India, the considerable international emigration and its social (including political) consequences.

In appraising the political processes in India since 1947, it is necessary to remember that it was impossible, at that point in time, to pick up from where the eighteenth century had left off. Between the time that the indigenous élites lost control over their own societies, and the moment of independence, the informational, technological, organizational and other changes had been such as to preclude a return to the pre-colonial arrangements, at least in any deliberate manner....

Excerpted from Satish Saberwal, 'On the Diversity of Ruling Traditions', in Sudipta Kaviraj and Martin Doornbos (eds.), *State-Formation in Europe*, Sage Publishers, New Delhi, forthcoming.

Apropos the earlier political traditions, one notices on the Indian side that there is a multiplicity of traditions. The political institutions and supporting arrangements are markedly divergent as between such polities as the Rajputs, the Mughals, and Vijayanagar, and no one case may serve as wholly representative.... The colonial state is the setting for the mixing of traditions to begin, and, in a major transformation, the process leads into the regime established by the Constitution in 1950. My central contention is that between the two sets of traditions there are tensions — weak or strong, latent or manifest — and I shall suggest tentatively four dimensions to indicate the major kinds of these tensions.

PRECOLONIAL TRADITIONS

Mobilizational energy

Confining persons into their segmental spaces may indeed be taken as the principal, if unintended, theme of the caste order. Yet it supported a complex civilization, that continued over millennia.... During the past two centuries, furthermore, the caste order has often provided considerable resources that were used by persons and groups for propulsion into activities and relationships of growing and sometimes vast, magnitudes.

Let us try then to identify the settings within the caste order in which social energies have historically been available for mobilization. I shall argue that the caste order allowed for a relatively limited set of institutions or...types of frameworks in which shared objectives must be set and pursued....

...The caste order could not easily sustain open institutions of an impersonal sort, institutions which would select their members without reference to prior ties of kinship and *jāti*: the kind of impersonal relationships...which began to spread in Europe by the twelfth century and the kind of institutionalization which has given Europe its muscle since then. Overall, I look for the limits of how far mobilization could go in a particular framework — and ask why it could go no further.

The Brahminical social order ensured that ties of kinship and *jāti* (that is, the caste group) would be available to virtually everyone — except perhaps the renouncers. Consequently, one could count on being able to mobilize at least some resources in this framework in virtually any setting; in recent decades, though, this assurance has been declining. To take measure of this protean resource — its diversity, its malleability, and also its limits — we may consider a variety of domains: physical and social mobility; mobilization for power; commerce; learning; and other specialist occupations, say that of the *devadasis* in the great southern temples. Here we shall examine only situations pertaining to power.

We begin by noticing several general processes which have been at work historically. Within the village, a particular land-controlling family could organize the full round of agricultural activity with its dependents (in northern India, the *kamins*), tied together in *jajmani* and cognate frameworks; and, collectively, the land-controllers could commandeer the whole village for their purposes, both secular and ritual. The social structure of the village was constituted with relatively small, sharply bounded units, able to resist attempts at fluidizing them into larger social spaces. Furthermore, the control over land rested ultimately on rights of conquest; and these rights of conquest needed continual renewal by way of defence against all comers. This defence was likely to be more effective if castemates would stand together and fight for the cause — unless a *rāja* or an imperial power, or an entrenched normative order, guarded particular land rights in a locality.

Kinship and *jāti* have been crucial because their webs have been important in conserving and including (and thus transmitting) attitudes, knowledge, and skills associated with a *jati*'s particular occupational niche. Indeed, consequently, the participation in, and the influence of, these webs of relations has been the mechanism which shaped the structure of personality characteristic of a *jāti*....

In the course of coping with changing milieux, members of a *jāti* could at times modify their occupational profiles markedly, even while the *jāti*-identity, anchored to a durable web of relationships and associated symbols, remained intact....

The *jāti* has also been a field for other kinds of mobilization, say for colonizing virgin lands, and for resisting expansive imperial centres. The latter effort has marked the Rajputs in northern India particularly: the use of force and power became their forte historically. The point made earlier concerning the importance of family and *jāti* for transmitting attitudes, knowledge, and skills, and indeed personality structures, has been documented particularly well for the Rajputs....

Rajput polity

Studies in social structure and social history through much of north India bear witness to the widespread dominance of Rajputs in large parts of this region. This pattern has been noticed in recent ethnographic work in rural areas, for Rajput polity has always included a large element of localized dominance; but we shall see that this was part of much wider struggles for control during the precolonial period.

B.D. Chattopadhayaya has documented the gradual constitution of the Rajput *jati* during the later first and early second millennia, out of the families ruling in localities in Gujarat and Rajasthan, and commonly known by such terms as *Rajaputras* (literally sons of kings) and its cognates. Marriages between these ruling families were a major device for constituting the caste. Over time the lines of descent received increasing recognition, though the social category has retained an openness to new groups admitted into the Rajput fold 'by virtue of their political initiative and power'.[1] 'The consolidation of Rajput structures may be viewed', Chattopadhyaya adds cautiously, 'as a result of collaboration between emerging clans, not only in terms of inter-clan marriage relationship but also in terms of participation at various levels of the polity and the circulation of clan members in different kingdoms and courts'. These themes continued to mark the Rajput style in later centuries.

Rajput styles of dominance have been supported by socialization for inter-personal aggression...and their willingness and ability to use force has undoubtedly served historically to reiterate the domination. The Rajput social frameworks for the exercise of power have been constituted out of two sometimes competing principles: one is kinship, including the ties of both descent and marriage; and other is the tie between patron and client or master and servant. Sometimes an official link would follow the line of clientship and, as we shall see, the social boundary within which this could be done has been subject to historical redefinition.

Interlinked, far-flung webs of kinship, affinity, and clientship helped constitute vast social networks. The resultant spread of social ties would provide a Rajput with unusual opportunities:

the sensing of political possibilities and for mobilizing the resources needed for pressing one's political ambitions. Consequently,
in the Rajput states of Rajasthan, the primary political relations
were intra-familial and intra-caste, within the Rajput *jāti*. These
social networks included the dominance both of numerous independent rulerships and of the lesser Rajputs in their villages.
At least in medieval Rajasthan, the Rajputs came to enforce a
virtual monopoly over exercising power, and indeed over competing for it, though this reflected in part their willingness to
open Rajput status to new groups emerging to dominance, including immigrant Muslim ruling groups as early as the 1400s....

In the formation of Rajput identities in a later medieval period,
Norman Ziegler[2] stresses the weight of the tie between a three-
to-six generational patrilineal group (*khamp*) and a territory over
which it claimed hereditary control, although the *khamp* was also
part of a much wider patrilineal brotherhood. In some regions,
as in western Marwar, ties within the brotherhood remained
egalitarian, and the distribution of lineage defined the effective
political framework; but elsewhere the brotherhood came to be
stratified internally in terms of wealth and access to power and
authority which was organized in terms of rulership and
clientship. Growth in the size of a state meant growth in ties of
the latter sort, for a ruler's authority carried best along these
lines, where expectations of allegiance and loyalty defined the
relationship with the client.

Later Rajput polity functioned around a hierarchy of rulerships;
the Thakur ruling over a locality, who would submit to the Raja
at the regional level, who in turn would acknowledge subordination, by the late 1500s, to the Mughal Emperor. Outside kinship,
access to land and to positions of authority lay through clientship
to ruler, a multistranded tie which, especially at the local level,
would be cemented 'with a vow, sworn before a *devata* (deity)
in a local temple'. The client would submit to and bear arms for
the ruler who would maintain and protect him; and these implications were expressed in several symbolic ways.

Clientship was at times buttressed by ties of affinity: the affinal
relationship provided a code in which to make political statements.
As in much of north India the wife-taker was culturally defined
as being superior to the wife-giver; and a person could acknowledge someone publicly as his master by giving him his sister or

daughter in marriage. This would be a statement of political submission and, in this idiom, the tie of affinity became one with that of patron/client; for it was common for a master so acknowledged to provide for his follower or client. Such provision commonly meant a *jagir*, one or more villages for the allottee, the *jagirdar*, to rule; and it carried too a commitment of mutual support over the long run. Many castes would live in a village so allotted, including lower ranking Rajputs; but the ranks of *jagirdars* would have few other than Rajputs.

Whereas during the run up to, and during, the early Saltanat, say the 1100s or even the 1200s, Hindu chieftains often stood aloof, seeming to ignore the Muslim rulers, ...in later centuries the fact of Muslim power in India came to be gradually accepted.... There was also the learning, on the other side, of the necessity to incorporate indigenous functionaries into the state structure centred in Delhi. During the 1500s, several Rajput rulers suffered numerous defeats at the hands successively of Sher Shah Suri and Akbar.... By then, Rajput ideology had been admitting Muslim warriors, who were rulers too, to Rajput status...; this would enable one to treat with the Mughals and the like as one would with other powerful Rajputs. The Rajput political repertoire included the affinal clientship strategy; and several Rajput princesses were married to Mughal royalty....

By the late 1500s, the implications of centralized Mughal power were being felt in Rajasthan. Rajput rajas were fitted into the *mansabdari* order, the Mughal cadre for military and administrative leadership. Ziegler notes the increasing Mughal preference for the relatively larger states in Rajasthan...; with the assurance of Mughal political support, Jodhpur — the case studied by Ziegler — was able to enlarge its span of territorial control. This made possible an increase in the number of those who would hold lands and villages as clients of the Raja of Jodhpur. Given the example of the Mughal revenue system and the obligations of being a *mansabdar*..., the administrative arrangements in Jodhpur moved towards greater systematization, as with the issue of written titles to land; yet the term 'bureaucratic' can apply to them...only in its looser, less stringent sense.

Rights to land within any particular Thakur domain, the *thikāna*, were becoming complicated by the 1600s.... The choicest lands and villages were held by the ruling family on the grounds of

birth, and these constituted an inner circle in the *thikāna* along
with the holdings of the cadet lines of the *khamp*, which were
based partly on service to the senior line and partly on rights of
birth in the lineage. Around this core was an outer circle of lands
and villages allotted to the ruling Thakur's clients from other
clans whose only claim to the land was service rendered to the
Thakurs; and some clients had given a daughter to the Thakur
too. Some titles to land were written, others were informal; some
were held individually, others collectively. Some rights, finally,
had been secured from the Thakurs, others from the Raja in
Jodhpur; and in similar *thikānas* elsewhere, rights could be secured
from the Mughal Emperor directly too.

There was thus a multiplicity of forms and ways of acquiring
land rights in one *thikāna*; and correspondingly there were considerable personal moves physically and wide range of possibilities open to a Rajput: persisting with the solidarity of one's
own kin group or seeking service with the ruler of one's own,
or of another clan, or with the Mughal Emperor. During the 1500s
and 1600s several Rajputs in Ziegler's cases move conspicuously
back and forth between these levels, giving their lives what Ziegler
calls a 'disconnected quality'.... This discontinuity was at times
particularly marked in the move to the Mughal Emperor, for
there the Rajput value of loyalty to one's master could be in
conflict with another Rajput value — of not killing a castemate
— for the latter might become necessary in service to the
Mughals....

The Rajput matrix of kinship, marriage, and clientship could
provide the energies for a congeries of little kingdoms in continual
flux — within which some were able to grow in scale when backed
by external, Mughal support. Beyond the village level, the Brahmin
purohit, as dispenser of sacredness, could organize a consecration[3]
and arrange other symbols of legitimation at modest cost. Depending on the magnitude of force commanded, and the quality of
manpower and territory controlled, the raja would have resources
in varying magnitudes. Relying on his revenue and his booty,
he could sponsor the construction of palaces, temples and forts,
organize raids and campaigns, oversee the temple's management,
provide landgrants for Brahmins' settlements, and so forth.

The Brahmin's consecrative activity was, however, freelance:
no conqueror or pretender appears to have had much difficulty

in finding a Brahmin to do the ceremonies. Indeed, rival Brahmins would have seen potential advantage in instigating rival pretenders. Seen comparatively with medieval Europe, there was a paucity of nodes around which the society's symbolic, normative, and material resources might congeal for application to larger social visions. Consequently, those who conferred the symbols of legitimation in India could offer very little else by way of institutionalized skills and resources for state construction over a long period reliably.

South India and the Mughals

Several elements from the Rajput style reappear in South Indian politics in markedly different configurations. The Pallavas (early first millennium, peaking in late 700s), the Cholas (peaking between 900s and 1100s), and Vijayanagar (dominating south India between the mid-1300s and the 1600s, its later career relying on Arab horses and Portuguese guns) — these polities cover a long time-span during which the relations of authority, the key institutions, and the associated myths and symbolic activities underwent interlinked transformations of remarkable continuity. Far-flung webs of kinship and marriage were missing here; and the ties of clientship, which loomed so large in the later Rajput state, were mediated in South India partly by the institutional setting of the temple.

The Cholas and Vijayanagar give suggestions of vast capabilities in the monumental temples and in the large territories acknowledging their suzerainty; yet the bonds between the royal centre and those who ruled in the provinces were rather insubstantial. Burton Stein's explanation for this puzzle lies in showing: (1) that the kingdom's centre, especially for the Cholas, drew the agricultural surplus from the fertile Kaveri delta, supplementing it with predatory raids on distant lands; (2) that much of this surplus went into endowing *brahmadeyas* — Brahmin settlements — and constructing the monumental temples, the ritual centres of the regime and core institutions of the society. The ideology surrounding the temple posited a strong mutuality between king and deity; and if the crowded cycle of temple liturgies ran into social difficulties, the king or his agent would intervene to help to resolve them authoritatively. These efforts were situationally oriented; the prevailing political style did not search particular experience for general principles; and (3) that the differential organizational capacities between the kingship and distant localities was not such that the former might enforce imperative co-ordination on the latter in the manner of a bureaucratically organized state. Rather, the locally-arising chiefs would bring their armed contingents to join the royal forces in their predatory raids, sharing in the booty accruing; and the localities sought, at their own initiatives, to try to reproduce the prestigious forms of conduct and relationships prescribed at the ritual centre — thus showing allegiance to it — but retained an essential autonomy in the disposal of resources as a segment. Hence Stein's label for the regime: a segmentary state.[4]

My third case, to be considered briefly, concerns the Mughals (mid-1500s to early 1700s, with a presence in Delhi until 1857), successors to the Saltanat and part of Islamic advance in India since the 700s. The ruling Mughal dynasty had come from central Asia; and, for several generations, central and West Asia supplied the bulk of its leadership for the army and administration too. Consequently, at least initially, the Mughal apparatus did not carry extensive webs of kinship — neither as asset nor as liability. Relatively small numbers of immigrants had been able to win an empire — given a long-standing pattern of difficulties of the segmented indigenous society over combining adequately in its own defence. The Mughals, on the other hand, kept their elite military and administrative cadre, *mansabdari*, open to powerful indigenes too: Rajputs initially, but Kayastha, Khatri, Brahmin, and Maratha also in later generations.

Akbar undergirded the cadre with ties of imperial 'discipleship' which established a personal link between the emperor and a *mansabdar* who was initiated into the discipleship, a practice continued under Jahangir too.... The symbolism of empire was focused on the Emperor's person, and individual *mansabdars'* fortunes remained dependent on the Emperor's goodwill. The consequences of this dependence became manifest as the regime was immobilized in periods either of the Emperor's incapacitation, as towards the end of Shah Jahan's reign..., or of the struggles for succession, as at the beginning and the end of Aurangzeb's reign....

Under Akbar there are signs of officialdom looking like a Weberian bureaucracy...a firmer differentiation and systematization of function in the state and cash salaries for officials. A strong social tug pulled the other way, however, and was expressed variously. Nobles preferred *jagirs* — prebends — over vast salaries, and pressed the Emperor — successfully by the early 1700s — to revoke the transferability clause for *jagirs* in favour of their permanent endowment.... The *mansabdari* was focused virtually exclusively on the Emperor; it did not become an internal hierarchy with authoritative commands issuing from generalized roles at an administrative centre; and, correspondingly, there was a lack of impersonal, general codes for the whole gamut of situations, succession of Emperorship onwards.

It would not be correct to say that the Saltanat and Mughal regimes were altogether lacking in general laws. However, their sway was severely restricted: much remained enclosed within the internally-regulated kin, village, and other bounded groups; the *kazi's* general law rested on the Koran and the *hadith* — traditions concerning the Prophet's sayings and actions; this law partook of the sanctity of the traditions, and therefore there were limits both to the innovations that this sacred law would permit and to the secular systematization that it would admit; and finally there were the secular royal announcements, but these were wholly unfiltered by a cumulative, long-term tradition of general principles in specialists' hands.

THE COLONIAL STATE

The colonial state was created by the British in the course of establishing their rule over a vast land and alien peoples. We have space only to consider it briefly. It did not work on a clean slate. The spectacular British success was due, rather, to their skill at drawing older, indigenous elements into their own design.... While they recognized the uses of the older Indian political symbolism, and absorbed it selectively, a major part of their strength was in their bureaucracy, backed by force; and it was oriented towards maintaining peace, part of colonial control — and all that goes with it....

British rule was established in India in the late 1700s and early 1800s; and its moves in India have to be seen against the backdrop of processes then active in Europe. For one thing, Europe had been discovering ways for creating legitimate political centres not through conquest but through a combination of formal constitutions, legal institutions, and elective processes; and the method of general legal codes in varied domains had been spreading there since the 1100s. Much governmental practice, furthermore, followed from explicitly formulated general policies; and these policies, in turn, were influenced by the prevailing trends in ideology....

The colonial state recognized an obligation to adjudicate cases of conflict, and colonial courts were operational by late eighteenth century. General codes of an European cast, tending to ignore one's group affiliations and differences in status, encountered in India a forbiddingly complex situation of predominantly customary law, with the doctrines of the *dharmasastras* serving only to set the limits.... The working of the hierarchy of colonial courts could not fail to impose a measure of uniformity in court law, though plurality continued to reign in customary practice....

The use of the Western political and legal forms, however, was only part of a manifold cultural encounter in India. The British search for authentic indigenous legal codes, applying modern scholarly techniques, led to the recovery of rich veins of texts: this was the beginning of a new understanding especially of ancient Indian history, and it inaugurated, too, an active Indian interest both in that history and in the methods of modern scholarship....

During the early 1800s, furthermore, the colonial government began to expand the use of the English language, and of modern bureaucratic and judicial forms, in its own functioning. The road to government jobs, and to the few professional opportunities available, led through the institutions of Western education in India.... There was a strong impulse here for entering these institutions, established not only by the government and the missionaries but also by Indians who recognized the importance both of the new learning and of creating their own institutions for organizing that learning.... The channels for the flow of Western ideas into the subcontinent were thus being widened.

The Western models so appropriated included those concerning mechanisms of a civil society...: 'the public meeting, the petition, visits to government officials, including to the Colonial Office in London, and press campaigns'; to these, Gandhi joined the indigenously rooted methods of non-violent confrontation with authority. The resources of that civil society served an inspired leadership first to push the colonial regime to its end in 1947 and then, as we shall see, to design the Constitutional framework in which the new Republic might define, and govern, itself. The origins and the premises of these resources were inescapably alien, however; and therefore the Republic's future passages would be rather more turbulent than its creators then realized.

A CHANGE OF PHASE

If we define 'democratic political structures' as consisting of a Constitution, a differentiated party structure, and periodic acts of choice, between parties, by an electorate for election to legislatures; then post-colonial India has seen a sharp expansion of these structures and processes: a move to universal adult franchise in numerous arenas, such as elective arenas at national and state levels, and trials of these structures at other levels from village and town to district; and their extension into the functioning of co-operatives and other voluntary associations. This sharp expansion of these structures has to be seen as one element within a larger change of system. In so far as, at Independence, India lay at the juncture of two sets of very different traditions, the Indian and the European, the systematic change spelt a radical change in terms of the relationship between the institutions drawn from these two traditions: namely, the increased reliance on institutions of western design at a time when the European tradition *per se* has been losing ground to the politically and socially resurgent Indian traditions. That is to say, essentially imported forms have been proliferating, but the meanings which are crucial for the vitality of the forms have not been available consistently....

A major aspect of what has been happening in Indian political arenas is the interaction between elements from the Constitution and from the indigenous traditions and social structures. Impulses and purposes of variable intensity, arising out of ingrained meanings and motivations, work themselves out in frameworks arising out of the Constitution. Let us consider the working out of the consequences of the tension between their disparate premises.

A JUNCTURE OF TRADITIONS

Let us review some of the specific kinds of differences between the two sets of traditions: differences which have had a bearing on the rise and functioning of Western style political institutions in India. These differences may be considered in terms of extremes, remembering always the caution that functioning societies invariably display some admixture of contrary attributes.

SEGMENTATION VS. INDIVIDUALISM/UNIVERSALISM

The caste order had served historically to segment Indian society and to set relatively hard-set boundaries, with persons embedded firmly within such groups as the *jâti* or the joint family; apart from the sect, the category 'voluntary association' would have had few tenants.

At the heart of an electoral, participative 'democracy' lies the citizens' capacity to relate to each other positively and widely, and to co-operate over a variety of purposes. The purposes at issue would include establishment of durable institutions which routinely mobilize support for making public representations on issues believed to be important, and the constitution of political parties with policies of open membership. These capacities are necessarily blunted by the habits arising in the segmentation of social space. The segmentation is not final; yet its erasure may call for ideas, effort, and motivation of an order which may not be taken lightly for granted. The economically disadvantaged sections have had much greater difficulty in overcoming the legacy of segmentation than the advantaged ones; it would seem that the latter have not only learned the advantages of co-operation (in class interests, if you will) more fully than the former, but have also had the resources for organizing the requisite institutions....

Crucial in a large, industrializing society today are its organizations and institutions, with personnel picked for their competence, achievements, and potential — more than for their family, faith, or similar attributes; and so we should ask how the tradition of social segmentation has affected the functioning of these organizations and institutions....

In contrast to the embedding of the person in the group, usually the group of one's birth, in India, scholars...see the idea of the individual as a creation of the eighteenth century European Enlightenment.... Growing numbers of men, intent on career paths more or less unrelated to their family backgrounds, became available for regrouping in organizations — which would have their own varying logic guiding their functioning. There are numerous instances of voluntary associations, based on the older models of the guild; ...and at times these led to sworn fraternities, able to act together politically. By the thirteenth century, one notices a growing capacity to generate new kinds of institutions — new social forms — for advancing particular purposes; such 'modern' institutions as the university take off in Europe at this time. Their members did not come randomly from the larger society; yet the membership was substantially open.

Two characteristics of these institutions may be noted: these served to provide social fields amenable, in principle, to indefinite extension; and, increasingly, these operated under regimes of impersonal general rules. In this sense the orientation of such institutions was universalist. Together these provided, too, the range of settings needed for undergoing the experiences necessary, and developing the motivations, to grow into public roles of wide range....

Use of force: polycentric or centralized?

In precolonial India, control over force lay at multiple levels. Control over land in particular localities originated ultimately in rights arising in conquest.... Larger politics did aggregate some force at the centre, but they rarely had the means to interfere much with the patterns of local dominance, except to appoint an agent to appropriate a part of the local produce. When the centre weakened, its regional agents or associates could commonly strike out on their own — and secure legitimacy for their own regime....

In contrast, the emergence of durable bureaucracies in Europe, from about the 1100s, facilitated both the centralization of force in the state and, to pay for it, the monopoly over taxation. The subsequent course of European history has often been turbulent. Participative frameworks for exercising power — assemblies for legislation, courts of justice — arose meanwhile, building on varying social and institutional bases in the different regions. Given access to such differentiated frameworks of power, and the growing, effective penalties for using force privately, the latter course lost its attraction.

A priori we may expect that confidence in democratic institutions depends on the regulated conduct of political processes,

including conflict, within and outside the legislatures; it is likely
to be sapped when these processes are vitiated through the use
of violence and other means which are disruptive and are seen
to be illegitimate.

Weakness in a tradition of impersonal general rules

A related issue is that of impersonal general codes such as the
rules for cricket, traffic rules for crowded highways, the Indian
Penal Code, the largely unwritten codes of scientific research,
and so forth. Such impersonal codes have come to India from
the West in the main.... The Indian tradition has not been sensitive
to the value of such codes because it began early on to organize
social space by cutting it up into *jātis* and the like; and how a
segment arranged matters like marriage, divorce, inheritance, and
social discipline did not much worry members of other segments.

Modern legislation and the Constitution represent, in contrast,
a resort to impersonal rules at a high level of generality. The
'democratic' process — electoral politics, legislation of laws, the
separation of legislation from the executive and the judiciary — all
this depends on high commitment to the corresponding 'rules of
the game', supported by appropriate normative orders. Where
the normative support is weak or missing, the 'rules of the game'
are flouted more easily, sapping the confidence in due political
process.

The 'will of the people', expressed electorally, may be the source
of legitimacy to a government; but when the dominant groups
over a wide region are able to pre-empt that will, say through
booth-capturing; or if an election is won by a party which rejects
this form of political legitimacy — under such conditions the instituted bases of legitimate government and political order are
seriously undermined. When the entrenched social order, and
the consequent political pressures, pull in a direction contrary to
the prerequisites for operating the Constitution, strong tensions
arise; there also arise large unpredictabilities in the course taken
by particular political happenings.

Of the several senses of the term 'autonomy', that of 'independence' or a groups' freedom to act unconstrained by external
interference or accountability tends to prevail often in India —
even though the idea of autonomous, self-directed conduct would

be consistent with a full sense of accountability in terms of shared general rules and principles.

Ethic of public responsibility: a weak tradition

One does not easily find, in Indian history or mythology, role models of wide-ranging accountability: one that goes beyond one's family or employer, to society at large and to generations unborn. The 19th and 20th centuries were richer, but the models there — men like Gandhi and Nehru — do not come clearly out of older Indian prototypes. The historic weakness of this ethic in India can also be traced to the social segmentation, to the embedding of persons in their own segment — joint family, *játi* and the like. The taking of wider public responsibilities calls for a range of skills, values, ideas, and motivations: that is, for personality types of a particular kind. As noted earlier, social frameworks appropriate for nurturing them have not been common in Indian history....

Yet an active ethic of a widely shared sense of public responsibility is vital to a 'democratic' polity. Open polities must have on call persons in adequate numbers willing and able to accept public responsibility accountably, so that the self-seeking urges are bridled. It is due to our historic weakness here that even the kinds of institutions which, elsewhere, have nursed the ethic of public responsibility — say universities or civil services — have been succumbing in India to self-aggrandizement.

Having defined 'democratic political structures' as consisting of a Constitution, a differentiated party structure, and periodic acts of choice, between parties, by an electorate for election to legislatures, it follows that their satisfactory operation necessarily needs support from substantial, extensively learned matching skills, values, ideas, motivations, and practices. That is to say, the formal structures and processes can follow from relatively simple legislative and bureaucratic acts, while their sound, durable operation requires complex skills and attitudes — whose widespread availability may not be taken for granted. It will be remembered that these formal arrangements have been a historic European achievement, a device for constituting legitimate political centres without recourse to violent conquests; to work well, the device requires skilful, restrained, disciplined performance from large numbers of participants. The prerequisites for such performances are a cultural resource; their acquisition has to be a process of active learning.

Post-colonial India, as mentioned above, has seen these structures and processes expand sharply: a move to universal adult franchise in numerous arenas, at national and state levels, and trials of these structures at other levels from village and town to district; and their extension into the functioning of co-operatives and into sundry other settings. However, one cannot always claim that these have been instant, or long-term, successes. By and large, the formal structures have been instituted readily; but there has been only limited awareness of the complex range of skills, values, ideas, motivations and practices necessary for their satisfactory operation.

Propagating such unusual skills and attitudes, in a cultural milieu unused to them, is a task so demanding that one may not speak of it lightly; in any case, the will and the drive needed for making the effort have yet to arise. It is becoming clear, however, that while the participants do not learn the logics, the attitudes, and the techniques that have to enter participative institutions, violent practice will increasingly invade the 'democratic' routine and as this grows, the functioning of the state, for all its Constitutional trappings, will edge towards the style of a conquest state....

NOTES

1. Chattopadhyaya, B.D., 'Origins of the Rajputs: political, economic and social processes in early medieval Rajasthan', *Indian Historical Review*, vol. 3, no. 1, 1976.

2. Ziegler, Norman, 'Some notes on Rajput loyalties during the Mughal period' in J.F. Richards (ed.), *Kinship and Authority in South Asia*, Department of South Asian Studies, University of Wisconsin, Madison, 1978.

3. Coomaraswamy, Ananda K., *Sprititual Authority and Temporal Power in the Indian Theory of Government*, Munshiram Mahoharlal, Delhi, 1942, reprint 1978, ii.

4. Stein, Burton, *Peasant, State and Society in Medieval South India*, Oxford University Press, Delhi, 1980.

On the Construction of Colonial Power: Structure, Discourse, Hegemony

SUDIPTA KAVIRAJ

....Colonialism is both a set of institutions, and also, emphatically, a set of discourses. Both these sets — of structures and discourses — change in their constitution over the long history of the colonial period.... Any attempt to understand the structures of the field of power under colonialism must contend with three interconnected things. At the first level are the political power relations, which present no mean difficulty of theoretical description, because in the early period they constitute a very irregular structure without the focus of a regime at the centre. As colonialism in India becomes more powerful, and extends over the whole sub-continent, these congeal into the peculiar forms of the colonial state. To understand this regime, however, it has to be placed in the context of two networks of temporal and conceptual relations: that is, within the tangled complex of memories and structural legacies of earlier regimes; and in the space allowed it by the pre-existing structure of social relations. And these cannot be theorized or even described through the resources of conventional state theory with its traditional focus on linear transitions.

Excerpted from Dagmar Engels and Shula Marks (eds.), *Contesting Colonial Hegemony*, I.B. Tauris & Co Ltd., London, 1994, 19-54.

This state, secondly, is peculiarly dependent on and inextricable from certain discursive structures; its history must be written as part of the discourse of the Enlightenment, in terms of the rhythms, ruptures and punctuations of that different history. Its power is believed to be derived — by both its functionaries and its critics — from the grand discourses of European rationalism — its theories, self-definitions, narratives, delusions and strategies. It uses that discourse to define and describe itself, to negotiate and bring under control the alien social world it has entered. Others in this social world who have to deal with it, as enemies, friends, applicants for its favour, also see the centrality of this discourse to understanding its institutions and their logic of functioning. They pursue a great variety of strategies in order to do so. They were, after all, entering a myth-structure of Western invincibility and respected the indivisibility of myths. Some sought to master its occult powers by acquiring Western education and culture with an amazing, often ridiculous, thoroughness, not neglecting table manners and toilet styles. Others tried heroic translations, making figures of Hindu mythology speak flawlessly the language of English utilitarianism. Still others tried to avoid its mesmerizing and polluting contact by turning inwards into indigenous discourse. All produced interesting and complex unintended consequences. Conventions and concepts of rationalist discourse, if not high theory, surrounded this state on every side, mediating crucially its relations with the three dissimilar and largely unrelated publics between which it stood, carrying on three discrepant dialogues, trying to render them into some coherence. In its dialogue with British public opinion it adopted a tone of reasonableness; with the indigenous middle class it carried on a dialogue through education and legislation; while *vis-à-vis* the sullenly distant popular masses, it adopted primarily a monologue of force....

THE STRUCTURE OF SOCIETY AND THE SPACE FOR THE STATE

....When constructing the picture of a political field, the usual, almost reflex move of political theorists is to do so around the central concept of the state, to place it in our taxonomies of the state. Here it is worth alluding briefly to the debate about the connection between the concept of the state and the idea of publicity. The argument advanced by some theorists is that the state is not a name for any arrangement of power, but one that requires a certain publicity of its power arrangements. This affiliates the 'stateness' of regimes to modernity in a way that raises powerful and I think interesting questions, for in both imperial and nationalist arguments about the nature of the colonial regime there were considerations about the impersonal and public quality of political power....

It is valid to introduce the notion of publicity in the discussion of colonial political discourse, for it also serves to indicate the internal distances, disconnections and complexities with which rulers and their more voluble subjects had to contend. Power under colonialism was public in the sense of being at least a formal and impersonal set of laws and institutions, however, iniquitous. In trying to define its own institutions in the 'public sphere' — a European superstition brought, some thought gratuitously, into a colonial society — the imperial regime also provided a discursive space on which nationalist ideas could eventually be formed....

In India, the colonial state underwent a process of construction in the most literal sense. It did not emerge out of the internal logic of evolution of earlier Indian society, and had little by way of internal relation to do with the state it came to succeed in India. (As a corollary, I feel that the change it represents in Indian history cannot be fitted easily into the model of a transition process drawn from the model of European history; it is an excessively 'economic' picture of this change which confers plausibility on that approach.) But, clearly, the spread of British power from early insecure footholds in trading zones to large parts of the sub-continent was linked to the spacing of social institutions, and the determinate ways in which the earlier political forms (or state) were related to society.

Although both imperial and nationalist histories in their popular forms agree in seeing the battle of Plassey or the conquest of Bengal as the date of India's loss of independence, this is obviously anachronistic. The actual translation of commercial privileges into imperial power was a slower, considerably more complex affair.... In the contact between British imperial power and traditional Indian society there was also a contact between two very different principles of construction of society and state. Since these principles and constructs mediated their images of each other, and influenced their socio-political initiatives, this point needs to be made a little more fully. Ambitious merchants of the Company would probably have interpreted the world they were slowly coming to influence and control through the apparatus of rationalist social ideas and the bourgeois belief in the primacy of commerce and economic control. Yet in traditional Indian practical social thinking, commerce and the economic were treated as insignificant both in theory and in practical political arrangements. Local rulers considered merchants as politically insignificant, because they apparently did not work as a collective (or a class); rulers never expected a threat to their political power to come from that direction. To Indian rulers, accustomed to conceptualizing the social world in the traditional manner, a challenge to the political order by a commercial enterprise was as much a conceptual anomaly as it was an insufferable political interference. The Company, for its part, in stretching its reach towards the state was proposing not only a shift in the locus of political authority, but a change in the fundamental map of social relations.

....Capitalist societies are structurally similar, but each type of pre-capitalist society is traditional in its own way. Traditional Hindu society appears to have been decentred in a peculiar way (though that does not make it less repressive), and it had a determinate way of arranging its social space which has important implications for the relation between state and society. It did not have a clear hierarchy of classes presided over by a strong and fairly 'thick' state (in terms of the size of its bureaucracy and their functions) with the right, given to it by the predominant discourse, to interfere in and work around the patterns of authority and economic benefits....

Instead, traditional society seemed to work on a practical arrangement of a thin, rent-receiving, partly marginal state. The structure of the society, despite its obvious hierarchies, is less integrated in terms of its ordering discourses, and...can be likened to a circle of circles of caste and regional communities, with the state sitting at the centre. Of course the state impinges on these communities economically: but its right of economic extraction is more by 'squeezing' a sector than by restructuring it. In this scheme, the rulers were given a deep obeisance at the cost of a certain marginality, i.e. on condition, not legally but structurally enforced, that they did not intrude into the everyday life processes of the communities, and did not take upon themselves the right to legislate fundamental restructuring of relations as long as their appetite for a 'reasonable' rent was satisfied. Hindu social ontology was based on this internal balance between a dispersed, permanent and practically unalterable social order and the impermanence of political power at which society looked with perfect composure and indifference. As long as political regimes respected these ground rules of rent reception and non-interference, it mattered little which dynasty or set of rulers was actually transacting the political business. As long as the undoubted incremental alterations in social life did not threaten to alter its basic map of dispositions, and the state did not arrogate to itself the right to restructure relations, Hindu society could deplore with poetic detachment the tragic rise and fall of all eminence, including the political.

Given this relationship between state and society, the entry of Muslim rulers carrying a different religious doctrine, but not fundamentally different cognitive apparatus, does not seem to have altered the structure in any basic way. Although Islamic religious tenets were more egalitarian than Hinduism, the incursion was not in large enough numbers, nor were the conversions numerous enough to threaten the basic frame. The mechanism of distancing and marginalization allowed Hindu society and rulers to look upon the destruction of their principalities as a part of the necessary mutability of political fortunes, rather than as a civilizational threat, which should be collectively resisted. More importantly, the arrangement of a circle of circles could cope with such intrusions, allowing the entrants their own circle, at the expense of making the system a little more ragged and shapeless. This response was a strange combination of acceptance and rejection. Thus the Hindu and Muslim rulers who confronted the British at the stage of their passage from commerce to imperial power were singularly handicapped in dealing with them. This historical phenomenon was unprecedented in their political experience, and unrecognizable in terms of their dictionary of social identification. In dealing with the threat of the British, Indian rulers were not merely politically inept: at a more fundamental level, they were conceptually unprepared.

This conceptual mistranslation of what they saw was not confined only to the Indians. The British, equally, tried to make sense of an unfamiliar social ontology in terms of the familiar conventions through which rationalist modernist Europe had learnt to map its social space.... Political açtors, both individual and collective, do not react to discursively neutral 'objective' situations, but to threats and possibilities fashioned by their perceptions of the political world. Discourses also sometimes provide the vital connections between the various causalities through patterns of beliefs held by actors, which help us identify their intentions. This is a particularly fertile field for misunderstandings between contending forms of rationality.

What the British eventually did, or at least tried to do, to this asymmetric and dispersed traditional structure, can be understood not only in terms of their power compulsions in a brute data sense, but through the discourse they brought with them. No history of British rule can be complete until it is seen as part of the history of rationalist modernity, as distinct from the spread of extractive capitalism. On the British side, the entire grand business of colonization is affiliated to the grand structure of rationalist discourse. Groups of early colonizers, small enclaves in the vast Indian society, claimed invincibility in the name of the rationalist programme — a view of the world that is clear, precise, instrumentalist, technical, scientific, effective, true and above all beneficial to all who came in contact with it, both the rulers and the subjects.... Indeed, each of those adjectives flowed out of some central principle of rationalist discourse about society, unmodified at the time by hermeneutic scepticism. In particular, the early adventurers' belief in their invincibility and in the possibility of controlling a society of such enormous size was a product of their insertion into the mainstream discourse of rationalism — not its intellectual discourse, which was often full of self-doubt and criticism, but the popular mythic discourse — unself-critical, arrogant, aggressive. Thus, interestingly, both sides in the colonial transaction make sense of their historical experience in terms of large, necessary forces or powers: the British see their success not as a result of individual acumen or bravery, but as a function of a large, impersonal, invincible discourse of rationality of which they were products and 'bearers'. Indians, uninitiated in the intricacies of this cognitive apparatus, see in British power evidence of supernatural accreditation or the visitation of suffering for collective *karmic* sins. This was, if ever there was one, a theatre of Winchian incommensurable rationalities.

Early nationalist writers often wondered how a large society like 'India' could be colonized and held by such a small group of British people.... The simple answer to the puzzle (which is why the way they formulated their question was wrong) was that of course there was no pre-existing India which was conquered by British rule. India in that political sense was the result of comparable and increasingly coalescing indignities of colonial rule, and in this coalescing, which was conceptual and again not objective, ideas of conceptualizing political possibilities introduced by the discursive bestowals of colonial nationalism. This leads in turn to an interesting question as to how the process of cognitive identification of communities changed as a result of colonial rule and the incursion of Western education.

If we accept the meaning of the term 'imaginary'...as the internally accepted boundaries of a constituted social form, the principle of community construction in traditional India was different from the modern nationalist one.... The main difference between traditional communities and the modern community of the nation is not in their size, but in their internal constructive principles, of which size was a function. Earlier, people belonged to communities which did not make claims on their identity and strategies of self-description of the type modern states would make. Communities were fuzzy in two senses. Rarely, if ever, would people belong to a community which would claim to represent or exhaust all the layers of their complex self-hood. Individuals on suitable occasions could describe themselves as *vaisnavas*, Bengalis or more probably *rarhis, kayasthas*, villagers and so on; and clearly although all these could on appropriate occasions be called their *samaj* (if they were Bengalis), their boundaries would not coincide. The complex sum of these identities, now anachronistically termed 'selves', would be fuzzy in the first sense. More significantly, it would be fuzzy in a second sense as well.

To say their community is fuzzy is not to say it is imprecise. On the appropriate occasion, every individual would use his cognitive apparatus to classify any single person he interacted with and place him quite exactly, to decide whether he could eat with him, go on a journey with him, or arrange a marriage into his family. It was therefore practically precise, and adequate to the scale of social interaction. It would not, however, occur to an individual to ask how many of them there were in the world, and what they could wreak upon the world if they decided to act in concert. In other words they did not inhabit a conceptual world which could contemplate collective transformative actions on a large, universalist scale because all the crucial terms were absent from their vocabulary. They would not represent themselves as a large universalist collective group — i.e. every *vaisnava*, for the very fact of being one, being involved in some action. They would rarely contemplate action instrumentally to alter the balance of social advantages in their favour, because there would not be a sufficiently common register of social benefits. And it was at least partly because of this many-layered sense of community that those who were attacked severally, and destroyed by the colonial political regime, failed to make common cause. It was not lack of rationality in some transcendent political sense which failed them when dealing with the British, but precisely the operation of a rationality which had hitherto proved adequate. Thus, the revolt of 1857, which was undoubtedly anti-British, but equally certainly not 'Indian', represented an anti-colonial protest still trapped within the fuzzy and unenumerated community.

Into this carefully constructed equilibrium of the decentred totality held together by its internal distancing, the back-to-back spacing of groups, dispersal and countervailing power, the British brought a highly symmetrical, centralized, technologically effective apparatus of control. The earlier social form may have been technologically ineffective, but it was very stable and exceptionally difficult to reform; it is not entirely accidental that it was after an integrated structure was set up by the British, not before, that we find an increasing incidence of rebellious action by the popular masses. The system of social action that the British brought and gradually entrenched in urban India and its hinterland was instrumentally extremely effective. Yet because of its high salience and centralization — because it presented a clear and unambiguous institutional target — it could be challenged, and was vulnerable, as nationalists found out later, to pressures of collective action of its own type. Mature nationalists would turn the rationalist apparatus itself against the colonial state.

Once colonialism establishes itself in state or proto-state form, it faces the problem of constructing a 'hegemonic' discourse in its favour.... Though defiance and repression happened in dramatic episodes throughout colonial history, acquiescence was the rule rather than the exception. We must now ask how this acquiescence was arranged, its concepts constructed.

But before we enter into that discussion it seems necessary to ask how the terrain was structured upon which this question of legitimacy (or hegemony) was to be contested; the question is clearly related to the earlier one we noted of the publicity of power. The regime had to contend with the demands of publicity in several directions at once; and it was in terms of intelligibility and 'reasonableness' (which were different in each of these) that it had to present its policies. First, the colonial state was of course a subordinate arm of the state or regime in England. It was subject therefore to two kinds of pressure from that direction. It had to keep India a marginal subject and not allow problems arising out of the colonial entanglement to intrude too deeply or frequently into the agenda of domestic politics and demand an unreasonable share of attention. The less these questions were aired the greater the possibility of maintaining a low-level consensus on the colonial question. At the same time, the discourse of politics could not be fragmented and fractured beyond a point. Although it was possible to invite British public opinion to remain indulgently indifferent towards details of imperial politics in India while passively enjoying its material benefits and imperial glory, still significant issues in Indian politics were bound to be judged by the criteria of justice, effectiveness and honour that were current in internal politics in Britain. Imperial policy in India had therefore to remain legitimate in the internal terms of British political discourse.

The way this discourse was shaped historically displayed the plurality of possibilities contained within the alphabet of rationalist theory. Rationalism in politics was not a singular or entirely monolithic affair.... The discursive formation which provided Clive and Hastings with the crucial arguments of invincibility also, unfortunately for them, contained a puritanical side that condemned illegal gratification. Some important officials therefore had to pay the price of an inconsistent and self-servingly one-sided reading of what rationalist politics enjoined. Unsatisfactory and inadequate as these incidents may have appeared to the colonial peoples who suffered at their hands, this discourse had a reality in terms of a social ontology, and was forceful enough to claim occasional victims.

This was the first paradox of the colonial regime. Because it was in fact far more powerful (in the sense of the sanctioned or possible use of force in having its way) than the state in the mother country, it was entirely uncircumscribed by the democratic rules and demands which inconveniently restricted élite politics in the metropolis. It was an external, in a sense suspended, state which was not the product, or the terrain, of social conflict (as bourgeois states are) in the society over which it ruled. Compulsions arising out of publicity in England, only too real for its officials, were in large measure incomprehensible to its Indian subjects until quite late. Precisely because of its dual context, some of its domestic supporters also misunderstood the compulsions arising out of the fact that it was, after all, the *Indian* state, and had to respond in intelligible ways also to the pressures and the social logic of the country over which it sat with such imperial majesty. Its double publicity, the two publics it had to make itself comprehensible to, made it a possible area of misunderstandings.

Officials who were entrusted with the task of ruling India, however, were quick to realize the sharp difference between the dominant discourse they brought with them and that of the society they were to enter and hoped to hold in permanent, and preferably peaceable, control. And their ideas of the nature and limits of cognition, of social knowledge, its arguments of justification of political authority, its picture of society and the moral consequences of the division of social functions, even the levels of the social totality, were entirely different. Lively rationalist curiosity, driven by self-related prejudices into the familiar forms of early ethnology, made the British complete records about this society and its intellectual discourse (though often misleadingly classified). In a very short time early civilians had attempted, assisted by the more esoteric labours of the Asiatic society, to produce a reliable map of the social relations and modes of reasoning in this culture. Indeed, some of these early researchers affiliated themselves doctrinally to counter-Enlightenment tendencies in European culture like romanticism and came to the verge of questioning the comfortable civilizational hierarchies of rationalist thinking.

Under these circumstances two broad strategies of legitimation were possible. Since legitimation meant that political forms and strategies had to find the structures of self-evidence on their side it could be accomplished by fitting the patterns of the new political regime into the existing justificatory discourse, or at least appearing to do so. Alternatively, the discourses of Indian society could be remodelled by a serious and missionary spread of Western education, so that the activities of the colonial state would appear justified through the new structure of self-evidence acquired by the rationalist intelligentsia. In actual fact, the colonial regime followed a complex combination of the two strategies — to its immediate advantage and with some unintended long-term results.

CONSTRUCTION OF COLONIAL DISCOURSE

....To create legitimacy the colonial state had the choice between two mutually exclusive strategies, poised as it was between two civilizations with powerful discourses about the political world. Yet the colonial state failed to make a clear choice between the two strategies — to its great advantage, as it turned out. It followed variants of both in different periods, sometimes shifting emphasis with dramatic rapidity between two viceregal administrations.

Of course, above all the colonial state was the product of the discourse of the Enlightenment. That discourse stressed the possibility of Cartesian conceptions of knowledge in preference to asymptotic Aristotelian ideas and asserted as part of its cognitive programme the ready translatability of all knowledge into technical control over the world thus known. Enlightenment theories were proto-positivist (i.e. positivist before the recognition of a positivist position), and extended such general beliefs about the nature, means and consequences of knowledge from nature into the historical world. Another, equally significant, part of Enlightenment theory was not only its belief in the possibility of precise, incontrovertible knowledge, but also the impossibility of all men attaining it in equal measure. Externally affiliated to the doctrine of the rational equality of all men, this theory immediately resulted in a hierarchy of people as attainers of knowledge and users of technology. Moreover, apart from there being a possible exhaustive rank order of individuals on this cognitive scale, ...societies also could be placed in a rank order, using an implicit but ubiquitous premise of methodological individualism. This structure of reasoning, turned around, provided the principal frame of explanation and justification of Western imperial rule.

In the initial period, perhaps naturally, officials of the Company accepted traditional nomenclatures like the *dewani*, and generally tried to translate their own political existence into the earlier cultural and symbolic order. Historians have recorded in detail how self-consciously early and even later colonialists modelled themselves on the cultural and institutional legacy of the Mughal empire. The basic function of the Company's official structures was, of course, the extraction of rent and related revenue, and the classificatory schemes for rent and tenurial system were taken over from Mughal administration. But obviously the imitation of the Mughals could only proceed up to a point, and led to contradictions, for the civilizational discourse of bourgeois imperialism was incommensurate with Mughal social forms and cultural idioms. Although the Mughal system was more successful and long-standing than previous empires, it was still constructed on the traditional dualistic principle — a stable village social structure on the ground, based on caste rules, and on top a superordinate empire, which nevertheless left the business of social and cultural reproduction alone. The discourse of European rationalism did not allow such a policy of majestic aloofness for long. Once their political control was secure, the colonial administration went for a strategy which decisively infringed this dualism. It was no longer content to limit its majesty to the narrow space in the middle of the circle of circles. This was naturally related to the second strategy of legitimation. Western education, now extended with vigour, was calculated to produce a social group which would ensure an ideological relay of this language and structure of self-evidence — an expectation that was, ironically, both fulfilled and frustrated.

These British moves can be interpreted, in part at least, in terms of a Gramscian theory of common sense.[1] In the early period, when its control was confined to greater Bengal and it did not see itself capable of taking on the task of restructuring social relations, the regime followed the earlier strategy. But there was a price to pay, quite apart from the unconvincing pretence that the British were a small infeudatory power to the pitifully declining Mughal order. The price was that by accepting the logic of the traditional marginalization of the state, they abandoned their rationalist right to restructure society in their own image through enforced reform. It meant moreover adopting a sentimental feudal language which made it impossible to advance a Burkean traditionalist argument to justify their authority over Indian society. The early regime therefore spoke both languages — an idiom of reasonableness shown in its willingness to tolerate indigenous practices, a sort of conservative Winchianism, and also an idiom of rationality committing it to reform and an ideology of progress against domestic reaction. This curious incompatibility of 'reasonableness' and 'rationality' is reflected in successive viceroyalties as late as Lytton and his successor....

Despite the vestigial existence of the traditional language of authority, by the mid-19th century the colonial state had begun to speak in a more authoritative, rationalist, liberal voice. This stiffening of its tone could be attributed to several things. On the Indian side, by this time, colonial power was far more securely entrenched and began to entertain the normal illusions of untroubled permanence. The experience of the 1857 uprising (in which the Indian political coalition was between disgruntled elements of the old ruling classes and some elements of the peasantry in the form of the ordinary soldiery) made the British realize the vulnerability of their earlier line of non-interference and winning princes over by diplomacy and pressure. In short, the gradual entrenchment of the British destroyed the mutuality of interest between them and traditional rulers. By contrast, the new middle classes, particularly in rationalist Calcutta, showed exemplary loyalty, siding decisively with the forces of reason against the forces of freedom. They appeared a better candidate for political and pecuniary investment than traditional ruling orders.

Significant changes occurred in the climate of ideas in the West as well. Edward Said's work has popularized an exaggerated construction of Western rationalist orientalism, stressing the linearity in the rationalist discourse of otherness.[2] The actual structure and arrangement of ideas was more internally differentiated and varied. Indeed, contrary to Said's claims, in the early discourse of the Enlightenment the Orient fills the logical position of an other which in fact saves the sense of diversity of life-forms in the world and prevents a rash Eurocentric doctrine of superiority. To take only two well-known examples, Montesquieu and Voltaire, central intellectual figures of the Enlightenment, use a fuzzy and partly romantic conception of the Orient to set up imaginary archimedian points to tell the truth about European history.

This is a type of intellectual argument and comparison quite different from the confidently Eurocentric visions of the world unsurpassably classified, not only horizontally, but also vertically. The priorities and preoccupations of colonial administrators could not be unaffected by the shift in climate of opinion. This made the colonial regime more confidently interventionist. It remained dependent on rent, but it intervened in major ways to restructure the economy, the relation between state and society, and in the cultural constitution of social relations through its moves for social reform. It was not a state which could be treated in the old terms.

This is not to say that the earlier strategy of legitimation entirely disappeared. Indeed, as Bernard Cohn has tried to show, the attempt to incorporate the older symbolic order continued, and the more stable and expansive empire now deliberately sought to appropriate the whole train of symbolic memory of earlier empires.[3] But the new state required a new kind of legitimating discourse; and its earlier, more unsystematic initiatives in spreading Western education had created conditions for this shift. Earlier, legitimacy was really not the question; the major point was to produce a strategy which would prevent the rise of an overwhelming adversary coalition of political forces. From the mid-19th century that was no longer relevant, and the colonial regime required legitimacy of a deeper kind. It sought to create that at three different levels in the field of discourse, and it is to these to which we must turn.

HEGEMONY AND HISTORY: THE POLITICS OF THE PAST

....We find two *forms* of thinking about the problem of history — theoretical and narrative. Of course, theory and narrative are often inextricable, but what is interesting in this cultural context is how from one point of view the inextricability is sought to be maintained, and, from the other, sought to be riven apart.... The curricula of Western education contained not only theoretical tools, resources and techniques which could be applied critically to historical material to appraise and control them; they also contained and pressed upon their students a narrative of universal history, assigning values and places to civilizations. The whole story appeared very close to showing how human history was a preparation for the present Western colonial dominance. Rationalist thinking of course influenced the discourse of the Indian middle classes through both its theoretical apparatus and its narrative configurations. Soon, however, it was the narrative which came particularly to concern the Indian intelligentsia. The reasons are not far to seek. It was the legitimating discourse of imperialism which made the question of the past so political. In order to justify its claims, imperialist discourse, often assisted by missionary writing, had to advance a picture of the Indian past as one of indifferent civilizational achievements. On that depended the credibility of its claim that colonialism was the bestowal of the benefits of modern civilization by a distant and not wholly self-interested people. A favourable view of the accounts of British rule by the Indian intelligentsia depended on the acceptance of this picture of their past by the new élite, and their carrying it down by a relay of ideological common sense to the lower social orders.

....Particularly central to this view is the essentialist dichotomy between the self and the other. All dichotomies of this type are asymmetric: the self is portrayed as historical, determinate, laden with actual attributes, capable of the radical reformation of its structures, and the other is seen as empty, abstract, a repository of negative characteristics (negative not always in the sense of bad, but *non-x*). It follows that the 'self' would have a much thicker historical representation than the 'other'. After all, one purpose of the picture of the other is not simply to be true to its object, but to facilitate what is constructors wish to believe about the self. The thinness of the description of the other in turn reinforces essentialist thinking. Excessive historical details are apt to disturb the beautiful symmetries of negative belief....

Essentialism can assume various forms. One common form denies the privilege of history to social formations in this place of otherness, simply because the rhythms and forms of their historical evolution are different from those prevalent in Europe. A second and more refined form does not deny history in that elementary sense but argues that historical change occurred through a stable, almost transcendent structure of national characteristics which history can give form to, and refigure, but cannot really alter. Historiography of this kind produced two essentialist narratives — a narrative of European reason moving conveniently from ancient Greece and Rome, unmindfully through the 'dark ages' into a linear connection with the post-Renaissance history of Western Europe; and a narrative of India, which, in its most charitable forms, showed an early efflorescence followed by a linear decline down to the pre-colonial times of modern darkness. The European narrative, as some Bengalis pointed out, infringed some of the elementary rules of stability of narration, and fixity of its subject. Though there was some sense in this construction of a cultural tradition, Bengali authors pointed out sardonically the peculiarity of modern Englishmen choosing as their ancestors ancient inhabitants of Greece rather than the less philosophically engaged people of the British Isles. Above all, this seemed to show that historical narration was a political act, and provided one with a pleasurable freedom in choosing one's cultural ancestors. Bengali writers showed how well they had learnt these history lessons when they revealed their own deep conviction that they were incontrovertible descendants of the writers of the *vedas*. Imperial historiography constantly emphasized the rationalist character of its constructions. History not only uses critical tools of analysis, but, precisely because it does so, can provide a place from which fond fables about the past can be criticized and rejected. History was the best cure of cultural chauvinism. The proximate result of this history teaching was, in the first few generations of students at least, what was broadly expected. Later, however, it began to produce unintended and surprising results.

Two other elements in the legitimizing discourse of imperial power are worth mentioning — for both had serious consequences in the not too distant future. First, as practical students of the Enlightenment theory of knowledge the British imperial élite began its massive and unprecedented project of enumeration and classification — a procedure enjoined by the rationalist connection between precise knowledge and effective control. To control a society it was essential to locate it in taxonomic systems. The British administration accordingly inaugurated the great process of counting — through censuses, maps, and statistics, familiarizing the inhabitants of their empire with their great numbers, and offering them clearer pictures of their own land and peoples. Nationalists would quickly learn to count equally well and equally politically. Instead of seeing these as entities divided by the final lines on the census tables, they began to consider what they would look like, and what would happen, if they combined.

Secondly, another element of rationalist thought gradually removed the basis of the impossibility of collective action. As Indian society traditionally was a circle of circles it was unfamiliar with the processes of what Gellner has called social entropy.[4] This ruled out any possibility of conceiving Kantian, attributeless individuals who could, driven by self-interest, freely enter into *Gesellschaft*-like associations. Even a rhetorical disruption of the boundaries of those circles, turning them from a number of fuzzy communities into a single enumerated one — to be called, after European models, a nation — was a logically possible step. Finally, the rhetoric of rationalism attracted Western-educated intellectuals so powerfully because of its principle of an abstract universality of reason; it offered them the possibility of taking the slogan of all men being rational in quite a literal sense, ignoring the fine print introduced by constitutions and liberal theory. It was so inviting and irresistible because its theory, in a pure form, seemed to make all human beings eligible for entry into the rational condition. It was subject only to some cognitive accomplishments which no student of Hindu college and similar institutions considered beyond his reach. Rationalist education had provided these intellectuals with critical implements by which they rejected their society's traditions and its past. To be consistent, it had then to acknowledge their right to enter into the great narrative of reason, as reasonably respected if not equal participants. *Babus* in Calcutta particularly affected such inclusion, and very soon most of them knew in extraordinary detail events in European history at the cost of a condescending ignorance about the Indian past. But this was not just a matter of ignorance; rather it was a strategy for the constitution of the self. Historically, this was the hegemonic moment of imperial rationalist discourse.

But this hegemony was limited and unstable. Those *babus* who were convinced of their right to inclusion in this illumined side of humanity were bound to be deeply disenchanted and resentful when confronted with the arbitrary barriers of race and subalternity. The imperial narrativization of European history, and the colonial civilizing mission rhetoric, had held out a promise of the diffusion or reenactment of the great narrative of reason on alien soil. Some colonial intellectuals came to envy the Europeans and literally covet their history. If the colonial regime's policies systematically obstructed and belied such possibilities, this was bound to cause disillusionment. Thus, all these effects of structural and discursive change, after initially seeming to offer a secure base for hegemonic control, came to have contrary results. By integrating society, introducing symmetric trends of social hierarchy, enumerating society, familiarizing Indians with the theory of public power and democracy, placing before them the universality of reason and the great narratives of European nation-formation and introducing the skills of forming associations, this imperial discourse had also taught Indians how rationalism could be turned against the European colonizers themselves. The lessons of rationalism were learnt, unfortunately too well....

NOTES

1. Gramsci, Antonio, *Selections from the Prison Notebooks*, Lawrence and Wishart, London, 1971.
2. Said, Edward, *Orientalism*, Routledge and Kegan Paul, London, 1978.
3. Cohn, Bernard, 'Representing authority in Victorian India', in his *An Anthropologist among the Historians and Other Essays*, Oxford University Press, Delhi, 1987, 632-82.
4. Gellner, Ernest, *Nations and Nationalism*, Blackwell, Oxford, 1983.

The Study of State and Society in India

NICHOLAS DIRKS

THE LEGACY

The Indian state is barely visible to comparative sociology. When the state is evident at all it appears as a weak form of Oriental despotism, destined to disappear as suddenly, and as casually, as it emerged. It seldom possesses mechanisms — hydraulic or otherwise — that could enable it to sustain itself for long. It depends mostly on ruthless short-sighted taxation of the countryside, which eventually leads to such chaos that it dissolves on its own or is conquered by some new entrant on the political scene.

Weber, Marx, Maine, and more recently Dumont have all held that in India, in marked contrast to China, the state was epiphenomenal. Marx's view is typical.... Marx saw these village communities as the necessary complement of Oriental despotism:

These idyllic village communities, inoffensive though they may appear, had always been the solid foundation of Oriental despotism, in that they restrained the human mind within the smallest possible compass, making it the unresisting tool of superstition, enslaving it beneath traditional rules, depriving it of all grandeur and historical energies. While states came and went, village communities endured.

Excerpted from Nicholas Dirks, *The Hollow Crown*, University of Michigan Press, Ann Arbor, Michigan, 1993, 3-16.

For sociology, caste, not the state, held these village communities together. In a more general sense, caste is seen as the foundation and core of Indian civilization; it is responsible for the transmission and reproduction of society in India. Caste, like India itself, is represented as based on religious rather than political principles. The state is always about to dissolve into fragments made up of various 'communal' elements.... Weber writes that 'Caste, that is, the ritual rights and duties it gives and imposes, and the position of the Brahmans, is the fundamental institution of Hinduism. Before everything else, without caste there is no Hindu'. Weber goes on to say that the caste order is itself based on the greatest authority in the system, the sacerdotal Brahmans: 'Caste is, and remains essentially social rank, and the central position of the Brahmans in Hinduism rests primarily upon the fact that social rank is determined with reference to Brahmans'. For Weber as for sociology in general, Indian society, headed by a Brahmanic elite,[1] is based on other-worldly and spiritual principles.

While Louis Dumont has rightly been hailed as one of the most important writers on India in recent years, he has in many ways only updated the view of India found in Marx and Weber. Dumont holds that the political and economic domains of social life are 'encompassed' by the 'religious.' The religious principle becomes articulated in the Indian case in terms of the opposition of purity and impurity. For Dumont as for Weber the Brahman represents the religious principle, inasmuch as the Brahman represents the highest form of purity attainable by Hindus. The king, while important and powerful, represents the political domain, and is accordingly inferior to, and encompassed by, the Brahman. Caste is fundamentally a religious system.

Prevailing conceptions about Indian state and society reflect the larger history of Orientalism, in which the colonial and now post-colonial interest in controlling the East, an interest which entailed the delegitimization of pre- or postcolonial state forms, has merged with a nostalgia for spirituality and, more specifically, a religiously based society. India's represented past haunts not only studies of colonialism, but even the historical legacy handed down to modern India. India's need to invent the nation, the state, and to find the basis for a society which is neither narrowly religious nor ethnic is made far more difficult by prevailing forms of Orientalistic knowledge which have their immediate roots in representations of the old regime as despotic, decadent, and deformed by decontextualized versions of caste or the village community as the sole (and autonomous) basis of Indian society.

It is my contention...that until the emergence of British colonial rule in southern India the crown was not so hollow as it has generally been made out to be. Kings were not inferior to Brahmans; the political domain was not encompassed by a religious domain. State forms, while not fully assimilable to western categories of the state, were powerful components in Indian civilization. Indian society, indeed caste itself, was shaped by political struggles and processes. In using the term 'political' I am of course conscious of imposing an exogenous analytic term on to a situation in which, as I will argue, ritual and political forms were fundamentally the same. However, I must stress the political both to redress the previous emphasis on 'religion' and to underscore the social fact that caste structure, ritual form, and political process were all dependent on relations of power. These relations were constituted in and through history; and these relations were culturally constructed. And it is on the cultural construction of power, in the final analysis, that I rest my case.

This essay is about the relationship between the Indian state and Indian society in the old regime, and the transformation of this relationship under British colonialism, when the crown finally did become hollow. The particular focus for the study is a small region of southern India. This region was one of many similar political regions which constituted the lowest level of the late precolonial state, and is here called, borrowing a term from Bernard Cohn, a little kingdom. While what I write about the Indian state must always be qualified by the fact that I am not looking at large transregional states, my perspective is one that will reveal the complex and integral interrelations of political processes which ultimately culminated in larger kingdoms with the social forms that are held to be autonomous and nonpolitical. By focusing on the cultural, political, social, economic and ritual basis of the little kingdom, I will show the inherent problems of these analytic categories and the distinctions they imply.

The little kingdom under scrutiny is a place called Pudukkottai (Putukkōṭṭai), meaning 'new fort'. Pudukkottai, which at its most extensive did not exceed 1,200 square miles, was located in an exclusively rain-fed agricultural zone right in the middle of the Tamil speaking region of southern India, straddling the boundary between the two great medieval Tamil kingdoms. Ruled by Kallar kings from the end of the seventeenth century until 1947, it provides an excellent canvas for a study of the political history of Indian society, or, rather, a social history of the Indian state. Kallars were elsewhere thought to be highway robbers: the term itself is still used in Tamil for thief. Dumont, in his first work on India and his only ethnographic monograph,[2] used Kallars as example of a ritually marginal group that exemplified the Dravidian isolation of kinship from the influence of caste hierarchy. But in Pudukkottai Kallars were *kings*; they exercised every conceivable kind of dominance and their social organization reflects this fact.

I base my understanding of Pudukkottai on my reading of late medieval and early modern inscriptional and textual sources relating to local chiefs and kings, as well as on eighteenth- and nineteenth-century administrative and land records, colonial reports, and the results of my recent ethnographic fieldwork. Pudukkottai rose, as did other little kingdoms throughout southern India, within the context of a late medieval Hindu political order. In both its emergence to and its maintenance of power, it exemplified the social and military vitality of certain productively marginal areas in the seventeenth and eighteenth centuries before it began its long decline under a distinctive form of colonial hegemony engineered by the British.

Colonialism purposefully preserved many of the forms of the old regime, nowhere more conspicuously than in the indirectly ruled Princely State, of which Pudukkottai was the only one in the Tamil speaking region of India. But these forms were frozen, and only the appearances of the old regime — without its vitally connected political and social processes — were saved. The historical method in the book is thus both genealogical and archaeological; I trace connections but I also search for disjunctions in the historical, ethnographic, and textual shards I have found.

....Using eighteenth-century texts — genealogies, chronicles, ballads — as cultural discourses,[3] I find persistent motifs, events, narrative forms, tropes, and images, and I read the parts they play in the poetics of power. This textualized discourse suggests the key elements to which I must attend in my historiographic inquiry: the core conceptions of sovereignty; the interpenetrating transactions in gifts, service, and kinship; the structure and form of hegemony.

....I describe the political system of Pudukkottai in the old regime historically, as a dynamic system based on relations of service and protection, kinship and caste, lordship and gift, military might and discursive domination. In particular I show how rights to landholding were political rights, which reflected the structure of the little kingdom at the same time that they revealed the pervasive importance of royal honour.

But then, abandoning chronological consistency, I present my ethnographic evidence about the structure and ideology of social organization, both among Kallars and between them and other castes. Only through my fieldwork was I able to reconnect society and state; caste and kinship were profoundly political in their operation and their conceptualization. My conclusions directly oppose those of Dumont: thus I consider and often argue against his general writings about the nature of caste hierarchy, his technical writings about kinship, and his ethnographic conclusions about the nearby Pramalai Kallars of Madurai.

Specifically, I argue that caste was embedded in a political context of kingship. This meant, among other things, that the prevalent ideology had not to do, at least primarily, with purity and pollution, but rather with royal authority and honor, and associated notions of power, dominance, and order.[4] My analysis reintroduces this concern with power and dominance into studies of culturally determined structures of thought. It is a mistake to try to separate a materialist *etic* from a culturalist *emic*: even the domain of ritual action and language is permeated with the complex foundations and lived experience of hierarchical relations. At least this is true for the Kallars of Pudukkottai, less affected perhaps than most other groups by colonialism and the demise of the old regime in the nineteenth century. The concerns of comparative sociology are not only the products of a nineteenth-century Orientalism, but also of the colonial intervention that removed the politics from colonial societies. It was not merely convenient for the British to detach caste from politics; it was necessary to do so in order to rule an immensely complex society by a variety of indirect means. Colonial sociology was an out-growth of letters and reports which represented the eighteenth century as decadent and all legitimate Indian politics as past.[5] But caste — now disembodied from its political contexts — lived on. In this dissociated form it was appropriated, and reconstructed, by the British. Paradoxically, they were able to change caste only because caste in fact continued to be permeable to political influence. Ethnohistorical reconstruction is thus important not only for historians confronting new problems of data and analysis, but for anthropologists who confront in their fieldwork a social system that was decapitated by colonial rule.

....Colonialism changed things both more and less than has commonly been thought. While introducing new forms of civil society and separating these forms off from the colonial state, colonialism also arrested some of the immediate disruptions of change by preserving many elements of the old regime. But by freezing the wolf in sheep's clothing, it changed things fundamentally. Paradoxically, colonialism seems to have created much of what is now accepted as Indian 'tradition,' including an autonomous caste structure with the Brahman clearly at the head, village based systems of exchange, the ceremonial residues of the old regime state, and fetishistic competition for ritual goods that no longer play a vital role in the political system. A picture of the Princely State as the 'theatre state' (Geertz 1980) is the final and only realization in the south Indian context of a state where ritual has been set apart with dramatic but ultimately only fictional power for the anonymous audience.

My work on Pudukkottai and other little kingdoms in the south has led me to the realization that the history of these little kings (called 'poligars' by the British) has been substantially based on the writings of colonial administrators who had developed a systematic view of old regime state and society in order to justify and facilitate their own land settlements, including the Permanent Settlement, the subsequent *ryotwari* settlement, and finally the settlement of *inams* (tax-free lands) in the late nineteenth century. The land settlements were predicated on the dual aim of securing order and extracting revenue, the cornerstones of colonial policy. Taxonomies of land type and use, caste constituency and status, and political relations under the Raj became first fixed and then reified through the colonial institutions that promulgated and implemented this colonial sociology. This process of the reification of new forms took place against the background of the old regime. Whether we are concerned with the changing nature of the state, the implementation of new forms of private property and revenue collection, the creation of new forms of social relations and communal tensions, or the formalization of a colonial sociology in which the immediate past of India was represented for the purpose of controlling and appropriating the political dynamics of Indian society, the old regime must be studied.[6]

If it be argued that my interpretation, though perhaps true for marginal regions like Pudukkottai, can hardly apply generally to south India, let alone to the subcontinent as a whole, I reply that it is precisely the marginality of Pudukkottai that makes it possible to detect there the forces that were at work elsewhere. Because Pudukkottai was not brought under patrimonial control — neither that of the Islamic rulers in the south nor later that of the British — caste was never set completely loose from kingship. Many current theories of caste, particularly those emphasizing Brahmanic obsessions concerning purity and impurity, or the proper and improper mixing of substances, are in large parts artifacts of colonialism, referring to a situation in which the position of the king has been displaced, and sometimes destroyed. However much Dumont's theory is predicated on an a priori separation of what he describes as the domains of religion and politics, Dumont was also almost certainly influenced by an ethnographic reality in which kingship played only a very small, residual role. As for the ethnosociological marketplace of cultural theories of caste, Inden has himself recently noted that his early work is largely derived from texts which were generated only after the demise of kingship as a powerful cultural institution.[7] The texts, he now says, reflected new traditions which attempted to deal with the problem of regulating caste interaction in an environment in which there was no longer a king.

To resolve in such a clear-cut historical manner the 'great conundrum of Indian social thought' — whether the Brahman or the king had precedence — is perhaps to do injustice to the

complexity of the issue. However, the historical case of Pudukkottai strongly suggests that the caste system, and its attendant
hierarchical forms, reached a particular stage of development
and articulation under a social formation in which the king was
supreme. The demise of kingship, in some areas as early as the
twelfth and thirteenth centuries, progressively later in southern
India, and perhaps last of all in Sri Lanka, led to major changes
in the caste system. The demise of kingship was accompanied
by the steady ascendancy of the Brahman, as the maintainer of
social order and the codes of caste. Brahmans reached a new
high under British colonialism both in their participation in the
development of Hindu Law and in their preponderance in colonial
administration.[8] Even in the realm of the ideological basis of the
caste system, the role of Brahmans, not as honoured and valued
members of kingdoms, but as the colonially constituted arbiters
of caste order, has changed in major ways in the last two centuries.

The importance and reference of a study of a region such as
Pudukkottai should now be clear. Kings in Pudukkottai continued
to rule until very recently. And Brahmans were heavily patronized
by these kings. The ethnohistorical case before us facilitates rather
than obstructs the reconstruction of a caste system that was
profoundly political....

The contexts discovered in fieldwork can lead to more general
insights as well. Through context we learn that all knowledge,
all meanings, are used. As Sidney Mintz writes, 'I don't think
meanings inhere in substances naturally or inevitably. Rather, I
believe that meanings arise out of use, as people use substances
in social relationships'.[9] Fieldwork, particularly ethnohistorical
fieldwork, reveals just how true this is. For one of the principal
activities of ethnohistorical fieldwork is the 'collection' of texts:
ballads, folklore, family histories, temple *puranas*, genealogies,
land records, even locally held copper plate inscriptions. As soon
as the ethnohistorian becomes interested in these texts, they become valuable in new ways; we can infer the significance of
these texts in part from our sense of context, and in part from
reflecting about our own experience of creating new meanings
for texts.

Even when using what would seem to a historian to be neutral
texts, for example the eighteenth-century family histories collected by Mackenzie and his men, we must be aware that we

are confronting meanings and texts that have been used and contested. Returning from my first stint of fieldwork by way of India Office Library in London, I was stunned to discover a letter written by one Nitala Naina about his difficulties in procuring the Tondaiman Vamcavali (the family history of the Tondaiman kings of Pudukkottai) in 1804. The letter reveals that as soon as it became known that an agent of a Company servant was seeking to collect the palm leaf manuscript, the royal court became worried and protective; the king and his ministers no doubt wondered why the British sought information about the royal family. At the same time, incentives were created for the production and delivery of the text; many court retainers represented themselves as capable of procuring it, hoping all the while to gain influence if not employment with the Company Master. It took Nitala several months of wrong leads and frantic misunderstandings finally to procure a copy of the text.[10] Thus the text Nitala sought, like all texts everywhere, was not neutral: as soon as he began seeking it, he produced new contexts and meanings. Knowledge is never neutral, and the stakes are no less important today.

NOTES AND REFERENCES

1. In a recent review of two books, one by a Sanskritist and the other by an anthropologist, Wendy D. O'Flaherty confirms this by writing that 'In Indological Studies, it appears, all roads lead to the Brahman', in 'The Aura of Renunciation', *Times Literary Supplement*, no. 4., 23 November, 1984, p. 1357.

2. Dumont, L., *A South Indian Subcaste*, Oxford University Press, Delhi, 1986.

3. My use of the term 'discourse' is influenced by Foucault's view of the structure and power of discourse, and of the practical nature of its formation and implementation: i.e., power and its technologies. For an anthropological reading of Foucault which I have found particularly helpful, see Dreyfus, H., and Rabinow, P., *Michel Foucault*, Chicago University Press, Chicago, 1983.

4. This is not a totally new proposal. The following, among others, have raised various aspects of this agenda in important ways: Appadurai, Arjun, *Worship and Conflict under Colonial Rule: a South Indian Case*, Cambridge University Press, Cambridge, 1981; Breckenridge, Carol, 'The Sri Minakshi Sundaresvrar Temple: Worship and Endowment in South India, 1833-1925', Ph.D. thesis, University of Wisconsin, 1976;

Daniel, Valentine, *Fluid Signs: Being a Person the Tamil Way,* University of California, Berkeley, 1984; McGilvary, Dennis, 'Mukkuval Vannimai: Tamil Caste and Matriclan Ideology in Batticaloa, Sri Lanka', in McGilvray, D. (ed.), *Caste Ideology and Interaction,* Cambridge University Press, Cambridge, 1982. I hope, however, that this essay will provide the ethnohistorical evidence to give still greater credibility and sharper clarity to this alternative to the dominant view on caste.

5. Cohn, B., 'Representing Authority in Victorian India', in Hobsbawin, E., and Ranger, T., (eds.), *The Invention of Tradition,* Cambridge University Press, Cambridge, 1983.

6. This period, sometimes labelled the 'old regime,' sometimes 'late pre-colonial India', and sometimes not labelled at all, has recently received some important, if as yet only preliminary, attention. See Bayly, C.A., *Rulers, Townsmen and Bazaars,* Cambridge University Press, Cambridge, 1983; Dirks, Nicholas, 'The Structure and Meaning of Political Relations in a South Indian Little Kingdom', in *Contributions to Indian Sociology,* n.s. vol. 13, no. 2, 1979, 169-204.

7. Inden, R., 'Orientalism and India', Paper presented to South Indian Anthropologists Group, LSE, London, 1983.

8. Dirks, Nicholas, *Brahmans in South Indian History,* mimeographed.

9. Mintz, S., *Sweetness and Power: the place of Sugar in Modern History,* Viking, New York, 1985.

5. 'Letters and Reports from Native Agents Employed to Collect Books, Traditions, etc., in the Various Parts of the Peninsula', India Office Library Records, Mackenzie Collections, unbound Translations, Class XII, vol. 1, no. 3.

FURTHER READINGS

Alam, Muzaffar, *The Crisis of Empire in Mughal North India*, Oxford University Press, Delhi, 1986.
Discusses the decline of the Mughal empire, but avoids the traditional picture of a linear decline in the capacities of north Indian society.

Sarkar, Sumit, *Modern India*, Macmillan, India, 1983.
An excellent wide-ranging analysis of the historical confrontation between colonialism and nationalism in modern India.

Bayly, C.A., *India and Society and the Making of the British Empire*, Cambridge University Press, Cambridge, 1988.
A historical account which tries to capture the complexities of the situation in which British rule eventually established itself. It focuses attention on the complicated transactions of power between the early British power and regional rulers, and particularly interestingly, with Indian merchant capital.

Washbrook, David, 'Progress and problems: South Asian Economic and Social History, c. 1720-1860', *Modern Asian Studies*, no. 1, 1988.
A concise and searching critical analysis of recent trends in historiography of colonial India.

Chatterjee, Partha, *The Nation and Its Fragments*, Princeton University Press, Princeton, 1993.
The study questions the homogeneous form in which the nation is usually presented in historical narratives, and looks at its various fragments, suggesting a more decentered view of the nation's history. There is a chapter that deals with the recent literature on the colonial state.

Jalal, Ayesha, *Democracy and Authoritarianism in South Asia*, Cambridge University Press, Cambridge, 1995.
A historical review of the common social forms and divergent political trajectories of the different parts of the subcontinent. It is particularly interesting for its comparative perspective about the states of South Asia.

Brown, Judith, *Modern India: The Origins of an Asian Democracy*, Oxford University Press, Oxford, 1985.
A historical study of the colonial administrative attempts at reform and countermoves by Indian nationalism; but unlike most other 'historical' books, this tries to bring the story of political evolution into the period after independence.

III

Caste and Class

One of the most striking features of traditional Indian society was the relation between political power of royalty and the productive order based on castes. Basically, the allocation of individuals to productive occupations was done through the largely self-regulating system of ascriptive positions: people were born into the occupations they had to pursue for their entire lives within the caste system. There might be historical evidence of alterations in caste system, both by way of some room for individual movement, and movement for social groups; but such alterations were changes *within* the caste order, not of that order itself into something else. The role of the state was particularly limited in this respect. The Brahmins may have held crucial interpretative authority over questions of caste positions and practices, and helped groups with power to acquire benefits; but the state, by and large, acknowledged its role as the custodian of this order, rather than the sovereign. Some sociologists.[1] have generalized on such properties of premodern political forms and called these, generally, 'custodial' states. If that argument is to be trusted, then, this is not a feature of Hindu society alone, but of Islamic societies and Imperial China as well.

Modernity affects the world of work and occupations in several fundamental ways. The rise of modern technology and the new scale of modern social organization give rise to new occupational roles, and new structures of relations among them. Modern social theorists like Durkheim and Marx believed, on different grounds, that class identity tended to be large in scale and gradually broke down and dissolved more localized and segmented traditional identities with which people worked in politics. Earlier we have seen the strongly functionalist view of modernity which expected that the development of industrialization and operation of democratic parliamentary politics would slowly corrode caste identity and replace them by some unspecified modern ones. Schematically, the central principle of traditional stratification was caste, and of the modern industrial one is class. So one of the main problems of historical sociology is the relation between caste and class. How is the logic of one system different from another? And are they so different that there could not be any mixtures or graftings of one onto the other? Secondly, is this transition linear? Would caste eventually disappear? And, more significantly for politics, how do social groups, which can in principle think of themselves in both these ways, actually fashion their political self-descriptions? This problem is most acute when we try to understand and predict the political behaviour of the peasantry. Peasant society is caste ridden and highly unequal. When they act in the political arena, do peasants behave according to a logic of class differentiation, as Marxists expected; or do they think and act more in terms of caste solidarities?

Historically, the colonial state was the first form of the modern state in India, and it assumed its title to sovereignty emphatically. But there were ambiguities in its position on the relation between state and society in British India. Broadly, the response of the state oscillated between a stance of non-interference in the affairs of an alien society and a converse one of energetic reformism, but in general it did not enter into a direct intervention in the structures of caste society. For several reasons, the nationalist state after independence could not maintain a similar attitude of distance. It was committed to principles of social reform, which affected caste, and was pledged to abolish untouchability. Since it also accepted the idea that simply legal abolition did not eradicate longstanding social inequality, it undertook serious legislation introducing positive discrimination in favour of backward communities, giving them relative advantage in state employment and education. This was a process which, if successful, would have restructured caste divisions into class groups.

Modern states tend to displace all other ordering mechanisms of society, and become the sole source of mandatory rules. When the modern state arose in Europe, it had a very limited conception of itself, and therefore did not participate systematically in social engineering; rather, social changes, once complete, came to the state for formal ratification by law. In India, by contrast, the constitution itself introduces large programmes of social engineering and entrusts these to the state as their principal agency of realization. There are, therefore, two questions about caste and class which would be of interest to any historically interested political sociologist. The first is, to what extent and in what ways is caste changing into class? Do caste groups change their self-perceptions into class groups? If they do, their boundaries are drawn differently, just as their principle of membership are altered. Are groups like the Scheduled Castes, or the peasantry, or the bourgeoisie showing signs of such altered self-understandings? Secondly, both in the expected decline of caste-practice and the emergence of classes, the state plays a significant role. The state is, even statutorily, a major instrument for destruction of the caste system. Or, is this, as Partha Chatterjee has claimed recently, a plausible illusion? Social reform movements inside Hindu society had already undermined caste practices like hard distinctions and untouchability, and the state merely ratified what was already accomplished. The abolition of untouchability, etc. therefore should not be seen as a sign of the effectiveness of the state. Besides, the democratic state depends very heavily on political parties and their internal sociology. And if parties were using the logic of caste for their own electoral support and mobilization, could the constitutional order retain its formal opposition to caste?

It would be generally acknowledged that the modern state takes the Weberian principle of monopoly of coercive authority entirely seriously, and sends out signals to social groups to route their demands against each other through its agencies. Due to this, there is an inevitable rise in the demands made by groups on the state. Indeed, this is sometimes a subtler process: by making demands to the state, and through its formal recognition, social groups tend to mark their boundaries more sharply than before and historically constitute themselves. But the discussion about caste and class, central to any analysis of the nature of India's historical transition to modernity, has been unsatisfactory. Traditionally, Marxist analysis simply used class concepts without much modification to suit the specific conditions of Indian society, and generally avoided even standard Marxist questions like assessing the degree and depth of class formation, or about 'classness'. This drew understandable criticism that this entire mode of analysis was Eurocentric and misleading, that it assumed too casually that economic processes assume a causal primacy or centrality in all societies, not merely Western capitalism. Sociological analyses, with a few exceptions like Béteille, generally concentrated on caste, neglecting the possibility that there can be classes in precapitalist societies. In any case, to the extent social groups and territories came under the influence of modern capitalist productive organization, the question of class-formation would become increasingly significant. Although the caste- and class-based sociologies have recently overcome some of their former exclusivism, there are few direct analyses of these problems.

The extent to which social groups can influence governmental policy-making depends not only on the groups themselves, but also on the nature of regimes. The Rudolphs, in their recent work on political economy, introduce a refinement to escape from the simply formal description of the constitution as democratic. With democratic governmental forms, there are often significant refigurations of political authority and styles of dealing with group demands. The distinction between 'demand' and 'command polity' captures an essential, if conceptually elusive, difference between government under Nehru and Indira Gandhi, and they try to analyse the manner in which demands from social groups have influenced public policy. Although this is not a study of class-formation, the material contributes to an understanding of how government policies affect and shape group identities and cohesion.

One of the major groups in Indian politics is of course the peasantry. We include in this part an analysis of how peasant groups have responded to electoral politics in Uttar Pradesh, the largest state, by Paul Brass. Marxists expected the peasantry to gradually differentiate into four distinct classes of rich, middle and poor peasants and a lower class of agricultural labourers without any landed property, and their politics to show increasing signs of these fractures. In fact, peasants have, over large parts of the country, not responded to processes of class differentiation in their political behaviour. This blocks off two simple generalizations. The first is that, if economic differentiation exists, this would be translated into political action; the second is the converse, that if there is no political difference, this shows economic differentiation has not taken place. But if the peasantry has not broken up into its class fractions, it has also failed to make common cause on a national scale. Intermittent attempts to put together coalitions of peasant interests on a national scale have failed. It is interesting to speculate about why peasant mobilizations have never risen above their regional horizons.

Finally, one of the most significant historical initiatives of the constitutional system was the scheme of positive discrimination in favour of lower caste groups. Originally, the constitution-makers realized that there is a contradiction between the universalist liberal principles on which the constitution was based and the principle behind reservations on the basis of communities. Their expectation, quite explicitly, was that these arrangements were to be temporary — to be revoked after these discriminations were obliterated. The record of the reservations have been mixed. The appointment of low-caste individuals to high positions, some would argue, is itself a symbolic and significant fact of empowerment. However, it is also easy to point out that the effect of these measures on the general deprivation of these communities has not been very significant. These measures, it can be argued, have created a small stratum of people who have gained advantage, and who have turned it into a mechanism of individual advance rather than collective improvement of living conditions. Thus some view these measures as having failed, since they have produced an élite from among the backward, rather than reducing the backwardness of the whole community. These debates have become much more intense after the acceptance of the recommendations of the Mandal Commission by the government. Marc Galanter's essay provides a careful and well-judged account of the consequences of this 'pursuit of equality'.

REFERENCE

1. Hall, John, *Powers and Liberties*, Penguin, Harmondsworth, 1988.

Regime Types and Economic Performance

LLOYD I. RUDOLPH
SUSANNE HOEBER RUDOLPH

The relationship between politics and economics is one that continues to perplex politicians and social scientists. Does poverty lead to revolution or fatalistic apathy? Does economic growth yield explosive rising expectations or contented co-optation? Are the open, competitive politics associated with democracy compatible with economic growth, or does growth require the firm hand of authoritarian rule? In this article we will examine the historical association in India since independence between regime types and economic performance. We find the widely held intuitive judgement, that there is a positive relationship between authoritarian regimes and economic performance ('the trains run on time'), more contradicted than supported by the historical evidence. Both good and bad economic performance occurred under authoritarian and under democratic regimes.[1]

We will show, instead, a decline in state autonomy over the thirty-five years since independence, a decline that encompasses both authoritarian and democratic regimes. This long-run deterioration in state autonomy is associated with two phenomena: (i) a

Excerpted from Dilip Basu and Richard Sisson (eds.) *Social and Economic Development in India*, Sage Publications, New Delhi, 1986, 43-66. The argument in this paper has been expanded in Rudolph, L.I. and Rudolph, S.H., *In Pursuit of Lakshmi*, University of Chicago Press, Chicago 1987, and Orient Longman, Delhi, 1987.

long-term increase in social mobilization as measured by indicators of demand politics; and (ii) de-institutionalization — i.e.,
a secular decline in the authority and capacity of state agencies
and political parties to articulate a public philosophy and to
respond to and broker political demands within the framework
of that philosophy.

The intuitive presumption that authoritarian regimes are better
for economic performance is based on the notion that they invest
states with higher levels of autonomy and capacity. This
presumption is contradicted by the fact that the best economic
performance in India was achieved under a democratic regime
with a strong state. A more complex formulation of the relationship between politics and economics is required to explain such
'real world' outcomes. We begin by explicating two ideal typical
constructs — demand polity and command polity — which we
use to analyse and explain the relationship of regimes to economic
performance.

We approach this relationship by distinguishing four periods
since India's independence. Each manifests a different combination of regime types (democratic and authoritarian) and types
of polity (demand and command). Next we relate the four periods
to various measures of economic performance and to indicators
of demand politics. We conclude that demand and command
politics are more associated with economic performance than
are regime types *per se*, but that neither association is very compelling. We also note that the higher mobilization plateau of the
post-Nehru era lowered the range within which economic performance varies.

DEMAND POLITY AND COMMAND POLITY: IDEAL TYPES

Abstracting and simplifying, we posit that in a demand polity
extractive and allocative decisions are governed by voter
sovereignty expressed through elections and through the
demands of organized interests and classes, political parties,
social movements and agitational politics. In the theory of voter
sovereignty voters are said to be analogous to sovereign consumers in a competitive market economy insofar as their preferences and choices in markets and elections are not 'distorted' by
widely asymmetrical distributions of wealth, power and

information. In a command polity, extractive and allocative decisions are governed by state sovereignty expressed through state policies. The preferences of political leaders and bureaucrats largely determine investment decisions and policy choice. They favour, repress, license, or co-opt economic classes, organized interests, and elites. Using the economic analogy again, the role of the state is like that of monopolistic or oligopolistic producers who can determine what and how much is produced because they can control investment and shape consumer preferences and structure their choice in accordance with their investment decisions.

The demand polity is oriented towards short-term goals, competitive processes for determining policies and the public interest, and the provision of private goods. It is constrained and directed by the imperatives of electoral victory and pluralist and class bargaining. It is also oriented toward the 'rationality' of incremental policy choice.[2] The command polity is oriented towards state-determined long-term goals and formulations of the public interest and the provision of public and collective goods. Rationality in command politics derives from the calculations of systematic long-term planning rather than incremental change. A necessary condition for the command polity to formulate goals and choose strategies and policies is the state's ability to free itself through leadership or repression from the constraints of societal demands.

Command polities sacrifice short-run for long-run benefits and private goods for public goods while demand polities do the reverse. Legitimacy, support, and producer commitment in command and demand polities require equity in the allocation of benefits and sacrifices. Command polities tend to maximize legitimacy, support, and producer commitment by stressing equity with respect to sacrifice while demand polities stress equity with respect to benefits....

PERIODIZATION OF POLITICS

Our explanatory project encounters the phenomenon of circular causation. While we are primarily interested in analysing the effect of type of politics and regime on economic performance, we recognize that economic performance affects the type of politics and regime. The relationship is mutually determined.

The era 1956-80 was characterized by alternating periods of types of regimes and politics. Our periodization starts with the second five year plans (1956-61) when India embarked on a strategy of limited autarky based on investment in heavy and basic industry and import substitution. Each period specifies types of regime and politics which we shall examine in turn.

(a) 1956-7 to 1965-6: democratic regime/command politics (main-ly Nehru)
(b) 1966-7 to 1974-5: democratic regime/demand politics (mainly Indira Gandhi)
(c) 1975-6 to 1976-7: authoritarian regime/command politics (emergency)
(d) 1977-8 to 1979-80: democratic regime/demand politics (Janata)[3]

1956-7 to 1965-6: Democratic Regime-I/Command Politics-I

The Nehru era was characterized by a democratic regime and non-authoritarian command politics. Nehru-led Congress governments were able to invest in the future because they could rely on his persuasive leadership, the effectiveness of the Congress party's organizational wing at the centre and in the states, and autonomous and authoritative state institutions. Nehru-led Congress governments benefited from the residual consensus of the nationalist era and a less mobilized, more dependent society and electorate. Quantitative indicators of demand politics (such as, voter turn-out, work-days lost due to strikes, incidents of student indiscipline and riots) remained low.

The Congress party exercised firm control, winning two-thirds or more of the parliamentary seats and three-fifths or more of the assembly seats in the 1952, 1957 and 1962 general elections. Economic performance was good to outstanding.

The era encompassed the second and third five year plans which, in retrospect, appear as a kind of political and economic golden age. The government's investment effort, as reflected in the central government's capital formation, grew vigorously from about 25 per cent of the total expenditure of the central government just prior to the first five year plan (1950-1) to an average just below 50 per cent during the second and third plans. Industrial production sped forward during the last two years of the second plan and the first four years of the third five year plan (1959-60 through 1964-5). Subsequent industrial production has not equalled the 12 point average annual gain of these remarkable six years. Food-grain production increased 19 per cent between the last year of the first plan (1955-6) and 1964-5, the year before the great monsoon failure of 1965-6, staying abreast of population growth. In only two years of the 1956-66 period did the price index rise more than 10 points.

1966-7 to 1974-5: Democratic Regime/ Demand Politics I

The first phase of demand politics commenced in 1965-6, the last year of the third plan, and continued through 1974-5, with a brief remission in 1971-2. Factors exogenous to a political economy framework of explanation contributed to the manifestation of demand politics. The exogenous factors took the form of shocks caused by security, political, and economic events: military failure in wars with China (1962) and Pakistan (1965); the deaths of two prime ministers (Nehru in May 1964 and Shastri in January 1966); and the 'worst weather on record' in 1965-6 when food production plummetted and prices soared. Together they created the necessary but not the sufficient conditions for the rise of demand politics.

....One of the first acts of the inexperienced new Prime Minister, Indira Gandhi, was rupee devaluation (June 1966). Perceived as being imposed on India, it politically embarrassed the Gandhi government and weakened its standing and authority. Poor economic performance both reflected and compounded the effects of exogenous shocks on the rise of demand politics. Economic indicators for the fifth year of the third plan (1965-6) turned sharply downward. Industrial as well as agricultural production declined; plan investment, already adversely affected by the doubling of defence spending after the China war (October 1962), slumped further; and prices shot up.

The fourth general election (February-March 1967) illustrates the mutually determinative relationship between type of regime and politics and economic performance. Voters turned out in unprecedented numbers to protest poor economic performance and to vote against the government's domestic and foreign economic policy failures. The result was virtual repudiation of the Congress, the party of nationalism and independence.... In circular fashion, the outcome fostered demand politics, as narrow and uncertain Congress majorities at the centre and unstable and warring opposition coalitions in the states rendered governmental authority more suspect and vulnerable.... With the writ of the government enfeebled, it became much more difficult to combine a democratic regime with command politics.

Quantitative and historical evidence for the rise of demand politics after 1965 includes increases in electoral participation (turnout), riots, strikes, student 'indiscipline' and agrarian unrest.... Between April and August 1966, when food shortages were acute, there were widespread *bandhs* (suspension of business) and demonstrations demanding food rationing and protesting price rises, tax increases, hoarding and profiteering. Industrial unrest as indicated by work-days lost more than doubled between 1965 and 1966, rose about 25 per cent the following year and continued to rise through 1970.... Participation in the 1967 election increased by 11.7 per cent over the 49.6 per cent average of the first three general elections.

An agrarian version of demand politics began with alarming intensity after the defeated Congress government of West Bengal was replaced in February 1967 by a United Front government that included the CPI(M). Taking its name from Naxalbari (a village in the narrow neck of Darjeeling district that precariously connects Bengal to Assam) the Naxalite movement of tribal landless labourers spread west to Bihar and south along the tribal belt of the Eastern Ghats to Andhra and Kerala. By 1970, Naxalite rebellions had been crushed. They were followed by a new version of agrarian protest, the land-grab movement. Led by leftist parties (the CPI, SSP and PSP), landless labourers engaged in symbolic occupation or harvesting of over-ceiling land. A Union Home Ministry study reflected the national alarm. In language uncharacteristic of Indian bureaucratic speech, it observed that 'an explosive situation' existed and attributed it to the state governments' failure to carry out necessary land reforms. The patience of the cultivating classes was 'on the verge of boiling over', and the resulting explosion 'could rock India'.

....In 1971 the electorate voted against bad government again by using the 'delinked' parliamentary election to signal its repudiation of coalition governments in the large north Indian states and in West Bengal. In a 1972 election for state assemblies held soon after India's victory over Pakistan in December 1971, the electorate not only confirmed its 1971 judgement but also rewarded Mrs. Gandhi's conduct of the war by returning Congress majorities in most states. Formal indicators of demand politics receded: the number of work-days lost declined in 1971, and the Home Ministry reported a respite in challenges to law and order.[4]

However, the party credibility and governmental authority gained in these elections were soon dissipated. Mrs. Gandhi failed to exploit her mandate and began a process of party deinstitutionalization and centralized personal rule. The opportunity offered by the 1971 and 1972 elections to combine, as in the Nehru era, a democratic regime with command politics was lost.

The intense pressure on government that characterized the 1965-70 period quickly resumed. It was exacerbated by new exogenous shocks that lowered production and raised prices, the first oil price rise (1973), and a series of poor monsoons. The deterioration of party credibility and governmental authority quickened. The number of work-days lost jumped from 16 to 20 million between 1971 and 1972 and reached an unprecedented 40 million in 1974 — the year a national railway strike challenged Mrs. Gandhi's government. The incidence of student indiscipline increased greatly after 1966 reaching new heights. The reports in part reflect student participation in the mobilization of discontent by Jayaprakash Narayan (JP) that eventuated in the proclamation of emergency in June 1975. JP's anti-Congress movement for 'total revolution' (i.e., fundamental transformation of Indian society) was most active in Bihar and Gujarat where students were an essential component. On 26 June 1975, Mrs. Gandhi imposed an emergency regime on the country.

1975-6 to 1976-7: Authoritarian Regime/Command Politics II

Mrs. Gandhi's authoritarian and corporatist version of command politics ended the 1965-75 period of demand politics by banning strikes and demonstrations arresting opposition leaders, censoring the press and depriving citizens of their civil and political rights. The declared purpose of the emergency regime was to restore civil order and economic discipline. Reported incidents of student indiscipline declined dramatically in 1976 as did the number of work-days lost due to strikes.

1977-8 to 1979-80: Democratic Regime II/Demand Politics II

The Janata party's unexpected election victory in March 1977 abruptly ended authoritarian rule. When its government restored constitutional government, a liberal state, and democratic political cal processes, quantitative and qualitative evidence indicate a resurgence of demand politics. The rate of student indiscipline and the number of work-days lost surpassed those of the sixties. The Home Ministry reported serious law and order problems for 1978-9 and 1979-89. It specially noted the appearance in 1980-81 of 'farmers' agitations for remunerative prices, a development that signalled the emergence of a new constituency for demand politics.[5]

Economic performance is to some extent determined by non-political variables (for instance, the exogenous 'shocks'...or the level of household savings, the availability of foreign aid, etc.). Economic performance is also affected by leads and lags associated with the variable gestation time of investments and the recurring bottlenecks of uneven development. Recognizing that economic performance is determined in part by non-political variables, we would like to examine the proposition that regime types and/or types of politics account in some measure for variations in economic performance.

...[We next analyse] democratic and authoritarian regimes against four economic indicators: government capital formation, industrial production, food-grain production and wholesale prices. Wide variations in all four measures are apparent during democratic regime I (Nehru-Gandhi).... During the authoritarian regime, performance varied narrowly within plateaus reached just prior to its imposition. Under democratic regime II (Janata), investment and industrial production showed marked gains while food-grain production and prices performed well for two of the three years. Overall, there is no consistent time-bound association between type of regime and economic performance. Put differently, the conventional view that economies perform better under authoritarian than under democratic regimes is disconfirmed.

....[considering, however,] the periods for type of politics against the same measures of economic performance used in discussing regime types, we find they show only slightly more marked relationships than do the graphs relating to regime types. The most striking contrast is between command politics I (1956-7 through 1965-6/Nehru) and demand politics I (1966-7 through 1974-5/Gandhi). Economic performance on all indicators (except food-grain production) was better during the earlier period. However, there was little difference between economic performance under command politics II (1975-6 through 1976-7/emergency) and under demand politics II (1977-8 through 1979-80/Janata). Capital formation and industrial production did slightly better under demand politics II (Janata), while prices did slightly better under command politics II (the emergency). Overall, the relationship between type of polity and economic performance is slightly more discernible than that between regime types and economic performance.

What is most striking about the relationship presented in the graphs on type of polity and economic performance is the contrast between levels of economic performance before and after 1965-6. The contrast parallels the quantitative increases in demand politics indicators evident at the end of the Nehru era. What has changed is the mobilization and participation conditions under which state actors pursue economic growth. In the post-Nehru era, both command and demand politics face a differently constituted political universe that makes economic growth more problematic. Its higher levels of mobilization cannot be as readily enlisted in the cause of economic growth or repressed in its name by leadership, corporatist representation, or bureaucratic controls....

NOTES AND REFERENCES

1. For a review of the evidence, see Zagoria, Donald S., 'China by Daylight', *Dissent*, vol. 22, Spring, 1975.
2. A classic statement is found in Lindblom, Charles, 'The Science of Muddling Through', *Public Administration Review*, vol. 19, Spring, 1959.
3. The calibration and synchronization of political periods (regime types and types of politics) with our measures of demand politics and economic performance are complicated by the fact that demand politics and economic performance data are sometimes given on the basis of calendar years (1 January-31 December) and sometimes on the basis of financial years (1 April-31 March); that political events occur stochastically and that five year plan periods (starting in 1951) have been modified by a plan 'holiday' (or annual plans) (1966-7 through

1968-9) and by a one year reduction in the·fifth plan (from 1974-9 to 1974-8).
4. See the data and discussion in Government of India, Home Ministry, *Annual Report*, 1972.
5. Government of India, Home Ministry, *Annual Report*, 1974, 1.

Pursuing Equality: An Assessment of India's Policy of Compensatory Discrimination for Disadvantaged Groups

MARC GALANTER

Independent India embraced equality as a cardinal value against a background of elaborate, valued and clearly perceived inequalities. Her constitutional policies to offset these proceeded from an awareness of the entrenched and cumulative nature of group inequalities. The result has been an array of programmes that I call, collectively, a policy of compensatory discrimination. If one reflects on the propensity of nations to neglect the claims of those at the bottom, I think it is fair to say that this policy of compensatory discrimination has been pursued with remarkable persistence and generosity (if not always with vigour and effectiveness)....

Few in independent India have voiced disagreement with the proposition that the disadvantaged sections of the population deserve and need 'special help'. But there has been considerable disagreement about exactly who is deserving of such help, about the form this help ought to take, and about the efficacy and

Excerpted from Dilip Basu and Richard Sisson (eds) *Social and Economic Development in India*, Sage Publications, New Delhi, 1986, 129-52.

propriety of what the government has done under this head. There is no open public defense of the *ancien regime*. Everyone is against untouchability and against caste. Public debate takes the form of argument among competing views of what is really good for the lowest castes and for the country. These views involve a host of assertions about the effects — beneficial and deleterious — of compensatory discrimination policies....

The evaluation of these compensatory programmes involves a two-stage inquiry. First there is what we might call the problem of performance: does the programme actually deliver the goods (for instance, more jobs or housing or better performance in schools). In making such judgements we must be wary of all the pitfalls of measuring programme effects. Having satisfied ourselves that the programme has the projected effect, we then face what we might call the problem of achievement. Has the programme produced the results that it is supposed to achieve — do more jobs for Scheduled Castes produce considerate treatment by officials, or stimulate educational accomplishment, or produce social integration? To what extent does delivering the jobs entail the costs alleged by critics of preferential treatment — stigmatizing the beneficiaries, fomenting group resentments, lowering self-esteem, and so on.

A COSTLY SUCCESS

Have these policies 'worked'? What results have they produced? And at what costs? ...Performance is difficult to measure: effects ramify in complex interaction with other factors. Compensatory policies are designed to pursue a multiplicity of incommensurable goals in unspecified mixtures that vary from programme to programme, from time to time, and from proponent to proponent. Evaluation of a specific scheme for a specific group during a specific period is itself a daunting task....

What I want to do here is draw a crude sketch of the effects of the compensatory discrimination policy in their largest outline. What has the commitment to compensatory discrimination done to the shape of Indian society and to lives lived within it? The limited clarity of such a sketch is dimmed by the necessity of distinguishing between compensatory discrimination for the Scheduled Castes and Tribes on the one hand, and for the OBCs on the other. The following summary focuses on programmes for Scheduled Castes and Tribes and adds some qualifications in the light of experience with schemes for the OBCs.

Undeniably, compensatory discrimination policies have produced substantial redistributive effects, though redistribution is not spread evenly throughout the beneficiary groups. Reserved seats, for example, provide an important legislative presence and swell the flow of patronage, attention, and favourable policy to SCs and STs. The reservation of jobs has given to a sizeable portion of the beneficiary groups earnings, as well as the security, information, patronage, and prestige that go with government employment. At the cost of enormous wastage, there has been a major redistribution of educational opportunities to these groups. In the utilization of these opportunities, however, there is evidence for substantial clustering, which appears to reflect structural factors (for instance, the greater urbanization of some groups) more than deliberate group aggrandizement, as is often charged.[1] The better situated among the beneficiaries enjoy a disproportionate share of programme benefits.[2] This tendency, inherent in all government programmes — quite independently of compensatory discrimination — is aggravated here by passive administration and by the concentration on higher echelon benefits. Where the list of beneficiaries spans groups of very disparate condition — as with the most expansive lists of OBCs — the 'creaming' effect is probably even more pronounced.

The vast majority are not directly benefited, but reserved jobs bring a many-fold increase in the number of families liberated from circumscribing subservient roles, enable them to utilize expanding opportunities and support high educational attainments. Although such families constitute only a tiny fraction of all Scheduled Caste families — an optimistic guess might be 6 per cent — they provide the crucial leaven from which effective leadership might emerge.

Reserved seats afford a measure of representation in legislative settings, though the use of joint electorates deliberately muffles the assertiveness and single-mindedness of that representation.[3] The presence of Scheduled Castes and Scheduled Tribes in legislative settings locks in place the other programmes for their benefit and assures that their problems are not dismissed or ignored. Even so, there is evidence that Scheduled Castes and

Tribes are not accepted politically — few are nominated for non-reserved seats, only a tiny number are elected, and there is massive withdrawal by voters from participation in election for reserved seats in the legislative assemblies. Apparently large numbers of people do not feel represented by these legislators and do not care to participate in choosing them.[4] Job reservations promote their presence in other influential roles, and educational preferences provide the basis for such participation. Of course these positions are used to promote narrower interests — although we should not assume automatically that those they displace would bestow the benefits of their influence more broadly. If, for example, reserved seat legislators are disproportionately attentive to the concerns of their fellows who already have something, it is not clear that this is more the case with them than with legislators in general seats.

Preference programmes are integrative in several ways. Reserved legislative seats are generally occupied by members of national political parties. They must aggregate broad multi-group support in order to get elected and, once elected, must participate in multi-group coalitions in order to be effective. In the office settings, too, there are relations of reciprocity and interdependence. The broad participation afforded by reserved seats and reserved jobs is for many others a source of pride and warrant of security.

If, as critics of preferential programmes charge, receiving separate and special treatment in itself wounds and alienates the members of beneficiary groups, this is surely amplified by the hostility encountered on being identified as a recipient. As sources of alienation, these experiences must be placed against the background of more devastating manifestations of hostility, such as the much publicized assaults and atrocities perpetrated on Scheduled Castes.

In the long run, education and jobs help weaken the stigmatizing association of Scheduled Castes and Tribes with ignorance and incompetence, but in the short run they experience rejection in offices, hostels, and other set-ups into which they are introduced by preferential treatment.[5] Resentment of preferences may magnify hostility to these groups, but rejection of them obviously exists independent of compensatory programmes.

Compensatory programmes provide the basis for personal

achievement and enlarge the beneficiaries' capacity to shape their own lives. But in other ways the programmes curtail their autonomy. The design of legislative reservations — the dependence on outside parties for funds and organizations and needs to appeal to constituencies made up overwhelmingly of others — tends to produce compliant and accommodating leaders rather than forceful articulators of the interests of these groups. The promise of good positions offers a powerful incentive for individual effort. But reservations in government service — and educational programmes designed to provide the requisite qualifications — deflect the most able to paths of individual mobility that remove them from leadership roles in the community. Constraints intrude into central issues of personal identity by eligibility requirements that penalize those who would solve the problem of degraded identity by converting to a non-Hindu religion.

Although preferential treatment has kept the beneficiary groups and their problems visible to the educated public, it has not stimulated widespread concern to provide for their inclusion, apart from what is mandated by government policy. This lack of concern is manifest in the record of private sector employment — as it was in public employment before the introduction of reservations. Against a long history of such lack of concern, it is difficult to attribute its current absence to compensatory discrimination policy. But this policy has encouraged a tendency to absolve others of any responsibility for their betterment on the ground that it is a responsibility of the government. The pervasive overestimation of the amount and effectiveness of preferential treatment reinforces the notion that enough (or too much) is already being done and nothing more is called for.

Compensatory preference involves a delicate combination of self-liquidating and self-perpetuating features. Reservations of upper-echelon positions should become redundant as preferential treatment at earlier stages enables more beneficiaries to compete successfully , thus decreasing the net effect of the reservations. A similar reduction of net effect is produced by the extension to others of benefits previously enjoyed on a preferential basis (for instance, free schooling). Judicial requirements of a more refined and relevant selection of beneficiaries (and of periodic

reassessment) and the growing use of income cut-offs provide
opportunities to restrict the number of beneficiaries.

The diversion of resources by compensatory discrimination
programmes entails costs in the failure to develop and utilize
other talents. The exact extent of this is unclear. It seems mistaken,
for example, to consider compensatory discrimination a major
factor in the lowering of standards that has accompanied the
vast expansion of educational facilities since independence. The
pattern in education has been less one of excluding others than
of diluting educational services while extending them nominally
to all. Similarly, the effect of Scheduled Castes and Tribes on
the effectiveness of a much enlarged government bureaucracy
is overshadowed by a general lowering of standards combined
with the assumption of a wide array of new and more complex
tasks.

As a forced draft programme of inclusion of Scheduled Castes
and Scheduled Tribes within national life, compensatory discrimination has been a partial and costly success. Although few
direct benefits have reached the vast mass of landless laborers
in the villages, it has undeniably succeeded in accelerating the
growth of a middle class within these groups — urban, educated,
largely in government service. Members of these groups have
been brought into central roles in the society to an extent
unimaginable a few decades ago. There has been a significant
redistribution of educational and employment opportunities to
them; there is a sizeable section of these groups who can utilize
these opportunities and confer advantages on their children; their
concerns are firmly placed on the political agenda and cannot
readily be dislodged. But if compensatory discrimination can be
credited with producing this self-sustaining dynamic of inclusion,
there is at the same time a lesser counter-dynamic of resentment,
rejection, manipulation, and low self-esteem. And these gains
are an island of hope in a vast sea of neglect and oppression.
This mixed pattern of inclusion and rejection, characteristic of
urban India and of the 'organized' sector, is echoed in the villages
by a pattern of increasing assertion and increasing repression.

Since independence India has undergone what might crudely
be summarized as development at the upper end and stagnation
at the bottom. With the boost given by compensatory discrimination, a section of the Scheduled Castes and Scheduled Tribes

have secured entry into the modern class populating the organized sector. What does this portend for the bulk of untouchables and tribals who remain excluded and oppressed? Are they
better or worse off by virtue of the fact that some members of
their descent groups have a share in the benefits of modern
India? The meaning of these achievements ultimately depends
on how one visualizes the emergent Indian society and the role
of descent groups in it.

Even this kind of crude characterization of the overall impact
of policies is not possible in dealing with measures for OBCs.
Policies diverge from state to state, and very different groups
of peoples are involved. In some states the OBC category is
used to address the problems of a stratum of lowly groups who
are roughly comparable in circumstance to the Scheduled Castes
and Tribes. In other places this category has been used to tilt
the distribution of government benefits in favour of a major section
of the politically dominant middle castes. The latter doubtless
produce substantial redistributive effects, if less in the way of
including the most deprived. But these expensive preferences
for OBCs are of immense consequence for the Scheduled Castes
and Tribes. They borrow legitimacy from the national commitment to ameliorate the condition of the lowest. At the same time
they undermine that commitment by broadcasting a picture of
unrestrained preference for those who are not distinctly worse
off than non-beneficiaries, which attaches indiscriminately to all
preferential treatment. And because the OBC categories are less
bounded and are determined in the states rather than at the
center, they carry the threat of expanding into a general regime
of communal allotments....

To prefer one individual over another on grounds of caste,
religion, or other ascriptive criteria is specifically branded as
unfair by the anti-discrimination provisions of the Indian Constitution. The ban on the use of these criteria is, as we have
seen, qualified to allow preferential treatment to a certain range
of groups, whose history and condition seemed distinctive. There
was agreement that some groups were burdened by a heritage
of invidious discrimination, exclusion, and/or isolation that made
their condition distinct from that of their fellow citizens; the
deprivations of their past and present members were thought
to justify a special effort for their improvement and inclusion.

Those representing the Backward Classes sometimes call for measures specifically to remedy the wrongs of the past. If one thinks of the blighted lives, the thwarted hopes, the dwarfing of the human spirit inflicted on generations of untouchables, or of the oppression and exploitation of tribal peoples, the argument for a measured vindication of these historic wrongs has an initial appeal. But there are many kinds and grades of victimization; deprivations are incommensurable. Perpetrators and victims sometimes stand out in stark clarity, but infirm and incomplete data often leave unclear precisely who were brutally exploitative, who willing or reluctant collaborators, who inadvertant beneficiaries of what we now see as systems of oppression. These arrangements interact with many other factors (climate, invasions, technology) in their influence on the present distribution of advantages and disadvantages. The web of responsibility is tangled and, as we try to trace it across generations, only the boldest outlines are visible. Without minimizing its horrors, the past provides a shaky and indistinct guide for policy. It is beyond the capacity of present policy to remedy these wrongs: in the literal sense these injustices remain irremediable.

But if our perception of past injustice does not provide a usable map for distributing reparative entitlements, it can inform our vision of the present, sensitizing us to the traces and ramifications of historic wrongs. The current scene includes groups that are closely linked to past victims and that seem to suffer today from the accumulated results of that victimization. In a world in which only some needs can be met, the inevitable assignment of priorities may take some guidance from our sense of past injustice — thus providing the basis for a metaphoric restitution.

All remedies involve new distinctions and thus bring in their wake new and, it is hoped, lesser forms of unfairness. Singling out these historically deprived groups for remedial attention introduces a distinction among all of the undeserved inflictions and unfairness of the world. One batch of troubles, but not others, are picked out for comprehensive remedy using extraordinary means. Those afflicted by other handicaps and misfortunes are left to the succour and aid that future policy-makers find feasible and appropriate within the framework of competing commitments, including commitments to equal treatment. But drastic and otherwise outlawed remedies were authorized for victims of what was seen as a fundamental flaw in the social structure. The special quality of the commitment to correct this flaw is dramatized by the Constitution's simultaneous rejection of group criteria for any other purpose.

The line of distinct history and condition that justifies compensatory discrimination is of course less sharp in practice than in theory. There are borderlines, grey areas, gradual transitions. There is disagreement about just where the line should be drawn. And once it is drawn, the categories established are rough and imperfect summations of need and merit; there are inevitable 'errors' of under-inclusion and over-inclusion.

We arrive then at an ironic tension that lies at the heart of the compensatory discrimination policy. Since the conditions that invite compensatory treatment are matters of degree, special treatment generates plausible claims to extend coverage to more groups. The range of variation among beneficiaries invites gradation to make benefits proportionate to need. These preferential policies create new discontinuities and it is inviting to smooth them out by a continuous modulated system of preferences articulated to the entire range of need and/or merit. But to do so is to establish a general system of group allotments.

Compensatory discrimination replaces the arbitrariness of formal equality with the arbitrariness of a line between formal equality and compensatory treatment. The principles that justify the preference policy counsel flexibility and modulation. We may shave away the arbitrary features of the policy in many ways. But we may dissolve the arbitrary line separating formal equality and preferential treatment only at the risk of abandoning the preference policy for something very different.

If there is to be preferential treatment for a distinct set of historically victimized groups, who is to bear the cost? Whose resources and life-chances should be diminished to increase those of the beneficiaries of this policy? In some cases, the costs are spread widely among the tax-payers, for example, or among consumers of a 'diluted' public service. But in some cases major costs impinge on specific individuals, like the applicant who is bumped to fill a reservation. Differences in public acceptance may reflect this distinction. Indians have been broadly supportive of preferential programmes — for instance, the granting of educational facilities and sharing of political power — where the 'cost' of inclusion is diffused broadly. Resentment has been focused on settings where the life-chances of specific others are diminished in a palpable way, as in reservations of jobs and medical college places.

There is no reason to suppose that those contenders who are excluded from valued opportunities are more responsible for or benefited by past invidious discrimination than are those whose well-being is undisturbed. Reserved seats or posts may thus be seen as the conscription of an arbitrarily selected group of citizens to discharge an obligation from which equally culpable debators are excused. The incidence of reservations and the effectiveness with which they are implemented tends to vary from one setting to another. Reservations impinge heavily on some careers and leave others virtually untouched. The administration of compensatory discrimination measures seems to involve considerable unfairness of this kind. If some concentration of benefits is required by the aims of the preference policy, it seems clear that more could be done to distribute the burden among non-beneficiaries more widely and more evenly.

SECULARISM AND CONTINUITY

Fairness apart, to many Indian intellectuals compensatory discrimination policies seem to undermine progress toward the crucial national goal of a secular society. Secularism in this setting implies more than the separation of religion and state — religious freedom, the autonomy of religious groups, withdrawal of state sanction for religious norms, and so forth. It refers to the elimination (or minimization) of caste and religious groups as categories of public policy and as actors in public life. In the 1950s and 1960s this was frequently expressed as pursuit of a 'casteless' society. Proponents of such a transformation were not always clear whether they meant the disestablishment of social hierarchy or the actual dissolution of caste units. But at the minimum what was referred to was a severe reduction in the salience of caste in all spheres of life.

The Constitution envisages a new order as to the place of caste in Indian life. There is a clear commitment to eliminate inequality of status and invidious treatment and to have a society in which government takes minimal account of ascriptive ties.

But beyond this the posture of the legal system toward caste is not as single-minded as the notion of a casteless society might imply. If the law discourages some assertions of caste precedence and caste solidarity, in other respects the prerogatives previously enjoyed by the caste group remain unimpaired. The law befriends castes by giving recognition and protection to the new social forms through which caste concerns can be expressed (e.g., caste associations, educational societies, political parties, and religious sects).

If the legal order's posture toward caste is ambivalent, public denunciation of caste has universal appeal. For the lower castes it provides an opportunity to attack claims of superiority by those above them; for the highest castes it is a way to deplore the increasing influence of previously subordinate groups, either the populous middle castes that have risen to power with adult suffrage or the lowest castes whose inclusion is mandated by compensatory discrimination programmes. Looking up, the call for castelessness is an attack on the advantages retained by those who rank high in traditional terms; looking down, it denies legitimacy to the distributive claims of inferiors and insists on the even-handed application of individual merit standards.

The use of caste groups to identify the beneficiaries of compensatory discrimination has been blamed for perpetuating the caste system, accentuating caste consciousness, injecting caste into politics, and generally impeding the development of a secular society in which communal affiliation is ignored in public life. This indictment should be regarded with some skepticism. Caste ties and caste-based political mobilization are not exclusive to the backward classes. The political life within these groups is not necessarily more intensely communal in orientation, nor are the caste activities of greatest political impact found among these groups. Communal considerations are not confined to settings that are subject to compensatory discrimination policies but flourish even where they are eschewed. Although it has to some extent legitimated and encouraged caste politics, it is not clear that the use of caste to designate beneficiaries has played a preponderant role in the marriage of caste and politics. Surely it is greatly overshadowed by the franchise itself, with its invitation to mobilize support by appeal to existing loyalties. But the avowed and official recognition of caste in compensatory discrimination policy combines with the overestimation of its effects to provide a convenient target for those offended and dismayed by the continuing salience of caste in Indian life.

The amount of preference afforded the Scheduled Castes and Tribes is widely overestimated. The widespread perception of ubiquitous and unrestrained preferment for these groups derives from several sources. First, there is the chronic overstatement of the effects of reservation: large portions of reservations (especially for cherished higher positions) are not filled; of those that are filled, some would have been gained on merit; the diversion of benefits to a few may be perceived as a deprivation by a much larger number. The net effect is often considerably less than popularly perceived. Second, ambiguous nomenclature and public inattention combine to blur the distinction between measures for Scheduled Castes and Tribes and those for Other Backward Classes. The resentment and dismay engendered by use of the OBCs category to stake out massive claims on behalf of peasant middle groups (particularly in some southern states), are readily transferred to discredit the more modest measures for Scheduled Castes and Tribes.

If caste has displayed unforeseen durability, it has not remained unchanged. Relations between castes are increasingly independent and competitive, less interdependent and cooperative. 'Horizontal' solidarity and organization within caste groups have grown at the expense of 'vertical' integration among the castes of a region. The concerns of the local endogamous units are transformed as they are linked in wider networks and expressed through other forms of organization — caste associations, educational societies, unions, political parties, religious societies.

If secularism is defined in terms of the elimination of India's compartmental group structure in favour of a compact and unitary society, then the compensatory discrimination policy may indeed have impeded secularism. But one may instead visualize not the disappearance of communal groups but their transformation into components of a pluralistic society in which invidious hierarchy is discarded while diversity is accommodated. In this view compensatory discrimination policy contributes to secularism by reducing group disparities and blunting hierarchic distinctions....

The compensatory discrimination policy is not be judged only for its instrumental qualities. It is also expressive: through it Indians tell themselves what kind of people they are and what kind of nation. These policies express a sense of connection and shared destiny. The groups that occupy the stage today are the repositories and transmitters of older patterns. Advantaged and disadvantaged are indissolubly bound to one another. There is a continuity between past and future that allows past injustices to be rectified. Independence and nationhood are an epochal event in Indian civilization which makes possible a controlled transformation of central social and cultural arrangements. Compensatory discrimination embodies the brave hopes of India reborn that animated the freedom movement and were crystallized in the Constitution. If the reality has disappointed many fond hopes, the turn away from the older hierarchic model to a pluralistic participatory society has proved vigourous and enduring.

NOTES

1. Shah, Vimal P. and Patel, Tara, *Who Goes To College? Scheduled Caste/ Tribe Post-Matric Scholars in Gujarat*, Rachana Prakashan, Ahmedabad, 1977, 149 ff.
2. Malik, Suneila, *Social Integration of Scheduled Castes*, Abhinav Publications, New Delhi, 1979, 158.
3. The seats are reserved in the sense that the candidates who stand for them must belong to the specified group, but the electorate is joint in that all voters participate in choosing from candidates so qualified.
4. This evidence is presented in Galanter, Marc, 'Compulsory discrimination in Political Representation: A Preliminary Assessment of India's Thirty-year Experiment with Reserved Seats in Legislaures', *Economic and Political Weekly*, vol. 14, 1979, 437-54.
5. C. Malik's finding that middle class Scheduled Castes experience more exclusion than do their less educated fellows.

The Politicization of
the Peasantry in a North
Indian State

PAUL R. BRASS

INTRODUCTION

....My purpose in writing this article is to demonstrate how a
programme of modest land reform, designed to establish a system
of peasant proprietorship and reenforced by the introduction of
the technology of the 'green revolution', has, in the context of a
political system based on party-electoral competition, enhanced
the power of the middle and rich peasants. The landholding classes
in UP, particularly those with landholdings above 2.5 acres, have
become the arbiters of the fates of governments and parties and
their interests have become decisive in critical areas of government
policy making affecting economic development. The rise to political prominence of these peasant classes also has forestalled both
peasant revolution and class polarization as the leading political
parties in the state have vied for the support of those who control
most of the land.

In order to understand how the politicization and political
dominance of the peasantry have developed in UP, it is necessary

Excerpted from Paul Brass, 'The Politicization of the Peasantry in a North Indian
State: I & II', *Journal of Peasant Studies*, vols. 7&8, nos. 4&1, July 1980 & October
1980, pp. 395-426 & pp. 3-36.

to refer back to the period of British rule. Before Independence, the British controlled the countryside in what was then known as the United Provinces of Agra and Oudh with the collaboration of a group of tax-farmers known as *zamindars* in most parts of the province, and as *talukdars* in the region of Oudh. Most of these tax-farmers owned lands of their own, whose cultivation they supervised personally or through their agents, but they collected revenue also on lands held in various types of tenures by others. There were more than two million of these tax farmers at independence, but the vast majority of them had only medium-size landholdings and collected only a petty revenue for the state. The biggest tax-farmers, those who collected rent on hundreds of villages and paid revenues to the state of more than Rs 5,000 per year, numbered less than a thousand. It was upon these larger tax-farmers whom the British authorities relied to maintain political control in the countryside and whom they rewarded with titles of honour and positions of political weight in the provincial government and in the districts.

For its part, the Indian National Congress, which was the principal nationalist organization in the province and which emerged to lead the government after independence, based its rural organization and its rural appeal on the high caste tenants of the big *zamindars* and *talukdars* and on the petty and middle *zamindars*, those paying less than Rs 100 per year in land revenue. The Congress supported struggles and demands for security of tenure, for rent reductions, for cheap credit facilities, and for an end to abuses such as forced labour, fines, and 'illegal exactions'. These tenant movements were strongest in the region of the state known as Oudh, where the *talukdars*, holding semi-princely status and privileges, allegedly oppressed the tenantry more relentlessly than the *zamindars* did in other parts of the state....

The Zamindari Abolition Act, as its name implies, eliminated the former system of tax-farming by removing the *zamindars* and *talukdars* from their positions as intermediaries between the cultivator and the state.[1] It also eliminated the heterogeneous forms of land rights and types of tenancy that had existed previously and created in their place two principal categories of landholders, called *bhumidhars* and *sirdars*. The only difference between these two categories was that the *bhumidhars* acquired transferable rights to their lands and a reduced land revenue by making an initial payment of ten times their land revenue whereas the *sirdar*s could not sell their landholdings and paid a higher land revenue. A third category of land tenure also was created, called *asami*, but it was meant to be a minor form of tenure for persons engaged in 'shifting or unstable cultivation' and for those letting land from *bhumidhar*s and *sirdar*s who were not able to cultivate their own land.

It must be stressed that the Zamindari Abolition Act did not dispossess the former *zamindars* and *talukdars*. It removed them as tax-farmers and displaced them from control over lands they did not own, but it left them in possession of lands traditionally presumed to be under their personal cultivation or supervision, which were called *sir* and *khudkasht* holdings. It also provided for rather generous monetary compensation to the ex-*zamindars* and *talukdars*. In some cases, the former tax-farmers were able to retain both large incomes and possession of very large tracts of land.[2]

The Land Ceilings Act of 1960 was designed more with a view to reduce the size of the largest landholdings in UP than to redistribute and equalize landholdings on a large scale. It set a rather high ceiling of forty standard acres per individual, which meant that many families still could hold 150 to 200 acres of land. Moreover, the exclusion of grovelands left some of the former *zamindars* who had converted their lands to fruit trees in anticipation of the law, in control of quite substantial acreage and incomes. The act was stiffened somewhat in 1973 in conformity with the National Guide Lines established by Mrs Gandhi's government in 1971. The basic ceiling was reduced to 27 1/2 acres per family. Although most big farmers had by then divided their lands sufficiently among family members and relatives to avoid confiscation of their lands, some actually lost lands after the enactment of the amendments of 1973. Nevertheless, loopholes remained to be exploited by the skilful and politically well-connected farmers and ex-landlords, many of whom still retain hundreds of acres of lands by such devices as establishing bogus cooperatives or educational and charitable trusts....

In general, therefore, the Congress land reforms were designed principally to eliminate the old system of tax-farming, which was accomplished effectively, and to limit the size of the largest farms, which also was achieved for the most part. However, these reforms were in no sense radical. They left most landholders in possession of lands they and their families had always cultivated, they involved very little redistribution of land, and they left a considerable range in the size of land holdings in the countryside and, therefore, considerable inequality among landholders and between the landless and the landholders.

Although there have always been a minority of Congressmen in UP and in New Delhi who have argued in favour of more radical land reforms and for extensive redistribution and equalization of landholdings, the predominant leadership of the Congress in the state remained content to dismantle the system of intermediaries and to establish a land system in which most cultivators held exclusive rights to the land they tilled. In fact, the ruling Congress drew its local leadership from the leading rural proprietary groups.[3] During the 1960s and 1970s, moreover, several measures were taken by government which further strengthened the position of the peasantry and which made it nearly impossible to carry out policies that were contrary to the interests of the more prosperous among them. These measures included consolidation of landholdings, the introduction of a system of rural self-government known as *panchayati raj*, an effort to increase rural taxation that encountered stiff opposition, and the introduction of the technological changes in agriculture known as the 'green revolution'.[4]

Consolidation of landholdings brought together into compact and contiguous plots of land the fragmented holdings of the peasantry in U.P. The consolidation operations, which began after the passage of the U.P. Consolidation of Holdings Act of 1953, had encompassed more than half the cultivable area of the state by the end of the Fourth Five Year Plan (1971).... Although consolidation made more efficient cultivation possible for all landholders, it clearly had even greater significance for the middle and larger landholders, who were now in a position to make effective use of the new agricultural inputs and, in the case of the bigger farmers, to adopt some forms of mechanization.

The introduction in the 1960s of the system of rural self-government known as *panchayati raj* enhanced the political position of the peasantry, again favouring the middle and larger farmers among them....

It was apparent in the early 1960s that any measure that ran contrary to the interest of the peasantry as a whole would be politically difficult to enact in U.P.....

Finally, in the late 1960s, the new emphasis placed by Indian government on agriculture and the introduction of the package of improved seeds and agricultural practices that goes by the name of the 'green revolution' also affected the peasantry in U.P.....

This brief survey of government policy towards the landed classes in U.P. since independence has revealed four important features. First, the old system of tax-farming was eliminated, but the ex-*zamindars* and former *talukdars* retained some economic power and potential political influence in the countryside. Second, a number of laws, structural changes in government, and policies were introduced that enhanced the economic and political positions of the peasant cultivating classes generally. Third, however, most of those measures benefited the peasants with larger landholdings more than others. Finally, it became apparent in the 1960s that no state government could function effectively if it attempted to extract resources from the peasantry or in other ways went against their interests....

Rural Social Structure in Uttar Pradesh

....It is evident...that the political stability of the U.P. countryside depends to a considerable extent on the contentment of the middle peasantry. On the other hand, their numbers alone, even if concerted action on their part were assumed, are insufficient to provide majority support for an agrarian-based party in a one man-one vote system. Moreover, there are important internal divisions among the dominant peasant classes both with respect to the size of their holdings and with respect to caste.

Although the Zamindari Abolition Act benefited the former occupancy tenants and the small and middle ex-*zamindars* irrespective of caste, the leading castes among these groups in size of landholdings and local influence were Brahmans and Rajputs in most of the state, Jats and Tyagis in western U.P., and Bhumihars in eastern U.P.... These five castes together accounted for less than 20 per cent of the population of the state, but owned a much larger share of the land in U.P. before *zamindari* abolition. Although *zamindari* abolition affected adversely the very largest landlords among these castes, it left many of their members with substantial holdings of land. The result was that, as a body, the landowning segments of these castes retained their leading positions as landholders after *zamindari* abolition and acquired an enhanced political position in U.P. villages as a consequence of the reduction of the economic hold and the political authority of the former big *zamindars* and *talukdars*. The leadership of the Congress in the rural districts after *zamindari* abolition also was drawn overwhelmingly in all early cases from these locally dominant rural castes. Moreover, as the Congress established its control over local government and cooperative institutions and developed a new system of local self-government under *panchayati raj*, these castes became the principal beneficiaries of the considerable patronage that became available through these institutions. Thus, in the aftermath of *zamindari* abolition and the establishment of Congress rule in the rural districts of U.P., the middle and large peasantry from among the elite proprietary castes benefited economically and politically.

A second group of castes that benefited to some extent from *zamindari* abolition were the middle cultivating castes of Ahirs, Kurmis, Lodhi Rajputs, and a few other smaller castes, most of whose members were tenants of the élite castes before *zamindari* abolition. However, although these castes benefited psychologically by the removal of their former overlords as collectors, most members of these castes probably became *sirdars*, paying the same amount of revenue as before to the state instead of to the tax collector and not holding the right to sell their lands. Moreover, they did not acquire as much political influence after *zamindari* abolition as the elite proprietary castes. In many districts in U.P., these middle or backward castes often occupy secondary positions both in size of landholdings and in political influence in Rajput and Brahman-dominated villages. And, as already indicated, the Congress structure of rural influence was built upon the élite castes rather than the middle castes. Consequently, it should be expected that Congress would not receive strong support in areas where these middle castes are most heavily concentrated and that they would form a potential source for opposition mobilization.

The bottom of the economic hierarchy in rural U.P. corresponds strongly with the status hierarchy in the sense that most of the landless come from the lowest caste groups. Consequently, common action on economic grounds between the landless and the small and middle peasants would have to cross a social as well as an economic barrier. It should, however, be stressed here that the correspondence between caste and economic class or political influence is far from perfect. Many elite caste persons are small holders in U.P. whereas many middle caste households belong to the middle and big peasantry. There are also some small holders among the lower castes, but very few middle or big peasants. In general, therefore, the socio-economic structure of rural U.P. does provide a basis for political mobilization that plays upon the dual theme of economic and caste inequalities, but the cross-cutting of class and caste lines also limits the potential for such appeals....

How did...parties and independents fare over time in the electoral history of U.P.? ....Four features stand out in regard to the electoral strength of the Congress and its splinter, Congress (0). First, the Congress was consistently the strongest political party in U.P. Second, however, there was a steady decline in Congress strength over the first four elections, with a general levelling off from that point on through 1974 at the low level of less than a third of the popular vote. Third, the decline in Congress strength is clearly related to, though not necessarily entirely explained by, the spread of factional conflict at the state and national leadership levels of the party in the 1950s and 1960s, culminating in the split in the party in 1969 which largely reflected earlier factional cleavages in the state Congress. Fourth, Mrs. Gandhi did not succeed in U.P. even before the declaration of Emergency in 1975 either in rebuilding the party organization or in restoring the electoral strength of the Congress. However, it is also apparent...that Mrs. Gandhi's Congress succeeded in maintaining the electoral strength of the party intact up to 1974 at roughly the 1967 level in the face of the creation of the BKD and of an alternative Congress organization, both formed from former leaders and factions within the parent Congress. Moreover, despite the massive victory of the Janata coalition in the 1977 elections in which the party won 83 per cent of the seats in the U.P. Legislative Assembly, the Congress popular vote share declined only marginally from 1974 when it won 50 per cent of the seats against a fragmented opposition.

Among the more striking features revealed...is the sudden emergence of the BKD as the leading non-Congress party in U.P.

politics. Charan Singh's party emerged in its first election contest in 1969 not only as the strongest non-Congress party in U.P. in that election, but with the highest popular vote and the largest number of seats ever won by a non-Congress party in any election since independence. Even more impressive is the fact that the BKD maintained its strength in 1974 in the face of the massive intervention of Mrs. Gandhi and her lieutenants in state politics in their efforts alternately to absorb and destroy the power of the new party. One of the most important tasks of these articles is to explain the rise of the BKD and its social and economic significance and the relationship between the rise of the BKD and the great victory of the Janata coalition in 1977.

The third group of parties, comprising the parties of the non-Communist Left has been the most fragmented of all the groups of parties in U.P. In the first general elections of 1952, three parties from this group won seats, but only the SP and the KMPP won a significant percentage of votes. Moreover, the SP was clearly the dominant party in this group and the principal opposition party in the state at that time. After the 1952 elections, the SP and KMPP merged into the PSP, but the Lohia group split off in 1954 and re-formed the SP. The PSP, however, emerged as the stronger of the two parties in the 1957 elections in both electoral support and seats won. Once again also, a party from this group, the PSP, was the leading party of opposition in the state Legislative Assembly. The relative strength of the two parties in relation to each other was more or less maintained in the 1962 elections, but the PSP declined to third place in strength in the state party system after the Jan Sangh. From this point on, in fact, the Socialist movement entered a decline that approached disintegration in 1974, when the entire non-Communist Left polled only 3.59 per cent of the votes and won only six seats. Between 1962 and 1974, the movement went through several splits and mergers whose cumulative impact was to weaken the main Socialist parties irretrievably. Its principal wing in U.P., the SSP, merged with the BKD after the 1974 elections into the BLD.

For a time, it appeared that the party system in U.P. might be moving towards a dualistic competition between the Congress and the Jan Sangh, which showed a steady increase in its electoral strength and seat-winning capacity over the first four elections. However, the rise of the BKD in 1969 contributed to a decline in Jan Sangh strength and to its relegation to third position in the U.P. party system in the 1969 and 1974 elections. Nevertheless, the Jan Sangh remained a strong force in 1969 and even more so in 1974. Thus, by 1974, there were two leading parties in opposition to the Congress — the BKD, presenting an economic appeal and a direct challenge to Congress dominance in rural areas among the leading proprietary groups, and the Jan Sangh, whose appeal emphasized Hindu nationalism and Hindi-speaking regional sentiment more than economic issues, but which also appealed to the general body of peasant proprietors. These two parties also formed the principal components of the Janata coalition in the 1977 election....

It is desirable at this point to summarize the detailed and complex data that have so far been presented.... In particular, it will be useful here to show how the data provide a basis for inferring a) the extent to which areas dominated by different social categories in the countryside were persistent sources of satisfaction or of discontent with the dominant Congress party, and b) the degree to which class differences were translated into the party system. The data suggest both the persistence of rural discontent with the Congress and a considerable degree of socio-political differentiation within the party system, which can be summarized in the following points:

1. At the top of the rural class structure, among the former *zamindars* and the modern capitalist farmers, the evidence presented is that the political influence of these classes was not concentrated effectively, but was diffused and fragmented. As a consequence of the Zamindari Abolition Act and its anti-landlord bias, the Congress generally polled poorly in areas dominated by the ex-*zamindars*, especially in the 1957 and 1962 elections. However, the *zamindars* and big farmers did not succeed in organizing a coherent opposition to the Congress, even though two parties — the UPPP and Swantantra — formed largely to pursue their interests. On the contrary, most of the politically active ex-zamindars pursued individual interests rather than class interests and divided their support among several political parties, including Congress, UPPP, Swatantra, Jan Sangh, the SP, PSP, independents, and others. In Oudh, for a time, the Jan Sangh received strong support from the former landlords. However, over time, the personal economic interests of the ex-landlords and the

capitalist farmers pulled many of them into the Congress orbit of influence, and into the nexus of Congress patronage, in search of the capital, the inputs, and the political influence required for them to prosper as the 'green revolution' began to spread. It is noteworthy in this regard that the *only* strong positive correlations — in the state as a whole, in the whole state controlling for region, and in the plains districts treated separately — between the Congress vote and the peasantry with more than 5 acres of land were with big farmers holding at least 30 acres of land.

2. At the bottom of the rural social structure, among the agricultural labourers, dwarf landholders, and poor peasants, there has been a similar dispersion of political support. If there has been no successful landlord — big farmer party in UP, neither has there been any successful party of agrarian protest nor, for that matter, any major radical agrarian movements. Only the SSP attempted to appeal explicitly to the interests and needs of the rural poor. Although it had some success in doing so, its poor organization and internal divisions prevented this party from consolidating its support among these rural social classes.

Although the support of the rural poor has been partly dispersed among opposition parties and groups, the Congress was persistently the strongest political force in areas where the rural poor are concentrated. Although the class interests of the lowest rural social classes were not pursued by the Congress, many economic measures were passed during the years of Congress rule that benefited large numbers of the poor, and much patronage was also distributed to persons from these categories. The correlations have shown that the Congress in turn received support in areas where agricultural labourers and poor peasants were concentrated.

The Congress then was not, truly speaking, a party of the centre in rural UP, but a party of the extremes, one which combined both ends of the rural social structure without the middle. Class polarization and conflict, therefore, were warded off in UP partly by the dispersion and political fragmentation at opposite ends of the rural social structure, partly by the integration of the extremes into the patronage network of the dominant Congress organization.

3. The most striking finding in the data is the evidence of persistent discontent with the Congress among all classes of the

peasantry holding between 2.5 and 30 acres of land, and particularly those holding between 5 and 30 acres. This discontent,
which revealed itself first in the correlations for the 1957 elections,
did not become translated into political support for either parties
of the far left or the far right, but was dispersed among independent
candidates. This pattern persisted for three elections. Among the
established political parties, only the Jan Sangh received any positive support in areas where these peasant social classes were
dominant, primarily in Oudh. Then, in 1967, Charan Singh, the
leading spokesman of the peasant proprietors as a body and the
principal supporter of the aspirations of the middle or 'backward'
cultivating castes, who had left the Congress to lead the first
non-Congress government in the state's history, formed the BKD.
The BKD, which appealed in the 1969 elections specifically to
the interests of all the peasant classes holding between 2.5 and
27.5 acres of land, and which also drew into its fold many persons
who in previous elections had contested against the Congress as
independents, clearly succeeded in mobilizing the discontent of
the bulk of the middle and big peasantry. The success of the
BKD in 1969, therefore, which appeared at the time as a flash-
in-the-pan success based on the gathering together of a horde of
defectors and non-party persons, had a genuine socioeconomic
basis in the support of the most important social force in the
state, the peasant proprietors as a body.

PARTY SUPPORT BASES AND SIZE OF LANDHOLDINGS IN THE 1974 ELECTIONS

Two important changes in the structure of the party system and
of the contesting parties occurred before the 1974 elections. One
was the split in the Congress, in which by far the largest segment
of the party joined Mrs. Gandhi while a much smaller but not
insignificant section joined the INC(O). In the state as a whole,
Mrs. Gandhi's Congress polled 32.24 per cent of the vote while
the INC(O) polled 8.36 per cent. The second change was the disintegration of the socialist parties in the state. Several socialist
parties contested the elections, but the largest, the Socialist Party,
polled less than 3 per cent of the vote. Most important, the SSP,
the major remnant of the socialist movement in UP, effectively
merged with the BKD in an alliance in which SSP candidates

contested on the BKD ticket. Although the BKD vote share did not increase in the state as a whole as a consequence of this alliance, it did increase markedly in the eastern districts, where the SSP had had one of its major areas of strength, from 17.74 per cent in 1969 to 25.08 per cent in 1974. Aside from the two Congress parties and the BKD, the only other party that polled a substantial share of the vote in the state as a whole was the Jan Sangh, which secured 17.12 per cent of the valid votes polled. The CPI polled only 1.45 per cent of the vote. Independents and a veritable host of minor parties polled approximately 20 per cent of the vote.

The shifts in the structure of the party system had some effect on the support areas of the parties that contested, but the broad patterns of differentiation in the party system in relation to agrarian social structure remained comparable to previous elections. The correlations for the two Congress parties were similar to those for 1969 in the absence of strong associations with any size category, with the sole exception of the positive correlation between the INC(O) vote share and the marginal landholding category of 1 to 2.4 acres.... The absence of strong correlations, positive or negative, suggests the persistence of some support across all size categories for the Congress without a concentration of support or opposition among any of the size groups. It also suggests, however, that the dominant Congress was losing one of its principal support bases among the marginal landholders in both the 1969 and 1974 elections. In most other respects, the 1974 correlations are consistent with the support bases of the main parties in previous elections. There were no strong correlations between independent vote shares and any of the size categories in the plains districts as a whole, as in 1969. However, there was a strong negative correlation with marginal farmers in the rice districts and with small farmers.... The Jan Sangh pattern in 1974 also was consistent with previous results in showing strong positive correlations with marginal landholders and strong negative correlations with middle peasant categories, particularly in the wheat districts. The sharpest pattern once again was that for the BKD, showing a very strong negative correlation with marginal landholders and strong positive correlations across the whole range of middle and rich peasant classes holding between 7.5 and 50 acres of land in the plains districts as a whole.

However, the regional break-up for the BKD shows that the pattern was a phenomenon largely of the wheat districts. In the rice districts, the BKD did *not* show strength among the middle peasantry in 1974, despite the general increase in its strength in the predominantly rice-growing eastern districts. In the wheat districts, in contrast, the middle peasant areas were virtually BKD territory, with all other parties and independents except the Congress showing negative correlations in areas of middle peasant concentration. Only the Congress was in a position to compete with the BKD for support in such areas, but none of its correlations with the middle peasant categories were at significance levels of 05 or better. Finally, the strong positive correlation between the BKD vote and the smallest landholdings in the rice districts suggests that the previous support of the SSP in smallholder areas in Oudh and the Lower Doab was successfully transferred to the BKD in this election....

THE MIDDLE PEASANTRY AND THE TRANSFORMATION OF THE PARTY SYSTEM

The foregoing survey of the electoral history of UP in relation to rural social structure and regional imbalances suggests two broad conclusions in relation to the middle peasant sectors. One is that the small and middle peasantry, who control the bulk of the land in the countryside, have played a critical role in the transformation of the party system. The available evidence suggests that the discontent of the middle peasantry developed in the 1950s and intensified in the 1960s. That discontent arose out of frustration both with government policies on prices and procurement and with the fact that control over agricultural patronage in the districts was maintained by Congress supporters among the local landed elites, who naturally favoured themselves and their closest allies in distributing inputs and credit. During the 1950s and 1960s, the middle peasantry lacked a political spokesman with whom they could identify and whom they could trust to promote their interests. Consequently, their discontent was diffused among independent candidates. When Charan Singh broke from the Congress in 1967 and later formed the BKD, that discontent was gathered up and consolidated. It provided the principal base for BKD support in both the 1969 and 1974 elections and for the Janata party in 1977.

The second broad conclusion is that the discontent of the middle peasantry had a strong regional basis in the agriculturally more modernized western wheat-growing districts. Although it was demonstrated above that the BKD-SSP alliance in 1974 and the Janata coalition overcame the regional division between the western and eastern districts, the support bases of the BKD/BLD in 1974 and of the Janata in 1977 appeared to be different. BKD/BLD and Janata did not seem to be so firmly based on the middle peasantry in the rice-growing eastern districts. The BKD/BLD did succeed in capturing some support in 1974 in areas of concentration of marginal landholders, who are far more important numerically in the eastern districts than in the western districts, but Janata did not retain this support in 1977. There remained, therefore, a continuing underlying regional difference in the political geography, as in the agricultural economy, of UP between the more prosperous, more market-dependent, more technologically oriented western wheat- and sugarcane-growing districts and the less prosperous, less market-dependent, less technologically oriented eastern districts, where rainfed paddy grown on smallholdings is the principal crop.

CONCLUSION

Hobsbawm has argued that 'democratic electoral politics do not work for peasants as a class', who 'tend to be election fodder, except when they demand or inhibit certain specialized political measures'. These statements have a bold ring to them, but they are actually vague since Hobsbawm never makes clear his definition of the peasantry or what their class interests are. Linz, in contrast, after surveying patterns of voting behaviour in the rural areas of several European countries, concludes that European peasants in democratic countries were able to 'articulate and defend their divergent interests' through the party system and that, although 'democratic politics did not always serve rural interests', they 'gave the rural population a voice without forcing it to revolution or sullen apathy, as in most of the world'. The evidence from the history of democratic electoral politics in UP supports Linz's point of view. In this Indian state the system has worked for the peasantry in ways that go beyond blocking or achieving specific 'political measures'. While the system has provided little more than specific ameliorative measures for the rural poor, it has provided an effective vehicle for the articulation of both the interests and the discontent of what P.C. Joshi calls the 'intermediate classes' of former big tenants and medium landlords, who in UP are the 5- to 30-acre cultivators.

The post-Independence political and economic system of UP functioned for its first two decades under something of a contradiction. The Zamindari Abolition Act was designed to establish a social and economic order based on peasant proprietorship, but it did not dispossess the former *zamindars* and *talukdars*. Moreover, many of the predominant leaders of the Congress in UP came not from peasant classes, but from professional classes, who accepted the Nehru ideology of planned, rapid, large-scale industrialization, with agriculture taking second place. Most also paid lip-service to the goal of establishing a system of cooperative farms in India, though it is difficult to believe that any but a few socialist diehards took this idea seriously. At any rate, the history of electoral politics in UP has been very largely influenced by this dual contradiction between the interests of the peasant proprietors and the interests of the former landlords on the one hand, and between the values associated with a political economy based on small-scale owner-cultivation and the values associated with rapid industrialization on the other. It is this dual contradiction which offers the most satisfactory explanation for the discontent of the peasantry in the 1950s and 1960s and its articulation ultimately through the BKD. The contradictions manifested themselves in political recruitment, in land reform, in economic development policies, and in the party system.

With regard to political recruitment, it is known that in the first three legislatures, MLAs whose fathers were former big and middle *zamindars* or peasant cultivators comprised a majority of the legislators in the UP legislative assemblies from 1952 to 1962. Many of those legislators whose fathers were cultivators did not themselves continue to practise agriculture, but in fact derived their main source of income from non-agricultural occupations, particularly the professions. Only 24 per cent of MLAs from 1952 to 1962 actually derived their principal income from cultivation.[5]

The available data on the social composition of legislators in the 1967 assembly do not differentiate MLAs with agricultural backgrounds. It is known that only 40 per cent of the Congress members and 54 per cent of the Jan Sangh members gave their occupation as agriculture.... On the whole, therefore, the available evidence indicates that the peasantry have been underrepresented in relation especially to former landlords, big farmers, and professional persons. It was also mentioned above that the middle agricultural castes have been relatively less well represented than persons from elite caste backgrounds. Nevertheless, it is also clear that a considerable proportion of the legislators in UP have come from peasant backgrounds. Moreover, the peasantry in UP have had an effective and articulate spokesman in Charan Singh, who himself belonged to the category of a legislator whose occupation at the time of his entry into politics was the law, but who came from a peasant background. In terms of political leadership and party cadres, therefore, one source of peasant discontent in the 1950s and 1960s may well have been the underrepresentation of peasants in politics, but it cannot be argued that the UP peasantry lacked class representation in the political system.

A second manifestation of both the dual contradiction and the influence of the peasantry in UP was the character of land reforms. The abolition of *zamindari*, the imposition of land ceilings, and the consolidation of landholdings all benefited principally the middle and large peasant proprietors. Proposals to introduce joint farming in UP, as elsewhere in India, were blocked. Land reform in UP clearly did not eliminate the political and economic influence of the former *zamindars*. Moreover, land ceilings in the state were placed at a level which permitted the biggest farmers to mechanize their operations. While in some respects, therefore, the interests of the bigger peasants and the capitalist farmers have converged, the evidence from the correlations suggested a divergence in their political identifications, with the biggest farmers identifying with the Congress and the middle and large peasantry identifying with independents, the Jan Sangh, and the BKD.

Third, although economic development policies oriented towards large-scale industrialization and mechanized agriculture, to be financed by extraction of resources from the peasantry, were put forward in UP as elsewhere in India, they have been effectively blocked in UP. Large-scale industrial development has been very limited in UP since independence, the state government has been unable to tax the peasantry, and economic policies have increasingly been oriented toward providing agricultural inputs to the peasantry. The 'green revolution' has been spreading during the past decade in this state, particularly in the wheat-producing regions. By all accounts, the big farmers have had greater access to and have benefited most from the new inputs associated with the 'green revolution'. Consequently, although the interests of the 5-to 30-acre peasants again converged with those of the big farmers on economic development policies favouring agriculture, they diverged on the question of differential access to the new inputs and on differential ability to make use of them. The BKD, in its opposition to large-scale mechanized farming and its explicit support for an agricultural policy favouring the middle cultivating owners, appealed specifically and with considerable success to the class interest of the self-sufficient and the better-off peasantry.

Finally, the contradictions also found expression in the electoral system in UP. The evidence from the correlation analysis suggests that from 1957 onward the middle peasantry withdrew their support from the ruling Congress. Although the discontent of the peasantry was for a decade partly fragmented, finding expression largely through voting for independent candidates, it was more clearly channelled into support for the Jan Sangh in Oudh and ultimately was expressed in the striking success of the BKD in 1969 and in 1974. Moreover, the electoral support of the peasantry for the BKD brought the party and its leader, Charan Singh, to power. Although no government lasted for long during the turbulent period of coalition politics between 1967 and 1974, Charan Singh and his party were a leading force in the party system throughout this period. During this period, the state government passed a few acts and amendments to existing legislation to assist the peasantry, such as an amendment to the Zamindari Abolition Act that extended the right of transfer of their lands by *sirdars* to enable them to obtain bank loans for agricultural development and an amendment to the Land Revenue Act to provide cultivators with certified records of their land holdings. An amendment to the Land Ceilings Act also was passed, permitting the distribution of surplus land on a permanent basis to eligible persons, rather than only to cooperative farming societies, as originally specified in the legislation. Parties of the left also took up the cause of the poor peasantry by securing exemption from the land revenue for cultivators holding less than 6.25 acres of land. While numerous taxation measures were passed during these years, none increased the taxes or rents of the peasantry and no moves were made to reduce land ceilings. The full impact of the rise to power of the non-Congress parties cannot be seen through legislation, however, for many important decisions that affect agriculturists are taken at the local level in the cooperative credit societies and in the government agencies distributing agricultural inputs. In this respect, it is probable that the non-Congress parties wasted no time in shifting the distribution of resources and benefits to their supporters from the intermediate peasant classes.

The support of the middle peasantry also comprised a central component of the Janata victory in the 1977 state assembly elections, which brought the non-Congress groups to power again after their displacement by the Congress in the period between 1974 and the end of the Emergency in 1977. The second period of non-Congress rule in UP saw an even more vigorous attempt to promote peasant interests and agricultural development. Government policies were oriented virtually exclusively toward rural development, including agriculture, irrigation, rural small-scale cottage industries, construction of link roads, regulation of markets to prevent exploitation of the peasants by middlemen, flood protection schemes, and the like. Most important from the point of view of the peasantry was the UP Government's determination to insure a good return to the cultivators for sugar cane, the leading cash crop of the state. When production was high, the state government compelled the factories to continue crushing until all the cultivators had disposed of their cane. The state government went so far as to add its own subsidy to the cane price on top of the support prices awarded by the central government.[6]

Far from having been only 'election fodder', therefore, the middle and upper peasantry in UP have played a critical role in the electoral system, have found effective spokesmen for their class interests, and have had their class interests protected. At the same time, the relatively weak representation of the middle peasantry in the Congress of Mrs. Gandhi, the break-up of the Janata coalition, and the return of Mrs. Gandhi to power at the central government in 1980 represent serious potential threats to peasant interests. The danger to the middle peasantry lies in the possibility that Mrs. Gandhi and the Congress will move resolutely to resolve the dual contradiction between agrarian social structure and economic development strategy at their expense, by reverting to policies of rapid large-scale industrialization combined with measures to keep the poor content, such as rural works programmes, cheap food, and tolerable wages for the industrial workforce. More drastic measures of agrarian reorganization such as land redistribution or the encouragement of large-scale joint or commercial farming are also possible, if less likely in the short term. Since many of these policies would involve diversion of resources from the rural to the urban sector, lower prices for farm products, and increased hostility between the middle peasantry on the one hand, and the rural poor and the biggest commercial farmers operating through bogus cooperative farms on the other hand, such policies would, without doubt, also be accompanied by widespread violence and the end of the parliamentary system in India. It is more likely, therefore, that Mrs. Gandhi's Congress will strive to divide the middle peasantry by co-opting particular leaders, appealing to specific middle caste groups, and adopting economic policies that will ensure that the middle peasantry have access to inputs at reasonable cost and can sell their products at good prices. The adoption of such an accommodative policy toward the peasantry also would be more consistent with the maintenance of a competitive political regime.

NOTES AND REFERENCES

1. Uttar Pradesh Zamindari Abolition and Reform Act, 1950, cited in Singh and Mishra (1964), 68.
2. For a concise summary of the Zamindari Abolition Act, see Thorner, Daniel, *The Agrarian Prospect in India*, 2nd ed. Columbia, Missouri, South Asia Books, 1976, 22-7; for a more detailed analysis, Johnson, Michael H., 'The Relation between Land Settlement and Party Politics in Uttar Pradesh, India, 1950-69: with Special Reference to the Formation of the Bharatiya Kranti Dal', unpublished Ph.D. Dissertation, University of Sussex, ch. 3.
3. Brass, Paul R., *Factional Politics in an Indian State: The Congress Party in Uttar Pradesh*, Berkeley: University of California Press, 1965 describes these measures and the political conflict surrounding the land tax issue in its early phase.
4. For an analysis of the 'green revolution' technology and its political consequences, see Frankel, Francine P., *India's Green Revolution:*

Economic gains and Political Costs, Princeton: Princeton University Press, 1971, ch. 3.

5. The data in the previous paragraph are from Meyer, Ralph C., 'The Political Elite in an Underdeveloped Society: The Case of Uttar Pradesh, India', unpublished Ph D dissertation, University of Pennsylvania, 1969, 91 and 156-60.

6. Interview in Lucknow, 25 July, 1979.

FURTHER READINGS

Rao M.S.A., and Frankel Francine, (eds.) *Dominance and State Power in Modern India*, Oxford University Press, Delhi, 1990.

An excellent collection of studies of the relation between caste and class in specific regions. The individual studies try to follow the sociological trajectories of regions historically, and do not start abruptly from the institution of democracy in 1947. Precisely because it is impossible to make generalizations across the whole of India, regional studies are the most insightful.

Brass Paul, and Franda Marcus, (eds.) *Radical Politics in South Asia*, MIT Press, Cambridge, Mass, 1976.

Collection of sociologically informed analyses of radical politics in South Asian societies. Although the structure and electoral fortunes of radical parties have changed fundamentally since the seventies, the analyses are perceptive and useful for understanding the sociological bases of radical aspirations.

Kohli, Atul, *State and Poverty in India*, Cambridge University Press, Cambridge, 1985.

Combines a theoretical analysis of the nature of state power in India with intensive discussion of Left party governments in power.

Omvedt Gail, (ed.), *Land, Caste and Politics in Indian States*, University of Delhi, Delhi, 1982.

A collection of essays pursuing the historical connection between caste and class in various regions of India.

Bardhan, Pranab, *Political Economy of Development in India*, Clarendon Press, Oxford, 1986.

A excellent concise argument about the nature of the ruling coalition of classes which dominate Indian politics, and a sophisticated class analysis of the making of development policy.

Frankel, Francine, *India's Political Economy*, Princeton University Press, Princeton, 1978.

A detailed historical account of the making of economic policy by the central government, and the play of political pressures on parties and bureaucracy. Although this is not written in the formal style of political sociology, it provides excellent detailed analyses of social pressures on policy-making.

Rudolph I. Lloyd, and Rudolph, Suzanne H., *in Pursuit of Lakshmi*, Chicago University Press, Chicago, 1985.

A detailed exposition of the process of formation of classes and their operation in the political field. It investigates some important general questions of political theory about the impact of democratic government on rates of economic growth by analysing the political sociology of the Indian state.

Vanaik, Achin, *The Painful Transition: Bourgeois Democracy in India*, Verso, London, 1991.

A detailed Marxist account of the politics of India after independence, using a complex understanding of the processes of class formation and state power, and informed by recent Marxist theory about the state.

IV

Sociology of Identities

The modern state emerged in Western Europe and the colonies in fundamentally different ways. The processes which led to its growth in the modern West were endogenous, and happened over a long period. Political changes from the period of the Renaissance first produced modern territorial states with highly effective absolutist regimes. Gradually, these states devised patterns of modern bureaucratic control over the human, economic and other resources of the territory which fell under their stable control. The emergence of modern nationalism, centred on the coincidence of the boundaries of political administration and culture, finally provided these territorial states with their typical modern form. Historical research has recently shown how much this development of a single national culture was based on drives towards cultural homogenization, internal coercion, and the perpetual threats of the constant wars of the eighteenth and nineteenth centuries, which forced their populations to associate themselves to their countries with a new and more intense and obligatory form of attachment. None of these circumstances existed in precolonial India, at least in a straightforward form.

In precolonial India, although state forms like kingdoms and occasional large empires existed, sometimes for appreciably long periods, these structures never established anything like the deep and detailed control modern states routinely exercise over territories under their control. The colonial state, in the late nineteenth century began to introduce some of the major instruments of control over populations and resources tried out in Europe, with suitable modifications for colonial adaptation. The colonial administration simultaneously inducted cognitive and statistical projects of modern rule, like census and cartography. Yet the colonial state could not enjoy the kind of cultural legitimacy that modern nation-states acquired in the West. It was the emerging political imagination of mature nationalism which invested this state with an idea of nationalist legitimacy.

As British rule expanded from its original coastal bases, the colonial administration adopted territorial divisions to carry out the task of ruling this vast empire with some efficiency. But these territorial units were not constructed on the basis of any obvious principle, except administrative convenience, and the quite accidental timing of conquests. When political influence of the Congress grew across the whole of British India, it slowly articulated an alternative principle for organizing political space. The internal organization of the Congress implicitly recognized a 'democratic' principle in the proper territorial organization of the state on the basis of linguistic regions. There could be a theoretical argument to reinforce this arrangement. Linguistic regions would, it could be argued, make it possible to use the vernacular as the effective language of political transactions, and therefore bring the administration closer to ordinary people by making affairs of the state transparent to them. Also implicit in this practice was an idea that the great diversity of India precluded the realization of any homogeneous cultural nationalism on the lines of European nation-states, and a recognition of the legitimacy of regional cultures based primarily, but not exclusively, on languages.

It was natural that after independence demands would come from linguistic regions for a greater recognition of their identity. Colonial administrative practices had entrenched solid sub-colonial advantages for some linguistic groups, simply because those were the first to receive colonial education and formed the natural reservoir for personnel for colonial administrative expansion. The Bengali middle class, for instance, exceeded the demands of the Bengal provincial economy, since it provided professionals for the whole of northern and eastern India. Resentment against this kind of sub-colonial dominance was bound to find expression after independence. Not surprisingly, movements for regional autonomy began soon after independence with the demand for the recognition of an Andhra state. The response of the Nehru government was, at first sight, incomprehensibly unsympathetic. But Nehru's hesitation was due to understandable anxiety that more homogeneous regional units might lead to a weakening of the political imagination of the Indian nation. Linguistic states were granted by the States Reorganization Commission of 1956; but two types of anomalies remained. Some were simpler cases, like the Bombay state which was divided into two linguistic units of Gujarat and Maharashtra after a time. But there were other areas, like the Northeast and the former state of Punjab, which were in principle more difficult to settle on linguistic lines. Consequently, the Indian state has faced repeated trouble in arranging an acceptable territorial reorganization of these areas.

Historically, there were three waves of regionalist movements. The first was the demand for linguistic states in the mid-fifties; the second was a wave of 'sons of the soil' movements in the sixties and seventies; and finally, there was a third wave of much harder problems with regionalist agitations in areas like Punjab, Assam and Kashmir which swung, at times, towards secessionism. Although, generally, these were all regionalist movements, in the sense that they pressed the demands of particular regions against the central government, their character and their significance for Indian politics and the fate of the nation-state were often dramatically different. The Central government found the first wave relatively easy to deal with, partly because they grew out of a principle that the Congress movement itself acknowledged, and partly because these demands could be settled by a rearrangement of constitutional forms. But, as Gupta's paper in this section points out, despite their conflict with the Centre, these movements presupposed the existence of a central national authority against which such demands could be made, and which alone could fulfil them in actual terms. Granting their demands did not involve taking either assets or prestige away from some others. 'Nativist' mobilizations of the next two decades were similar to the earlier ones in that in most cases these had strong popular support. But these led to more intractable conflict as they pressed actively for discrimination against other citizens who, in principle, should have enjoyed equal rights in matters of state employment. Still, these were also demands made to a Central government which was thus seen as a part of the essential scheme of political things. Regional dissent in the eighties proved more long-drawn, intractable and occasionally displayed irreconcilable hostility towards the basic assumptions of the Indian state. The states of the Indian federation have now existed in a reasonably stable constitutional framework for about five decades, and used a common set of constitutional democratic rules. Theoretically, these trends would have been assisted by the significant growth of the capitalist economy and the national labour market. The explanatory question is, why has regionalist dissent become more intractable?

Among various contending explanations two are particularly notable. The first uses a distinction between two types of goods for which political agitations are launched. The first type of goods are like constitutional recognition and rights which do not necessarily produce conflict between different claimants. In fact, the success of one might give to others an advantage they did not work for. Recognition of the right of all linguistic groups to states of their own might have been conceded due to pressure from one particular region. But once it is acknowledged, it benefits other regions as well, irrespective of whether they have agitated for it or not. Thus recognition of one group enhances the claims of others similarly placed, instead of standing in their way. Demand for enhanced economic resources, by contrast, divide claimants, because what is given to one is taken from a common pool which could go to others. On this view, the first wave of regionalism centred on the first type of demand, which could be met relatively easily. Subsequently, the demands made against the Centre were primarily about redistribution of economic resources which exacerbated conflict both between the Centre and the individual states, and indirectly, between the states themselves.

A second strand of explanation would look in the direction of the specific nature of capitalist development in India to account for regionalist politics as expressions of uneven development. Colonial industrialization and its spread social effects were concentrated in certain coastal centres. Although early plans of state-led industrialization after independence sought to locate industries deliberately in backward areas, these did not always create new nodal points of industrial growth. Market-led capitalist development through the private sector, in any case, accentuated the earlier regional inequalities and created new ones on top of the old. But the existence of a democratic constitution and the implicit concession to regional equality through federalism has encouraged political expression of resentment against these trends. It is interesting to note that, in purely economic terms, industrialized regions have not always done better. Agriculturally successful regions, in some cases, like Punjab, have higher levels of income than more industrialized states. It is also important to note that two types of regional demands have been persistently advanced against the central government. Some are for greater rewards for relatively faster growth, which, if conceded, would intensify and aggravate regional imbalances still further. Others are more conventional redistributive demands advanced by backward regions. Both these grievances lead to political agitations that are seen as regionalist, and they might indeed make common cause against a Centre which they view as their common enemy. But it is difficult for any regime of economic administration to satisfy both types of demands within one internally consistent policy. These two types of explanation are clearly not mutually exclusive. The second type of analysis can easily subsume the first. Additionally, some observers of Indian politics have argued that purely contingent political trends, like spells of frenetic centralization under Indira Gandhi, went against the underlying framework of political relations between the traditionally-recognized regions and a historically modern central authority, and brought forth intense reactions.

The readings in this section are dissimilar, though their concerns partly overlap. Dipankar Gupta's essay provides a historical analysis of the three waves of regional assertion in Indian politics, and attempts to build a theoretical argument to account for their distinctions. Weiner is more concerned with the fundamental processes by which groups come to see themselves as majorities and minorities, which then determine the nature of their political initiatives.

Ethnicity and Politics

DIPANKAR GUPTA

Even though four decades have passed since India became independent, this has not yet stilled the doubts in the minds of many regarding her future as a viable nation-state. Every now and again commentaries on the Indian political situation are awash with speculations as to how long Indian unity will hold.... These speculations are inspired by Western notions of the nation-state where, ideally, language, religion and political sovereignty have coterminous boundaries. Notwithstanding the fact that such notions disregard the historical processes by which some nationalities were subsumed by more powerful nationalities in the making of modern Western nation states, the belief that language and religion, in their pristine form, are the twin ballasts of nation-states is almost universal.

India, very self-consciously, rejected this understanding of the nation-state. From the early decades of this century when a cogent national independence movement began to take shape in the subcontinent, it was clear to the Indian nationalists that liberation from colonial domination must necessarily be all Indian in character. There were certain contrary tendencies in the political condition of India in those times, many of which were assiduously encouraged by the British rulers. One such tendency was in the

Excerpted from Dipankar Gupta, 'The Indispensable Centre: Ethnicity and Politics in the Indian Nation-State', *Journal of Contemporary Asia*, vol. 20, no. 4, 1990, 521-39.

shape of the Muslim League which argued that only religion could be the basis of an enduring nation-state. Hindu nationalist organizations which believed in an identical formulation indirectly helped the British to rationalize their administrative decision to undermine secular nationalist parties, such as the Indian National Congress, which had from 1920 onwards been the most dominant representative of the nationalist urge in the subcontinent....

In this paper we shall argue that the acceptance of cultural and linguistic differences is no superficial acquiescence but is the enduring basis on which Indian politics is played out. In the following pages we hope to test this proposition against empirical instances where cultural chauvinism (or should one say, passions?) of one form or another have loomed large on the political space of India since independence....

NATION-STATES AS ORIGINAL COMBINATIONS

But before we begin on this exercise we believe it will be useful to quickly recall some of the peculiarities that characterize India which, we are convinced, make the Indian experience as a modern nation-state not only different from the Western model, but also different from the experiences of other newly liberated nation states all over the world.

It is not as if the Indian subcontinent was unified for the first time under British Imperial rule. The boundaries of the Mauryan Empire which flourished from the fifth century BC to first century BC were also confined largely to the limits of the subcontinent. This was true of the Gupta empire which came five centuries later, and of the more recent medieval Mughal Empire, especially during the sixteenth and seventeenth centuries.... Are the high mountains in the north and the great waters in the south responsible for India's uniqueness? Or should the responsibility be placed at the door of the caste system whose peculiarity characterizes Indian society and culture? Does one also have to factor in the fact that places of education and religious centres all over the subcontinent were esteemed and revered by different regional and linguistic groups over the length and breadth of India? What will however be difficult to controvert is that India existed as a cultural and social entity, in spite of all its internal variations, even before it became a modern political entity.[1]

Apropos of the above we should also like to distance ourselves from the issue which Benedict Anderson raises in his impressive work entitled *Imagined Communities*. According to Anderson colonial administrative boundaries with localized centres of higher learning provided a kind of ready-made map for the newly emerging nation states[2]. The division of India between British India and the Princely states did not however hold back in any appreciable manner the unified formation of the Indian nation-state .... If nation-states are imagined communities then the only way to do justice to this conceptualization is if one were not to impose formats along which such imaginings must necessarily take place. Nor should one be tempted to consider the historical depth of post-colonial countries as one limited to the colonial experience alone. The Indian case should at least make this much clear....

THE TEST CASES: LINGUISTIC, NATIVIST AND REGIONAL POLITICS

There have been three great occasions in India's short history after independence which have darkened the optimists' sunny projections. The first erupted soon after independence when the demand for unilingual states (or provinces) engulfed large areas of the subcontinent. The second followed soon after when the 'natives' of these unilingual states demanded that economic opportunities in their states be reserved preponderantly for them. The third great occasion is a contemporary one. It demands greater regional autonomy for the states in economic matters. Superficially viewed these three instances can be seen as manifestations of an original, and unquenchable, primordial sentiment which the structure of the Indian nation-state cannot contain. The political centre is viewed as coercive for it forcibly endorses centripetal pressures to draw in culturally separate and obdurate masses in various stages of recalcitrance. According to this line of reasoning, the linguistic, the nativistic and the more contemporary regional movements, are all expressions of an original and restless cultural disaffection in the breast of different 'nationalities' forced to cohabit in the Indian nation-state.

It would be more revealing, however, if one were to separate these three kinds of movements on the basis of their central demands, their constraints and the nexuses they activate. Such an exercise is rarely, if ever, undertaken. This would eliminate the instinctive appeal of the superficial similarities between the three kinds of political mobilizations. These ostensible similarities persuasively argue for the merger of the three different mobilizations into one such that the last is visualized as a fuller efflorescence of the first.[3] In our opinion this does an injustice to the realities of the situation....

In the case of linguistic movements, i.e., those movements demanding a unilingual state, it was the reiteration of primordial identity on the basis of language that bound the partisans into a coherent political group and signified them as 'natives'.... But soon after the major demands for linguistic states had been met on a national scale. India witnessed the emergence of 'nativistic' movements. The protagonists of these agitations claimed that the gift of the tongue was not enough, it had to be supplemented by tangible economic opportunities....

In the case of regional movements, the third case, language and nativism *per se* were not the crucial condensing factors. The demands were now primarily economic and were specific to the region, and the fact that the region also happened to be preponderantly populated by members of one linguistic group did not vitally alter the secular character of their charter. It is in this sense that regional mobilization and parties moved beyond language and nativism — from the tower of Babel finally to the truct farm of Mammon....

OBJECTIVES

It is important to establish the separate identities of nativist, linguistic and regional mobilizations because the respective careers of the three markedly differ from one another.[4] This difference is also accentuated to a significant extent by the way in which the Centre and other national parties interact with them. It is only by concentrating on this web of interaction, even if it is to amass aggregative generalities, that the distinctions between the three kinds of mobilization and organizations can be validated. Moreover, if our earlier contention that such political occurrences are not inimical to the political unity of India (nor to the notion of a political Centre) is to hold, then it is just these types of objective factors that need to be focused on as they not only reflect the constraints of subnational movements and their respective organizations, but also reflect the conditions of their origin.

Finally, this paper has been prompted by a somewhat paradoxical observation. It appears that as these movements progress from primordial to secular economic demands, the Centre seems to progressively become more and more maladroit. In other words, it would seem that the Centre and the Indian Union seem more at home and comfortable with ethnic based movements than with those generated by secular economic demands. The pages that follow will try to substantiate this formulation.

INDEPENDENCE AND THE HINDU-MUSLIM DIVIDE

Independent India inherited a great many things from its colonial past. Among them was the fear, a persistent undertow, that the cultural diversity of the subcontinent would soon see to the fragmentation of the Indian State. Immediately a grand fact, viz., the partition of the subcontinent into India and Pakistan, took place as if to concretize these apprehensions. A moment's reflection will, however, tell us that the partition was not a necessary (or logical) outcome of the Indian national movement.

The stated objective of the participants in the national movement, including the communists, was not the division of India between Hindus and Muslims, but political independence from the British in the subcontinent. As a matter of fact every time the Hindu-Muslim divide surfaced politically it constituted a setback for the national movement and weakened its viable bargaining power. The demand for division on pure religious grounds was not the logical culmination of the national movement, but grew on its fringes, preying on inconsistencies in the 'eventist' articulation of the nationalist ideology and on the situationalist contretemps in which the national parties and their leaders were often placed[5]....

Partition could have been an ideal setting for all these Hindu nationalists to make India a Hindu state[6]. The point is that this did not happen for which reason the Nehru-Gandhi secular vision of India won the day[7]. This however, would not have been possible unless centrifugal forces detrimental to the unity of India as a political unit had not been politically overwhelmed during the years of the nationalist movement. This too is an aspect of India's

'original' combination. Hence the first instance of political separation was not an outcome of the given diversity of Indian society,
but grew predaciously at the margin of the nationalist movement
on leavings thoughtfully thrown its way by deliberate administrative decisions.

There is however no denying the fact that the nationalist movement under the Congress was unable to handle this extraneous
intervention adroitly enough. When it did not in its eventist postures aid the cause of the separatists, it made concessions to it
for short term gains believing, perhaps incorrectly, that the long
term was forever perjured by the graffiti — green and saffron —
that were appearing on the interstitial walls. In other words, there
were two movements. One brought about the partition of India
and the other political independence from the British. The former
never participated in the mass upheavals of the latter; content
instead to remain angularly positioned, elbowing and tugging at
the seams of the latter, willing it to fall apart. The Muslim League
did not demand a Pakistan for the Muslims free from British
domination, but from what it saw as Hindu domination. It was
because India got independence that the Muslim League got its
Pakistan.

But after independence, and after the partition, the Centre and
its 'men of straw' did not come crashing down, like a pack of
cards. Slowly, almost unbelievably, the Centre consolidated itself.
Cultural diversities remained, regional inequalities continued and
sometimes got heightened, and yet a separatist phenomenon could
not work itself to the fore. Cultural disparities and regional inequalities continued to spur dissatisfaction as they had in British
India, but now the mobilizations on their behalf were better organized. But at all these flash points the existence of the Centre
was never seriously threatened....

LINGUISTIC MOVEMENTS

In the mid fifties the demand for unilingual states enveloped the
whole country, necessitating the formation of the States Reorganization Commission. All national parties including local
branches of the Congress, participated in these movements, sometimes contrary to the stated positions of the Congress at the Centre.
While it is true that the majority of participants were explicitly

parochial and even primordial in their outlook, the leaders of
the movements were not portrayed simply as regional heroes,
but as nationalists who had the interests of the nation uppermost.
They were thorough patriots and it was their patriotic duty
towards India to demand unilingual states.

The demand for unilingual states was not seen either by its
partisans or by the Congress at the Centre as anti-India or anti-
national. This is because the Congress in the twenties had explicitly
proclaimed, as part of its charter, that once independence was
won India would be administratively demarcated on linguistic
lines. It was felt that provincial boundaries thus delineated would
enhance greater participation at the lower levels and help in root-
ing democracy deep in Indian soil. This is why national parties
had little ideological reluctance to enter the agitation for linguistic
states.

The other reason why national parties could participate wholly
in these linguistic movements was because the demand that each
state should be linguistically demarcated could be carried out
without damaging the linguistic rights of any other major linguistic
community in the country....

Since the demand for a unilingual system was activized under
the aegis of the national parties, the various linguistic movements
were complementary to each other and thus bonded to the grid
of national politics. The entire polity through its segments was
activated on a single demand which in principle did not do injustice to the other constituent segments. From a single universal
principle, several particularistic, even primordial, demands were
satisfied. The Centre did not in principle, or in practice, oppose
the formation of linguistic states as such a policy had been formulated by the Congress much before independence came to
India. The problem the Centre faced was not the principle behind
the demands, but how to best realize it without sacrificing its
existing political bases, or potential ones, in different geographical
areas and among different linguistic communities....

The linguistic movements also demonstrate that they were not
antagonistic to the Centre, and were if anything, hostile to the
neighbouring states, not because of their opposition to the formation of linguistic states elsewhere, but because of rival territorial
claims.... But at no stage was the political unity of India even
questioned, nor as we have tried to demonstrate, were the or-

ganizations that were set in motion by linguistic movements, and propagated their cause, even remotely separatist or anti-federal in character.

NATIVIST MOVEMENTS

But before the sixties were over, and well after linguistic divisions had been accepted as basis for the formation of states in the Indian Union, another movement began. The 'sons of the soil' began to demand that they be given the major, if not the sole, right to work on the soil of their linguistic states and reap the economic benefits therein without interference from people belonging to other linguistic communities. The demand was economic but was mediated through specific linguistic identities. The national parties could not lumber up to take advantage of this groundswell, and organizations explicitly local and nativistic in their nomenclature and orientation emerged. They began haltingly and unambitiously, but before many could look back to redefine their positions they were swept to the top on a staggering wave of popular sympathy.

The Shiv Sena of the sixties and seventies and the Assam movement, which culminated in 1985, may be considered to belong to this genre. In both cases the enemy is within, the 'aliens', who by careful manipulation deny the native sons of the soil the benefits of economic advancement that their native state offers. These movements thus carry with their economic demands a vital linguistic element, and it is on the basis of discrimination on linguistic grounds that the economic demands are sought to be worked out.... The major enemies of such movements are not other states so much as the linguistic groups from these other states who are seen as threats by the natives.... Only some states are singled out as particularly offensive and never is the whole country held responsible. In fact, nativist movements acknowledge that it is only through the machinery at the Centre that their grievances can be redressed.... In other words, if the Centre at all becomes the enemy it is not a generic one, and the hostility shown towards it occurs on the rebound.

Neither were the Congress and the other national parties, with the exception of the communists, averse to arriving at agreements with these nativist forces. This was of course difficult in the first flush of these movements because the nativist forces chose other linguistic groups in the country as their targets. Thus, no national party could align with them without risking its political bases elsewhere in the country. Gradually the Shiv Sena in Bombay shifted its attention away from the South Indians and concentrated instead on the Communists.... The Assam movement too moved away by 1980 from being anti-Bengali to becoming hostile to the Muslim migrants from Bangladesh....

National parties and national politics surely had a role to play in altering the principal focus of these nativist movements. However, the major beneficiaries were the nativist forces who won a measure of national legitimacy which was essential for their continued survival. This also sheltered them from a full scale attack by the Government's coercive apparatuses, a fate reserved .for all oppositionist elements who can be successfully portrayed as anti-national by the ruling party. Additionally, it was now legitimate for national parties including the Congress to openly negotiate with the Shiv Sena or with the All Assam Students' Union (AASU). The right wing Bharatiya Janata Party supported the major demands of the AASU and all non-communist parties nationwide, including the Congress, have from time to time come to adjustments with the Shiv Sena in Bombay....

REGIONAL MOVEMENTS

Unlike nativist movements and their somewhat shaky transformation into political parties, regional movements give rise to stable party formations. The Akali Dal, the DMK and the Telegu Desam are convincing examples of this.

Over time the Centre learns to treat them as it would to any opposition group, but in the initial stage it views the emergence of regional parties with great alarm as they are not only stable political contenders, but also because the growth of such parties, and their subsequent viability, are consequent upon their being single-mindedly nurtured on hostility towards the Congress at the Centre. So unlike the other two movements, viz., the linguistic movement and the nativist movement, the regional movement is manifestly against the government at the Centre first and foremost. Consequently the development of regional party formations indicates the attenuation of·political support for the party in power at the Centre. The Centre's response to such regional parties is not equivocal as it sees such parties as clear political rivals.

The opposition parties which are national in character may react to the emergence of regional parties variously. Usually, however, they seek some kind of political understanding with the regional organizations hoping thereby to share their mass support and weaken the party in power at the Centre which, in the long run, they believe, is the main obstacle to their coming to power at the national level. This also aids the regional party for it enhances its degree of credibility which is very crucial in its fledging years.

Unlike the case with nativist parties, when the opposition parties support such regional organizations they do not necessarily endanger their bases in other states. An important feature of regional parties is that they have no essential quarrel with other states, they have a bone to pick only with the Centre. If they do attack any one state in particular, it is usually a peripheral issue, and then too the Centre is seen as the provocateur egging that province on into taking a hostile stand.

The appeal of these regional movements is limited to the boundaries of particular states (or provinces). The Akali Dal, the Telegu Desam, the Dravida Munnetra Kazhagam, as their very nomenclatures suggest are limited to Punjab, Andhra Pradesh and Tamil Nadu respectively. By virtue of circumscribing their areas of influence in this fashion these parties can never hope to capture power at the Centre on their own. This however does not deter them from playing politics at the national level by aligning with other regional and national parties. This is true of all the known regional parties in India today.

It needs also to be acknowledged that none of these regional parties have ever publicly or actively disowned a particular section of the population belonging to their state (or province) and classified it as 'alien'....

The point that we are driving towards is that in spite of their ethnic labels and provincial sway, these regional parties have no ethnic enemies. Therefore, their strivings for power must necessarily be weighted towards economic demands such that they specifically address the specific demands of the region. The question that naturally crops up here is the following: given the economic nature of the demands, why is it that it is regional and not national parties who are more successful in mobilizing local sentiment on these demands? Tentatively, we might answer the problem in the following way.

The primary and most important aim of national parties is to win power at the Centre. They thus find it difficult to identify themselves exclusively with the demands of a particular state. As long as the demands from several states overlap or coincide there is no major difficulty. But when people in specific states demand specific considerations from the Centre, the national parties find themselves unable to sponsor such demands. If they did and could, regional politics in the form of regional parties would probably not have become so dominant in the first place....

But does this mean that with the emergence of such regional parties the Centre is likely to collapse? Or, to put it more sharply, will regional movements place the future of India as a political union in serious jeopardy?

In this context one has to pay attention to two further features that characterize the relationship between regional parties and the Centre. Firstly, the one supreme fact that may rob a regional party of its significance as a regional party is the absence of a Centre. Parties are regional when they are opposed to the party in power at the Centre. Moreover, they get additional justification when the Centre, i.e. the party controlling it, is strong and cannot be easily dislodged. If the Centre is itself unstable much of the motivation behind regional parties is lost....

We would like to go further and state that as the structural properties of the Indian union are put under severe tension by economic and secular regional demands, the government at the Centre tries to convert regional and secular issues to ethnic and cultural ones. The Punjab case is a pointer to this.

Nowhere in the much disputed Akali Dal resolution (the so-called Anandpur Sahib Resolution of 1978) did the Akali Dal demand the dissolution of India. More than nine-tenths of the resolution is concerned with secular and economic issues....

The Congress at the Centre however chose not to look at the major demands of the resolution but publicized instead the view that the Anandpur Sahib resolution was secessionist in character. This falsehood was proclaimed by everyone including the late Mrs Indira Gandhi. The mass media were pressed into service for this cause and everyone but the Sikhs were convinced about the secessionist character of the Anandpur Sahib Resolution. The

Centre also played upon spurious versions of the Anandpur Sahib Resolution which did not bear the imprimatur of the Akali Dal leadership. In this manner a secular and regional movement was ethnicized in reverse by the Centre — another version, perhaps, of the empire striking back. The Army operation in the holiest of Sikh shrines, the Golden Temple, in June 1984, and then the senseless assassination of Mrs Indira Gandhi by two Sikhs, con- solidated this process of ethnicization. Rajiv Gandhi used it to great advantage by corralling in an unprecedented number of votes for the Congress on the ground that the country must unitedly oppose Sikh secessionism, and the nation responded overwhelmingly. The success of the Congress left the established opposition parties like the Bharatiya Janata Party (BJP) in shambles. Large numbers of those who had in previous years voted for the BJP or its predecessor, the Jana Sangh, deserted it for Rajiv's Congress for they felt that under Rajiv India would be safe, and India would remain one. This once again demonstrates how regional parties get side-lined if the people perceive the Centre as being threatened.

It should not be forgotten that during this phase of Akali agitation in Punjab the Centre was quite responsive to many of the ethnic aspects of the Akali demands, but never to the secular and economic aspects....

Minoritizing, or ethnicizing, politics is a tool which the Centre is resorting to increasingly. It may be argued that if the government in power paid attention to the specific nature of economic demands coming up from different regions it would disadvantage the class coalition on which it survives. Or one might also add that redress of economic grievances is no easy task at all. Such an effort would never be fully successful and the structural properties of the Indian State (with a Capital 'S') would be tested to exhaustion....

Each nation-state is constructed differently. There are unique and original features that go into the making of the sentiments and structures of nation-states. But as all nation-states are 'constructed' there is a certain self-consciousness that must accompany all imaginings of the nation-state, Indian or Western. This essay has argued, through the three test cases of linguistic, nativist and regional politics, that for any mobilization to function in the political mainstream of India it must deliberately stay in line with this self-conscious sentiment that upholds the sanctity of the Indian nation-state. This argument runs parallel to the empirical and substantive demonstration that cultural differences have never empirically threatened or inauthenticated the viability of the Indian Union.

REFERENCES

1. Nehru, J., *The Discovery of India*, Garden City, New York, 1960, 27-32.
2. Anderson, B., *Imagined Communities: Reflections on the Origin and Spread of Nationalism*, Verso, London, 1983, 54-6, 124-8.
3. Sheth, D.L., 'State, Nations and Ethnicity: Experience of Third World Countries', *Economic and Political Weekly*, vol. 24, 1989, 624-5.
4. Weiner, M., *Sons of the Soil: Migration and Ethnic Conflict in India*, Oxford University Press, Delhi, 1978.
5. Thorner, D., *The Shaping of Modern India*, Allied Publishers, New Delhi, 1980, 85, 188.
6. Kothari, R., 'Nation-building and Political Development', in Dube, S.C. (ed.) *India Since Independence: Social Report on India*, Vikas, Delhi, 1977, 514.
7. Das Gupta, J., *Language Conflict and National Development*, Oxford University Press, Bombay, 1970, 118-19.

Minority Identities

MYRON WEINER

Any attempt to forecast relations between India's minority and majority communities through the year 2000 is bound to be coloured by recent turmoil.... If, as some argue, education is increasing aspirations, economic growth is enlarging economic opportunities, and political democracy is resulting in increased politicization, then one can expect more, not less, competition and conflict among India's many social groups. And, it is further argued, if the competition and conflict continue to result in violence, then the central government is likely to make increasing use of the army, and suspend civil liberties in disturbed areas. Could the fragile Indian democratic political system survive the combined assaults of group violence and state force?

An alternative view is that violence among caste, linguistic, and religious groups is endemic in India's variegated social structure, and that there is no reason to believe that the situation is worse now than in the past or that it is likely to grow significantly worse in the future....

This essay argues still a third perspective: group conflict is indeed endemic in India and there are forces — some new — that seem likely to worsen minority-majority relations, but what seems most likely to intensify ethnic conflict is the deterioration of

Excerpted from Myron Weiner, 'India's Minorities: Who are they? What do they want?', in James Roach (ed.) *India: 2000*, Riverdale Publishers, Maryland, 1985, 99–134.

political institutions. The capacity of institutions to manage conflict in the eighties and nineties is what is at issue. In a period in which majorities are becoming more self-aware, a sense of territorial nationalism is emerging both among majorities and selected minorities, and the international ties of some minorities are growing, political coalitions are in flux, and the problems of conflict management are likely to mount.

WHO ARE INDIA'S MINORITIES?

....Theodore Wright quotes a Hindu writer as saying that 'it is taken for granted that the Hindus are a majority...but to say so is totally wrong. The vast mass of people that are called Hindus are a vast congeries of sub-caste minorities...whereas the Muslims form the actual majority'.[1] These quotes highlight the point that minority and majority status is a matter of self-ascription as well as objective definition. What is a majority from one perspective is a minority from another....

Clearly India contains such a medley of religious, caste, and linguistic groups that the sense of belonging to a minority depends upon where one lives, how much power and status one has, and one's sense of community threat. Many Indians narrowly use the term 'minority' to refer to those who are not Hindu, a conception which implies that somehow the dominant core of Indian identity is Hinduism, the 'mainstream' (to use a favourite Indian word) with which minorities should identify if they want to be regarded as wholly Indian. Thus, some Hindus speak of the need for the 'Indianization' of minorities, by which they mean that minorities should adopt 'Indian' (i.e., Hindu) names, observe Indian (i.e., Hindu) national holidays, identify with India's historical (i.e., pre-Islamic Hindu and Buddhist) past, its heroes and great events, and be attached to the soil of India (not to Mecca or Rome).

Needless to say, this is not the way India's minorities define the problem. It is not only religious groups who regard themselves as minorities. Caste, tribal, linguistic as well as religious groups can be self-defined minorities for any one of a number of reasons: they have a distinctive group identity that they fear is eroding; they regard themselves as socially and economically subordinate to others; or they believe that they suffer from discrimination, either from others in the society or from the state itself. To regard oneself as part of a minority in India is to suggest that one ought to take group action to remedy one's situation. To declare one's group a minority is, therefore, a political act. In the Indian context, it is a way of calling attention to a situation of self-defined deprivation.

A people who do not share what they regard as the central symbols of the society invariably view themselves as a minority. It is not simply that a community lacks power but rather that the symbols of authority, the values that are propagated from the centre, and the culture that emanates from the centre are viewed as not theirs. To members of a minority community symbol sharing may be no less important than power sharing. Members of a minority community may refer to those of its members holding high office as having been 'co-opted' if they share power without the symbols. Moreover, a community may feel threatened because its own members are coming to partake of the symbols, the values, and the culture of the 'centre' even in the absence of explicit repression.

Once we conceive of a minority as a category defined by the observed rather than by observers, a self-definition by a community itself rather than by others, we are faced with a methodological problem of considerable proportion. If we understand the term 'minority' as a socially negotiable concept, then a community that regards itself and is regarded by others as a minority may under some circumstances cease to be a minority, while other communities may become minorities....

Since we are the observers and not the observed we must fall back upon the communities' self perceptions regarding their minority status. We can then engage in some informed speculation as to which other communities might actively put forth minority claims. It is useful to think of four types of minorities in India: linguistic, religious, caste, and tribal. These can be further divided along three dimensions: whether minorities have a conception of a territorial homeland; the extent of the sense of cohesion within the community; and whether the community regards itself as a disadvantaged or as an achieving minority.

Linguistic Minorities

Since each of India's states has an official language, those who speak another language as their mother tongue regard themselves as belonging to a linguistic minority....

Some minorities speaking 'unrecognized' languages have demanded statehood. This demand is often made by those linguistic groups concentrated in a particular region of a state and where the group has a strong sense of its own distinctive identity....

Special note should be taken of the concern by some linguistic majorities that they are in danger of becoming a minority within their own state....

There are a number of cities in which speakers of the state language are a minority. The Maràthi-speaking population constitutes only 42.8 per cent of Bombay. Kannada speakers in Bangalore (23.7 per cent) are outnumbered by Tamils (31.7 per cent). The Assamese lack a majority in Gauhati and in several other towns along the Brahmaputra. It is no surprise, therefore, that these towns have active 'sons of the soil' movements.

Religious Minorities

According to the 1981 census, Muslims constituted 11.4 per cent of the Indian population (75.5 million), Christians 2.4 per cent (16.2 million), Sikhs 2.0 per cent (13.1 million), and Buddhists and Jains 1.2 per cent (7.9 million). Hindus constituted 82.6 per cent of the population....

Two features of India's religious minorities warrant special note. The first is their internal divisions and the second is their relationship with Hindus.

None of the three major religious minorities is cohesive. Sikhs are divided between scheduled caste and non-scheduled caste Sikhs and between Jat Sikhs and other high-caste Sikhs. These divisions have enabled the Congress party to win substantial support from among the Sikhs and have prevented the consolidation of the Sikh vote in the Punjab around the Akali Dal.

Muslims are even less cohesive. The Muslims of the southwest have had long-term ties with Arab countries and they continue to migrate in large numbers to work in the Persian Gulf. They speak Malayalam and in their diet and dress are close to Hindus in the region. The Muslims of Kashmir form a majority of the state, have a strong Kashmiri identity, and overwhelmingly speak Kashmiri rather than Urdu. The Muslims living in the Hindi-speaking region, from the Yamuna north through the Gangetic plains, live in the mainstream of the Turkish, Afghan, Mughal and Persian invaders, and overwhelmingly (64 per cent) speak

Urdu. It is here that the Two-Nation Theory had its greatest support and where the Muslim League developed. Still further eastward Bengali Muslims speak Bengali rather than Urdu. Of the nine million Muslims in West Bengal less than one million speak Urdu. These are mostly migrants from Bihar, eastern Uttar Pradesh, and Orissa. The Muslims of Andhra form still another distinctive group. They lived under a Muslim ruler until 1947; their upper classes (some of Persian origin) formed part of the governing élite. Unlike most Muslims living in the south, they are overwhelmingly (91 per cent) Urdu-speaking. It is particularly noteworthy that the Muslims in south India, especially in Andhra and Kerala, have formed their own confessional political parties while north Indian Muslims, perhaps 'tainted' by their association with the League and the Two-Nation Theory, have frequently participated in mainstream political parties.

Finally, ...the Christians of the northeast, most of whom are tribal people, are culturally distinctive from the Christians of the south.

The attitude of Hindus toward religious minorities is guided by one central feature of Hinduism: it is an inclusive religion. Unlike Christianity, Judaism, Islam, and Sikhism, which are 'exclusive' religions that prescribe rules for membership, insist on adherence to specific dogmas and rules of conduct, and purge the heterodox, Hindus have no clear rules as to what constitutes a Hindu. Hindus view anyone who observes any Hindu rituals, worships any Hindu deities, or philosophically subscribes to any elements of Hinduism as a Hindu. Hindus have no conception of heterodoxy, no notion of apostasy....

Hinduism is inclusive in a second sense as well. Hindus regard religions that originated in South Asia, including Buddhism, Jainism, and Sikhism, and variants of Hinduism, such as the Brahmos, Lingayats, and other sects, as Hindu. Article 25 of the Indian Constitution stipulates that Sikhs, Buddhists, and Jains cannot be excluded from Hindu temples, a provision seen by Sikhs as intending to include Sikhs among Hindu communicants. Hindus see no apostasy when members of their religion worship at Sikh Gurdwaras, or at the tombs of saints; it is not unusual for Hindu families to declare one of their male children a Sikh and to give him a Sikh name. Similarly, Hindus incorporate tribal gods into their pantheon as reincarnations of Hindu deities.

Orthodox Hindus do not regard 'heterodox' and 'reformist' Hindu movements as threatening. India has been rife with religious movements during the past century: the Arya Samaj, theosophists, Vedantists, Brahmos, Lingayats, and numerous 'Godheads' or self-proclaimed religious leaders with their own followings. Religious Hindus regard the proliferation of such movements as a sign of religious vitality, not as a threat to any particular orthodoxy....

This tolerance for internal diversity and a readiness to incorporate others is, paradoxically, regarded with distrust by the exclusive religions of Islam, Sikhism, and Christianity. Each has sought, not always successfully, to resist the tendency of their communicants to adopt Hindu customs. Hindus, in turn, regard with equanimity Muslims and Sikhs who succumb to Hindu syncretism. Thus, the Mughal ruler Akbar is highly regarded by Hindus for his efforts to build a composite Indian culture, but by Muslims as an apostate who failed to keep faith. Hindus do, however, regard mass conversion to Islam and Christianity with alarm. The hostility to conversions is largely a reflection of nationalist opposition to religions of foreign origin, but it also reflects the Hindu antipathy towards exclusive religions.

Hindus regard with aversion a philosophical position shared by orthodox Sikhs and Muslims that politics and religion are inseparable. The classical Indian view is that the state preserves order, but it does not impose any particular moral code. Hinduism, unlike Christianity, Islam, Sikhism, and Judaism, has no conception of a universal moral code of conduct and no notion that rulers should act in moral ways according to some religious code. Politics is viewed as an amoral sphere, a notion partly rooted in the conception that Kshatriyas, not Brahmins, are rulers. Men like Maulana Moududi and Sant Jarnail Singh Bhindranwale are regarded by Hindus as 'fanatics' for their exclusive attitudes toward their own religion and for their rejection of political secularism....

Conclusion: A Statistical Recapitualtion and Projection

India's religious minorities, scheduled castes, and tribes constituted 37.2 per cent of the country's population in 1971, while the linguistic minorities were 17.5 per cent. These two categories overlap substantially since virtually all Urdu speakers are Muslims and a majority of speakers of non-regional languages are members of Scheduled Tribes. Taking these overlaps into account, approximately 45 per cent of the population belongs to linguistic, tribal, religious, or caste groups that regard themselves as minorities....

A projection of these figures for the year 2000, extrapolating from current growth rates, gives us 172 million Muslims, Christians, and Sikhs, 255 million scheduled castes and tribes, approximately 42. 3 million linguistically 'stateless' people (without a state of their own), and another 73.7 million people living outside of their 'home' state (some of whom, of course, are members of religious minorities or scheduled castes). The number of minorities for the year 2000 thus ranges from 472 to 545 million, the difference including many who are 'double' minorities. In short, if we think of the dominant majority as those who speak the official regional language as their mother tongue and are caste Hindus, then perhaps only 45 per cent to 52 per cent of the population can be regarded as part of this 'majority' in the year 2000, as compared with a 51 to 58 per cent range in 1971. It is likely that the 'majority' will fall below 50 per cent in several states. Assam, with its Assamese-speaking caste Hindu population already below 50 per cent may foreshadow the anxieties that other 'majorities' may feel as their majority status becomes precarious.

INDIA'S EMERGING MAJORITIES

To be part of the 'majority' is no less a matter of self-identification than to be part of a 'minority'. The growing articulation of minority claims in India is matched by an assertion of 'majority' claims as well. What remains problematic, however, is what constitutes this self-conscious 'majority'. Two overlapping identities have been competing for majority status: one is Hinduism; the other is determined by various regional languages.

The much noted 'revivalism' of Hinduism in recent years is hardly a reassertion of religious piety, for on that score there is no evidence of any decline in the performance of rituals, devotion to deities, participation in religious festivals, religious observance or whatever else one chooses as an indicator of religiosity in a religion that defies easy categorization. Hindu revivalism, or what some Hindus prefer to call a Hindu 'renaissance', is a political statement, a reassertion less of religion than of nationalism....

Linguistic regionalism (a form of linguistic 'nationalism' as distinct from an all-India nationalism) is the other claimant for majority status. Its perception of the majority-minority distinction is, however, at the regional rather than at the national level. It takes the form of 'sons of the soil' sentiments, protection in education and employment against 'alien' migrants, the insertion of regional histories, regional symbols, and regional pride into school textbooks and, above all, the demand for greater regional autonomy in relation to the central government. If Hindu revivalism stirs anxieties among Sikhs, Muslims, and Christians, then linguistic regionalism stirs anxieties among linguistic minorities in each of the states and among élites in the centre who see regionalism as undermining the creation of an all-Indian nationalism. These latter anxieties are most deeply felt by Hindi-speaking Hindus of the north who see themselves as the centre of the centre, so to speak.

If the emphasis on group claims and rights for minorities has served to strengthen group assertiveness on the part of various majorities, it is also the case that this new assertiveness has further intensified the anxieties of the minorities. To religious minorities, the embrace of Hindu tolerance, its eagerness to absorb others, is psychologically threatening. To linguistic minorities, the protective, assimilative, and exclusionary stance of linguistic majorities is a cultural threat and a barrier to educational, occupational, and spatial mobility. It is in this context of the new majorities that one must understand the demands of India's minorities.

WHAT DO INDIA'S MINORITIES WANT?

The Demand for a Homeland

…The sense of attachment to 'place' in India is as powerful as attachment to group and the two are closely intertwined. Groups often regard the territory in which they live as the site of their exclusive history, a place in which great events occurred and sacred shrines are located. Tribal and linguistic groups often regard a homeland as exclusively their own and would, if they could, exclude others or deny others the right to enjoy the fruits of the land or employment provided within the territory. Hence, India's linguistic majorities define themselves as 'sons of the soil' with group rights to employment, land, and political power not granted to those who come from 'outside'. It is not sufficient that the group occupy the territory that is their homeland; they also seek to exercise political control.

For this reason many minority groups with a territorial base have pressed for statehood. Statehood converts minority status into majority status. It enables minorities to resist assimilation (linguistic or religious) by the majority. And in more practical terms it gives them control over the resources of the government, employment, patronage, and education. In India, where the state exercises so much control over the market, ethnic groups believe that it is essential to hold political power to enable their members to redistribute public goods into their own hands....

Linguistic Recognition

A major demand of a number of linguistic groups is that their language be included in the eighth schedule of the Constitution. Inclusion in the list enables a linguistic group to take all-India examinations in their own language. Similarly, recognition as an official language of a state enables a people to compete for positions in the state services without having to take examinations in another language. Official recognition, linguistic minorities argue, reduce the pressures for linguistic assimilation and enables the group to strengthen its identity and solidarity....

Reservations

The alternative to statehood for dispersed minorities is to have reserved seats in legislative bodies and in the administrative services. The Indian Constitution...legitimizes claims for groups' rights. The Constitution provides for group benefits for Scheduled Castes, Scheduled Tribes, and other backward classes. In addition to group representation through reserved constituencies in elected bodies, the government can provide for quotas for appointments in the administrative services, and admissions into colleges, universities, and medical and technical schools....

State and central governments in India have moved toward the principle that membership in educational institutions, in state and central administrative services, in the military and in public sector employment should ultimately reflect the demographic division of the country. While that policy is welcomed by some minorities (and some majorities!), it leaves two groups unhappy: those who are left out and those who lose....

....The more successful reservations become at improving the capacity of Scheduled Castes and Tribes to compete for jobs in the administrative services, the less willing are others to support a system of employment based on group membership. Reservations in India, as elsewhere, has left all communities dissatisfied — beneficiaries because they believe that the reservations are not satisfactorily administered and those who are excluded because they view the system as discriminatory.

Security

Minorities in India, as elsewhere, are particularly concerned over their security. Poor and dispersed minorities, most especially members of the Scheduled Castes, are particularly vulnerable to attacks from the majority. In recent years, there have been repeated charges from minorities that they can no longer rely upon the police to assure them of protection and that the police themselves have attacked minorities or provided support for attackers. There is considerable evidence from media reports that the police in India have become increasingly politicized and that factions of the governing party and their supporters within local communities have used the police to their own advantage. The collusion of sections of the police with sections of the Congress party against minorities was particularly evident in the attacks against Sikhs in the capital city following Mrs. Gandhi's assassination. Not until the army was called in did the attacks subside....

....There is in India a deep and justifiable fear of uncontrollable violence among religious, caste, and linguistic groups. This fear serves to legitimate armed intervention by the state and can easily be played upon by a government. A government whose leaders and supporters deliberately or through inaction enable such conflicts to grow, however, is in danger of unleashing controllable forces that could ultimately lead to its own undermining.

POLITICS: THE PROBLEM OR THE SOLUTION?

Indians have two views of the impact of politics on ethnic group conflict: that it worsens group relations and that politics is the way to reduce group conflict. Both views are correct.

The distribution of education, employment, and wealth in India is largely determined by the political process. This central feature of political life means that each ethnic group can best improve its share of education and employment by increasing its political power. The twin objectives of all ethnic groups in India — to strengthen their group identity and to improve both the social status and economic well-being of the group — can best be achieved through the route of politics. It is this central fact that induces politicians to appeal to their ethnic group for votes....

· ....Ethnic groups have interests no less than do classes. In India, as in other multi-ethnic societies, individuals are members both of a class and an ethnic group. In a society without ethnic divisions class consciousness develops more easily, but in a society divided along ethnic lines historical and comparative evidence over-whelmingly suggests that ethnic group consciousness is likely to prevail. The fictive ties of kinship that characterize ethnic groups provide a more affective sense of attachment than do the appeals to interests made on behalf of classes. Class has its affective appeals, but the sense of class comradeship is often of a lesser pull than the attractions of blood ties, real or imagined....

Heightened group consciousness does not necessarily result in intergroup conflict. Group consciousness may lead to a sense of pride, may result in a more strict observance of cultural and religious practices, may lead members of a group to help one another. Conflicts arise when a group asserts its identity by attacking the identity of other groups and, above all, when a claim for group rights and group power is perceived by others as threatening.

....Weak political institutions are more often a cause than a consequence of growing social conflict.

Conflict Management in the Eighties and Nineties

The organizational decline of the Congress Party at the state and local level, and the politicization of the police and the lower levels of administration, do not augur well for conflict management by government. Moreover, a number of public policies which had mitigated group conflict in the past have now themselves become sources of conflict. Reservations ameliorated the plight of scheduled castes and scheduled tribes but the pressure for their extension to other groups has now made reservations a divisive issue. Federalism and the rearrangements of state boundaries to provide statehood for linguistic, tribal, and (in the case of Punjab) religious minorities worked well for reducing conflict in the fifties and sixties, but it is not working well in the eighties, as many of the states now seek a rearrangement of centre-state powers and resources. The earlier government policy of seeking to reduce foreign influence (particularly with respect to foreign missionaries) works less well when India's Muslims employed in the Gulf are sending remittances home, Sikhs are living in western Europe and North America, Bangladeshis are moving into Assam, and Tamil-Sinhalese conflicts in Sri Lanka arouse south Indian Tamil sentiments. Even the language formulas of the sixties are questioned as Urdu-speaking Muslims, Nepalis, and other linguistic minorities press for official recognition. Nor do strategies of sitting it out, waiting for ethnic feelings to dissipate, or of incorporating leaders of ethnic groups seem to work as well in the eighties as those strategies did earlier....

....Of critical importance in the future of majority-minority relations in India is the viability of the state governments. ....Should minorities become more assertive and conflict prove to be unmanageable by state government authorities, then the powers of the central government will increase.

A pessimistic scenario is one in which majority-minority conflicts increase, state governments do not demonstrably increase their capacity to deal with these conflicts, the centre by its actions provokes opposition to central authority, and the growth of violent conflict leads to greater coercion and the use of the armed forces.

An optimistic scenario is one in which leaders at both the national and state levels demonstrate their skill at accommodating the demands for substantial administrative decentralization and prove skilful at reassuring minorities without threatening the cultural identity and interests of majorities. We can make no predictions about which scenario is most likely.

FURTHER READINGS

For a discussion on the thinking that went into constitutional arrangements of Indian Federalism the following works provide considerably detailed analyses.

Austin, Granville, *The Indian Constitution: Cornerstone of a Nation*, Clarendon Press, Oxford, 1964.

Chapters 8–10 deal with the federal principles in the Constituent Assembly of India.

Chapter 10 refers to linguistic demands. Austin's scrupulous account of the debates in the Constituent Assembly clearly presents the thinking that went into the institutional design devised for dealing with regional and other types of social diversity.

Chanda, Asok, *Federalism in India*, George Allen and Unwin, London, 1965.

This is a predominantly legal-consitutional analysis of various aspects of Indian federalism, in great detail. It describes the functioning of the federal system down to the mid-sixties, and there is very little interest in the sociology of regional politics.

Brass, Paul, *Language, Religion and Politics in North India*, Cambridge University Press, London, 1974.

This is a fine sociological study of the dyamics of religious and linguistic identities in North India. Though the analysis is from the early seventies, since the basic structure of identities remain the same in broad terms, the discussion remains interesting and relevant.

Dasgupta, J., *Language Conflict and National Development*, University of California, Berkeley, 1970.

An excellent study of the problem of linguistic identity in the context of the institutional arrangements of Indian federalism.

Weiner, Myron, *Sons of the Soil: Migration and Ethnic Conflict in India*, Princeton University Press, Princeton, 1978.

This work is among the very few dealing with the problem of migration and the political conflicts it spawns. It brings the discussion up to the wave of 'sons of the soil' movements of the late seventies, but provides an acute analysis of the sociological processes which contribute to these political conflicts.

V

Sociology of Political Parties

Democratic politics functions through a relation between the constitutional structure and the operation of political parties. Parties are not mentioned in the constitutions, but they constitute an essential part of the democratic system. For, theoretically, in a democracy governments are chosen by individual electors expressing their choice for candidates in free elections. Actually, it is political parties which set up the candidates, and campaign actively for votes in favour of their nominees. This arrangement imparts a necessary degree of flexibility to the world of democratic politics. Constitutional and legal structures are usually inflexible: and some aspects of the political system are deliberately cast in that inflexible form, so that some things, like the rights to be enjoyed by citizens, cannot be easily altered. But since parties function informally, their activity reflects the constant flux of interest formation in society. It is through the parties that a democratic constitution remains contemporary with political aspirations and pressures. The actual politics of a particular country can change dramatically without any formal alteration of its constitutional structure. The interests that are aggregated by parties in Western democratic systems are usually economic; often they are related, albeit in complex ways, to the interests of social classes. But in countries of the Third World, and in India, the situation is different. Usually, when parties try to aggregate interests they make appeals not only to the common economic interests or class, but also to other identities that ordinary people commonly use to identify themselves — like caste, or religious community, or region and language. The way political parties use these appeals often leads to paradoxical results, some of which are reflected in the readings selected in this section. The parties chosen for attention are the Congress in Karnataka, the Communist Party of India (Marxist) in Kerala and the Jana Sangh, which drew electoral support traditionally in North Indian states. These represent three *types* of political parties with wide national influence; but evidently, there are further questions to be asked. Congress obviously was influential over the whole of India, thought its appeal rested on arguably different factors in different regions. Communist influence has been deeply entrenched in some regions, especially Kerala, West Bengal, Andhra Pradesh, but insignificant elsewhere. Similarly the Jana Sangh's influence, and subsequently of its successor, the BJP, has been primarily restricted to the North. These parties are obviously different in terms of their ideology. The ambiguity of Congress ideology has been in some ways its great strength, since it can draw in support from the most diverse social groups. Communists represent a political group which is more ideologically distinct, highly disciplined in its party organisation, and expecting to draw its support from working class, peasant and lower middle class elements in society. The Jana Sangh, and now its successor, the BJP, represent the primary political party based explicitly on the ideology of Hindu communalism. The essays presented here offer us sociological accounts of how these parties worked and mobilised their support from social groups; but it is important to remember that these come from a period before the two major contemporary issues broke on the scene — disputes about economic liberalism and Hindu communal politics.

Although the constitutional system explicitly discourages appeals to caste, party politics has been dominated by caste mobilisations of various kinds. But there is a clear paradox in the use of caste in elections. To what extent a direct appeal to caste by nominating a candidate from a group which constitutes the main caste element in a particular constituency actually helps win an election is quite doubtful. Usually, such advantage can be easily neutralised, since all parties can find candidates from the same caste group. So, eventually, the outcome depends not on the membership of the dominant caste (since all candidates belong to it) but on other factors. But though this cancels out the contingent advantage any single party would have gained, this has a long term effect by creating a pronounced bias in favour of caste nominations, and making the language of politics generally casteist. Parliamentary processes, thus, instead of diluting caste identification of ordinary voters, conspire to reinforce them. On the other hand, this has altered the structure of caste affiliation, most significantly in some cases. The clearest example is the slow erosion of traditional segmented identities of the untouchable groups, and their replacement by a new, constitutionally created category of Scheduled Castes. For similar reasons, more recently a new identity of 'intermediate castes' has appeared in political life. Categories like Scheduled or Intermediate Castes are clearly not traditional identifications, but new ones, created out of the vocabulary of caste, by pressures of modern parliamentary politics. Just as electoral politics has been overrun by caste, caste has been transformed by modern politics.

Interestingly, contrary to traditional expectation, the pressure from the more assertive among the lower order groups of Indian society has come through caste forms rather than class ones. A wide range of traditionally lower castes have built large coalitions, and exerted successful pressure on the political system, though the actual process has taken somewhat different expressions in North and South India. The leadership provided by Devaraj Urs to Congress politics in Karnataka provided one of the first examples of this political potential. James Manor's essay gives us a careful sociological account of the way Urs' political support was built and deployed to win electoral campaigns and subsequently to carry through government policies.

Theoretically, Communist politics is the organised expression of the interests and aspirations of the industrial working class. But in India, industrialisation and thus the presence of an industrial working class in extremely uneven. If a communist movement agrees to do its politics within a constitutional and electoral framework, its success would depend vitally on drawing support from the peasantry and the urban petty bourgeois groups. These groups undoubtedly share some sociological features with the proletariat, but have significant differences as well. The peasantry, or at least its poorer sections, face great economic deprivation and poverty; but, as classical Marxist thinkers acknowledged, they often display a fierce attachment to private property. Secondly, peasant communities do not always break up along class lines at times of political action, preferring to behave politically as a single, unfractured community. The urban poor are often unorganised, unlike industrial workers, and difficult to bring into any organisational net. The lower middle classes display a combination of education, political articulateness and resentfulness against deprivation, but their economic interests do not always exactly coincide with the workers'. A successful communist movement, therefore, faces a considerably complex task of coalition-building of the parallel, but often distinctive grievances of disadvantaged groups in society. Political sociologists unsympathetic to communism had pointed out conventionally that the success of communist politics is often based surreptitiously on caste mobilisation in cases of Andhra and Kerala under a thin veneer of class assertion. This is evidently not true of West Bengal. In fact, communist politics appears to have used two different, but complementary axes in search of electoral success. In industrialised areas, communists have been most energetic in building trade union movements, and consequently, their success in both regionally based and nation-wide industrial trade unionism is no surprise. Though this creates internal problems of reconciling the demands of various segments of trade union movements and their often incompatible interests. For example, highly paid white collar workers in banks or airlines transport are highly unionised, and use their organization and strategic placement in the economy to raise salaries. But any success in this, while an undoubted achievement for trade unionism, makes it more difficult to compose their interests with those of the very poor unorganised workers. Around this core of industrial working class support, communist parties have been obliged to seek electoral support from other, rural and non-proletarian groups.

The slow, but definite alterations in the political world also affected communist politics more subtly. From the eighties, it became evident that violent revolutions were historically unlikely, and even established socialist systems were in a state of deep crisis. Communist parties within democratic constitutional systems were thus more firmly inserted into the logic of electoral power. Indian communist groups, particularly the CPI (M) which was, despite its revolutionary rhetoric, remarkably successful in electoral politics, sought to increase their appeal to social groups not traditionally considered their usual social base. Communist regimes have at times sought to reassure business groups that they were not hostile to legitimate entrepreneurial interests, and due to their firmer control over trade union movements, could offer a more predictable industrial climate than other parties. Like other political forces in India, communists however have to contend with great regional variations. In West Bengal, the other traditional base of stable communist power, caste is a negligible factor. Thomas Nossiter's essay analyses the specific complexities of social support for the communists in Kerala, along several different axes — class, income, caste and generational divides. Nossiter also uses technical means of aggregate data analysis from elections, census and other statistical sources, with some reflection on attendant methodological difficulties.

The Congress party has always based its electoral politics on the width of the coalitions it could put together, which was consistent with its ideological principles of a pluralistic nationalism. Ideologically, this was challenged by the communists, using a more pronounced class based politics, and by parties which contested the idea of pluralistic nationalism by an alternative conception of a Hindu nationalism. The primary vehicle of the idea of a Hindu nation has been the Jana Sangh, and later the BJP. The fortunes of Hindu nationalists constitute one of the most perplexing problems of modern Indian politics. There is, first, a problem of the elementary characterisation of this force. Is this a fundamentalist force, like some powerful movements in modern Islam, on something distinctive in character? Some analysts would hesitate to call them a 'fundamentalist' force for two reasons. The BJP seeks to use Hindu religion as its ideological base, but Firstly, Hinduism has been marked historically by an ineradicable pluralism of doctrinal and structural forms. Therefore, there simply are no fundamental ideas of principles around which the movement could ask its adherents to rally. There is no consensus among practising Hindus about what should constitute Hinduism's fundamental texts. Are these the Gita, the Vedas (but which part of them?), the Upanishads, the Manusmriti? Each of these, even assuming there are no interpretative debates about their individual messages, would give to Hindu religion a distinctive and different emphasis. Secondly, fundamentalist movements are usually traditionalist, openly and intensely opposed to forces of modernity. The Jana Sangh/BJP position on this point is ambiguous. However, there is no ambiguity about their hostility to Muslims as a community, and their characterisation of them as representing an 'alien' presence in India. So, even if there are difficulties about calling the BJP fundamentalist, there are none in seeing it as communal. Even the early programme of the Jana Sangh was fanatically anti-Muslim, but not seriously anti-modernist. After some limited success initially, its electoral support reached a plateau, and remained stagnant for a long time. This appears to have occasioned some internal discussions within the party about the most profitable strategy it could follow. It appeared in the seventies that the Jana Sangh, or an influential section within it, wanted to present itself as an increasingly centrist force, offering to replace the Congress which showed signs of unmistakable institutional decline. But in the eighties, the BJP experimented successfully with a far more aggressive, refurbished communal strategy centring on emotive issues like destruction of the Babri Masjid at Ayodhya as a preliminary to systematic attacks on other mosques in other parts of the country. This was a considerable radicalisation of communalism. Earlier, Muslims were a target of attack as a social group distinguished by religion in terms of political and social arrangements, but now it devised a way of attacking religious beliefs and practices more directly. It is difficult to assess what the long term consequence of this shift, and the destruction of the Babri Masjid in Ayodhya, is going to be. Initially it appeared to give the BJP instant results in winning elections. But systematic attacks on Muslim religious places would lead to political instability on a scale quite unprecedented in independent India, and is unlikely to be seen with favour by groups like big business. The BJP lost elections in the relevant states soon after, indicating that the extremism of the destruction of the mosque might have scared voters off rather than enticed them. Clearly, the appeal of the BJP is also deeply linked to issues like separatist militancy in Kashmir and long-standing regional problems in the Punjab and Assam. The more extreme forms of nationalism and separatist movements reinforce each other by supplying, paradoxically, each other's justification. Traditionally, the Jana Sangh was unable to organise and mobilise the whole Hindu vote as it expected; support for its politics came from identifiable social groups like small traders, lower government employees, and others in urban North India. In recent years, the party has clearly sought to widen its appeal to other social groups, particularly the urban middle class professionals and industrialists. Bruce Garham's analysis identifies the bases of social support for the party in its earlier form, as the Bharatiya Jana Sangh; but the social bases of its support remain similar. In its new form, the BJP faces an evident political dilemma. To use Hinduism effectively for political purposes, it must transform its historically pluralist structure, and to profess an explicitly Brahminical Hinduism would surely alienate the lower castes. To advocate a homogenised and casteless form of Hinduism would appear to be a travesty of what Hinduism has historically been.

Karnataka: Caste, Class, Dominance and Politics in a Cohesive Society

JAMES MANOR

This [essay] seeks to understand the interplay of caste, class and patterns of dominance in the political and social history of the state of Karnataka. My contention is that this state has long possessed what must, within the Indian context, be seen as a comparatively cohesive society....

It is difficult to find in Karnataka's history, much evidence of groups feeling or demonstrating the severe alienation from the social order which tends to arise more often in many other regions of India.... To call Karnataka a relatively cohesive society is not to imply that it is destined to remain so forever. Social historians have a great deal to say about regions or nations which had acquired reputations for stability and cohesion, but later underwent rapid decomposition or radicalization.... Nor is there any suggestion that a 'cohesive' society is necessarily a 'harmonious' society, or that Karnataka is a blissful place, devoid of inéquities. They exist, patently and ubiquitously, and disadvantaged people face serious indignities at every turn. But the disparities in wealth,

Excerpted from 'Karnataka: Caste, Class, Dominance and Politics in a Cohesive Society,' in Francine Frankel and M S A Rao (eds.) *Dominance and State Power in Modern India*, vol. I, OUP, Delhi, 1990, 322-61.

status and power have not been so severe as to undermine the comparative cohesion of society throughout most of this state.... Two things, apart from the relatively stable, well-integrated character of Karnataka society which underpins all of this, are worth mentioning at the outset. First, the pace of change has been moderate enough to prevent extreme stresses from developing, and the number of people who get torn loose from the fabric of society amid change has been kept to a manageable minimum. In this connection the state's moderate growth rate in agricultural production should be noted. This enabled it to move from deficit to surplus in foodgrain output around 1970, but it has not occurred with the rapidity seen in Punjab over the same period or in Sri Lanka since 1977 — places where high speed growth appears to have caused disorientation and social dislocation.

Second, the character of change has been such that the social order has faced only limited disruptions.... It is also true that some of the successes and some of the failures of successive governments in the state since independence have tended to ensure that change did not place the existing social order under undue stress. Among the successes are the various ameliorative programmes directed at the rural poor between 1972 and 1980 and again since 1983.... Among the failures of all Karnataka governments, mention must be made of lack of any major progress with irrigation projects that might have created opportunities for landowning groups to make rapid economic advances relative to their disadvantaged neighbours....

DOMINANCE AT THE LOCAL LEVEL

The problem of socio-economic and political 'dominance' in Karnataka needs to be studied first at the local level, in the villages where the vast majority of the state's population is to be found. This is an essential prerequisite to the discussion later in the essay of the separate problem of 'dominance' at supra-local levels — especially in state-level politics.

Throughout the nineteenth and twentieth centuries — even to the present day — life in most Karnataka villages has been dominated by powerful minorities within village societies. The kind of people that one finds in dominant roles has barely changed over the decades. They tend, with few exceptions, to be peasant proprietors whose wealth derives mainly from the cultivation of crops (as opposed to the rearing of animals) which is to say that they tend to be members of the two well-known *jati*-clusters, the *vokkaligas* and the *lingayats*.

'Dominance' is a very strong word. When used in this discussion, it implies a very substantial quantum of power and influence over the life and resources of the village and over the behaviour of the people within it: it implies *control* or something very near to it. It is impossible to speak of 'dominance' being very widely shared or divided among different groups within an arena, or of it being diluted to any degree. Diluted dominance is no dominance at all. Of what does the dominance of the *lingayats* and *vokkaligas* consist? The answers have been familiar since M.N. Srinivas set most of them out in his classic essay on the subject.[1] Dominance is multi-stranded. It consists of the control of a substantial proportion (though not necessarily an overwhelming proportion) of the land around the village (including the better land); numerical strength, which usually means that dominant groups are a sizable minority in the village; possession of the village headman's post; the leadership of patron-client networks, often based in part on money-lending, and relatively high (though seldom supreme) status in the traditional caste hierarchy. The dominant groups tend to dominate, whether we measure their power in terms of action (their capacity to do things which others cannot do, and to persuade or compel others to act in ways that suit them) or in terms of structure (the impediments to life chances, the actions and the aspirations of poorer groups).

There are at least three other things that need to be said about this more or less ubiquitous dominance at the village level in Karnataka. The first is that one measure of it is the capacity of locally dominant groups to prevent the reformist elements operating in the modern mode of supra-local politics from catalyzing major changes in the villages....

The second point about village-level dominance in Karnataka is that it is bound up with both caste and class.... Indeed, given the lack of class awareness or consciousness that one finds so often in rural Karnataka, given the complications and ambiguities that so often arise, given the predominance of caste consciousness, given the still potent capacity of caste to erect impediments to solidarity among people sharing similar economic circumstances,

and given the heterogeneity in caste and class terms of most of
the important coalitions which have surfaced from time to time
in state-level politics, it is perhaps advisable to use a more vague term
like 'stratum' than 'class' as a means of describing aggregations
in rural areas based largely on similar economic circumstances....

I should also stress that although caste tends to predominate
over class in the identities of most rural — though *not* most urban
— dwellers in Karnataka, that is, at the level of ideas, perceptions
and ideology, I do not regard caste as simply a matter of ideology.
Caste possesses material substance. It exists not only at the level
of ideas but at the level of concrete social structure, at the level
of action and interaction. Rural social organisation and village-
level dominance are not based wholly on caste.... Karnataka's
poorer villagers *do* perceive inequalities and exploitation which
are to a large extent products of class differences, but they tend
to express this in language heavily laced with caste cliché. And
that is not entirely inappropriate since caste, as a material reality,
plays an important role in sustaining inequalities and exploitation.
The problem is to sort out the varying admixtures of class and
caste elements in shaping social, economic and political relations
in rural areas of varying regions.

The third point about dominance in village Karnataka is that
it tends to be less severe and oppressive than that which exists
in the villages of most other parts of India. This also makes it
more resilient and more capable of maintaining a certain legitimacy in the eyes of the dominated than the forms of dominance
which are found elsewhere.

Village-level dominance in Karnataka is less severe than in
most other regions because some of the various strands of which
it is composed elsewhere are either missing or only loosely woven
into the fabric of dominance. Dominant groups in Karnataka villages do not possess supreme social status within the traditional
hierarchy. This is particularly true in *vokkaliga* areas where *brahmans* still serve as priests and often as teachers and accountants.
But even in *lingayat* areas the dominant group in the village power
structure is generally drawn from one of the *lingayat* cultivating
jatis while priestly functions are left to members of the small
jangama jati. Nor in any part of Karnataka do locally dominant
groups claim to be twice-born, and this absence of a *varna* barrier

between those groups and poorer Shudras who usually comprise a majority of the dominated again reduces status distances....

CASTE AND CLASS IN OPERATION AT THE RURAL LOCAL LEVEL

...Many scholars have stressed the importance of class divisions within castes or *játis*, and the tendency of élites within castes to forge alliances with their class fellows in other castes while stimulating caste consciousness to maintain both solidarity within and their own influence over their castes. But this is not the only thing that is happening and this process is no longer as simple as this. If we assume that this is the *only* thing or the *main* thing that is happening, then it is quite logical to conclude that class has greater importance than caste, that caste is on the wane and that relations within classes are based on substance while relations within castes are largely based on sentiment and on elite manipulation of ideology and symbolism.

The view tends to overlook or underrate the *materiality of caste*. Caste possesses material substance. This can be seen to be true both in the way that it tangibly reinforces ties between people within the same caste, and in the way that it erects or strengthens tangible divisions between people from different castes. Numerous examples can be provided of members of the same *játi* — whether they be of similar or dissimilar wealth and status — sharing concrete resources preferentially with one another.... Members of a *jati* who have some success in politics or who obtain an education and settle in towns or cities where they have access to government agencies and banks, often act as intermediaries between such agencies and poorer, less educated members of their own *játi* in nearby rural areas who desire the money, material and opportunities that those agencies provide. Whether they do so out of self-interest or for altruistic reasons — and both sorts of motives appear to be at work — the result is that *jati* membership yields *material* returns.

Caste also possesses material substance in at least two other senses which are linked to its more traditional forms and roles. First, it is still intimately bound up with the division of labour in villages, since a great many — indeed most — people there continue to pursue traditional caste occupations or occupations of a closely related nature. This clearly has major implications for the material conditions in which people find themselves, and for *class* divisions and structures within the village....

The second thing to notice about the more traditional features of a caste or *játi* is that it serves as an arena that is often well-integrated by networks of marriages that are constructed in part out of a desire to link the material resources of pairs of families. A large number of such interlocking alliances, taken cumulatively, lend considerable substance to a *jati*....

POST-INDEPENDENCE STATE-LEVEL POLITICS

....Within a short period after the end of British rule, every area of Karnataka came under the control of the Congress Party. It eventually presided over the unification of the disparate parts under a single administration in 1956, and it remained in power until 1983. *Vokkaligas* and *lingayats* — the two groups that were dominant at the village level — already controlled the Congress in most areas by 1947. And since Congress quickly developed into a highly effective political machine that controlled the institutions of government at state, district and subdistrict levels, *vokkaligas* and *lingayats* soon came to dominate politics at the state level and all other supra-local levels too. The spoils which became available to those in control of state power went disproportionately though not exclusively to *lingayats* and *vokkaligas* on the land, thereby strengthening their dominant position at the local level. Those on the land responded by using their influence at the grassroots level to deliver majorities in the state assembly for Congress....

It must be stressed, however, that there was a second element in the strategy of Karnataka's Congress in the period between 1947 and 1972: a policy of very modest reform and very limited representation for and concessions to less prosperous groups. This was always far less important than preferential treatment for *vokkaligas* and *lingayats*, but it was not entirely insignificant. Congress politicians in the state, particularly those who held power before the mid-1960s when *lingayat* chauvinism took hold for a few years, were sufficiently canny and enlightened to see that a relatively generous approach to the weaker sections of society made good political sense. After all, *lingayats* and *vokkaligas* together constitute only about 32 per cent of the population....

Most of the concessions by these leaders to poorer groups amounted to little more than tokenism, and those resources which reached the disadvantaged were often manipulated by *vokkaliga* and *lingayat* middle-men with Congress in such a way as to co-opt and disarm potentially troublesome leaders of less prosperous groups. But important recent research by A.R. Rajapurohit[2] indicates that certain programmes — most notably the land reform of 1961 which was the handiwork of Kadidal Manjappa had a somewhat greater impact than most commentators, including this writer and Manjappa himself,[3] have previously believed. Indeed, it is appropriate to view these early, highly tentative initiatives as precedents for the more forceful reforms and the more substantial concessions to poorer groups which became the main thrust of a new set of Congress leaders in Karnataka between 1972 and 1980....

The trend towards a more equitable distribution of land in Karnataka, which began under the impact of the 1961 land reform, appears on the basis of available evidence to have continued and to have accelerated gradually under the much more formidable land reform of 1974....

The land reform of 1974 was the central element in a whole array of programmes created by the Congress government of Chief Minister D. Devaraj Urs between 1972 and 1980 to assist disadvantaged groups. Let us now look at the conditions under which that innovative government achieved and maintained power, and at the impact that it had in the state. We have already noted that when Karnataka was unified in 1956, *lingayats* outnumbered *vokkaligas*, so that every Chief Minister between 1956 and 1972 was a *lingayat*.... It led many *vokkaligas* to feel that they were being left out, even though in the period up to 1972 the Congress machine in the state kept delivering sizable quantities of spoils to its *vokkaliga* clients. These feelings were part of a more general political awakening in this (and other) states which had caused the appetites of most social groups — both privileged and disadvantaged — for patronage from the government to grow quite noticeably. By the late 1960s frustration had become quite a common emotion among members of the two dominant landed groups, especially among the large number of people in both groups who had never been particularly well-off economically.

Curiously enough, in what was clearly a time of *lingayat* supremacy in state politics, these frustrations appear to have been more acute among *lingayats* than among *vokkaligas*. Many *lingayats* claimed that an inordinate share of resources had gone to a tiny élite within their sect.... By the late 1960s and early 1970s the solidarity of *lingayat raj* and of dominant landed 'caste' *ráj* had been undermined to a modest but nonetheless significant extent.[4]

These frustrations and the consequent erosion of solidarity within the *vokkaliga/lingayat* bloc or alliance — it was and is too heterogeneous to allow us to describe it as a class — aided Devaraj Urs in his efforts to gain control of state politics in the early 1970s. ....After the 1969 split in the Congress, Urs had worked hard to put together a network of supporters in every part of the state who were tied to him largely by the hope that he might attract the endorsement of Mrs Gandhi and the fact that they had nowhere else more rewarding to go. For a long time this seemed a rather unpromising line to pursue: until the 1971 general election Mrs Gandhi's own prospects seemed rather uncertain. After the split the regional Congress machine in Karnataka remained largely in the hands of Mrs Gandhi's opponents. In addition, far more eminent Karnataka politicians than Urs — for example, the prominent Union cabinet minister K. Hanumanthiah — had stood by Mrs Gandhi. As a result, Urs had to go for support to people in the district and *taluk* towns who were left over after more potent figures had developed their networks of clients. In many cases, these were people from less exalted communities, often without much previous political experience, people with secondary and perhaps some tertiary education who were in small businesses, minor government posts or the co-operative sector. He rightly saw their obscurity as something of an advantage, since it meant that they would be (at least for a time) heavily dependent on him. Urs was also gambling that the disadvantaged social groups from which many of his new recruits came and to which some of the others had good connections, thanks to services which the recruits had rendered to them, had experienced a sufficient political awakening since 1947 to vote for a party that promised to deliver major new resources to them rather than to the dominant landed group.

It is worth noting here, however briefly, that this awakening appears to have been the result not of *economic* changes at the grassroots, but of ordinary voters' exposure to the *political* process. This took the form mainly of a popular realization that in exchange for electoral support, *lingayats* and *vokkaligas* gained access to resources. Over time, less exalted groups began to feel that resources should come their way too, and they altered their voting behaviour accordingly. This suggests that politics can enjoy a certain autonomy and occasional primacy as an agent for change....

....Urs put together a slate of Congress candidates at the 1972 state election which contained a higher proportion of people from disadvantaged groups and a smaller number of *lingayats* and *vokkaligas* than ever before. Success at that election enabled him to break *lingayat/vokkaliga* control over state politics. He then developed a series of gradualist, reformist programmes to assist disadvantaged voters. ...Urs also redirected the flow of a substantial portion of political spoils toward poorer groups. This was less widely advertised and less easily discernible than his new reformist programmes, but (as Urs himself stated[5]), it may have had as great an impact as all of them put together. It should be stressed, however, that he wisely kept *some* spoils flowing to traditional recipients to prevent a severe backlash from *lingayats* and, especially, *vokkaligas*.

In order to give his programmes some prospect of success, Urs found civil servants who either came from disadvantaged communities (and he recruited such people in large numbers to the state's Administrative Service) or who appeared to sympathize with his aims and inserted them into key positions where they might expedite implementation....

His programmes penetrated downward to the grassroots only imperfectly, intermittently and unevenly. Some, although only a limited minority of his initiatives, were intended as window-dressing, particularly those unveiled just before the assembly election of 1978. The result of all of this therefore fell far short of major social change. But to say this is not necessarily to pass a particularly negative judgement on Urs, since he always intended to proceed gradually, to push things further and deliver more effectively at a later stage. What he did was to make a substantial beginning in giving substantial numbers of disadvantaged people in most parts of the state quite modest doses of new resources....

Urs timed his other major initiative — the introduction of measures to channel government concessions to the state's Backward Classes — very carefully in relation to the programmes outlined above. Urs waited five years, to give these programmes some chance to make an impact at the grassroots (and three years after his Land Reform Act had taken effect) to announce that he proposed to act on the recommendations by a commission that a major share of places in schools and government service go to the Backward Classes.[6] He delayed the decision until then because he understood that it was important to consolidate his government's position via the distribution of tangible patronage to disadvantaged groups before making an announcement that would be far more alarming to organized *lingayat* interests than nearly all of his other schemes. *Vokkaligas* were included among the Backward Classes with some justice in many cases, but more for reasons of expediency. Urs also knew that such an announcement carried considerable risks since there were unlikely to be enough places for Backward Class people to meet the expectations that would be generated. But those risks were significantly reduced because he had first developed considerable support among poorer people that could not be extinguished overnight by frustration. It is also true, of course, that the relatively cohesive character of Karnataka society, provided a relatively congenial setting for an attempt by politicians to redirect resources to less prosperous groups....

The important point is that Urs was adapting machine politics to modestly progressive purposes. This was an achievement of no small historical significance since, in this writer's view, machine politics was the central feature of the Indian political system during the first quarter-century or so after 1947. It was becoming difficult and in many areas impossible during the late 1960s and early 1970s — as the political awakening caused interest groups to crystallize and conflict between social groups to sharpen — to maintain Congress' very broad and heterogeneous social bases in the regions through spoils distribution. Urs showed that it was possible to use the machine to distribute patronage mainly among a more selected clientele — the weaker sections of society — without being run out of office....

Urs' Coalition

One of the great difficulties with seeing Urs' coalition of disadvantaged groups as an emergent 'class' force — a term that has
often been used rather loosely, not least by Urs himself — lies in
Urs' stimulus of 'caste' (that is, *játi* or *játi*-cluster) sentiments in
his efforts to develop his new political base. Urs was very active
in attempts to revive flagging or dormant caste associations among
artisan and service castes....

....These actions do not appear to have been based on the
assumption that there was latent class sentiment waiting to be
brought to the forefront of people's consciousness.... Urs saw
that rural dwellers were very firmly locked into a world-view
in which *jati* (after family) was the dominant social category, and
he did not expect this to change in his or their lifetimes. He also
believed that their world-view was for the most part not an example of false consciousness, but that it was essentially well-rooted
in the concrete realities of village life.

Urs also understood three other things which caused him to
believe that the development of caste associations might help
rather than hinder his efforts to construct a broad-based coalition
of support among disadvantaged groups from the same broad
stratum of society. First, he saw that in the years since 1947, a
great many people from these groups had developed a certain
limited political awareness. They understood many of the implications of the electoral system, and in many — though not all
— parts of the state they were now deciding for themselves how
to vote, and they were often basing their decisions on hopes for
some assistance from the government. Second, he saw that those
hopes — however tenuous — were attended by an awareness that
vokkaligas and *lingayats* had gained an inordinate share of the
resources which the government and ruling party had distributed
in rural areas. He therefore saw that resentment against those
groups might be tapped to unite what were otherwise socially
disparate groups into a coalition. Finally, he realized that in most
parts of Karnataka (particularly in the southern districts from
which he came), his efforts at coalition-building would not be
vitiated by severe antipathies between groups within the broad
stratum at which he was aiming. He saw that no serious impediments existed to an alliance of disadvantaged Hindu groups and
Karnataka's Muslims, most of whom are also disadvantaged.

Above all, he saw that the comparatively less wretched condition — economically and socially — of the Scheduled Castes meant that they were somewhat less alienated from the poorer caste Hindu groups than was the case in most of the rest of India. This was a comparatively cohesive society.

....Urs was above all a *pragmatic* progressive who did what he did because it was the only way that he could achieve and keep power. Therein lies his considerable importance in modern Indian history....

NOTES AND REFERENCES

1. Srinivas, M N, 'The Dominant Caste in Rampura', *American Anthropologist*, vol. lxi, 1959, 1-16
2. Rajapurohit, A. R, *Land Reform and Changing Agrarian Structure in Karnataka*, (mimeographed) Institute for Social and Economic Change, Bangalore, 1982.
3. This comment is based on numerous discussions over several years with Kadilal Majappa. My earlier comments on his land reforms are in Manor, J, 'Pragmatic Progressives in Regional Politics: The Case of Devaraj Urs', *Economic and Political Weekly*, Annual Number, 1980, 201-13.
4. Discussed in greater detail in Manor, J., 'The Dynamics of Political Integration and Disintegration', in Dalton, D. and Wilson, A. (eds.), *State of South Asia: Problems of National Integration*, London, 1982, 89-110.
5. Interview with Devraj Urs, Bangalore, 23 March, 1982.
6. Karnataka Backward Class Commission, *Report*, 4 vols., Bangalore, 1975.

Jana Sangh and Social Interests

BRUCE GRAHAM

The Jana Sangh...was one of a number of non-Congress parties endeavouring to attract various social groups whose material interests were being adversely affected by the policies of Congress governments, both central and state. The Jana Sangh's manifestos reveal that the party had firm views about which sections of society would sympathize with its general approach to questions of social and community relations. At the centre of its focus was a cluster of urban groups, chiefly small industrialists, traders and people on the lower rungs of the professional and administrative hierarchies, but it also saw itself as a party which could represent those sections of the working class employed in small enterprises and in the service industries. Within rural society, besides speaking for small traders, it was prepared to take the side of the peasants against landlords and big farmers....

THE JANA SANGH AS THE PARTY OF SMALL INDUSTRY AND COMMERCE

The Jana Sangh's rhetoric was directed neither to the closed world of the village nor to the open world of India's modern cities but to the middle world between these two extremes, that of the rural towns, the provincial professions, small industry, and country

Excerpted from Bruce Graham, *Hindu Nationalism and Indian Politics*, Cambridge University Press, Cambridge, 1990, 158-95.

trading and banking. The party made much of the precariousness of this middle world, which it characterized as being threatened from two directions: from above, by the competitive individualism and the secular values of capitalism and from below by the first expressions of urban and rural populism, the growing power of caste associations, and the increased militancy of the Communist-led trade unions.

To provide a way forward for those placed in the middle world, the Jana Sangh offered a social ethic which stressed the principles of corporatism and of family solidarity. At a general level it depicted an organic society in which social groups, though dif-ferentiated by their economic functions, were at the same time integrated within the whole community by relations of reciprocity and mutual support instead of being divided by conflict and competition....

Here was an social ethic which abstracted one aspect of caste, the joint-family system, and fused it with some of the positive aspects of capitalism such as enterprise, profit-making and advancement. It provided something of a half-way house between the economic and social restrictiveness of caste and the unrestrained individualism of modern urban life.

Convinced that this ethic was more likely to flourish in modest rather than large firms, the party argued that the organizational principles of small industries were in harmony with Indian social tradition and that they were the best means of providing employ-ment and producing consumer goods. It therefore called upon the government to break up excessive concentrations of private industry and to ensure that small firms were given reserved sectors of the domestic markets and were not placed at a disadvantage in the competition for services, raw materials and licences. Although it supported the nationalization of industries related to essential defence needs, it believed that the state could foster a private-enterprise economy provided that it was prepared to intervene occasionally to protect the weak against the strong....

The Jana Sangh's early policy resolutions had given the impression that its support for small industries involved support for village and cottage industries as well, but [Deendayal]...Upadhyaya began to question the value of government assistance to the latter....

The *Principles and Policy* document of 1965 proclaimed that

Most of the traditional village and cottage industries have ceased to be economic. By use of power and machine they should be rationalised and brought into the category of small industry. Unless their productivity is raised they can not survive. Protection is useful and necessary in the early stages, but it should not become a permanent feature.

It went on to note that artisans

have an important place in the village economy. With the advance of modernisation most of them are being displaced. Arrangements should be made to rehabilitate them.[1]

The 1967 manifesto did not even pretend that the party's championship of small industries was also a defence of the handloom, khadi, village and cottage industries; it simply stated that

Decentralisation, Swadeshi and labour intensity should be the criteria for our industrial development. It will reduce unemployment, inequalities and the foreign exchange shortage and in physical terms our achievement will be greater. Jana Sangh will evolve a pattern suited to the needs and conditions of our country and integrate it with the existing industries. Bharatiya Jana Sangh considers small scale decentralised industries to be most suitable for country's industrialisation. It will, therefore, give priority to small scale mechanised industries and provide them all facilities[2]....

However, although it was possible for the Jana Sangh to generalize about the weaknesses of small industries as a class, it failed to recognize that different categories of small industry faced quite different problems in their relationships with other economic sectors. There were, in fact, three clearly distinguishable categories: firstly, those small factories specializing in various branches of engineering, in chemicals and in scientific instruments, for example, which produced goods for large manufacturing industries and were not in competition with cottage and village industries; secondly, those factories which represented some degree of concentration and rationalizaion in what were mainly specialized handicraft industries, such as the manufacture of brass utensils and ornaments, carpets, lace, carved wood, bangles and pottery; where the skill of the individual artisan was the most valued asset and where factory methods did not threaten the predominantly cottage basis of production to any significant extent; and thirdly, those small units involved in the processing of agricultural, pastoral and forest products in such fields as wheat and rice milling, *dal* manufacture, oil crushing, cotton ginning, leather working and cloth making, in which factories were in direct competition with cottage and village industries for raw materials and primary products, local markets, and local supplies of specialized labour.

When the Jana Sangh went beyond its defence of small industries in general to make an appeal to specific sections, it tended to ignore the second category, the handicraft industries, and to appeal in quite different terms to the first and the third. In addressing the third category, the small agro-industries, it used the language of economic liberalism and, as we have seen, spoke of the need to rationalize village and cottage industries by ending their protected status and making them 'economic' and 'self-reliant'. However, in representing itself as the champion of 'modern' small industries, the first category, it adopted the language of planning and of state-regulated capitalism, arguing that the government had an obligation to help small manufacturing industries in the issue of licences, the allocation of raw materials, the reservation of markets, and the provision of technical and other services. Congress was identified as the villain, too closely bound to big business to respond to the needs of small industries....

In fact, however, both the central and the state governments were paying increasing attention to the needs of small industries, especially during the period of the Second and Third Five-Year Plans (1956-66)....

....While the Jana Sangh's advocacy of the cause of small industries undoubtedly earned it the goodwill and support of individual firms, in general neither small businessmen nor their interest groups were tied closely to the party

The Jana Sangh was also interested in the possibility of establishing a base in the country and market towns among the wholesale and retail traders who bought produce from cultivators and supplied them and the urban population with consumer goods. Traders were better organized than small industrialists and occupied a secure position within the economic structure, but they were threatened by the government's willingness to increase indirect taxation at their expense and by the growing demand that the foodgrains market should be brought under control. They were prepared to face both challenges through their own town-based and regional associations, which were well established and resilient, but they had an obvious interest in searching out allies amongst the non-Congress parties.

In the early 1950s further series of increases in indirect taxation was the most immediate source of anxiety to traders. State governments relied on several sources of taxation income, including land revenue, but they soon found that the most elastic of these was the general tax on the sale of commodities, levied either at a single point of sale or at several points in a chain of distribution, at percentage rates which varied between different classes of goods. Sales taxes were first introduced in Madras Province in 1939-40 and were instituted in most other provinces during the 1940s, but after independence they were increased rapidly and in the tax-year 1959-60· they provided 30.53 per cent of· the total tax revenue in all states.[3] In its early years the Jana Sangh was prepared to attack this system without quarter and its first national session in Kanpur in December 1952 adopted a resolution criticizing the taxation policy of the state governments....

However, in the 1960s the party's pronouncements on sales taxation were considerably toned down. Its 1962 manifesto simply stated that the necessities of life 'shall be exempt from indirect taxes'[4] and the 1967 manifesto, while calling for a taxation inquiry commission, restricted itself to supporting the abolition of sales taxes and other taxes on food articles.[5] This change of emphasis must have been forced on it by expediency: as a party with a reasonable prospect of taking power as a coalition partner in one or two states, it was obliged to discuss issues of general finance in responsible and realistic terms. By the 1960s it would have been quite impossible for an aspiring party of the government to propose the ending of sales taxation without at the same time recommending an increase in either land revenue or state excise rates or both and arousing considerable opposition in the process. Thus constrained, all that the Jana Sangh could offer the traders was the promise of some reform of sales-tax procedures and the abolition of indirect taxes on food and other essential items.

For somewhat different reasons, the Jana Sangh did not form a direct and functional relationship with organized interests in the field of small industry and country trading. The small industrialists' associations, such as the FASII, had no need of a party to mediate between them and the state because they had no difficulty in attaching themselves to the framework of public agencies in the small industries field. As for the traders, they were usually well represented by hardy and resilient associations, often called Beopar (or Vyapar, meaning 'trade' or 'business') Mandals, which were capable of exerting considerable pressure on state ministries and departments without assistance from any political party. What links there were between the party and these two groups were based on their shared outlook; however, the party was not expected to represent their specific material interests beyond certain clearly understood limits.

THE JANA SANGH AS A PARTY OF THE WORKING CLASSES

The Jana Sangh also claimed to speak for two important components of Indian urban society, white-collar workers and industrial employees, but only in terms which were compatible with its essentially corporatist view of social organization. In one sense, the party kept faith with its clientèle in small business by refusing to use the rhetoric of class conflict in its appeals to employees. It began as and remained a party of class conciliation and co-operation.

At first glance, the Jana Sangh's manifestos and policy statements give the impression that the party was prepared to accept industrial relations based on contract. It readily acknowledged the rights of workers to form trade unions, to strike and to use collective bargaining, it supported the establishment of a permanent wage board and a specified national minimum wage, acknowledged the right of labour to share 'in the management and profits of industry', and recommended the use of conciliation and arbitration in the settlement of industrial disputes. At the same time, however, it warned that workers should avoid serving the purposes of the Communists by taking part in strikes or joining trade unions which were against the national interest....

The Jana Sangh's chief aim in the industrial relations field was to gain the allegiance of white-collar workers....

The Jana Sangh and other political parties found difficulty in organizing support amongst government employees because of various conduct rules which governed the latter's conditions of service....

The Government Servants' Conduct Rules prevented trade unions of government employees from affiliating with any general federation, a category which included unions of private employees. Exceptions were made for certain categories of government employees in industry, such as railway servants and civilian employees of the Defence Department, but otherwise organizations such as the National Federation of Post and Telegraph Employees and the Confederation of Central Government Employees were independent of INTUC, AITUC and the other national federations.

Although it was not the only party to support the demands of government employees, the Jana Sangh was always prepared to argue their case in detail. Its first concern was to defend their right to form associations and to have their demands considered within an adequate machinery of negotiation and arbitration....

The Jana Sangh's second concern was to endorse the demands of government employees for an alternation in the terms of their salary payments. The party's 1962 and 1967 election manifestos declared in favour of uniform pay-scales for central, provincial and local government employees and proposed improvements in the methods of awarding increments to take account of price increases (the system of dearness allowances)....

Thirdly, the party was concerned to deal with charges of inefficiency and corruption in government departments. It suggested that the chief fault lay not with the lower ranks but with senior officials, and with the hierarchical nature of the profession....

In general, the Jana Sangh cast its appeals to urban working-class groups within the framework of a corporate ideal of the state, rather than within that of a pluralist or a class-based ideal. It represented politics as a process whereby social groups constitute themselves as corporate entities and enter into co-operative and mutually supportive relations with each other. This approach was at least consistent with its general social philosophy and was presumably acceptable to the party's backers in industry and commerce; it also had some appeal for civil servants, whose employer was the state and who saw in the Jana Sangh an opposition party prepared to press their claims for a less restrictive right of association and for better material rewards. However, such an approach limited the party's ability to appeal to industrial workers who were looking for a rapid and substantial improvement in their income and living conditions, even if this entailed open conflict with their employers and managers. On balance, then, the Jana Sangh was not in a good position to build up a substantial following as a workers' party.

THE JANA SANGH AND REFUGEE INTERESTS

Another group in whose welfare the Jana Sangh claimed to have a special interest was that of the refugees who had emigrated from the areas which had become Pakistan to the towns and cities of northern India....

The Jana Sangh's general policy that India should take a hard line in dealing with Pakistan gained it some sympathy in refugee circles but the government's schemes for rehabilitating and compensating refugees were so comprehensive that the party had little opportunity for acting as a benevolent mediator between refugees and the state. All that it could do was to draw attention to alleged deficiencies in procedures and policies by demanding, for example, better terms of compensation for those with property left behind in Pakistan, more generosity in the allotment and sale of houses to refugees, and more assistance to refugees who were taking up new occupations. It also opposed restrictions on the entry of further immigrants from East Pakistan and criticized the implementation of the Dandakaranya scheme. It is difficult to estimate the extent to which refugees identified themselves with the Jana Sangh as a result of such advocacy. In general, their support for the party was strongest amongst the western immigrants who settled in the towns and cities of north-western India and were drawn towards occupations in small industry, trading and government service....

THE JANA SANGH AND THE POLITICS OF LAND

In the year immediately following independence the central issues in rural politics were not those concerning marketing or credit or production but rather those relating to the tenure and use of land, and it was the Congress Party's land policies which set the standard against which agrarian radicalism and agrarian conservatism were measured. The Congress argued that landlordism should be abolished, that individual peasant proprietorship was the ideal form of land tenure, that land-users should pay land tax (or revenue) direct to the government rather than through intermediaries, and that village panchayats should be fostered in the interests of local democracy. To these ends it proposed that tenants should be given the right to acquire permanent land rights, provided that landlords were duly compensated and allowed to retain some land for personal cultivation, that ceilings should be imposed on the size of landholdings and the surplus redistributed, that scattered holdings should be consolidated into single units, and that co-operative farming should be encouraged for the benefit of poor cultivators. However, the problem of translating these policies into a concrete programme was a formidable one, given that land systems varied so much from region to region and that, under the Constitution of India, land and agriculture, along with taxes on land and agricultural income, had been placed under the legislative competence of the state governments. The task of implementation was therefore effectively delegated to Congress governments at the state level, and these varied considerably in their willingness to proceed with reforms.

The Jana Sangh was formed just at the time when some of these Congress ministries, most notably those in Uttar Pradesh and Bihar, were trying to carry the first wave of legislation into effect and when the landlords were still trying to protect their rights in the courts. In its first election manifesto of 1951, the new party endorsed the principle of individual proprietorship and set out a land policy which came very close to that favoured by moderate Congressmen. The relevant passage stated that

In the interest of increase in production and the betterment of the lot of the actual cultivator the party would take all steps to introduce land reforms so as to make the cultivator 'Kshetrapala', i.e., virtual owner of land. In the interest of the economy of the country the party would abolish Jagirdari and Zamindari as with compensation and distribute the land to tillers. Enough land, however, would be left with such Zamindars and Jagirdars as would settle down as cultivating farmers.[6]

This stand reflected the peculiar rural romanticism of the party's early workers and supporters, who looked on the villages and the country areas generally as places which had kept alive social and religious traditions which had been smothered in the cities and towns of northern India during centuries of Mughal and later British rule. They idealized the simple peasant and, while extending some sympathy to resident Hindu landlords, were generally hostile to the class of absentee landlords, whether Hindu or Muslim, who lived in the towns and sustained an Indo-Persian culture.... ·

Both the First and the Second Five-Year Plan documents recognized that the economic precariousness of small cultivators constituted a problem and proposed that, as a possible solution, the state might provide them with opportunities to form voluntary co-operative associations for credit purposes and for processing, marketing and farming activities, while strengthening village communities on a democratic basis....

Nehru made clear his own commitment to this proposal, despite the lack of enthusiasm for it on the part of the state Congress leaders, and the opposition parties were therefore able to represent the Nagpur resolution as the sign of a major shift in the land policies of the ruling party. The Central Working Committee of the Jana Sangh claimed that the reference to farmers' retaining property rights after the pooling of land was 'futile and misleading', and argued that

such entry of property rights in the books of the farm is farce, since the owners are prevented from operating on their lands as masters with the full rights of disposal and management on their own responsibility and in accordance with their own plan of life.

In actual effect, co-operative farms are not radically different from the next state of collectives after the Russian and Chinese patterns (before the Communes).[7]

The party's Central General Council later decided to stage a campaign in October 1959 against the scheme[8] and its Central Working Committee envisaged this taking the form of conferences aimed at 'awakening the peasantry against inherent dangers of co-operative farming and prepare them for future struggle'.[9]

Both the Jana Sangh and the Swatantra Party were able to exploit for several years the propaganda opening provided by the Nagpur resolution: even as late as the 1962 election campaign Nehru was still referring to the ideal of co-operative farming in his local speeches and the Jana Sangh was continuing to claim that the proposal was 'detrimental to democracy and unsuited to the needs of increasing production per acre of land'.[10] By this stage, however, it was already becoming clear that the Congress Party as a whole was not pressing for major changes in the system of land tenure, and that future reforms would be restricted to the enforcement of ceilings legislation, the consolidation of holdings, and the improvement of tenancy conditions; when it was mentioned, co-operative farming was characterized as a voluntary arrangement, dependent on consent.

By 1963, indeed, the central question in land politics was whether the state Congress governments could continue to surmount the legal obstacles which were being raised against the implementation of the early reforms.... To solve this problem, the Government of India decided to propose the amendment of Article 31A to avoid restrictive interpretations of the term 'estates'.

The result was the Constitution (Seventeenth Amendment) Bill, which was first considered by Parliament in 1963 and which proposed to amend Article 31A (2) so that 'estate' would include any land held under *ryotwari* settlement and indeed any land held or let for agricultural purposes. In December 1963 the Jana Sangh's national session at Ahmedabad declared that this proposal indicated that the Union government was 'seeking powers to seize land from the tiller of the soil under any kind of tenure for any purpose'.

Besides, in view of the Government's objective of collectivisation of agriculture under the guise of co-operative farming, this step cannot be looked at with equanimity. In creates apprehension that this power is being sought by amending the Constitution to put an end to peasant proprietorship and family farming.

The resolution declared the Jana Sangh to be totally opposed to this particular provision and directed all its units 'to organise a mass movement in support of the rights of the tiller to his land and labours'. However, neither the Jana Sangh's opposition not that of the Swatantra Party proved a serious obstacle to the passage of the bill and, having been considered by a joint select committee of the two houses of Parliament, it was finally adopted at a special session of Parliament in June 1964.

As its position on this legislation revealed, the Jana Sangh had by this stage settled for the policy of defending the tenure rights of those peasant proprietors who had been the principal beneficiaries of the land reforms of the 1950s. By keeping open the possibility of a further redistribution of land, however modest, the Congress showed that it was still a reforming party and thus enabled the Jana Sangh and the Swatantra Party to claim that they alone understood the need to strengthen and consolidate the principle of individual proprietorship embodied in the early legislation. The Jana Sangh dressed up this conservative message in radical language....

The party which had once recommended the abolition of *zamindari* and *jagirdari* without compensation was now prepared to envisage the approval of a different form of 'landlordism', that of the peasant proprietor:

There are many farms which remain untilled because of restrictions on subletting. This has affected capital investment also towards the development of land. Bharatiya Jana Sangh will get records corrected and then allow subletting to tenants with uneconomic holdings and to landless farmers.[11]

THE JANA SANGH AND THE POLITICS OF AGRICULTURAL MARKETING

The Jana Sangh at first tended to be more responsive to the interests of traders in foodgrains, moneylenders and small industrialists in the food-processing sector than to the interests of the agricultural producers themselves. In the 1950s it, like the Congress, tended to reduce rural politics to a single issue, that of land ownership, and to argue that the chief aim of the state should be to provide land to the tiller, as if this action alone would create the conditions for increased production and higher returns for the peasant cultivator.

However, it was quite impossible for any political party to ignore the importance of peasant agriculture, which formed the life of the great majority of the Indian people....

The Jana Sangh's early manifestos envisaged the state intervening to foster and protect a traditional scheme of peasant agriculture rather than to produce a system of modern farming capable of reducing the power of the moneylenders and the grain traders at the level of the village economy. Thus although the party's 1957 election manifesto, for example, spoke of establishing cottage and village industries, cooperative banks, and schemes of insurance for the villagers and for their crops and cattle, it dealt with the central problem — of increasing yields and profits for peasants — as if it were basically one of motivation. It mentioned steps to supply better seeds and manure but declared that the use of chemical fertilizers would be discouraged, as would the use of tractors for 'normal ploughing purposes'. The manifesto said that the party would try to establish parity between the prices of agricultural and industrial products, but did not mention the possibility of price incentives for farmers or of marketing reforms. The task of increasing productivity was assigned to 'country-wide campaigns' by means of which peasants would be 'encouraged and enthused to work harder for increased yield'.[12] By comparison, the corresponding passages in the Jana Sangh's manifestos for the 1962 and 1967 elections had become bland, technical and 'modern' in their style and prescriptions; they no longer declared against chemical fertilizers and tractors, and even proposed advance-price arrangements for the government purchase of farm produce.[13]....

Thus, in formulating its agrarian policy, the Jana Sangh faced a dilemma: on the one hand it wanted to demonstrate that it was a modern party, capable of making rational and constructive proposals for the improvement of the conditions surrounding peasant agriculture, but on the other it was anxious to demonstrate its faith in traditional practices and arrangements. As a result it seldom took a clear stand on an issue but was inclined to balance mild prescriptions for increased public control with arguments that the peasant should be left to work out his destiny without interference. Postponement of choice was possible only so long as the Congress Party was similarly cautious in its agrarian policies, but once Congress began to edge towards more radical measures the Jana Sangh was forced to reveal its conservatism. This pattern can be illustrated most clearly in the politics of agricultural marketing in the 1950s and 1960s....

CONCLUSION

The nature of the Jana Sangh's sectional appeals throws some interesting light on its assumptions about the function of the state in regulating social and economic life. Claiming that producer- and consumer-groups could achieve a harmonious relationship within a corporate framework of society, it treated each group as if it were, potentially, an integral part of an organic whole; that is to say, it assumed that each group had its own function to perform within a social system in which the relations between groups were reciprocal and mutually beneficial. The party saw small industry not as a residual category within the industrial structure but as coherent economic sector which drew upon the talents and skills of local entrepreneurs and met important consumer demands; it treated peasant proprietors not as petty producers but as small farmers who were perfectly capable of supplying sufficient foodgrains for the country's needs, provided that the government offered them the appropriate assistance and incentives; and it depicted the grain trade as an established business profession capable of making foodgrain markets work for the benefit of the community. Of course, the Jana Sangh acknowledged that certain conflicts of interest would have to be resolved to establish a fully functional relationship between the various groups within society; it took account of those conflicts which separated small industry from large industry, peasants from landlords, and traders from producers and consumers but regarded the state as a mechanism within which they would be minimized and controlled.

None the less, the party's corporatism was partial; it tended to offer the extension of the state's protective and regulatory framework specifically to those activities which it valued most highly within the economic structure — small industries, country trading and small-scale peasant agriculture — and to ignore social groups on the margins. To take some examples: the party's proposal that the state should help small industries in various ways was accompanied (in the 1962 election manifesto and in the 1965 *Principles and Policy* document in particular) by suggestions that village and cottage industries should be 'rationalised'; the party had very little to say about the provision of economic security for poor peasants and agricultural labourers beyond expressing its support for ceilings legislation; and its strong opposition to the joint cooperative farming proposal of 1959 showed that it had no wish to see the state go further towards incorporating the rural poor within the organized economy.

The Jana Sangh's appeals to groups of workers were more complex, but held to the same pattern. In this case, the need for corporate solidarity was attributed not to the workers as a group but to industry as a form of social organization; the party assumed that workers and employers should be bound together by a reciprocal, family-like relationship and that, as an organic unit, they would develop functional ties with other groups in society. The formation of the Bharatiya Mazdoor Sangh as a trade union associated with the party was justified on the grounds that it would serve to regulate and settle industrial disputes within an ordered framework of common values and thus prevent the growth of class conflict.

The deficiencies of the Jana Sangh's social strategy go a long way towards explaining its comparative lack of electoral success in the 1950s and 1960s. In the first place, its preferred interest base was an extremely narrow one and could not have produced electoral majorities except in a limited category of constituencies; a party which was directing its appeals mainly to small industrialists and traders, and, more generally, to the lower-middle classes to the northern towns and cities was concentrating on a potential clientéle which was relatively small and comparatively isolated. When the party turned to address other more substantial social groups, such as the peasants and the workers, its statements of interest were inevitably coloured by its sensitivity to the values of its essential reference groups. In the second place, it was over-cautious in formulating its economic policies and was reluctant to strike out on its own. Although it stood up to the Congress on some issues, such as the 1959 proposal for joint co-operative farming and the demand for the complete nationalization of the foodgrains trade, it generally conformed to the government's line on economic policy. It could, for example, have formulated radical taxation policies instead of accepting the notion that land revenue and sales- and excise-taxes were the most reliable sources of public revenue at state level; or, anticipating the position taken later by the Swatantra Party, it could have come out much more strongly in the mid-1950s for a thorough-going liberalization of the domestic economy. Even the party's corporatism was presented in a hesitant and partial way, rather than as a systematic and convincing philosophy. For all its criticism of the ruling party, the Jana Sangh was very much a prisoner of the Congress Raj, accepting many of its economic and social values and unwilling to explore the possibility of a direct and radical attack on its basic assumptions about how the economy should be managed.

Notes and References

1. Bharatiya Jana Sangh (BJS), *Principles and Policy*, New Delhi, 1965, 37-8.
2. BJS, *Election Manifesto*, 1962, 1967, 22-3.
3. National Council of Applied Economic Research, *Techno-Economic Survey of Uttar Pradesh*, 324-6 (table 105).
4. BJS, *Election Manifesto*, 1962, 21.
5. BJS, *Election Manifesto*, 1967, 18, 25-6.
6. BJS, *Manifesto*, 1951, 5.
7. *BJS Documents*, vol. II, 64-6, quote from p. 65.
8. Ibid, 68-9.
9. *Hindustan Times*, 23 September, 1959, 10.
10. BJS, *Election Manifesto*, 1962, 16.
11. BJS, *Election Manifesto*, 1967, 19-20.
12. BJS, *Election Manifesto*, 1957, 15-16.
13. BJS, *Election Manifesto*, 1962, 13-16, and 1967, 17-21.

FURTHER READINGS

Kochanek, Stanley, *The Congress Party of India: The Dynamics of One-Party Democracy*, Princeton University Press, Princeton, 1968.

A detailed sociological study of politics of the Congress Party, and its broader relation with the functioning of the state in India. The account is of what was known once as 'the Congress system'. The present structure of the Indian party system is very different from that system, as the Congress has lost its general legitimacy and its centrality in the political process.

Brass, Paul R., *Factional Politics in an Indian State: The Congress Party in Uttar Pradesh*, University of California Press, Berkeley, 1965.

An excellent sociological account of how the Congress party functioned in one of the most crucial states, since the dominance of the Congress in the central legislature depended on the support it enjoyed in UP.

Kothari, Rajni, *Politics in India*, Orient Longman, Delhi, 1970.

The most influential account of the operation of 'the Congress system', which remains important for its excellent exposition of the 'one-party dominant' party structure, and its social bases.

Morris-Jones, W.M., *Politics Mainly Indian*, Orient Longman, 1978.

A series of perceptive essays on the operation of the political system, ranging from its political culture to the military, and with some acute analyses of crucial elections.

Franda, Marcus, *Radical Politics in West Bengal*, MIT Press, Cambridge, Mass, 1971.

A study of radical politics in West Bengal which investigates the social roots of the movement instead of focusing exclusively on political programmes and policies.

Banerjee, Sumanta, *In the Wake of Naxalbari: A History of the Naxalite Movement in India*, Subarnarekha, Calcutta, 1980.

An excellent overall account of the history of the Naxalbari movement which seeks to analyse its historical context and sociological origins, and covers its political evolution.

Ostor, Akos, *Culture and Power*, Sage Publications, Delhi, 1984.

An interesting anthropological study of everyday life in a town dominated by leftwing ideology and political power.

Jaffrelot, Christopher, *The Hindu Nationalist Movement and Indian Politics*, C Hurst, London, 1996.

Probably the most detailed historical account of the rise and growth of Hindu nationalism in India. It covers the politics of the demolition of the Babri Masjid, and the recent electoral results of the BJP.

VI

Sociology of Religion

Among the social forces which affect political life in India, religion is clearly one of the most significant. It is essential to understand the historical transformations in the nature of religious practices and of religious communities for several reasons. In conventional sociology of modernization, religion was seen as an unambiguously traditional force. There is nothing wrong in this, unless tradition is seen as unchanging, affecting social behaviour of people deeply precisely by its power to remain obstinately static. This view of tradition is now undergoing serious revision, and it is recognized that religion, like other social practices also has 'history'. More specifically, it appears that the power of traditional forms lay precisely in their adaptability and flexibility; they were able to change in response to historically altered circumstances — often surreptitiously, without formal declaration. Sometimes traditional structures contain mechanisms which erase the evidence of change after these have taken place, producing an illusory quality of changelessness. It is hardly surprising, given this view of what traditions are really like, that they would also respond and adapt to the pressures of political modernity.

In many pre-modern societies, religious doctrine determined the role of political power. In the Hindu system, ordinarily, the caste order could not be altered by the power of the state; rather, those who had power had to abide by rules of the caste order in important respects. Modernity generally engenders process of secularization of society in which first some aspects of social practice are taken out of the control of religious rules; and subsequently, if western experience is any indication, the practices of religious communities come under the supervision of secular laws enacted by the state. It is at least plausible to argue that the relation between religion and state, as two sources of providing the general rules by which a society has to live, has been turned around through the forces of modernity.

In India as well, one of the main features of modernity was a fundamental change in the character of religious communities. Through processes of modern enumeration, census and mapping, religious communities came to have much clearer self-perception. This was helped in part by the influence of Orientalist knowledge which drove the thinking of colonial administrations. Europeans saw Indian society as strange, and essentially different from their own, and considered religious communities as fundamental to Indian social life and political behaviour. Colonialist politicians also encouraged clearer self-definition of the major religious communities with the belief that their resultant conflict would make the colonial authority an essential mediator between them and help preserve colonial power. All sides to the political conflicts of the twentieth century found ways of dealing with the unprecedented power of these religious communities risen to a sudden self-recognition and feeling of political agency. There were four different strands of political thinking within Indian nationalism about the relation between religion and state power. The first two were Hindu and Muslim communalism, which saw religion as the basis of nationhood and thought, quite consistently, that it was impossible for the two communities to live in a mixed state. The result of the second trend was the creation of Pakistan; but the power of Hindu nationalism inside the Congress was also quite considerable. Gandhi's thought represented a third strand. It considered religion to be central to social and political life, but believed that most religions advocated tolerance and mutual respect. He therefore wanted the state to be based on principles of religious tolerance, which he saw as a common feature of all religions. A fourth trend was a modern atheistic secularism adopted by liberals like Nehru and leftists like the communists. Although the practical suggestions of the third and the fourth view were very similar, these were based on significantly different principles.

Secondly, the immense historical event of the Partition determined the nature of constitutional arrangements in India. Revulsion against the horrors of the Partition riots, the murder of Gandhi by a Hindu communalist, and apprehension about further communal mobilization came together to provide the context for the adoption of a secular constitution, extremely careful about the protection of the rights of religious minorities. This constitutional order was not able to prevent small-scale rioting and occasional tension, but for a long time explicitly communal political groups remained ineffective in national politics. The future of communal politics seemed so unpromising at one point that the Jana Sangh agreed to merge into the Janata Party after the Emergency.

The last decade has seen a sudden and unexpected revival of Hindu communal politics, most prominently through the successes of the BJP. Communalism had conventionally been associated with the power of tradition, the alleged unwillingness of religious people to accept modern notions of secular democratic politics. Yet the career of communal politics in India raises many doubts about this simple thesis. Leading political figures engaged in the inflammatory use of religious divides were not necessarily themselves religious people. Also, if communalism is to be attributed to the power of traditional superstitions, it should have been more powerful at the time of independence, and not emerged as a major political force after fifty years of unfolding of economic and political modernity. In the last decade at least three different types of re-assertion of religious identities can be observed. First, there is a sudden and spasmodic rise of Hindu communalism through the BJP, but careful analysis would show that other parties have not been entirely above using Hindu communal sentiments. Political parties which do not base their electoral appeal predominantly on the sensitivities of religious communities, have often, for short-term reasons used them. On the other side, the politics of militancy in Punjab and Kashmir bear some relation with Sikh and Muslim religious identities. Clearly, the majority and minority communalisms reinforce and justify each other, not least because the militant minorities wish to assert majoritarian control over their own regions, if they are able to establish their power.

It is difficult to account for this upsurge of communal passion after forty years of modified success of capitalism and democracy. And it is particularly odd for the conventional way of making a clear binary distinction between traditional and modern forms of social practice. Several, occasionally conflicting, explanations have been offered for this surprising re-emergence of communal politics. It has been forcefully argued by T.N. Madan that institutions of secularism are inextricably linked to dualistic conceptions internal to Christianity. Since Christian doctrine recognised the distinction between the domains of the spiritual and the mundane, this facilitated the eventual development of secular ideas about division of jurisdiction between the church and the state. Besides, a secular constitution which denied religion any significant role in public affairs was at odds with popular common sense in a deeply religious society. Secularism can thus be seen as an ideal of a small highly westernized élite which sat uneasily on a society dominated by religious beliefs. Ashis Nandy has suggested that the brand of political intolerance that marks communal politics does not stem from traditional religious practice, but rather from modern ideas of using the state for political purposes. Communalism, in this view, is a *modern* phenomenon, associated with the specific pathological forms of violence related to modern states, rather than an expression of *traditional* religion, which is held, somewhat romantically, to have been essentially tolerant.

There can be several counter-arguments to this line of thought. First, the essential premise of Madan's well-known essay, reproduced here, is that a secular state requires a secular society, and is a reflection of its preferences. But the historical experience of the West can be interpreted differently. Secularism is a political ideal or doctrine, but secularization was a long historical process which passed through different equilibria. The idea of a secular state arose first in early modern Europe as a response to the danger of perpetual religious civil wars. The theoretical argument suggested that if a society was deeply religious but divided, it was natural for people to expect that public affairs of the whole society should be governed by the principles which their religion commanded people to obey. But if such principles differed between various religious communities, societies would suffer endless political strife precisely because religious principles were held to be fundamental by believers. In this case, the only solution to perpetual civil war was to ensure that the state did not consider the religious beliefs of its subjects as relevant. If this reading of Western history is correct, then the opposite of Madan's thesis is true. A secular state is required precisely because society is not only deeply religious, but also divided. A secular state would thus appear particularly appropriate for India, if religious strife is to be avoided. But there is obvious truth in what Madan asserts if it is applied to modern secularised western societies, which have secular states. But here too, the example of modern Britain leads to a different conclusion. Britain does have a state religion; but since British society is secularized, it does not matter that the state is not. The historical experience of the West can thus be read in a way that offers exactly the opposite conclusions to Madan's.

There are important and interesting differences between those who regard communalism as a force of tradition and others who attribute it to modernity. Nandy's argument suggests that traditional religious communities engaged in less violent transactions principally due to a doctrinal adherence to principles of tolerance. Undoubtedly, in all religious doctrines there are teachings of tolerance; but it appears misleading to deny that, equally, religious doctrines also justify exclusivism and a firm belief that one's own religion is superior to others. The more peaceable relations between religious communities in pre-modern times can then be attributed to more sociological causes, like the relative insignificance of the traditional state, or the unenumerated character of the social world. However, it would be irresponsible not to recognize that modernist beliefs can also exhibit aggressively uncritical and in that sense 'fundamentalist' qualities which can bring forth an equally fundamentalist reaction from religious believers. But whether the rise of Hindu communalism is a response of an embittered and endangered group is a matter of serious debate. They constitute the largest religious community, and therefore, could not be encircled like a minority. The Indian state did not engage in an atheistic campaign against its principles or observances, except on the matter of untouchability. In any case, this debate has serious practical implications for politics. If communalism is based in tradition, it can be expected to weaken over the long run; if, on the contrary, it is caused by forces of modernity itself, it can be expected to continue. If the historical longevity of traditions is to be explained by their adaptability then religious practices could also adapt to circumstances of modernity rather than simply wither away. There is also the question of what can be the nature of the impact of the contemporary irruption of communal politics. It is possible that the forces of Hindu communalism represented by the BJP might not become overwhelmingly strong in electoral terms and gather enough support to alter the fundamental pattern of political life in India. For it has to contend with very serious obstacles. Most other parties would combine against it. Its attempt to unify the Hindu vote might be wrecked by the contending effort of the lower castes to mobilize a different type of consolidation. Its own attempt to unify and homogenize Hinduism goes against the historical logic of doctrinal and iconic pluralism of the Hindu faith. However, its effect can be more insidious and far reaching. It is possible that the electoral fortunes of the communal parties may decline, but communalism might affect the everyday 'common sense' of Indian society.

The readings in this section are more numerous than the earlier ones simply because of the practical importance of this question in current Indian politics. The reading from Chandra illustrates the orthodox Marxist view that communalism is a case of 'false consciousness', and it really represents a distorted manifestation of fundamental economic and class interests. Pandey does not reduce communalism to a simple expression of economic interests, and emphasizes the historical understanding of the processes of formation of this 'imagination'. Madan and Nandy offer critiques of the practices and theoretical bases of Indian secularism, though their arguments diverge at important points. Oberoi's paper offers a detailed account of the imaginative world of Sikh fundamentalism. But the argument about secularism is not just a sociological problem; most arguments cross over into theoretical disputation of its major principles and premises. Bilgrami's essay provides a theoretical justification for secularism in the Indian context.

Communalism as False Consciousness

BIPAN CHANDRA

Basically, communalism was one of the byproducts of colonialism, of the colonial character of the Indian economy, of colonial underdevelopment and, in recent years, of the failure and incapacity of capitalism to develop the economy and society. Colonialism provided the social structure which produced communalism and in which it could grow.... This was particularly true of the impact of colonialism on the middle classes, which were, in particular, torn by fears, jealousies and frustration.

First of all, I would like to draw attention to the middle class or petty bourgeois base of communalism under conditions of relative economic stagnation.

Throughout the twentieth century, in the absence of the development of modern industries and modern social and cultural services, such as education, health services, the press, libraries, music, dance, drama, radio and films, and because of shrinking governmental expenditure, there existed extremely poor and worsening economic opportunities and increasing unemployment, especially for the educated middle and lower middle classes who

Excerpted from Bipan Chandra, *Communalism in Modern India*, Vikas, New Delhi, 1984, 34-54.

could not fall back on land and who found government jobs to
be getting scarce and the professions overcrowded....

Furthermore, the distorted pattern of the colonial economy,
which continues in some aspects till this day, produced a large
middle or service or tertiary sector which was neither integrated
with the productive sectors nor capable of being productively
absorbed by the colonial economy or by underdeveloped
capitalism today. In other words, the growth of the middle classes
constantly outpaced economic development. There was,
moreover, an acute shortage of superior jobs carrying high salaries
and social status, most of these being reserved for Europeans till
the 1920s. This led to intense competition for those remaining.

....The lower middle classes were increasingly placed in a position of economic misery, lack of opportunity, constant threat to
their existing position and increasing breakdown of their class
position and social status and value systems. A certain edge and
urgency was imparted to their worldly struggle to maintain their
class position and identity. In fact, this struggle became increasingly sharp and even bitter though often also frustrating. This
frustration, a sense of social deprivation and a constant fear of
loss of identity and status often created an atmosphere of violence
and brutality which when triggered off by a religious issue led
to communal riots. The petty bourgeois identity and ego got tied
up with the cow or *peepal* tree protection and music before a
mosque; protection of such supposed rights — a cow must not
be sacrificed, a music procession before a mosque must become
silent — was seen as a life-and-death question because it came
to represent symbolically the preservation or destruction of the
petty bourgeois ego.

In this social situation of the potential or actual loss of their
old world by the middle classes, the far-sighted intelligentsia,
the national movement, left-wing groups and parties, and other
popular movements worked for the long-term radical solution
of the social condition by the overthrow of colonialism and the
restructuring of the social system and the national economy....

But those individuals and sections of the middle classes who
lacked a wider social vision or faith in the capacity of the national
and social movements to transform the reality within a reasonable
span of time, when faced with an immediate social and personal

condition, looked to their narrow immediate interests and sought short-term solutions to their individual problems....

Because of economic stagnation, middle-class Indians were compelled to compete with each other for scarce opportunities and resources. There existed a perpetual and increasingly intense, tough and unhealthy competition among individuals for jobs, in professions, and among traders and shopkeepers for customers.... Every available means was used in this competition, and no weapon was too lowly if it could bring success within one's grasp....

But to give their struggle a wider fighting ground, the middle classes also used other group identities, such as caste, province, region and religion, to enhance the individual's capacity to compete through a group....

Thus, the crisis of the colonial economy and society constantly generated two opposing sets of ideologies and political tendencies among the petty bourgeoisie. On the one hand, when social change and revolution appeared as immediate possibilities — for example, the slogan of Swaraj in one year or Quit India — the petty bourgeoisie enthusiastically joined the struggle for the radical transformation of their existing social condition and therefore also of society. It then took up the cause and demands of the entire society from the capitalists to the peasants and workers.... On the other hand, when revolutionary change receded into the background, ...the petty bourgeoisie shifted to short-term considerations and advantages, to the struggle for individual survival, to egoistic and selfish politics, that is, to the strategy of trying to recover or maintain the existing social position....

Groupings around religion leading to communalism, and other similar groupings and ideologies, could and did play an important role in this struggle. The enemy was a group which could be collectively dislodged to improve one's personal position as a member of an alternative group. Or one promoted a group whose membership would enable one to maintain a situation with a better opportunity and opposed a group whose entry would reduce one's own opportunity.... Consequently, in colonial India, the struggle of the individuals within the middle classes and their desire to find scapegoats acquired mainly a communal form in the end.

....The competition for jobs among individuals could be given the turn of being a struggle between two 'communities', even though the colonial underdevelopment which had led to and intensified this competition was affecting both Hindus and Muslims equally and simultaneously. The larger proportion of Hindus in jobs in an area could be declared to be 'Hindu economic domination', while the larger share of Muslims in the same jobs could be pronounced a 'Muslim threat' to the 'Hindu position'....

The colonial economy had one other particular aspect that favoured communal politics. In the absence of openings in industrial and commercial establishments, social services, and the fields of culture and entertainment, government or municipal bodies' service was the main avenue of employment, especially for the educated middle and lower middle classes who possessed little capital or land....

Sectional groupings around individual interests became particularly important when competition over government jobs, educational opportunities, contracts, etc., occurred, for they involved administrative action and therefore politics directly. Political power could not, however, be thrown into the scale till some wider group was formed. But once formed, communalism could be most 'fruitful' in this sphere, especially when encouraged by the government. For this reason, constitutional reforms increased the rivalry among upper and middle classes. Even the petty political and administrative power devolved under them could now be used as a counter in the struggle. It is therefore not accidental that the communal struggle occurred mostly over government jobs, educational concessions, etc., and the political positions in the legislative councils and municipal bodies which enabled control over them.

Almost all the basic guarantees that the communal leaders demanded for their 'communities' referred to these two aspects. Moreover, the dependence of the middle classes on government services, educational facilities, contracts, etc., placed the crucial levers of patronage in the hands of the colonial state and the communal leaders capable of influencing appointments from within or without the administration. This patronage could be used to encourage communalism and discourage nationalism among the job-hungry middle classes....

Some individuals from the middle classes did, in the short run, benefit from communalism, especially in a relatively stagnant economy and in the field of government employment. this gave a certain 'validity' to communal politics which enabled one to improve one's chances in government service. This partly explains why communal propaganda succeeded among the middle classes....

The middle class tendency to think and act communally combined with the greater weight of the middle classes in Indian politics in general and in the national movement in particular tended to weaken the nationalist struggle for secularism and against communalism....

Jawaharlal Nehru was in this sense quite right in suggesting that communalism was an inherent weakness of a national movement largely based on the middle classes. In other words, the Congress would have found it easier to engage in a resolute struggle against communalism if the centre of gravity of its social and ideological base had been shifted from the petty bourgeoisie to the mass of the peasantry and the working class; or if it had possessed control over the social condition so that the petty bourgeoisie could be rescued from the socio-economic dead-end which led it to take to communal politics. The third alternative was to undertake an intense educative ideological and political campaign among the petty bourgeoisie.

It was also perhaps politically counter-productive to carry on negotiations with communal leaders on the question of communal reservations in government services, educational institutions, etc. These negotiations enabled the communal leaders to emerge in the public eye as the champions of the 'interests' of their respective 'communities'. Moreover, they led even secular leaders to get contaminated with communalism and to think in terms of their 'communities'. Any debate or discussion with the communalists in these terms meant playing into the hands of the communal leaders and the colonial rulers who were practising the policy of reservations.

The failure to fight communalism and communal-type movements in post-independence India, Pakistan and Bangladesh can also perhaps be best explained on a similar basis. Even political parties which have been fully free of the communal-type outlook, ideologies and politics have failed to do so effectively because of the fear of alienating their petty bourgeois base. Instead they have tended either to compromise with communal-type movements or to keep quiet, preferring to let the whirlwind blow over.

The middle classes formed the main mass social base of communalism for one other reason. The middle class individuals alone had the capacity to move up or down socially as individuals; in their case alone could personal motives and social questions be integrated. Other numerically significant social classes could do so only on the basis of class. Thus, workers and peasants could not benefit form communalism in any way. Communalism could not be an inherent property of these social classes....

....In fact, there were no communal interests, only individual interests masquerading as such. This is what we mean when we say that communalism neither comprehended the problem correctly nor provided a correct solution — it represented a false consciousness of the reality....

....There could be no final solution to the communal problem within the colonial situation and the existing social order. This does not mean that communalism and such other social phenomena should not be opposed. They should be and can'be opposed successfully but with a clear recognition that they will not totally disappear from the social scene so long as the social soil for them remains fertile. Till the economy starts developing and the petty bourgeoisie loses its predominance over the political and social ethos, such phenomena and ideologies would continue to appear and grow, and, when not vigorously opposed politically and ideologically, even prevail.

Communalism as Construction

GYANENDRA PANDEY

Historical reconstructions...were clearly part of a more general assertion of community and status by many different groups and classes. What such assertions and counter-assertions did, paradoxically, was to transform the very sense of 'community' and redefine it at every level. In an earlier period the discourse of community had perhaps been stronger, in the sense of being more universal and unchallenged by any other discourse. At the same time, however, the sense of the individual community had also been 'fuzzier' — capable of apprehension at several different levels (sub-caste, sect, dialect and other regional or religious groupings) and not greatly concerned with numbers or the exact boundaries between one community and the next. Much of this survived...into the late-nineteenth and even the twentieth century. But the balance of forces was against its long survival in the old form.

The new 'communities' were now often territorially more diffuse than before, less tied to a small locality, less parochial, on account of the changes in communications, politics and society more generally. They were at the same time historically more self-conscious, and very much more aware of the differences between themselves and others, the distinctions between 'Us' and 'Them'. The new 'community', or 'enumerated community'...also became increasingly a part of a rationalist discourse — centrally

Excerpted from *Construction of Communalism in Colonial North India*, OUP, Delhi, 1990.

concerned with numerical strength, well-defined boundaries, exclusive 'rights' and, not least, the community's ability to mount
purposive actions in defence of those rights.

Once again, this is not to suggest that collective actions in
defence of a community's claimed or assumed rights had never
occurred before. But the explicit statement of objects and rights
now became a feature of such actions, their scale expanded, and
they brought diverse 'communities' into more and more frequent
confrontation with state. In Mubarakpur, ...opposition to the
encroachments of the state constituted an important aspect of
the local community's acts of resistance in the nineteenth century.
It is noteworthy that in the long-drawn-out dispute between the
Hindus and Muslims that followed the building of a *shivalaya* in
the *qasba* in 1877, the state had ultimately to back down under
the pressure, as it were, of the 'traditions' of Mubarakpur. This
in spite of the expressed opinions of the officials on the spot
(most of whom, in 1877, happened to be Hindus) and the British
District Officer's initial decision to let the *shivalaya* stand — on
the ground that it was inside the compound of a Hindu
moneylender's house and that the buildings round about were
mainly the dwellings of other Hindus.

....The threat of violence weighed heavily with the administration in their reversal of this initial position. The Muslims pointed
out repeatedly that since the *qasba* was established, there had
never been a temple or *shivalaya* inside the habitation. The one
instance when this tradition was ignored led to the nine days
and nights of bloodshed that occurred in 1813....

A similar retreat by the state occurred after the Banaras outbreak
of 1891. What was in question here, as in so many other areas,
was the right of the state to intervene where it had not intervened
before. Such intervention created new grounds of contention, and
focused the question of who was to have control over a whole
range of activities in a whole range of areas — 'government' or
'public', and, implicitly, which 'public'? The Age of Consent Bill,
the demolition of a temple in Darbhanga, the proposal to demolish
the Banaras temple, the decision to close the access road to the
public — these events, coming in quick succession, brought matters to a boiling-point in Banaras.

Following the resulting confrontation, the administration was
forced to back down in this instance too. Large numbers of Hindus

and Muslims in Banaras were united in their anger and resistance to this colonial encroachment. The Municipal Councillors who had acquiesced in the administration's plans were widely condemned and written off as 'toadies' and traitors; some of them also had their property attacked in the riots....

We have seen a striking example of such resistance by the community at a much earlier date, in the Banaras anti-house-tax hartal and dharna of 1810-11. The boundaries between the rights of the state and the rights of the community were not easily settled, then or later. Nor were those between the rights of different communities, or indeed of different sections within the same community; and frequently the struggle to establish the boundary between one set of contestants spilled over into struggles regarding boundaries between other sets of contestants as well. In the following pages, I examine one of the more conspicuous examples of such a struggle in the period under study — the attempt to define the identity and assert the rights of the 'Hindu community' at large in the later-nineteenth and early-twentieth centuries, through concerted action to protect the cow as a symbol of the Hindu religion and, hence, of the 'community'. In this, as in other instances of this kind, however, the attempted demonstration of unity also showed up the fissures in the community, and pointed to the persistence of other unities and solidarities that often acted in defiance of the unities sought to be established here.

The contradictory processes and tendencies that went to make up the struggle to establish an all India 'Muslim community' have attracted considerable scholarly notice. The parallel struggle to forge a united 'Hindu community', with its own organizations and representatives, has received rather less attention — presumably because this 'community' was far more numerous, more widely dispersed, and, plainly, less in need of presenting the kind of 'unity' that sections of the Indian Muslim community were constrained to seek....

....Cow-Protection was of special importance, too, as the scholars have noted, in bridging the gap between urban and rural Hindus and élite and popular levels of 'communalism'.[1] The question I wish to ask here is *how* all this happened: what did the call for cow-protection amount to, and how was it received by different sections of the putative Hindu community?...

....Some recent writers have sought to distinguish two phases

in the Cow-Protection movement — an urban and a rural, corresponding perhaps to a less militant phase, under a moderate,
'upper class' leadership, and a more militant one that was guided
by 'extremist' leaders from less privileged backgrounds.[2] One
writer has also suggested that the movement in its earlier, urban
phase was more unambiguously 'ideological', i.e. concerned with
religion, distinction between people on grounds of religion and
attacks upon people of other religious persuasions. It is said that
this 'ideological' component of Cow-Protection activities was not
quite so marked in the country-side, concerns were more parochial
in this later phase and the villains of the piece in Cow-Protection
propaganda included a whole variety of local castes, Hindu as
well as Muslim.[3]

There is some evidence as well that the Cow-Protection movement became more aggressive as it advanced from the 1880s to
the 1890s and from Punjab and the Central Provinces to eastern
U.P. and Bihar, although this shift did not correspond very closely
to a move from 'urban' to 'rural'. The great majority of the Gaurakshini Sabhas not only in Punjab and the Central Provinces, where
no major violent clashes occurred, but also in the areas where
serious riots broke out in the 1890s, were established in order to
set up *gaushalas* (homes for sick and aged or deserted cattle) and
propagate the usefulness of cattle and the religious and other
reasons for protecting the cow. They gained support not only
from prominent Hindu *rajas* and landlords, traders and bankers,
but also from Hindu officials, honorary magistrates and members
of local boards and, in the form of attendance and participation
at Cow-Protection meetings, even from Muslim and English local
officials. Many of these wealthy and highly-placed patrons appear
to have taken a back-seat as the Gaurakshini Sabhas became more
militant, turned to coercive practices and threatened 'law and
order'....

Whatever the actual motives and sympathies of the great *rajas*
and landlords, the experience of their withdrawal from the lime-
light, along with that of sundry titled folk, English and Muslim
officials, honorary magistrates and other aspirants to colonial
patronage, was widespread; and the initiative in organizing Cow-
Protection activities in the late 1880s and 1890s passed to people
who were described officially as 'half-educated English-speaking
agitators', small *zamindars*, professionals and traders with little

direct bureaucratic connection, and a motley crew of *swamis, sanyasis* and *fakirs* whose propaganda proved to be remarkably effective. 'One "Pahuari Baba" did more in a month to stir up disaffection [in the Patna Division]', wrote Anthony Macdonnell, Lieutenant-Governor of Bengal, Bihar and Orissa in 1893, 'than the whole Native Press has probably done in a year'.[4]

The suggestion made by Sandria Frietag that with this move from lesser to greater militancy ('urban' to 'rural'?), the Cow-Protection movement also moved from a stronger 'ideology', greater clarity about requirement of 'religion', to a more diffuse, parochial and, as it were, pragmatic appeal, seems to be more questionable. There are often specific, local conflicts that feed into wider movements which may explain the choice of particular targets for attack or the active participation of particular groups of people....

....But the general proposition that pre-existing contradictions — quarrels between landowners, tension between weavers and moneylenders, anger against shopkeepers or officials or police — feed into wider political movements applies as much to urban areas as to rural.

Frietag's other evidence for the 'parochial' concerns of 'rural' Cow-Protection — that in Gorakhpur, the Cow Protectionists attacked the travelling and trading groups of Nats and Banjaras and the untouchable Chamars, along with the Muslims[5] — cuts both ways. Rather than representing a concession to some local resentments, in fact, these attacks appear to me to represent the demand of an increasingly aggressive and determined movement that all erring Hindus ('betrayers') must fall into line — those (like the Nats and Banjaras) who might conduct cattle from one place to another for sale to the commissariat or to individual non-Hindus, and those (like the Chamars) who sometimes responded to the degraded position assigned to them in Hindu society as cow-herds, lifters of carcasses and curers of animal-skins by turning to cattle poisoning and the sale of cattle skins.

In any case, none of the evidence from the militant, 'rural' phase of the Cow-Protection movement suggests any lessening of the religious element in the appeal to the Hindus. Pratap Narayan Mishra's Kanpur monthly, *Brahman*, stressed in the 1880s that Cow-Protection was the supreme *dharma* of the Hindu, that the wealth of Hindustan too was largely dependent upon the welfare of the cow, and that without Cow-Protection the 'Hindu nation' and the country of 'Hindus' could never prosper. Mishra wrote also that the supreme importance of *gaumata*, the 'Mother Cow', was attested to by the invocation, 'Gaubrahman', in which Hindus made their obeisance to the cow even before they bowed their heads to the repositories of the faith, 'those who are venerated universally', the Brahmans.[6] The 'rural' literature of the later phase of Cow-Protection — poorly printed leaflets, pictures and 'snowball' (or relay) letters — did nothing to dilute this religious appeal focussed on the cow as mother: on the contrary it made the appeal even more direct and urgent.

Several motifs appear again and again in the broadcast appeals of the late 1880s and early 1890s. One is that of the cow as the 'universal mother', based on the proposition that all human beings drink the cow's milk: in consequence of this, the killing of a cow is represented as matricide. Another is that of the cow as the dwelling place of all the major Hindu gods and goddesses, as a result of which cow slaughter becomes doubly heinous in Hindu eyes. A third, which gains prominence by the end of the 1880s is the representation of the Muslim — and to a lesser extent the Englishman, the Indian Christian and others — as the killer of cows and, hence, the enemy of Hinduism.

A picture displayed at a Cow-Protection lecture in Bahraich in 1893 combined two, or, if one accepts the interpretation of the local officials, all three of these themes. It showed a cow, inside which several Hindu deities were depicted, waiting to give milk to the assembled Hindus, Muslims, Parsis and Christians. Near the cow was a demon, half-human and half-animal, with a raised sword. A man representing *Dharma Raj* appeals to the demon: 'Oh! Demon of the iron age! Why art thou going to kill this useful animal. Have mercy on her.'

The *Hindustani*, reporting the case that arose out of the display of this picture, declared that the demon here was in the common form of such creatures in 'Hindu books'. But the Deputy Commissioner of Bahraich was convinced that the demon's animal head was that of a pig, and intended as a deliberate insult to Muslims. Other pictures more simply portrayed a (Muslim) butcher ready to slaughter a cow, and Hindus of several different castes crying out to him to desist. 'The effect of this symbolical teaching on the rustic mind may be readily conceived', as a colonial official superciliously commented, '[for] to the Hindu the symbol has in everything displaced the symbolised entity'.

It was, however, not only the 'rustic mind' that was disturbed by all this propaganda. In an article on the anti-cow-killing agitation, Mohammad Ali wrote in 1911 of a picture that was printed in Bombay and then widely circulated in many different parts of the country. The picture represented a cow standing meekly with its head turned to one side, while 'a huge inhuman monster, a Malechh [*mleccha*, non-Hindu untouchable]' rushed forward, sword in hand, to kill the animal. A Brahman, 'with a look of mingled wrath and horror', stood with arms upraised in front of the cow to ward off the attack. Several gods and goddesses, as well as ordinary Hindu folk, were drawn 'in symbolical configuration across the body of the cow, with appropriate writings and texts to explain their significance'. Among them, Mohammad Ali noted, was an extract from the Koran in Devanagri characters, placed insultingly below the hind feet of the cow, 'A mere glance at this picture unmasks the real spirit in which the anti-cow-killing agitation has been conceived', he concluded.[7]

The 'religious' appeal remained just as central, but was in some ways even more strident in the course of the mobilization for Hindu demonstrations that turned into such a colossal outbreak of violence in Shahabad in 1917. This is amply illustrated by the contemporary *patias* that survive in the colonial records....

The basic form of these *patias* appears to be the same. It consists of:

1. Invocation
2. Information
3. Appeal for (a) propaganda, and (b) action
4. Promise of support
5. Sanctions

This structure, and the remarkable brevity of the *patias*, is determined to a large extent by the constraints of the form itself — the need to keep the relay-letter short and sharp for quick reproduction and further distribution. Recall the use of '*dharm-patris*' for the mobilization of forces in Banaras in 1809 and again 1810-11. The process was described as follows by the local Magistrate:

Swift and trusty messengers run full speed all over the city, *proclaiming in a single word* the place of rendezvous, and *invoking infamy and eternal vengeance* on any who do not at the hour appointed repair to it. From the city the alarm is spread over the country. The first messenger conveys the symbol which is a Dhurmputree or paper containing a mystic inscription to the next village. From that to the next, till all know where, when, and wherefore they must meet. This practice is common not only among the Hindoos but the Mohamedans also and in the disturbances of 1809 and 1810 was the means of collecting together an innumerable multitude at one spot in the space of no more than a few hours[8]....

The *patias* of 1917, prepared in haste in the midst of a rapidly growing confrontation, betray a greater sense of urgency. They begin usually with an invocation to Ram, probably the most popular deity among the Hindus of the Bhojpuri region, or to 'Mother Cow', which follows naturally from the matter at stake. The information that they go on to provide tends to be a bare minimum; that the cow, which has committed no sin, is dying at the hands of 'others' (*'dusre ke haath se marta hai'*), that fighting has broken out between Hindus and Muslims on the question of *qurbani*, that the cow has been publicly paraded and sacrificed in certain places to heap additional humiliation on the Hindus, that some Hindus (acting against the dictates of their *dharma*) are sheltering and helping Muslims, that the village of Mauna is to be attacked, and so on....

That appeal for action, of course, constitutes the next component of the *patia*.... A part of the appeal is the simple one of passing on the information and message contained in the *patia* to other Hindus, the injunction to anyone reading a *patia* to relay it to 5, 10, 12, 25 or other given number of 'Hindu brothers'. The other part relates to the physical action to be undertaken: that Hindus must not allow cows to pass into the hands of Muslims, must prevent the sacrifice of cows already in Muslim hands, must not shelter Muslims in villages where *qurbani* has been performed or even that they must kill all Musalmans.

The promise of support from additional Hindu (and certain interesting non-Hindu) forces is an unusual feature of the *patias* .circulated in Shahabad in 1917, pointing to the quite remarkable expectations and anti-British rumours aroused by the exceptional circumstances of the First World War,[9] as well as to the fairly long-drawn-out nature of the fighting in Shahabad, the Muslim resistance encountered and the strength of military and police contingents that the rioters had to combat. Different *patias* thus contain the promise of calling in reinforcements from Hindu *zamin-dars* and *rajas* who were well known in the region, from distant kings (including the German), from the Bengalis (the particular force the authors have in mind here is unclear; the 'Bengalis' as a race were already being described as 'non-martial'), and of course from the great mass of the 'Hindu community'.

The *patias* almost invariably ended with a listing of the extreme consequences that would overcome those who responded or failed to respond to the appeals for action and propaganda contained in them: recipients could acquire the merit accruing from the gift of five cows or the de-merit flowing from the slaughter of five, or the consequences of a sin equivalent to sleeping with one's daughter, sister, mother or marrying any of these to a Musalman.

The sin of incest looms large in these *patias*. The violation of the chastity of women of one's family is repeatedly invoked as a spiritual punishment in these appeals for action to protect 'Mother Cow'. The fear of incest and the question of cow-slaughter are presented as being equally critical to the life of the community. The notion of the sacred duty of cow-protection, the sanctity of the *family* and the inviolability of the *community* are thus collapsed together. As in the case of the proposition that the killing of a cow (whose milk all human beings drink) is 'matricide', it is the image of the community — here, the 'Hindu community' — as a family that binds the elements of the *patia* together.

Prior to the sin of incest, and central to the demand to preserve the sanctity of the family and the community, is the insistence on action to prove one's faith. Action on behalf of the community appears in the *patias* as the one means of proving oneself a Hindu. 'We appeal to Hindu brothers....' 'Hindus have no choice....' 'If you are a Hindu, you must save the cow....' 'Those who are Hindus should assemble for cow protection....' 'What Hindu, on seeing this *patia*, will not come, shall incur the guilt of killing 7 cows' 'It is your duty (*dharma*)....'

If you do not do your duty, you forsake your *dharma*, you are no Hindu. For which Hindu would willingly take a step that is equivalent to the crime of killing a cow (or, worse, five cows, or seven), or sleeping with one's daughter, or marrying one's mother to a Muslim. Those who respond to the call at this time, they alone are Hindus: all others are traitors, enemies, Others.

It is difficult, then, to sustain the view that Gaurakshini

propaganda was less religious (or 'ideological') in the 'rural' phase
of this movement than in its urban. The appeal to Hindus to
devote themselves to the service of the cow, to work for the care
of sick and aged cattle, to do their utmost to prevent cow-sacrifice,
was always religious, even if it was backed up by statements
regarding the economic benefits to be obtained from 'Mother Cow'.
In the later, more aggressive stages of the Cow-Protection movement, this appeal was reinforced, as we have seen, by the appeal
to bonds of family and threats of excommunication. In spite of
the forthrightness and urgency of Cow-Protection propaganda
in the 1890s and the 1910s, and the terrible sanctions that were
invoked alongside the appeal to 'all Hindu brothers', however,
only certain sections of that 'community' called 'Hindu' responded
readily to the appeal for action....

While it is necessary to emphasize the leading part played by
upper-caste *zamindari* elements in organizing the Hindu demonstrations and attacks in September and October 1917, it would
be a very one-sided statement that did not recognize a similar
initiative (and leadership) on the part of rather less privileged
communities who were organizing their own autonomous movements at this time and who were able to use the issue of cow
protection, perhaps, as another lever in the bid to improve their
social status....

Most colonial officials, of course, were firmly convinced of the
upper classes' monopoly of enterprise and brains, and paid little
attention to the role of such subordinate groups in the rise and
spread of large-scale political movements. Historians, with less
excuse, have often reproduced this official view....

....The caste breakdown of those arrested for participation in
the widespread rioting that followed confirms these indications
of the special role of the Ahirs, a role that cannot be explained
away by the suggestion that they were drawn in by the *zamindari*
groups. Of the 140 trials instituted in consequence of the Shahabad
riots, I have seen the detailed evidence and judgements in only
seven cases. Out of 560 men sent up for trial in these, as many
as 85 were Rajputs, 90 Brahmans and 55 Bhumihars. Other upper
castes, fairly thin on the ground in any case, were represented
by a handful of Kayasthas and Banias from one or two villages.
Ahirs, however, were 'very prominent' in the riots, 127 of them
being convicted in these seven cases alone. Doubts about the

representative character of any sample are heightened in this instance, of course, by the feeling that privileged men of the upper
castes would be far more readily noticed in the course of a riot.
Yet, if this is granted, the identification of the lowly Ahirs in
such large numbers becomes all the more significant.

I would suggest that we have evidence here of a relatively
independent force that added a good deal of power to Cow-
Protection activities in the Bhojpuri region — marginally 'clean'
castes who aspired to full 'cleanness' by propagating their strict-
ness on the issue of cow slaughter....

....Whatever one might make of those later, confused stages
of general rioting and looting, it emerges clearly from the evidence
that the handful of upper *zamindari* castes and a few of the lower
castes, like the Ahirs and Kurmis, took the dominant part in the
actions to save the cow in the Bhojpuri region in 1893 and 1917.
The same kind of circumscribed 'Hindu community' moved to the
defence of a 'general' Hindu interest in Banaras in 1809....

All this is not to suggest that 'Hindu' (and 'Muslim') interests
or the notion of a 'Hindu (or Muslim) community' had no meaning
for the vast majority of local castes, in the Bhojpuri region or
elsewhere. We have seen that quite the opposite was the case
with the Muslim weavers of Mubarakpur, in spite of the strength
of 'caste' feelings and of their own caste organization in the *qasba*
and beyond. But the relevant point, perhaps, is that apperception
at the local level during the early nineteenth century, and well
into the twentieth, was very much in terms of *jati* and *biradari*,
caste and kinship, that the strength of local caste and community
organization mattered (in that decisions were most often taken
and/or channelled through them), and that the feeling of belonging to a wider 'Hindu' or 'Muslim' community did not mean —
in spite of all that colonialist historiography and sociology had
to say on the subject — that 'Hindus' and 'Muslims' responded
automatically and in unvarying ways to every appeal for action
on behalf of 'Hindu' or 'Muslim' interests.

The point possibly applies with greater force to the Hindu
community than to the 'Muslim', because, unlike the latter, the
'Hindu community' was far from being small, concentrated in
any particular localities, or bound by anything in the way of a

'revealed' book or a 'united' church. The all-India 'Hindu community' (and, to a large extent, the all-India 'Muslim community' too) was a colonial creation for, the social and economic changes brought by colonialism, Indian efforts to defend the indigenous religions and culture against western missionary attacks, the 'unifying' drive of the colonial state — which was marked at the level of administrative structure and attempted political control ('Muslims' must not be antagonized, 'Hindu' sensibilities must not be touched), and the very history of movements like that of Cow-Protection, widely publicized as they were by the end of the nineteenth century, tended to promote the idea of an all-India 'Hindu community' and an all-India 'Muslim community' which were supposedly ranged against one another for much of the time. In spite of a widely felt sense of 'Hinduness' and 'Muslim-ness', I would suggest that until the nineteenth century at any rate, people always had to work through caste, sect and so on to arrive at the unities implied in the conception of the 'Hindu community' and the 'Muslim community'.

Given the strength of local community solidarity until well into the late colonial period, and of collective decision-making at many levels, it is not surprising that in different conjunctures, and on different issues, different constellations of local groups, castes and communities are to be found coming together — 'Hindu' or 'Muslim' or both. Of course the very act of coming together, especially when this occurred repeatedly in particular combinations, gave rise to new feelings of solidarity and new strains in the indigenous society. And yet, in spite of the many instances of Hindu-Muslim strife in the nineteenth century, and the powerful movements that arose to promote 'Hindu' and 'Muslim' unity in northern India, the new solidarities that emerged did not everywhere and indubitably add up to 'Hindu' versus 'Muslim'....

....And in the 1910s and '20s, as we have seen, when the Koeris, Kurmis and Ahirs became organized and increasingly militant in pressing their demands for a more respectable status the upper-caste Hindu *zamindars* joined hands with the upper-caste Muslim *zamindars* of the region to keep these 'upstart' peasant castes in their place — through physical violence, rape or any other method that served their purpose. That divide between upper and lower castes and classes, and the strife attendant upon it, remained the predominant feature of the rural political scene in eastern U.P. and Bihar, more marked than any perceptible rift between local Hindus and Muslims, at least until the 1940s.

NOTES

1. Sarkar, Sumit, *Modern India*, Macmillan India, Delhi, 1983, 79.
2. Pandey, Gyanendra, 'Rallying round the cow', in R. Guha, (ed.) *Subaltern Studies II*, OUP, Delhi, 1983, and Freitag, 'Sacred symbol as mobilising ideology'.
3. Freitag, Sandra, 'Sacred symbol as mobilising ideology', 607; also her 'Religious rites and riots', in *Comparative Studies in Society and History*, vol. 22, no. 4, October, 1980. 127 ff.
4. Macdonnell-Forbes, 9 November, 1893, 'Confidential Correspondence' of Sir A.P. Macdonnell, Bodleian Library, Oxford, Ms. Eng. Hist. d. 235.
5. Freitag, Sandra, 'Sacred symbols as mobilising ideology', 607.
6. Mall, Vijayshankar, (ed.), *Pratapnarayan Granthavali, pt I*, Kashi, 1958, 178, 563, 601.
7. Jafri, R.A., ed. *Selections from Moulana Mohammed Ali's Comrade*, Lahore, 1965, 258.
8. (IOR) Home Misc., vol. 775, Report on Benares City by W.W. Bird, 20 August 1814 (pp. 451-506), para. 12.
9. Pandey, Gyanendra, 'Peasant revolt and Indian nationalism', in R. Guha (ed.) *Subaltern Studies, I*, Oxford University Press, Delhi, 1982, 164-5.

Sikh Fundamentalism

HARJOT OBEROI

....Fundamentalism among the Sikhs today is primarily a movement of resistance. While Sikh fundamentalists certainly envision a separate nation-state in the Indian subcontinent, in the last decade much of their energies have been spent in assailing and battling the Indian state. Denied political authority and engaged in constant struggle for survival and legitimacy, Sikh fundamentalists have not succeeded in articulating their vision of the world in any great detail. This lack of an elaborate model, say on the lines of Iranian clerics, of what the world should look like is closely tied to the social origins of Sikh activists. A great majority of them come from the countryside and would be classified as peasants by social anthropologists. Historically, peasants have not been known to come up with grand paradigms of social transformation. Peasant societies are by definition made up of little communities, and their cosmos is invariably parochial rather than universal. To speak of Sikh fundamentalism and its impact is to enter a universe that until recently was largely characterized by marginality, incoherence, and disorder....

....I would like to defend my usage of the term Sikh fundamentalism on three grounds. First, in the Punjabi word *mulvad*, Sikhs possess a term that exactly corresponds to fundamentalism

Excerpted from Martin E. Marty and R. Scott Appleby (eds.), *Fundamentalism and the State*, University of Chicago Press, Chicago, 1993.

and stands in stark opposition to *adharma*, a Punjabi word for secularism. Although the term *mulvad* is of recent coinage, resulting from the need to have a Punjabi counterpart to fundamentalism, Sikh journalists, essayists, and politicians, in discussing contemporary religious and political movements, now constantly use the term *mulvad*, connoting a polity and society organized on the basis of religious (particularly scriptural) authority. Thus, in the Sikh case the commonly voiced objection, that non-Christian religious groups to which the term fundamentalism is applied have no such equivalent in their own lexicon, does not fully hold.

Second, there are strong cultural reasons for adopting the term 'Sikh fundamentalism'. Much like Protestant church groups in the United States that at the turn of the century insisted on the inerrancy of the Bible and opposed liberal theology, Sikh fundamentalists have no patience for hermeneutic or critical readings of Sikh scriptures. Their scriptural absolutism precludes any secular or rational interpretation of what they consider to be a revealed text....

....A critical textual analysis of the Sikh scriptures that may introduce an element of historicity and plurality of interpretations, thus undermining scripturalism, would certainly be constructed as an affront — one that would bring quick retribution. Jarnail Singh Bhindranwale (1947–84), a key figure in the rise of Sikh fundamentalism, repeatedly reminded his audience that they should not tolerate any form of insult toward the Sikh scriptures and that, where required, Sikhs were morally obliged to kill an individual who dared to show disrespect toward the holy book.

Third, the current Sikh movement, ...amply manifests many tendencies like millenarianism, a prophetic vision, puritanism and antipluralism, trends that have been commonly associated with fundamentalism. For these three reasons — linguistic, cultural, and associative — I think we are justified in speaking and thinking in terms of Sikh fundamentalism.

Having said this, I must stress that in Foucault's terms there is no archaeology to Sikh fundamentalism. It is an episteme that is still in the making, and its canon, ideology, objectives, and practices are being gradually defined. In this sense, for all those who are interested in fundamentalism, the Sikh case is of particular value, for here we can clearly see how a group of fundamentalists invent and reproduce themselves in the late twentieth century.

Given its relatively recent origins, the success of Sikh fundamentalism has been staggering. In less than a decade Sikh fundamentalists not only established a multitude of relationships with
ethnicity, political economy, and nationalism but also eventually
came to encompass these materially and conceptually varied conditions. To speak of Sikh fundamentalism is therefore to address
simultaneously issues of Sikh identity, the crisis of agrarian
development, class antagonisms, and the process of state formation in India, including popular resistance to this process....

THE BACKGROUND

Despite the powerful normative notion of a Sikh collectivity, popularly known in the Punjabi language by the term *panth*, Sikhs
are not a monolithic religious community. Much like other religious
communities, the Sikhs are divided by geography, ethnicity, social
hierarchy, sects, ritual practices, and individual preferences. Consequently, when it comes to political participation, Sikhs have
never been represented by a single political party. They have
always opted for a wide variety of political platforms, ranging
from arch-conservative to ultra-radical....

POLITICAL ECONOMY AND SIKH SUBJECTIVITY

There is no denying the fact that the nature of the contemporary
Sikh polity is closely tied to the social and economic transformations undergone by the province of Punjab over the last three
decades.... Following the capitalist path of development, the accelerated growth in the agrarian sector made Punjab the first
region in South Asia to experience what is commonly known as
the 'Green Revolution'. The social costs of such agrarian innovation have been extremely high, and Punjabi society over the last
two decades has become highly polarized.

The benefits of agrarian development have primarily accrued
to those sectors of rural society which already possessed substantial resources like land and capital.... In contrast to rich cultivators, small and marginal farmers have fared poorly in the
Green Revolution. They are faced with a situation where their
small land holdings, ranging from two to five acres, have increasingly become less viable.... The negative returns have made

it hard for the small and marginal farmers to sustain their family farms. Consequently, in recent years a large number of small holdings have disappeared.... ِ

Suffering this decline were countless Sikh peasants from the small and marginal sector. As yet it is not clear what exactly has been their fate. In classical models of development those who are dispossessed either join the ranks of the agrarian labor force or turn to jobs in the burgeoning industrial sector. In Punjab there is no such simple transition. The bulk of the small and marginal farmers are from the high-status Jat caste, and even when they find themselves without land to cultivate they are most unwilling to become agricultural laborers. This would imply working in the midst of low-caste Harijans, a clear loss of face for the status-conscious Jats. (The strong sense of egalitarianism of the Sikhs does not easily extend to others, particularly non-Sikhs.) The other alternative — working in the industrial sector — is equally difficult, for two reasons. First, Punjab does not have the large-scale industries which could absorb the depeasantized Sikh cultivators. Second, even where such jobs exist, particularly in medium- and small-scale industries, the work force is made up of migratory labor from the poorer areas of northern India....

In entering the final quarter of the twentieth century, the Akali Dal, led almost exclusively by rich kulaks, had no solution for the crisis in Punjab's political economy.... For the most part the Akali Dal leadership had prospered from the Green Revolution, and they were unconcerned about those who had lost out in the process.[1] ....

The rising tide of inequalities in the Punjab did not easily blend with the dominant ethos of Sikh religious tradition, which demands a just moral economy based on an equitable distribution of wealth and resources. From its inception in the early sixteenth century, Sikh discourse has sought the creation of an egalitarian society where all men, if not all women, would be equal and share the ritual, sacred, profane, and economic resources collectively. The appeal of such teachings was considerable in a society where the organizing ideology gave open recognition to principles of human inequality, expressed in the caste system. Over a period of roughly three centuries the Sikh movement launched an offensive against the theory and practice of the 'Hindu' social structure, particularly its acceptance of the notion that inequality was inherent in the human condition. It set up the institution of the *sangat* (congregation) and *langar* (communal consumption) to combat social distinctions and moulded a collectivity called the *panth*. All practitioners had equal access to the holy scripture, and there was no institutional priesthood that could act as the sole custodian of the Sikh holy book. During the eighteenth century, Sikh militants further sought to implement the egalitarian paradigm of Sikhism. The Sikh movement attracted the rural poor, the urban underprivileged, and others who persisted on the margins of Punjabi society. No efforts were spared by the peasant armies of the Sikhs to destroy all modes of authority, all order, and all mechanisms of social control. They succeeded in doing away with a whole range of intermediaries, those who extracted the much-hated land revenues for the state and often acted as instruments of oppression. Large estates were dissolved, and the lands distributed to the peasantry....

Whenever this egalitarian thrust within Sikhism has been ably voiced, it has demonstrated an immense power to mobilize the faithful and lead them toward the inversion of the status quo, in order to establish a society free of religious and social inequalities. Such an ideology becomes most attractive in periods of intense social change. During the nineteenth and early twentieth centuries under British colonial rule, there were numerous movements within the Sikh community, like the Kukas, Ghadarites, and Babbar Akalis, which sought to recover the original message of Sikhism and establish a society relatively free of human distinctions. The Sikh past endowed its constituents with a highly developed vocabulary of social justice, and the community had a long experience of social movements that fought for greater social equality.

By the early 1970s then there was a serious crisis in Punjab's political economy that polarized class distinctions. The scope of this crisis was further enhanced by the nature of the Indian nation-state in general and the pro-rich policies of the Akali Dal in particular. While the crisis may have been more easily accommodated in the rest of India, the egalitarian impulse within the Sikh tradition was to make the voice of redistributive justice more compelling in Punjab. All those who perceived their lived experience in this sequence began increasingly to search for solutions. Some were readily convinced of the veracity of the Dal

Khalsa's 'final solution'. Others kept looking. Eventually in the late 1970s they were to shape a body — the Damdami Taksal — that was to articulate their aspirations forcefully and, by challenging the status quo, to turn the 1980s into a decade of Sikh fundamentalism.

DAMDAMI TAKSAL

....Millenarianism is hardly new to Sikhism. Of all the indigenous religious communities in India, Sikhism possesses the most advanced paradigm of millennial thought and practice. For much of their history, at least since the rise of the Khalsa, Sikhs have opted to deal with major social crises — state oppression, economic upheavals, colonialism, collapse of semiotic categories — by invoking the millenarian paradigm. Central to this entire model has been a prophetic figure of extraordinary charisma with the will to establish an alternative social system in which oppression would cease and people would lead a life of harmony, purity, and good deeds. Bhindranwale was heir to this cultural tradition. Perhaps nothing would have come of it without the Green Revolution and the social processes it unleashed. In hindsight it is possible to see how the Sikh past, an expanding network of communications, mechanized farming, and the Sikh identity became inextricably linked in the Punjab of the 1970s. As the first people to experience the Green Revolution in South Asia, Sikhs were confronted with unprecedented change in economy, lived experience, and social relationships. No one had prepared them to handle so much change in so little time. Failed by established political parties, they turned to a messianic leader and his seminary to make sense of a world they had helped create, but one they no longer fully grasped or controlled.

Bhindranwale knew little about economics or parliamentary politics. He turned the complex problems faced by the Sikhs into simple homilies. In his worldview, what I shall call the 'Sikh impasse' resulted from the prevalent religious depravity among the Sikhs and the ever-increasing Hindu domination over the Sikhs. As had happened with earlier social movements within the community, Bhindranwale sought a resolution to this new Sikh impasse by invoking the millenarian charter. In 1982 he agreed to participate in the *dharma yuddh*, or righteous battle, earlier launched by the Akalis. Unlike the Akalis, who viewed the *dharma yuddh* as a politically expedient campaign, Bhindranwale characterized it as an epic war where good was pitted against evil and only one side was to be victorious. His participation in the campaign was fired by the cultural logic of Sikh millenarianism....

Sikh fundamentalists are responding to prevailing socioeconomic conditions in the Punjab and envision a society free of distinctions based on birth, gender, and class. Their social programme seeks to invert the existing hierarchies of power and advance the rights of the subaltern over the elite....

Even if their rhetoric was for public consumption, such resolutions endorsed by tens of thousands of Sikhs are a powerful critique of the existing social norms and distribution of resources. The vision of an alternative universe has often proven to be incentive for a people to expend all in pursuit of it, particularly when the world to be ushered in will have none of the drawbacks of the old.

THE VISION

The utopia that fundamentalists envision is not a secular one. Its identity is to be defined in terms of Sikh religious tradition. The 1986 *Declaration of Khalistan* stipulates: 'The Sikh religion will be the official creed of Khalistan. Further, it will be a paramount duty of the Government to see that Sikhism must flourish unhindered in Khalistan.'[2] By proclaiming an official religion for the state of Khalistan, Sikh fundamentalists stand in direct opposition is to the present secular constitution of India that guarantees freedom of religious practice. Sikh militants are dismayed by several aspects of that constitution. One is its secular content. Another is its association of Sikhs with Hindus. Article 25, section 2b, states that all public Hindu shrines must be open to all Hindus, irrespective of their caste. The clause includes under the category 'Hindu' all 'persons professing the Sikh, Jain or Buddhist religion'. For Sikh fundamentalists there can be no greater affront than being included among the Hindus. In their view Sikhism and Hinduism are two diametrically opposed religions; there is no common ground between them. Angered by the insensitivity shown to them by the constitution, Sikh leaders in February 1984 took to the streets of major cities in Punjab and publicly defaced copies of the Indian constitution in order to protest article 25, section 2b. Behind this act of defiance stretches a long history of Sikh search for a personal law.

Fortunately or unfortunately, the first principles of Sikhism were never explicitly codified. The little that was formalized during the formative phases of the Sikh movement under the *gurus* or preceptors could hardly be enforced in the absence of an organized clerical hierarchy....

....What we have here are different subtraditions evolving within Sikhism, each claiming allegiance and constituents for its own version. The *rahit-nama* [(manuals of conduct)] textual materials reflect only the aspirations and worldview of the hegemonic Khalsa tradition and not of the entire Sikh tradition. A single orthodoxy for the entire Sikh community was not articulated until the late nineteenth century; many observers have mistakenly accepted this as the orthodoxy for all times and phases of the Sikh movement. Given the pluralistic nature of the Sikh tradition in the nineteenth century and the absence of a powerful orthodoxy, Sikh cultural, social, and economic transactions were based on Punjabi customary law and, more recently, on Anglo-Saxon law as it evolved during the colonial and postcolonial periods.

This ambiguity is not to the liking of Sikh fundamentalists. They have demanded a Shari'a-like personal law for the Sikhs. Such a demand was put forward in the Akali Dal's forty-five-point charter of demands submitted to the federal government in September 1981. What exactly is to be covered under the rubic of Sikh personal law (hereafter SPL) is still largely undecided. Though there is no agreement, it is possible to gain some idea of what its scope and nature would be from the sermons of Sikh leaders like Bhindranwale and Darshan Singh Ragi, a former head of Sri Akal Takhat Sahib.

The major thrust of the proposed SPL would be to define who is a Sikh. Although such definitions have been attempted in the past, particularly in the Sikh Gurdwaras Act of 1925 and the *Sikh Rahit Maryada* (Sikh personal code) of 1950, these enactments were ambiguous. A liberal reading of them would permit a person to consider him- or herself Sikh without undergoing initiation (the Khalsa *amrit* ceremony) and maintaining the famous five K's. To Bhindranwale one could not be a Sikh without undergoing initiation and upholding the five K's. As head of the Damdami Taksal, Bhindranwale spent much of his time touring the villages of Punjab and exhorting Sikh youth to take *amrit* (baptismal nectar) and be loyal to the external insignia of the faith. He constantly reiterated in his sermons, 'Only people without ambiguity in their heart have the right to call themselves Khalsa'. The ambiguity Bhindranwale was seeking to redress had to do with contemporary Sikh identity. Under the growing influence of a secular culture many Sikhs in the 1960s and 1970s turned indifferent toward their religious identity. To counter this trend, preachers like Bhindranwale advocated a stricter definition of Sikh identity. A more rigorous definition would clearly distinguish the true believers from nonbelievers, and help prevent Sikh assimilation into Hinduism....

The writings of Edward Said and Johannes Fabian have made us sensitive to the fact that power groups in all societies require an image of the Other in order to bolster their own identity and further their sociopolitical interests.[3] It is by cultivating a profound sense of Otherness that cultural groups promote their notions of superiority, insularity, and incompatibility. Secular and fundamentalist thought does not seem to be very different when it comes to distinguishing 'us' from the 'others.' Fundamentalists, be they Sikh, Shi'ite, or Hindu, always require the Other to sharpen their self-identity and appropriate a higher moral ground relative to their adversaries. A discourse of heightened religious boundaries helps religious groups to gain or retain power.

I have been arguing that the vision of Sikh fundamentalists is closely related to the problem of Sikh identity. Secular public culture in their view erodes morality and religion. To counter this threat, Sikh fundamentalists seek to inscribe their religious identity on all possible cultural resources: constitutions, dietary habits, and the environment of the body. The objective of all this is to leave no lacuna in definition. For Sikh fundamentalists it is ambiguity that breeds atheism, immorality, and denial of tradition....

....There is a fundamental chasm between the world-view of Sikh fundamentalists and what Habermas has described as the 'project of modernity.' A key element in the 'project of modernity' has been its separation of the domain of politics from the sphere of religion. It was this differentiation across 'cultural value spheres' that Max Weber convincingly used to distinguish modern from premodern polities. This distinction between the political and religious domains is anathema to Sikh fundamentalists. For them religion and politics are inseparable.

In the last decade all shades of Sikh politics — accommodative, intransigent, and millenarian — have been formulated within the walls of *gurdwaras,* or Sikh religious shrines. Sikh ideologues have justified this by invoking the long hand of history....

In the early 1980s Bhindranwale waged his battle against the Indian state from the Akal Takhat. When the government of India finally decided to launch a counter-attack in June 1984 the army operation, named Operation Blue Star, succeeded only after blowing up the Akal Takhat. The tragedy in no way altered Sikh perceptions concerning the relation between religion and politics. Possibly, the army action only further strengthened the Sikh resolve to articulate their politics in the idiom of religion. Indeed, the Sikhs have never known a truly secular movement of dissent. Opposition to political authority and the various institutions of the state has always been articulated in religious terms. Whether dealing with the oppression of the Mughal state in the eighteenth century or the economic exploitation of British colonial rule, the Sikhs have always responded with social movements mediated through religion.

Thus the Sikhs have no language of politics free of religion. The categories of thought, the heroic figures, the symbols, the costumes which have motivated Sikhs to react to the demands of the state or come to grips with ongoing social transformations have been of a purely religious nature. The most important qualification for a political leader among the Sikhs is his understanding of Sikh scriptures and his ability to expound on their meaning. It is no coincidence that Bhindranwale, the most important political leader of the Sikhs in the 1980s, belonged to a seminary which instructed Sikh students in the art of exegesis. Politics among the Sikhs is always explained and internalized by referring to the religious history of the party or by quoting from the writings of the Sikh masters. The vocabulary of political discourse and the goals of society are rooted in perceived Sikh experience. What happens outside that experience is unimportant. It is not from classical models of structural change — the French or the Russian revolution — that inspiration is sought. Nor is there an echo of the Indian struggle for freedom from colonial rule. Rather, political mobilization and the search for justice is solely based on Sikh texts and semantics. In recasting the world, Sikh militants today look to the emergence and consolidation of the Sikh movement for their theory and practice.

But it would be wrong to draw from all this the conclusion that the rise of Sikh fundamentalism was inevitable and a logical result of the Sikh past. Much as it would be oversimplistic to ascribe the rise of Nazism to German tradition, similarly Sikh tradition by itself is no explanation for the formation of Sikh fundamentalism. Fundamentalism is a modern ideology, and while it voraciously appropriates the past, the success of Sikh fundamentalism is to be traced to the massive crisis in contemporary Indian society....

NOTES

1. Narang, A.S., *Storm over the Sutlej: The Akali Politics*, Gitanjali, New Delhi, 1983, 198-9.
2. 'The document of the declaration of Khalistan' in Singh Gopal, (ed.) *Punjab Today*, Intellectual Publishing House, Delhi, 1987.
3. Said, Edward, *Orientalism*, Vintage, New York, 1979; and Fabian, J., *Time and the Other: How Anthropology makes its Objects*, Columbia University Press, New York, 1983.

A Critique of Modernist Secularism

ASHIS NANDY

FAITH, IDEOLOGY AND THE SELF

A significant aspect of post-colonial structures of knowledge in the third world is a peculiar form of imperialism of categories. Under such imperialism a conceptual domain is sometimes hegemonized so effectively by a concept produced and honed in the West that the original domain vanishes from our awareness....

....I seek to provide a political preface to the recovery of a well- known domain of public concern in South Asia, ethnic and, especially, religious tolerance, from the hegemonic language of secularism popularized by the westernized intellectuals and middle classes exposed to the globally dominant language of the nation-state in this part of the world. This language, whatever may have been its positive contributions to humane governance and religious tolerance earlier, has increasingly become a cover for the complicity of the modern intellectuals and the modernizing middle classes of South Asia in the new forms of religious violence. These are the forms in which the state, the media and the ideologies of national security, development and modernity

Excerpted from Veena Das (ed.), *Mirrors of Violence*, OUP, Delhi, 1990, 69-93.

propagated by the modern intelligentsia and the middle classes play crucial roles.

....I shall...first describe four trends which have become clearly visible in South Asia during this century, particularly after the Second World War.

The first and most important of these trends is that each religion in South Asia, perhaps all over the southern world, has split into two: faith and ideology. Both are inappropriate terms, but I give them...specific private meanings to serve my purpose. By faith I mean religion as a way of life, a tradition which is definitionally non-monolithic and operationally plural. I say 'definitionally' because unless a religion is geographically and culturally confined to a small area, it has as a way of life, in effect, to turn into a confederation of a number of ways of life which are linked by a common faith that has some theological space for the heterogeneity which everyday life introduces. Witness the differences between Iranian and Indonesian Islams, two cultures which can be said to be divided by the same faith. The two forms of Islam are interlocking, not isomorphic, in relation to each other.

By ideology I mean religion as a sub-national, national or crossnational identifier of populations contesting for or protecting nonreligious, usually political or socio-economic, interests. Such religion-as-ideologies usually get identified with one or more texts which, rather than the ways of life of the believers, then become the final identifiers of the pure forms of the religions. The texts help anchor the ideologies in something seemingly concrete and delimited, and in effect provide a set of manageable operational definitions.

The modern state always prefers to deal with religious ideologies rather than with faiths. It is wary of both forms of religion but it finds the ways of life more inchoate and, hence, unmanageable, even though it is faith rather than ideology which has traditionally shown more pliability and catholicity....

Second, during the last two centuries or so there has grown a tendency to view the older faiths of the region through the eyes of evangelical Anglican Christianity and its various offshoots — such as the masculine Christianity associated with nineteenth-century missionaries like Joshua Marshman and William Carey, or its mirror image in the orthodox modernism propagated by the likes of Frederich Engels and Thomas Huxley. Because this particular Eurocentric way of looking at faiths gradually came to be associated with the dominant culture of the colonial states in the region, it subsumes under it a set of clear polarities; centre *vs.* periphery, true faith *vs.* its distortions, civil *vs.* primordial, and great traditions *vs.* local cultures or little traditions.

It is a part of the same story that in each of the dyads, the second category is set up to lose. It is also a part of the same story that, once the colonial concept of the state was internalized by the societies of this region through the nationalist ideology — in turn heavily influenced by the western theories and practice of statecraft — the nascent nation-states of the region took upon themselves the same civilizing mission that the colonial states had once taken upon themselves *vis-à-vis* the ancient faiths of the subcontinent.[1]

Third, the idea of secularism, an import from nineteenth-century Europe into South Asia, has acquired immense potency in the middle-class cultures and 'state sectors' of South Asia, thanks to its connection with and response to religion-as-ideology. Secularism has little to say about cultures. It is definitionally ethnophobic and frequently ethnocidal, unless of course cultures and those living by cultures are willing to show total subservience to the modern nation-state and become ornaments or adjuncts to modern living. The orthodox secularists have no clue to the way a religion can link up different faiths or ways of life according to its own configurative principles.

To such secularists, religion is an ideology in opposition to the ideology of modern statecraft and, therefore, needs to be contained. They feel even more uncomfortable with religion-as-faith — which claims to have its own principles of tolerance and intolerance — for such a claim denies the state and the middle-class ideologues of the state the right to be the ultimate reservoir of sanity and the ultimate arbiter among different religions and communities. This denial is particularly galling to those who see the clash between two faiths merely as a clash of socio-economic interests, not as a simultaneous clash between conflicting interests and a philosophical encounter between two metaphysics. The westernized middle classes and literati of South Asia love to see all such encounters as reflections of socio-economic forces and, thus, as liabilities and as sources of ethnic violence.

Fourth, the imported idea of secularism has become increasingly incompatible and, as it were, uncomfortable with the somewhat fluid definitions of the self with which many South Asian cultures live. Such a self, which can be conceptually viewed as a configuration of selves, invokes and reflects the configurative principles of religion-as-faith. It also happens to be a negation of the modern concept of selfhood acquired partly from the West and partly from a rediscovery of previously recessive elements in South Asian traditions. Religion-as-ideology, working with the concept of well-bounded, mutually exclusive religious identities, on the other hand, is more compatible with and analogues to the definition of the self as a well-bounded, individuated entity clearly separable from the non-self. Such individualisation is taking place in South Asian societies at a fast pace and, to that extent, more exclusive definitions of the self are emerging in these societies as a byproduct of secularization.[2]

A more fluid definition of the self is not merely more compatible with religion-as-faith, it also has — and depends more upon — a distinctive set of the non-self and anti-selves (a neologism analogous to 'anti-heroes'). At one plane these anti-selves are similar to what the psychotherapist Carl Rogers used to call, infelicitiously, the 'not-me' — and to what others call rejected selves. At another plane the anti-selves are counterpoints without which the self just cannot be defined in the major cultures of South Asia. It is the self in conjunction with its anti-selves and its distinctive concept of the non-self which together define the domain of the self. Religion-as-faith is more compatible with such a complex self-definition; secularism has no inkling of this distinct, though certainly not unique, form of self-definition in South Asia. For, everything said, secularism is, as Madan[3] puts it, a 'gift of Christianity', by which he presumably means a gift of post-medieval, European Christianity to this part of the world.

It is in the context of these four processes that I shall now discuss the scope and limits of the ideology of secularism in India and its relationship with the new forms of ethnic violence we have been witnessing.

THE FATE OF SECULARISM

I must make it clear at this point that I am not a secularist. In fact, I can be called an anti-secularist. This is because I have come to believe that the ideology and politics of secularism have more or less exhausted their possibilities and that we may now have to work with a different conceptual frame which is already vaguely visible at the borders of Indian political culture.

....As we know, there are two meanings of the word current in modern and modernizing India and, for that matter, in the whole of this subcontinent. One of the two meanings is easily found by consulting any standard dictionary. But there is difficulty in finding the other, for it is a non-standard, local meaning which, many like to believe, is typically and distinctively Indian or South Asian....

The first meaning becomes clear when people talk of secular trends in history or economics, or when they speak of secularizing the state. The word 'secular' has been used in this sense, at least in the English-speaking West, for more than three hundred years. This secularism chalks out an area in public life where religion is not admitted. One can have religion in one's private life; one can be a good Hindu or a good Muslim within one's home or at one's place of worship. But when one enters public life, one is expected to leave one's faith behind. This ideology of secularism is associated with slogans like 'we are Indian first, Hindu second', or 'we are Indians first, then Sikhs'. Implicit in the ideology is the belief that managing the public realm is a science which is essentially universal and the religion, to the extent that it is opposed to the Baconian world-image of science, is an open or potential threat to any modern polity.

In contrast, the non-western meaning of secularism revolves around equal respect for all religions. This is the way it is usually put by public figures. Less crudely stated, it implies that while the public life may or may not be kept free of religion, it must have space for a continuous dialogue among religious traditions and between the religious and the secular — that, in the ultimate analysis, each major faith in the region includes within it an in-house version of the other faiths, both as an internal criticism and as a reminder of the diversity of the theories of transcendence.

....Most non-modern Indians...pushed around by the political and cultural forces unleashed by colonialism still operating in Indian society, have unwittingly opted for the accommodative and pluralist meaning, while India's westernized intellectuals have consciously opted for the abolition of religion from the public sphere.

In other words, the accommodative meaning is more compatible with the meaning a majority of Indians...have given to the word's 'secularism'. This meaning has always disconcerted the country's westernized intellectuals. They have seen such people's secularism as adulterated and as compromising true secularism. This is despite the fact that the ultimate symbol of religious tolerance for the modern Indian, Gandhi, obviously had this adulterated meaning in mind on the few occasions when he seemed to plead for secularism: as much is clear from his notorious claim that those who thought religion and politics could be kept separate understood neither religion nor politics.

The saving grace in all this is that while the scientific, rational meaning of secularism has dominated India's middle-class public consciousness, the Indian people and, till recently most practising Indian politicians, have depended on the accommodative meaning. The danger is that the first meaning is supported by the accelerating process of modernization in India. As a result, there is now a clearer fit between the declared ideology of the modern Indian nation-state and the secularism that fears religions and ethnicities. ....

Associated with this...is a hidden political hierarchy.... This hierarchy makes a four-fold classification of political actors in the subcontinent.

At the top of the hierarchy come those who are believers neither in public nor in private. They are supposed to be scientific and rational, and they are expected, ultimately, not only to rule this society but also to dominate its political culture. An obvious example is Jawaharlal Nehru.... It is the Nehruvian model which informs the following charming letter, written by a distinguished former ambassador, to the editor of India's best-known national daily;

M.V. Kamath asks in his article, 'Where do we find the Indian?' My dear friend and colleague, the late Ambassador M.R.A. Beg, often used to say: 'Don't you think, old boy, that the only Indians are we wogs?' However quaint it may have sounded 30 years ago, the validity of this statement has increasingly become apparent over he years.[3]

On the second rung of the ladder are those who choose not to appear as believers in public, despite being devout believers in private. I can think of no better example of this type than Indira Gandhi. She was a genuine non-believer in public life, dying at the hands of her own Sikh guards instead of accepting security advice to change them. But in private she was a devout Hindu who had to make her seventy-one — or was it sixty-nine? — pilgrimages. Both the selves of Indira Gandhi were genuine and together they represented the self-concept of a sizeable portion of the Indian middle class.... Though the westernized literati in South Asian societies have never cared much for this model of religious and ethnic tolerance, they have been usually willing to accept the model as a reasonable compromise with the 'under-developed' cultures of South Asia.

On the third rung are those who are believers in public but do not believe in private. This may at first seem an odd category, but one or two examples will make clear its meaning and also partially explain why this category includes problematic men and women. To me the two most illustrious examples of this genre from the Indian subcontinent are Mohammed Ali Jinnah, an agnostic in private life who took up the cause of Islam successfully in public, and V. D. Savarkar, an atheist in private life who declared Hinduism as his political ideology.

Such persons can be dangerous because to them religion is a political tool and a means of fighting one's own and one's community's sense of cultural inadequacy. Religion to them is not a matter of piety. Their private denial of belief only puts those secularists off guard who cannot fathom the seriousness with which the Jinnahs and the Savarkars take religion as a political instrument. On the other hand, their public faith puts the faithful off guard because the latter never discern the contempt in which such heroes hold the common run of believers. Often, these heroes invoke the classical versions of their faiths to underplay, marginalize or even delegitimize the existing ways of life associated with their faiths. The goal of those holding such an instrumental view of religion has always been to homogenize their co-believers into proper political formations and, for that reason, to eliminate those parts of religion which

smack of folk ways and threaten to legitimize diversities, inter-
faith dialogue and theological polycentrism.

At the bottom of the hierarchy are those who are believers
in the private as well as public domains. the best and most
notorious example is Gandhi, a believer both in private and public,
who gave his belief spectacular play in politics. This category
has its strengths and weaknesses. One may say that exactly as
the category manifests its strength in someone like Gandhi, it
shows its weakness in others like Ayatollah Khomeini in Iran
or Jarnail Singh Bhindranwale in the Punjab — both of whom
ended up trying to fully homogenize their communities in the
name of faith....

....Why is the old ideology of secularism not working in
India?.... First, in the early years of Independence, when the
national élite was small and a large section of it had face-to-face
contacts, one could screen people entering public life — specially
the upper levels of the public services and high politics — for
their commitment to secularism. Thanks to the growth of
democratic participation in politics...such screening is no longer
possible. We can no longer make sure that those who reach the
highest levels of the army, police, bureaucracy or politics believe
in old-style secular politics. .... India's ultra-élites can no longer
informally screen decision-makers the way they once used to;
political participation in the country is growing, and the country's
political institutions, particularly the parties, are under too much
strain to allow such screening. Religion has entered public life
but through the backdoor.

Second, it has become more and more obvious to a large
number of people that modernity is now no longer the ideology
of a small minority; it is now the organizing principle of the
dominant culture of politics. The idea that religions dominate
India, that there are a handful of modern Indians fighting a rear-
guard action against that domination, is no longer convincing
to many Indians. These Indians see the society around them —
and often their own children — leaving no scope for a compromise
between the old and new, and opting for a way of life which
fundamentally negates the traditional concepts of a good life
and a desirable society. These Indians have now come to sense
that it is modernity which rules the world and, even in this
subcontinent, religion-as-faith is being pushed to the corner. Much

of the fanaticism and violence associated with religion comes today from the sense of defeat of the believers, from their feelings of impotence, and from their free-floating anger and self-hatred while facing a world which is increasingly secular and desacralized.

....What the state says to a religious community, the modern sector often indirectly tells the individual, 'you give up your faith, at least in public; we also shall give up our faith in public and together we shall be able to live in freedom from religious intolerance'. I need hardly add that however reasonable the solution may look to people like us, who like to see themselves as rational non-believing moderns, it is not an adequate consolation to the faithful, to whom religion is what it is precisely because it provides an overall theory of life, including public life. For them life is not worth living without a theory of transcendence, however, imperfect.

Third, we have begun to find out that, while appealing to believers to keep the public sphere free of religion, the modern nation-state has no means of ensuring that the ideologies of secularism, development and nationalism themselves do not begin to act as faiths intolerant of other faiths. That is, while the modern state builds up pressures on citizens to give up their faith in public, it guarantees no protection to them against the sufferings inflicted by the state itself in the name of its ideology. In fact, with the help of modern communications and the secular coercive power at its command, the state can use its ideology to silence its non-conforming citizens. the role of secularism in many societies today is no different from the crusading and inquisitorial role of religious ideologies. In such societies, citizens have less protection against the ideology of the state than against religious ideologies or theocratic forces. Certainly in India, the ideas of nation-building, scientific growth, security, modernization and development have become parts of a left-handed technology with a clear touch of religiosity — a modern demonology, a *tantra* with a built-in code of violence.

....To many Indians today, secularism comes as a part of a larger package consisting of a set of standardized ideological products and social processes — development, megascience and national security being some of the most prominent among them. This package often plays the same role *vis-à-vis* the people of the society — sanctioning or justifying violence against the weak and the dissenting — that the Church, the *ulema*, the *sangha* or the Brahmans played in earlier times.

Finally, the belief that the values derived from the secular ideology of the state would be a better guide to political action and to a more tolerant and richer political life (as compared to the values derived from religious faiths) has become even more untenable to large parts of Indian society than it was a decade ago. We are living in times when it has become clear that, as far as public morality goes, statecraft in India may have some-thing to learn from Hinduism, Islam or Sikhism, but Hinduism, Islam, and Sikhism have very little to learn from the Constitution or the secular practices of the state....

In sum, we are at a point of time when old-style secularism can no longer pretend to guide moral or political action. All that the ideology of secularism can do now is to sanction the absurd search for a modern language of politics in a traditional society which has an open polity.

....In most post-colonial societies, when religion, politics or religion-and-politics is discussed, there is an invisible reference point. This reference point is the Western Man. Not the Western man in reality or the Western Man of history, but the Western Man as the defeated civilizations in this part of the world have construed him. This Western Man rules the world, it seems to the defeated, because of his superior understanding of the relationship between religion and politics. To cope with this suc-cess, every major religious community in the region has produced three responses — I should say two responses and one non-response....

The first response...is to model oneself on the Western Man. I do not want to use the word 'imitation' because something more than mimicking is involved. The response consists in cap-turing, within one's own self and one's own culture, the traits one sees as the reasons for the West's success on the world stage. Seemingly it is a liberal, synthesizing approach and those responding in this fashion to the West justify it as a universal response. However, one of the clearest identifiers of this response is its insensitivities to the new legitimacies and systems of domination and exploitation in the contemporary world....

The second response to the Western Man is that of the zealot.

The zealot's one goal is to somehow defeat Western Man at his own game, the way Japan, for instance, has done in economic matters.... In India at least, the heart of the response is the faith that what Japan has done in economy, one can do in the case of religion and politics. One can, for example, decontaminate Hinduism of its folk elements, turn it into a classical Vedantic faith, and then give it additional teeth with the help of Western technology and secular statecraft. Thus, it is hoped that the Hindus can take on and ultimately defeat all their external and internal enemies, if necessary by liquidating all forms of ethnic plurality, first within Hinduism and then within India, to equal Western Man as a new *übermensch*. The zealot judges the success or failure of his or her own religion only by this one criterion....

Such responses are...the ultimate admission of defeat. They constitute the cultural bed on which grows the revivalism of the defeated....

Usually, modern scholarship tends to see zealotry as a retrogression into primitivism and as a pathology of traditions. On closer look it turns out to be a by product and a pathology of modernity. For instance, whatever the revivalist Hindu may seek to revive, it is not Hinduism. The pathetically comic, martial uniform of khaki shorts, which the RSS cadres have to wear, tell it all. Unconsciously modelled on the uniform of the colonial police, the khaki shorts are the final proof that the RSS is an illegitimate child of western colonialism. If such a comment seems trivial, one can point out the systematic way in which the RSS ideology has always drawn upon the semiticizing Hindu reform movements under colonialism, upon the dominant Christian and Islamic concepts of religion (one Book and one God, for instance), and upon the modern western concept of the nation-state. Once such concepts of religion and state are imported into Hinduism, the inevitable happens. One begins to judge the everyday lifestyle of the Hindus, their diversity and heterogeneity, negatively, usually with a clear touch of hostility and contempt.

Likewise, there is nothing fundamentally Islamic about fundamentalist Muslims. As we see in Pakistan today, they are the ones who are usually the first to sell their souls at a discount to the forces which seek to disenfranchise ordinary Muslims on the pretext that the latter do not know their Islam well. And we are today witnessing the same process within Sikhism and Sri Lankan Buddhism too.

There is, however, a third sort of response. It usually comes from the non-modern majority of a society.... This response does not keep religion separate from politics, but it does say that the traditional ways of life have, over the centuries, developed internal principles of tolerance and these principles must have a play in contemporary politics. This response affirms that religious communities in traditional societies *have* known how to live with each other. It is not modern India which has tolerated Judaism in India for nearly two thousand years, Christianity from before the time it went to Europe, and Zoroastrianism for more than twelve hundred years; it is traditional India which has shown such tolerance. That is why today, as India gets modernized, religious violence is increasing. In the earlier centuries, according to available records, inter-religious riots were rare and localized; even after independence we had less than one event of religious strife a week; now we have about one and a half incidents a day. And more than ninety per cent of these riots begin in urban India, in and around the industrial areas.... Obviously, somewhere and somehow, religious violence has something to do with the urban-industrial vision of life and with the political processes the vision lets loose.

It is the awareness of this political process which has convinced a small but growing number of Indian political analysts that it is from non-modern India, from the traditions and principles of religious tolerance encoded in the everyday life associated with the different faiths of India, that one will have to seek clues to the renewal of Indian political culture....

....Modern India has a lot to answer for. So have the cosmopolitan intellectuals in this part of the world. They have failed to be respectful to the traditions of tolerance in Indian society. These traditions may have become creaky but so is, it is now pretty clear, the ideology of secularism itself....

The moral of the story is this: the time has come for us to recognize that instead of trying to build religious tolerance on the good faith or conscience of a small group of de-ethnicized, middle-class politicians, bureaucrats and intellectuals, a far more serious venture would be to explore the philosophy, the symbolism and the theology of tolerance in the various faiths of the citizens and hope that the state systems in South Asia may learn something about religious tolerance from everyday Hinduism, Islam, Buddhism, and Sikhism, rather than wish that ordinary Hindus, Muslims, Buddhists and Sikhs will learn tolerance from the various fashionable secular theories of statecraft....

Secularism has become a handy adjunct to this set of legimating core concepts. It helps those swarming around the nation-state, either as elites or as counter-elites, to legitimize themselves as the sole arbiters among traditional communities, to claim for themselves a monopoly on religious and ethnic tolerance and on political rationality. To accept the ideology of secularism is to accept the ideologies of progress and modernity as the new justifications of domination, and the use of violence to sustain these ideologies as the new opiates of the masses.

NOTES AND REFERENCES

1. Chatterjee, Partha, *Nationalist Thought and the Colonial World: A Derivative Discourse?*, Oxford University Press, Delhi, 1986.
2. Miller, D.F., 'Six theses on the question of religion and politics in India today', *Economic and Political Weekly*, July, 1987, 57-63.
3. Singh, G., 'Where's the Indian?', *Times of India*, 21 September, 1986.

Secularism in its Place

T.N. MADAN

We live in a world which we call modern or which we wish to
be modern. Modernity is generally regarded as both a practical
necessity and a moral imperative, a fact and a value.... By modernity I do not mean a complete break with tradition. Being modern
means larger and deeper things: for example, the enlargement
of human freedom and the enhancement of the range of choices
open to a people in respect of things that matter, including their
present and future life-styles. This means being in charge of oneself.
And this is one of the connotations of the process of secularization....

'Secularization' is nowadays generally employed to refer to,
in the words of Peter Berger, 'the process by which sectors of
society and culture are removed from the domination of religious
institutions and symbols'[1]. While the inner logic of the economic
sector perhaps makes it the most convenient arena for secularization, other sectors, notably the political, have been found to be
less amenable to it. It is in relation to the latter that the ideology
of secularism acquires the most salience.

Now, I submit that in the prevailing circumstances secularism
in South Asia as a generally shared credo of life is impossible,
as a basis for state action impracticable, and as a blueprint for

Excerpted from T.N. Madan, 'Secularism in its Place', *Journal of Asian Studies*,
vol. 46, no: 4, November 1987, 747-58.

the foreseeable future impotent. It is impossible as a credo of life because the great majority of the people of South Asia are in their own eyes active adherents of some religious faith. It is impracticable as a basis for state action either because Buddhism and Islam have been declared state or state-protected religions or because the stance of religious neutrality or equidistance is difficult to maintain since religious minorities do not share the majority's view of what this entails for the state. And it is impotent as a blueprint for the future because, by its very nature, it is incapable of countering religious fundamentalism and fanaticism.

Secularism is the dream of a minority which wants to shape the majority in its own image, which wants to impose its will upon history but lacks the power to do so under a democratically organized polity. In an open society the state will reflect the character of the society. Secularism therefore is a social myth which draws a cover over the failure of this minority to separate politics from religion in the society in which its members live. From the point of view of the majority, 'secularism' is a vacuous word, a phantom concept, for such people do not know whether it is desirable to privatize religion, and if it is, how this may be done, unless they be Protestant Christians, but not if they are Buddhists, Hindus, Muslims, or Sikhs. For the secularist minority to stigmatize the majority as primordially oriented and to preach secularism to the latter as the law of human existence is moral arrogance and worse....

....Social analysts draw attention to the contradiction between the undoubted though slow spread of secularization in everyday life, on the one hand, and the unmistakable rise of fundamentalism, on the other. But surely these phenomena are only apparently contradictory, for in truth it is the marginalization of religious faith, which is what secularization is, that permits the perversion of religion. There are no fundamentalists or revivalists in traditional society....

....Indian secularism has been an inadequately defined 'attitude'...of 'goodwill towards all religion', *sarvadharma sadbhāva*. In a narrower formulation it has been a negative or defensive policy of religious neutrality (*dharma nirpekshtā*) on the part of the state....

What exactly does the failure of secularism mean? For one thing, it underscores the failure of the society and the state to bring under control the divisive forces which resulted in the Partition of the subcontinent in 1947. Though forty years have passed and the Midnight's Children are at the threshold of middle age, tempers continue to rage, and occasionally (perhaps too frequently) even blood flows in some places, as a result of the mutual hostility between the followers of different religions....

Tolerance is indeed a value enshrined in all the great religions of mankind, but let me not underplay the historical roots of communal antagonism in South Asia. I am not wholly convinced when our Marxist colleagues argue that communalism is a result of the distortions in the economic base of our societies produced by the colonial mode of production and that the 'communal question was a petty bourgeois question par excellence'.[2] The importance of these distortions may not be minimized, but these analysts should know that South Asia's major religious traditions — Buddhism, Hinduism, Islam, and Sikhism — are totalizing in character, claiming all of a follower's life, so that religion is constitutive of society. In the given pluralist situation, both tolerance and intolerance are expressions of exclusivism. When I say that South Asia's religious traditions are 'totalizing', I am not trying to argue that they do not recognize the distinction between the terms 'religious' and 'secular'. We know that in their distinctive ways all four traditions make this distinction .... What needs to be stressed, however, is that these religions have the same view of the relationship between the categories of the 'religious ' and the 'secular'....

In our own times it was, of course, Mahatma Gandhi who restated the traditional point of view in the changed context of the twentieth century, emphasizing the inseparability of religion and politics and the superiority of the former over the latter. 'For me', he said, 'every, the tiniest, activity is governed by what I consider to be my religion'.[3] And, more specifically, there is the well-known early statement that 'those who say that religion has nothing to do with politics do not know what religion means'.[4] For Gandhi religion was the source of absolute value and hence constitutive of social life; politics was the arena of public interest. Without the former the latter would become debased. While it was the obligation of the state to ensure that every religion was free to develop according to its own genius, no religion which depended upon state support deserved to survive. In other words, the inseparability of religion and politics in the Indian context, and generally, was for Gandhi fundamentally a distinct issue from the separation of the state from the Church in Christendom. When he did advocate that 'religion and state should be separate', he clarified that this was to limit the role of the state to 'secular welfare' and to allow it no admittance into the religious life of the people. Clearly the hierarchical relationship is irreversible....

....Secularism as an ideology has emerged from the dialectic of modern science and Protestantism, not from a simple repudiation of religion and the rise of rationalism. Even the Enlightenment — its English and German versions in particular — was not against religion as such but against revealed religion or a transcendental justification for religion. Voltaire's 'dying' declaration was of faith in God and detestation of 'superstition' Models of modernization, however, prescribe the transfer of secularism to non-Western societies without regard for the character of their religious traditions or for the gifts that these might have to offer. Such transfers are themselves phenomena of the modern secularized world: in traditional or tradition-haunted societies they can only mean conversion and the loss of one's culture, and, if you like, the loss of one's soul. Even in already-modern or modernizing societies, unless cultural transfers are made meaningful for the people, they appear as stray behaviouristic traits and attitudinal postures. This means that what is called for its translation; mere transfer will not do.

But translations are not easily achieved. As Bankim Chandra Chatterji (that towering late nineteenth-century Indian intellectual) put it, 'You can translate a word by a word, but behind the word is an idea, the thing which the word denotes, and this idea you cannot translate, if it does not exist among the people in whose language you are translating'.[5] It is imperative, then, that a people must themselves render their historical experience meaningful: others may not do this for them. Borrowed ideas, unless internalized, do not have the power to bestow on us the gift and grace of living....

In short, the transferability of the idea of secularism to the countries of South Asia is beset with many difficulties and should not be taken for granted. Secularism must be put in its place: which does not mean rejecting it but of finding the proper means for its expression. In multi-religious societies, such as those of

South Asia, it should be realized that secularism may not be restricted to rationalism, that it is compatible with faith, and that rationalism (as understood in the West) is not the sole motive force of a modern state. What the institutional implications of such a position are is an important question and needs to be worked out....

....The Nehruvian state was first and foremost democratic, but in an economically poor and culturally diverse country it could hardly be truly democratic without being socialist and secularist. I am not here concerned with the course of democracy and socialism in India, but I must make some observations about the difficulties encountered by the secular state established under the Constitution.

.....We do not, of course, have a wall of separation in India, for there is no church to wall off, but only the notion of neutrality or equidistance between the state and the religious identity of the people. What makes this idea important is that not only Nehru but all Indians who consider themselves patriotic and modern, nationalist and rationalist, subscribe to it. What makes it impotent is that it is a purely negative strategy. And...in the history of mankind, nothing positive has ever been built on denials or negations alone.

An examination of Nehru's writings and speeches brings out very clearly his conviction that religion is a hindrance to 'the tendency to change and progress inherent in human society' and that 'the belief in a supernatural agency which ordains everything has led to a certain irresponsibility on the social plane, and emotion and sentimentality have taken the place of reasoned thought and inquiry'.[6] Religion, he confessed candidly, did not 'attract' him for 'behind it lay a method of approach to life's problems which was certainly not that of science'.[7] But, then, he did not worry too much about religion or its political expression, namely communalism, because he passionately believed that these epiphenomena would 'vanish at the touch of reality'.[8] Hence his insistence that, quoting from a 1931 speech, 'the real thing to my mind is the economic factor. If we lay stress on this and divert public attention to it we shall find automatically that religious differences recede into the background and a common bond unites different groups. The economic bond is stronger than the national one'[9]....

In the end, that is in 1947, Nehru knew that the battle at hand, though not perhaps the war, had been lost, that the peoples of the subcontinent were not yet advanced enough to share his view of secular politics and the secular state. A retreat was inescapable, but it was not a defeat....

What is noteworthy, therefore, is Nehru's refusal (or failure) to use the coercive powers of the state in hastening this [secularization] process. In this regard he invites comparison with Lenin and Ataturk, and, if you allow dictatorship, he suffers by it....

Contrast the internal coherence and sense of urgency of these two experiments — Lenin's and Ataturks — with the uncertainties of the 1949 Indian Constitution, which sought to establish a secular state (article 15) in a society which is allowed and even encouraged to be communally divided (articles 25-30). Under the rubric of 'freedom of religion', it allowed citizens not only the profession and practice of their respective religions but also their propagation. Besides, it allowed the establishment of educational institutions along communal lines. A direct reference to secularism had to wait until 1976, when it was introduced into the Preamble of the Constitution by the Forty-fourth Amendment.

It must be admitted here that the pluralistic situation which Nehru and the other framers of the Constitution faced was immensely more complex than anything that Lenin, and far less Ataturk, faced; yet the fact remains that Nehru did not use his undoubted hold over the people as a leader of the freedom movement and his vast authority as the head of government to bring communal tendencies under strict control. It is often said that he was too much of a liberal and a cultured aristocrat to think of strongarm methods; I think he was also too optimistic about the decline of the hold of religion on the minds of people. He did not seem to take into consideration the fact that the ideology of secularism enhances the power of the state by making it a protector of all religious communities and an arbiter in their conflicts.

No wonder, then, that secularism as an alien cultural ideology, which lacks the strong support of the state, has failed to make the desired headway in India. Instead what have made great strides are, apparently and by general agreement, Hindu revivalism and Muslim and Sikh fundamentalism....

....The principal question...is not whether Indian society will eventually become secularized as Nehru believed it would but rather in what sense it should become so and by what means. The limitations of secular humanism (so-called) and the falsity of the hope of secularists — namely, that all will be well with us if only scientific temper becomes generalized — need to be recognized. Secularized man can confront fundamentalism and revivalism no more than he may empathize with religion....

NOTES

1. Berger, Peter, *The Social Reality of Religion*, Penguin, Harmondsworth 1973, 113.
2. Chandra, Bipan, *Communalism in Modern India*, Vikas, Delhi, 1984, 40.
3. Iyer, Raghavan, *The Moral and Political Philosophy of Mahatma Gandhi*, Oxford University Press, Oxford, 1986, 391.
4. Gandhi, M.K., *An Autobiography or Story of My Experiments with Truth*, 1940, 383.
5. Chatterjee, Partha, *Nationalist Thought and the Colonial World: A Derivative Discourse?*, Oxford University Press, Delhi, 1986, 61.
6. Nehru, J., 1961, *The Discovery of India*, Asia Publishing House, Bombay, 543.
7. Ibid., 26.
8. Nehru, J., *An Autobiography*, Oxford University Press, Delhi, 1980, 469.
9. Nehru, J., *Selected Works of Jawaharlal Nehru*, Orient Longman, Delhi 1972-82, 5. 203.

Two Concepts of Secularism

AKEEL BILGRAMI

....My subject is the familiar dialectic between the concept of nation and that of religious community; and, though many of the conclusions drawn here are fundamentally generalisable, I will, for the sake of precision and detail, restrict my focus to India. The twin elements in the dialectic conspire toward my eventual theme of secularism, about whose precariousness in India I want to offer a philosophical diagnosis, and the very rudimentary beginnings of an alternative conception....

....What is it that we want explained? The answer on the surface seems obvious. For 17 initial years the leadership of independent India fell into the hands of Nehru and the Congress Party. Nehru's vision of a modern secular India is usually conceded by even his most vocal critics to be a genuine and honourable commitment. A comparison with the long stretches of either anti-secular or undemocratic regimes in Pakistan after the untimely death of Jinnah (who after leading a communal nationalist movement adopted much the same vision as Nehru's for the newly created Muslim nation), and also a comparison with what might have happened if other leaders such as Vallabhbhai Patel had been at the helm in India instead of Nehru, must allow the conclusion

Excerpted from Akeel Bilgrami, 'Two Concepts of Secularism', *Economic and Political Weekly*, vol. XXIX, no. 28, 9 July, 1994, 1749-67.

that, to a considerable extent, Nehru did succeed. But if we look around us today in the period before and after the destruction of the mosque at Ayodhya, we can only judge the secular success of his long rule as, at best, a holding process. To describe Nehru's success in terms of a holding process is of course to describe it as a success of a very limited sort. So the explanandum for which Nandy derives his historical analysis is just the following question: Why is it that the Nehruvian vision of a secular India failed to take hold?

Nandy's answer[1] and the general sense of the intelligentsia, including but not by any means exhausted by most in the academic community, is that there was something deeply flawed in the vision itself. On this there is a mounting consensus, and indeed I think it would be accurate to say that in the last few years there is widespread and accumulated deflation of Nehru's stature, to be found in the intellectual and political mood of the country. Though I have no particular interest in defending Nehru's achievements, nor even eventually his way of thinking about the secular ideal, which is in many ways muddled and mistaken, I want to briefly assess this mood because I think that there is much that is excessive in its main claims. I do also think that there is a strand of truth in it which may prove to be an instructive basis for how to re-think the methodological and philosophical basis for secularism in India....

The contemporary critique of Nehru...usually begins by laying down a fundamental distinction in the very idea of a religious community, a distinction between religions as faiths and ways of life on the one hand and as constructed ideologies on the other. This is intended as a contrast between a more accommodating, non-monolithic and pluralist religious folk traditions of Hinduism and Islam, and the Brahmanical BJP and the Muslim League versions of them which amount to constructed religious ideologies that are intolerant of heterodoxy within themselves as well as intolerant of each other. The critique's target is by implication modernity itself, for its claim is that it is the polity in its modern conception of nationhood and its statecraft which is the source of such ideological constructions that distort those more 'innocent' aspects of religion which amount to 'ways of life' rather than

---

[1] *See contribution by Ashis Nandy in this collection* Ed.

systems of thought geared to political advancement. The critique then suggests that once one accepts the inevitability of these ideological constructions, then there is nothing left to do in combating sectarian and communal sentiment and action than to formulate a secular vision which itself amounts to an oppressive nationalist and statist ideology. As they would describe Nehru's vision, it is one of a modernist tyranny that just as surely (as the narrow communalisms) stands against the pluralist and tolerant traditions that existed in the uncontaminated traditions of religions as faiths and ways of life prior to modernity's distortions. That was Nehru's primary contribution then: a perversely modernist and rationalist imposition of a vision that was foreign to the natural tendencies of Hinduism and Islam in their traditional pre-modern spiritual and societal formations, a vision accompanied by all the destructive modern institutional commitment to centralised government, parliamentary democracy, not to mention heavy industry as well as metropolitan consumption and displacement of traditional ways of life. The echoes of Gandhi here are vivid, and Ashis Nandy is explicit in describing this alternative secular vision in Gandhian terms.

This critique of Nehru is careful (though perhaps not always careful enough) to be critical also of contemporary Hindu nationalism in India, as was Gandhi himself despite his Hinduism and his traditionalism. Nandy makes great dialectical use of the fact that Gandhi was assassinated by a Hindu nationalist, arguing that Gandhi's politics and pluralist version of Hinduism posed a threat to the elitist pseudo-unification of Hinduism which flowered in the ideology of upper-caste Hindus and in orthodox Brahmanical culture, as represented paradigmatically in the Chitpavans, the caste to which Nathuram Godse (his assassin) belonged.

Now it should be emphasised that what is novel and interesting about this critique of Hindu nationalism is that it is intended to be part of a larger critique in two different ways. First, it is intended as part of a general diagnosis in which Hindu nationalism is to be seen as a special instance of the more general wrong that is identified in nationalism itself — which is a modern state of mind — in which the very ideal of 'nation' has built into it as a form of necessity the ideal of a nation-*state*, with its commitment to such things as development, national security, rigidly codified forms of increasingly centralised polity, and above all the habit of exclusion of some other people or nation in its very self-definition and self-understanding. There is apparently no separating these more general wrongs of nationalism from what is wrong with Hindu nationalism, for otherwise we would have missed the more hidden explanatory conceptual sources of this particular movement. And second, the critique of Hindu nationalism is intended to be *of a piece* with the critique of Nehruvian secularism. Such a communal nationalism, itself a product of modernity, owes its very existence to the oppositional but at the same time *internal* dialectical relation it bears to that other product of modernity, Nehruvian secularism. The claim is that the latter is an alien imposition upon a people who have never wished to separate religion from politics in their every day life and thinking, and therefore leaves that people no choice but to turn to the only religious politics allowed by modernity's stranglehold, i.e., Hindu nationalism. This secular tyranny breeds Hindu nationalist resistance, which threatens with the promise of its own form of tyranny. Such are the travails that modernity has visited upon us.

There is something convincing about this argument but its explanatory virtues are greatly marred by its narrowing and uncritical anti-nationalism, its skewed historiography, and its traditionalist nostalgia. What is convincing in it is much more theoretical and methodological than anything that surfaces explicitly in the critique's articulation....

First of all, though there is no gainsaying the humanism inherent in Gandhi's politics, it is also foolish and sentimental to deny the Brahmanical elements in it. There is the plain and well known fact that Gandhi, no less than the Chitpavan nationalist Tilak (however different their nationalist sensibilities were in other respects), encouraged the communal Hindu elements in the national movement by using Hindu symbolism to mobilise mass nationalist feeling. As is also well known, his support of the reactionary Muslim Khilafat movement had exactly the same motives and the same communalist effect on the Muslim population. I will not say a word more about this since this point is very well understood by many who have studied the national movement, even cursorily.

More importantly, there is some strenuous simplification in the critique's insistence that nationalism was the bad seed that turned a more pristine Hinduism and Islam into communal ideologies in India.

To begin with, there is the hardly deniable fact that Lenin pointed out quite explicitly. In a curious manner Nandy shares with the Hindu nationalists he criticises an idea that nationalism is a single and transparent thing, the very thing that Lenin denies. In fact, nationalism is far more omnibus and frustrating to analyse than either Nandy or the Hindu nationalists allow, and for that reason it is unlikely that it can be an explanatory concept at all....

....Though the underlying flaw in the prevalent anti-Nehru intellectual climate is to misdescribe the sense in which religion may enter politics in India, given the realities of a slowly consolidating bourgeois democracy and modern state, this is by no means to suggest that Nehruvian insistence on a separation of religion from politics is feasible either. Indeed, my acknowledging that his secularism amounted to no more than a holding process is an acknowledgement of the unfeasibility of that separation in a country with the unique colonial and post-colonial history of communal relationships that India has witnessed. Neither the pre-modern conception of an innocent spiritual integration of religion and politics, nor the Nehruvian separation of religion and politics can cope with the demands of Indian political life today.

What I see as a strand of truth in the contemporary critique of Nehru is roughly this: Nehru's secularism was indeed an imposition. But the sense in which it is an imposition is not that it was a modern intrusion into an essentially traditionalist religious population. It is not that because, as I said, the population under an evolving electoral democracy through this century willy-nilly has come to see religion entering politics in non-traditionalist modern political modes. It is an imposition rather in the sense that it assumed that *secularism stood outside the substantive arena of political commitments*. It had a constitutional status; indeed it was outside even of that: it was in the preamble to the Constitution. It was not in there with Hinduism and Islam as one among *substantive* contested political commitments to be *negotiated*, as any other contested commitments must be negotiated, one with the other.

I should immediately warn against a facile conflation. It may be thought that what I am doing is pointing to an imposition by *the state* of a doctrine of secularism upon a people who have never been secular in this sense. And in turn it may be thought that this is not all that different from Nandy's (and others') charge of an imposition made against Nehru, since states which impose entire ways of life upon a people are wholly a project of modernity. Let me leave aside for now, as in any case dubious, the idea that only modern states impose ways of life upon people, dubious because it seems to me a wholly unjustified extrapolation to go from the fact that the *scale* of imposition that modern states are capable of implementing is larger, to the idea that it is a *novelty* of the modern state to impose ways of life. That is not the conflation I had in mind. The conflation is the failure to see that in charging Nehru with imposing a non-negotiated secularism, I am saying something quite orthogonal to the charge that his was a statist imposition. Perhaps his *was* a statist imposition, but that is not what my charge is claiming. Rather it is claiming that what the state imposed was not a doctrine that was an outcome of a negotiation between different communities. This critique cannot be equated with a critique of statism, leave alone modern statism, because it may be quite inevitable in our times that, at least at the centre, and probable also in the regions, even a highly negotiated secularism may have to be adopted and implemented by the state (no doubt ideally after an inflow of negotiation from the grass roots). There is no reason to think that a scepticism about Nehru's secularism along these lines should amount in itself to a critique of the very idea of statehood, because there is nothing inherent in the concept of the state which makes it logically impossible that it should adopt such a substantive, negotiated policy outcome, difficult though it may be to fashion such a state in the face of decades of its imposition of a non-negotiated secularism.

Proof of the fact that my critique of Nehru does not coincide with a critique of statehood lies in the fact that the critique applies to a period before independence, i.e., before statehood was acquired. It is very important to point out that Nehru's failure to provide for a creative dialogue between communities is not just a failure of the immediate post-independence period of policy formulation by the state. There are very crucial historical antecedents to it, antecedents which may have made inevitable the post-independent secularist policies whose non-substantive theoretical status and non-negotiated origins I am criticising. For three decades before independence the Congress, under Nehru refused to let a secular policy emerge through negotiation between different communal interests, by denying at every step in the various conferrings with the British, Jinnah's demand that the Muslim League represent the Muslims, a Sikh leader represent the Sikhs, and a *harijan* leader represent the untouchable community. And the ground for the denial was simply that as a secular party they could not accept that they did *not* represent *all* these communities. Secularism thus never got the chance to *emerge* out of a creative dialogue between these different communities. It was *sui generis*. This archimedean existence gave secularism procedural priority but in doing so it gave it no abiding substantive authority. As a result it could be nothing more than a holding process, already under strain in the time of its charismatic architect, but altogether ineffective in the hands of his opportunist familial heirs. It is this archimedeanism of doctrine, and not its statist imposition, that I think is the deepest flaw in Nehru's vision and (as I will continue to argue later) it has nothing essential to do with modernity and its various Nandian cognates: rationality, science, technology, industry, bureaucracy....

....I should add several cautionary remarks in order to be fair to Nehru's position. For one thing, I do not mean to suggest that Jinnah and the Muslim League represented the mass of the Muslim people at these stages of the anti-colonial movement; he only represented the urban middle class and was not in an ideal position to play a role in bringing about the sort of negotiated ideal of secularism that I am gesturing at. Nor am I suggesting that these various elitist fora at which Jinnah demanded communal representation could be the loci for the sort of creative dialogue between communities that would have been necessary. However, neither of these cautionary remarks spoil the general point of my criticism of Nehru's position. That general point was to call attention to the horizon of Congress high command thinking about secularism in the pre-independence period, a horizon on which *any* conception of a *negotiated* ideal of secularism was not so much as visible. Putting Jinnah and the elitist conferrings aside, the fact is that even *Congress* Muslim leaders such as Azad were never given a prominent negotiating voice in a communal dialogue with their Hindu counterparts in conferrings within the supposedly *mass* party of which they were members. The question of the need for such a dialogue within the party in order to eventually found a substantive secularism in the future never so much as came up. The transcendent ideal of secularism Nehru assumed made such a question irrelevant.

However, the last and most important of the cautionary remarks I wish to make might be seen as attempting to provide an answer to this line of criticism of Nehru. It is possible that Nehru and the Congress leadership assumed something which to some extent is true; that the Congress Party was a large and relatively accommodating and (communally speaking) quite comprehensively subscribed nationalist party in a way that the Muslim League had ceased to be. And on the basis of that premise, they could draw the conclusion that an *implicitly and tacitly* carried out negotiation between the component elements in the subscription was already inherent in the party's claims to being secular. In other words, the secularism of a party, premised on the assumption of such a comprehensive communal subscription, had *built into it* by its very nature (that is what I mean by 'tacitly' or implicitly) the negotiated origins I am denying to it. This is a subtle and interesting argument which I think had always been in the back of Nehru's mind in his rather primitively presented writings and speeches on secularism. And I think the argument needs scrutiny, not dismissal.

I say that this argument was at the back of Nehru's mind partly because it was often pushed into the background by the rhetoric of a quite different argument that Nehru voiced, which was roughly the argument of the left programme, viz., that a proper focus on the issue of class and the implementation of a leftist programme of economic equality would allow the nation to bypass the difficulties that issued from religious and communal differences. Speaking generally, this argument is a very attractive one. However, except for a few years in the 1930s even Nehru did not voice this argument with genuine conviction; and in any case, if he were thinking honestly, he should have known that it would have been empty rhetoric to do so since he must have been well aware that the right-wing of the party was in growing ascendancy in Congress politics despite his central presence, and

there was no realistic chance of the programme being implemented. Given that fact, the negotiative ideal of secularism became
all the more pressing. And it is to some extent arguable that it
should have been pressing anyway.

To return to what I am calling Nehru's argument from 'implicit'
negotiation for his secularism, I strongly suspect that scrutiny of
the argument will show, not so much that its premise (about the
Congress Party's comprehensive communal subscription) is false,
but that the very idea of implicit or tacit negotiation, which is
derived from the premise and which is crucial to the argument,
is not an idea that can in the end be cashed out theoretically by
any confirmational and evidential procedure.... Hence the argument is not convincing because there is no bridge that takes one
from the idea that an anti-colonial movement and a post-colonial
party is 'composite' (a favourite word of the Congress to describe
its wide spectrum of communal representation) to the idea that
it stands for substantive secularism. My point is that to claim
that the *mere fact of compositeness* amounts to an *implicit* negotiation
among the compositional communal elements which would yield
such a secularism, is a sophistical move which does nothing to
bridge that gap in the argument. It is a mere fraudulent *labelling*
of a non-existing bridging argumentative link between compositeness and, what I am calling, a 'substantive' secularism. The label
'implicit' just serves to hide the fact that the commitment to
genuine negotiation (which alone could build the necessary bridge
from the party's compositeness to a substantive secularism) was
manifestly avoided by the Congress Party.

....In such circumstances, with no locus where negotiation between communities, however implicit, can be found or carried
out, the very idea of secularism is bound to seem an imposition
in the special sense I have claimed.

In reaction to this imposition it would be a mistake to formulate
an alternative vision of secularism which harked back nostalgically
to the idea of a pre-modern India. Since the sense in which it is
an imposition has not so much to do with modernist intrusion
as with its rarefied non-negotiable status, the right reaction to it
should be to acknowledge that secularism can only *emerge* as a
value by negotiation between the substantive commitments of
particular religious communities. It must emerge from the bottom
up with the moderate political leadership of different religious

communities negotiating both procedure and substance, negotiating details of the modern polity from the codification of law primarily to the distribution of such things as political and cultural autonomy, and even bureaucratic and industrial employment, education, etc....

An alternative secularism, emergent rather than imposed in the specific sense that I have defined, sees itself as one among other doctrines such as Islam and Hinduism. Of course there is still a difference of place and function in the polity between secularism and Islam or Hinduism. But once we see it as a substantive doctrine, this difference can be formulated in quite other terms than the way Nehru formulated it. In my conception, what makes secularism different from these specific, politico-religious commitments is not any longer that it has an archimedean and non-substantive status, but rather that it is an outcome of a negotiation among these specific commitments. This gives secularism a quite different place and function in the polity, and in the minds of citizens, than Islam or Hinduism could possibly have. Yet this difference does not amount to wholesale transcendence from these substantive religious commitments in politics. If secularism transcends religious politics in the way I am suggesting, it does so *from within*, it does not do so because it has a shimmering philosophical existence separate from religious political commitments, not because it is established by constitutional fiat by a pan-Indian elite unconcerned and unrealistic about the actual sway of religion in politics. It does so rather because *after* climbing up the ladder of religious politics (via a dialogue among acknowledged substantive religious commitments in politics) this emergent secularism might be in a position to kick that ladder of religious politics away. There is no paradox here of a doctrine emerging from its opposite, no more so than in any movement of synthesis, for the point is essentially Hegelian. Unlike the pure liberal fantasy of a secularism established by an ahistorical, philosophical ('transcendental', to use Kant's term) argument, the argument being proposed is essentially dialectical, where secularism emerges from a creative playing out (no historical inevitability is essential to *this* Hegelian proposal) of a substantive communal politics that is prevalent at a certain historical juncture.

When it is hard won in these ways, secularism is much more likely to amount to something more than a holding process. And this is so not merely because (unlike Nehru's secularism) it acknowledges as its very starting-point the inseparability of religion from politics, but also because, at the same time, it does not shun a realistic appreciation of the entrenched facts of modern political life, which Nehru (unlike his contemporary critics) was right to embrace wholeheartedly. This way of looking at things gives a philosophical basis to the widespread but somewhat vague anti-Nehru feeling (shared by a variety of different political positions today) that in a country like India we cannot any longer embrace a secularism that separates religion from politics. And it does so without in any way ceding ground to those who draw quite the wrong conclusions from this vague feeling: it cedes nothing to the Hindu nationalist, nor to the Muslim communalist, nor even to Ashis Nandy's nostalgia for a by-gone pre-modernism. The crucial importance of seeing things this way lies precisely in the fact that it counters what is a dangerously easy and uncritical tendency today, the tendency to move from this vague but understandable feeling of the inseparability of religion from politics to one or other of these conclusions. It counters this tendency by a very specific philosophical consolidation of this feeling, so that these conclusions which are often derived from it now no longer seem compulsory. Or, to put it more strongly (and more correctly), this philosophical consolidation of this understandable feeling allows us to see these conclusions derived from the feeling as simply *non-sequiturs....*

....In a very important sense, an aspect of Nandy's critique of Nehru, which I have not focused on, inherits a muddle that it uncovers in Nehru's thinking. There is a stand in Nehru's thinking that Nandy emphasises, which is Nehru's apparent linking of the scientific temper with a secular attitude. I have instead restricted my attention to Nandy's discussion linking Nehru's secularism with the modern phenomenon of nationalism and its accompanying statism. But this might seem unfair since his discussion makes so much of modernity and the enlightenment, and essential to the idea of these things, it might be said, is Nehru's optimism about the scientific outlook's power to overcome communal commitments. That is, it might seem unfair that in failing to take up this facile optimism in Nehru, I have left out an integral part of Nandy's critique of Nehru's modernism, and therefore rejected Nandy's outright scepticism about secularism too easily.

My only excuse for not taking up this aspect of Nandy is that it seemed to me obvious that this optimism on Nehru's part was based on a dumbfounding, though common, confusion. There is simply no dependable connection between communalism and the lack of scientific temper, because communalism is a *political* phenomenon (with economic underpinnings and cultural consequences) and not a matter of having an unscientific outlook. There is about as much connection between belief in the power of science and secular attitudes as there is between belief in god and moral behaviour. That is to say, none. The most scientific-minded can be party to a cynical adoption of religion in politics, and the most devout can be suspicious of the mix of religion and politics. Nandy is so obviously right to think that the canonisation of science and its method, and perhaps even its technological consequences in large-scale capital-intensive investments have failed to promote a secular polity, that it seemed to me hardly worth noting. That is why I focused on Nandy's more controversial and interesting argument against Nehru which linked his secularism *internally* with its opposite, Hindu nationalism, and in turn situated the latter too as a special instance of a general phenomenon of distinctly modern times. It does nothing to improve the genuine interest of this argument (nor to alleviate its dubious viability) to *throw into* the argument what is a quite separable strand, viz. these considerations critical of Nehru's commitment to science. Nandy, however, may not see it this way. For him, Nehru's wrongs regarding secularism are perhaps inseparable from the wrongs of that other commitment of modernity and the enlightenment, the fetishistic commitment to scientific knowledge. Thus for him to reject one is to reject the other as well.

But this is simply to buy into Nehru's confusion. The right criticism would have been to notice that Nehru confused the two things. And if that is so, that leaves it open...that each of those two things is right or that one of them is right, or even that both happen to be wrong. But to say that both things are wrong and *necessarily wrong together* (because they are both part of a post-enlightenment paradigm) is simply to have failed to see the strength and point of uncovering a confusion in Nehru's thinking. A critique of something as being confused should not then go on to inherit the confusion in its criticism. It is perfectly possible then to leave out of his critique of Nehru's commitment to secularism, his critique of his modernist commitment to science and technology, on the ground that these two commitments that are the targets of two separate critiques have no inherent inferential link and were only linked by a confusion in Nehru's thinking. But Nandy, and others who follow him, do not leave these separable things separate, and see their critiques of them as essentially linked. In doing so they make essentially the same confusion....

....Unlike those critiques of Nehru that criticise him for being too situated in the grand paradigmatic concepts of the enlightenment and of modernity, my criticisms acknowledge the determining fact of slowly evolving modern institutions and attitudes. As a result, my conclusions are less ambitious but also, I submit, less preposterously nostalgic and potentially more constructive. My (admittedly primitive and sketchy) proposal for an alternative conception of secularism seeks, by a posited process of reflection and internal negotiation, to arrive at a dialectical outcome uncountenanced either by Nehru or by the extravagantly extrapolative critiques of Nehru that I have been criticising.

FURTHER READINGS

The literature about politics and religion in India can be divided into
three types:
   (i) some deal with the recurrence of communal violence in many
   forms, especially riots;
   (ii) others try to analyse why religious identity has been mobilised
   with greater success in the recent decade; and
   (iii) a third group of studies go into the historical suitability of secular
   constitutional arrangements.
(i) Engineer, Asghar Ali, (ed.) *Communalism and Communal Violence in
   India*, Ajanta Publications, Delhi, 1985.
This book, as with much of Engineer's other work, seeks to understand
   the pattern of communal violence and discrimination against Indian
   Muslims, and tries to unravel the political instrumentalities at work
   behind them.
Das, Veena, (ed.), *Mirrors of Violence*, Oxford University Press, Delhi,
   1991.
This excellent collection of papers supplements the usual instrumental
   analyses of communal violence with a sophisticated understanding
   of their cultural dimensions, focusing on the processes of construction
   of religious communities, the narratives of the victims and the jus-
   tifiability of the standard arguments about religious traditions.
(ii) van der Veer, Peter, *Religious Nationalism*, University of California
   Press, Berkeley, 1994.
A sophisticated and theoretically informed study of the historical processes by which religious nationalism has been formed and propelled
   in South Asia.
Basu, Tapan, et al., *Khaki Shorts and Saffron Flags*, Orient Longman, Delhi,
   1993. Provides a concise history of the RSS movement, and concentrates
   on the technique of mobilisation and propaganda of the Vishwa Hindu
   Parishad in the recent years.
Jaffrelot, C., *Hindu Nationalist Movement and Indian Politics*, C. Hurst,
   London, 1996. Cited earlier in the readings on political parties, this
   book provides the most detailed account and a serious analysis of
   the mass mobilisation by the Hindu nationalist organisations in recent
   years.
Rajagopal, Arvind, 'Communalism and the consuming subject' *Economic
   and Political Weekly*, 10 February, 1996.
This, like other essays Rajagopal, tries to find a way of combining the
   political-economic and cultural arguments about communalism.
(iii) Smith, Donald E., *India as A Secular State*. Princeton University Press,
   Princeton, 1963.
The standard account of the institutions of Indian secularism. This offers

a careful analysis of the problems from which Indian secularism sprang, the institutions of the secular state and the policies it followed. Its account comes from the sixties when the secular state appeared solid and invulnerable.

Bhargava, Rajiv, 'Giving Secularism Its Due', *Economic and Political Weekly*, 9 July 1994.

This is a spirited and sophisticated rejoinder to the current arguments undermining the legitimacy of the secular state in India. Its thesis should be compared and contrasted with the readings from TN Madan and Akeel Bilgrami in the present volume.

Chatterjee, Partha, 'Secularism and Toleration', *Economic and Political Weekly*, 9 July 1994.

An excellent sociological analysis of the process of religious reform and its relation with secularization in India.

VII

Sociology of State Crisis

There is almost complete agreement among students of Indian politics that the national state that emerged from the freedom movement is in crisis. But this unanimity is misleading: there is no agreement about what caused this crisis, what is its exact nature, and what its most likely outcome. The crisis arguments can be classified in several ways. We can follow them historically. The first to develop a critical and sceptical view of Indian politics were the Marxists, but within that tradition too there was considerable variation of emphasis and explanatory models. Some Marxists entertained a radically sceptical view about possibilities of capitalist development and democracy. Since, under the historical conditions of colonialism, the essential preconditions for the development of capitalism had not matured, some Marxists argued, democracy, which was a specifically *bourgeois* form of governance, could never succeed in India. This minimized the force of the charge that Marxists did not believe in the democratic institutions of politics, by saying that, on solid theoretical grounds, they found it hard to believe that democracy would stabilise in India. There was no special culpability about undermining something that was fated to collapse in any case. Other Marxists, without subscribing to this radically sceptical view, generally emphasised two features of India's political economy: Firstly, the inadequacy of the spread of democratic rights to poorer segments of the population; and Secondly, the manner in which the disequalising effects of capitalist growth overwhelmed the egalitarian logic of democratic politics. But the main distinguishing feature of the Marxist views of crisis would be that all of them, despite considerable internal variation, would see the pattern of capitalist development in India as being central if not the primary causal influence. The more deterministic forms of Marxist analyses would conceive of the crisis as being one of capitalism, and being primarily caused by economic contradictions, which are merely being reflected in the political sphere as a crisis of the state. However, in recent decades, Indian Marxists have also widely used analyses of cultural processes and 'structuralist' ideas about the state itself being a 'site' of contradictions and power.

Till the 1970s other analysts did not see the Indian system as being in a state of 'crisis', certainly not a terminal one. The defeat of the Congress in many northern states in the elections of 1967 came to many as a shock; but the later recovery of Congress rule made that appear as a temporary and aberrant episode. In any case, the decline of the Congress was not necessarily a crisis of the state; and some observers saw the possibility of a movement from a monopolistic to a competitive system in party politics. The emergency, for the first time, created a widespread feeling of fragility of the democratic structure, and showed that the problem of authoritarianism, so common in Third World politics, could also arise in India. The fact that the coalition that defeated Indira Gandhi could not manage to say in power, or solve endemic problems of distributive justice and political stability indicated that the difficulty faced was not something that could be attributed to a single party; it indicated something was wrong with the 'system'. The persistence of instability since the late seventies has now shown that there is indeed a larger problem of political crisis, and various theories have been advanced to explain its exact nature.

Sociological analyses of Indian politics also developed views about the crisis, but these did not see the 'economic' as constituting the causal force. Among writers who did not use a Marxian explanation, there is a greater variety of hypotheses about what the crisis is about. Satish Saberwal has sought to understand the nature of the crisis and the logic of its movement for quite sometime, in a body of work that has enlarged its initial hypothesis into a long-term historical sociology. His work, deeply influenced by a coherent Weberian view of modernity, explains the crisis as a conflict between formal institutions of modernity which are based on rationalist liberal principles of impersonality, which enable modern institutions to increase their scale indefinitely, and the entrenched logic of segmentation of the traditional order. On Saberwal's view, the logic of segmentation of Indian caste society is replicated by other types of personalised conduct and segmentary behaviour which frustrate the modernist aspirations implicit in formal institutions. It also creates a dissonance between the formal and actual functioning of the institutions of modern life. Under conditions of modernity, it is impossible to go back to the consistency of segmentary behaviour of traditional society. But the requirement of impersonality and enlargement of scale is constantly undermined.

Political scientists have advanced theories of state crisis in a narrower sense. Rajni Kothari's work has moved in several stages towards a perception of crisis of the political system. Although his earlier analysis of Indian politics showed no sense of an impending crisis, since the emergency, his work reveals an appreciation of the a process of atrophy of the institutions of political democracy. Kothari observes a gradual establishment of monopolistic control over party and state institutions by a political elite which increasingly undermined some indispensable features of modern liberal democracy. First, there was a subtle, but increasingly explicit violation of the principle of state monopoly of legitimate violence, which by corollary outlaws use of private violence or threat of use of force. Clearly, a large number of groups in Indian politics have shown their willingness to use violence against opponents, and the state has not shown much initiative in curbing these attempts. Secondly, the format of political parties, which is supposed to articulate social demands into the political sphere has become so degraded as to be entirely

ineffective in functioning as a vehicle of democracy — either in
the procedural or the participatory sense. The state, as whole,
thus turns against democracy through large-scale bureaucratic
obstructiveness, civil service corruption and the use of private
force through the rising power of criminals. His stress on the
'criminalisation of politics', an unpicturesque and inelegant concept, however draws attention to a strangely uniform process of
increasing control of criminals in most parties, irrespective of
political ideology. Kothari has tried to devise alternative normative
perspectives for Indian politics by thinking about a 'non-party
political process' and the regeneration of democracy through 'civil
society'. Although, the positive, constructive parts of this view
are not unproblematic, the critique of politics is significant, and
searches out elements which might otherwise remain neglected.

A distinct line of argument, which recognises the crisis, but
explains it differently, comes from the work of Ashis Nandy and
T N Madan, who believe that it is the imposition of alien Western
institutions by an arrogant and unbending élite that has caused
the present situation of crisis reflected in the conflict over the
secular institutions of the state. Democracy, they imply, was largely a shallow consultative process in the first three decades after
independence. Ordinary people consider religion as the source
of determining principles by which social conduct should be
governed. It would be strange if they would readily agree to the
idea that the most important public questions should have nothing
to do with these principles which govern human conduct. The
Protestant idea of 'privatisation of religion' is thus an unintelligible
and unwelcome idea to them. The westernised elite, convinced
about its own rightness and faced with this incomprehensible
intellectual insubordination from the ordinary people, can only
take recourse to state violence. Evidently, this can easily lead to
a point where there could be a serious conflict between principles
of democratic rule and the secular character of the state.

All these suggestions advance our understanding of why Indian
society has tended to slide into a serious political crisis. And
there can, obviously, be modes of explanation which mix arguments drawn from a Marxian analysis that emphasises the intensification of inequality resulting from capitalist development
and a Tocquevillian theory that democracy alters the structures
of society irreversibly and generates political demands which

formal institutions might not be able to meet. In a sense of course, the various explanatory theories need not compete with one another, but relate to each other in a more complementary fashion. An explanation which emphasises the fact that social resentments, fuelled through democracy are finding it impossible to express themselves through the party format can be supplemented by an explanatory account of how the inequalities of modern capitalism has created this resentment in the first place. Both the essays chosen for this section offer multicausal explanations for the gathering crisis of the Indian state. Kohli's discussion seeks to weave strands of economic analysis about inequality and discontent into an analysis of the growing incapacity of political institutions to meet political demands from various assertive groups. Francince Frankel's essay puts somewhat greater emphasis on the decline of an order of relations based on caste precedence and the rise of new elites and political groups through the functioning of democratic processes.

The political situation after the general elections of 1996 in a sense demonstrates the validity of the historical surmise about the crisis. It has created a crisis evidently at two distinct levels. First, the result of the elections has led to a situation where stable government might become difficult because no party has received a clear majority. But obviously, the elections also raise a more fundamental question about the 'nature of the state' itself, since some groups with large electoral support, appear unreconciled to the principles on which the political institutions in free India have been based.

Decline of a Social Order

FRANCINE R. FRANKEL

ANALYSING DOMINANCE AND STATE POWER IN INDEPENDENT INDIA

'Transfer of Power' by the British Raj to the Government of India is a phrase which implies considerable continuity with the past. Yet, the governmental structures which were established after British rule introduced a complexity into relations within the state, and of the state with society, that marked an important break with the colonial period.

The standard definitions of the state, derived mainly from continental European experience, would have served adequately to describe the British Raj. Despite the series of constitutional reforms between 1909 and 1935 that provided for increasing Indian representation in the Central Legislature and Provincial Assemblies, the nature of the state was best captured by the classic concepts of sovereignty over a recognized territory, centralized public institutions and a monopoly over the legitimate use of force. The officials who served in the Indian Civil Service, the Indian Police Service and the Indian Army, in addition, were inculcated with

Excerpted from Francine Frankel and M. S. A. Rao (eds.), *Dominance and State Power in Modern India*, vol. II, OUP, Delhi, 1990, 482-517.

a sense of the public domain that transcended particular social groups. In an ironical transposition of the sacred and secular bases of power noted earlier, the Indian bureaucrats who filled key positions in the state were drawn from predominately Brahman and other small literati élites recruited across regions. After the departure of the British, they became, in a further irony, viewed from the perspective of Gandhi's vision, the backbone of the national class committed to modernizing India as an industrial nation.

The all-India services of the Indian state were the major institutional legacy of the British Raj. These public institutions laid the foundations for the successor bureaucratic and managerial state, whose functions, powers and personnel grew exponentially once India embarked upon its strategy of planned economic development. By the 1980s, the bureaucrats manning the public sector were far more powerful than their counterparts in the large private business houses. They presided over the 'commanding heights' of the economy in the organized industrial sector, and administered a formidable regulatory apparatus for the licensing and expansion of private enterprises, import and export of capital goods, allocation of foreign exchange, and clearances to raise capital from the public. Between 1969 and 1973 alone, their powers were expanded by nationalization of banks, general insurance, and the coal mining industry; the Monopolies and Restrictive Trade Practices Act (MRTP) devised to limit investment by the larger industrial houses to the heavy investment core sector, and the Foreign Exchange Act (FERA), restricting the role of foreign capital in Indian industry.

The bureaucracy's commanding presence was not confined to the organized industrial sector. The Planning Commission, established as an expert advisory body in 1950, enlarged its control over planning in the states through authoritative recommendations for 'discretionary' transfer of funds by the Centre for plan grants. By the 1970s, the power to legislate on economic and social planning, shared by the Centre and the States, was used by the Centre to introduce a plethora of centrally sponsored schemes in the rural areas across regions. These were administered at the district level by the Collector or Deputy Development Commissioner of the IAS. Education was also added to the powers on the Union List.

The bureaucracy's power grew in government affairs from the mid-1960s, reaching its apogee during the 1975-7 period of National Emergency. Even in normal times, the establishment of the Prime Minister's secretariat and its steady growth over successive decades into a set of offices parallel to the key Ministers, staffed by expert advisors and senior civil servants, extended bureaucratic reach into the policy-making process through direct access to the Prime Minister which bypassed the Cabinet on major questions of economic measures and foreign affairs.

The full panoply of the Indian state's power appears even more formidable once the steady expansion in its coercive institutions from the mid-1960s is taken into account. By the 1980s, the civil police forces officered by the elite Central cadre of the Indian Police Service numbered about 750,000; the Provincial (state) Armed Constabularies accounted for about 400,000; the proliferating paramilitary units under the control of central government ministries made up another 350,000–600,000, and the standing Army reached one million.

Nevertheless, for analytical purposes, it is important to preserve a distinction between the public institutions of the Indian state which represent a major continuity with British rule, and the political institutions of parliamentary democracy and division of powers that were fully elaborated only after Independence in the 1950 Constitution. The analytical advantages of maintaining this distinction become clear once questions are raised about the basis of political legitimacy, the dual foci of sovereignty involved in the separation of powers between the Union (Centre) and the states, and the autonomy of the Indian state from important social groups contending for control over the decision-making process.

First, it is quite apparent that the political legitimacy of the Indian state did not flow from those powerful public institutions which had their origins as instruments of colonial rule. Rather, it derived from the principle of popular sovereignty upon which the 1950 Constitution established the political institutions of parliamentary government. The Constitution was said to be given by the people to themselves, and despite assaults mounted on it in the interim, the position remained that the basic structure could not be changed except by another Constituent Assembly....

THE POLITICAL INSTITUTIONS OF THE INDIAN STATE

The political institutions of the Indian state were initially a gift to the masses by an elite political class of predominately Hindu men of the twice-born *varnas*, heavily weighted toward urban, English-educated Brahmans who shared a secular outlook. This gift from above represented in significant degree the political values of intellectuals who perceived the parliamentary system as the most highly developed form of modern politics. It provided to the weaker sections of the population in the principle of one person, one vote, their single greatest gain from Independence.

The consensus hammered out in the Constituent Assembly reflected other calculations of political realism. The very fact that after Independence India continued to be a patchwork of diverse regional, religious, caste and tribal groups argued for an accommodative approach to building coalitions capable of ensuring national integration. At the same time, the new political institutions, to be acceptable by entrenched elites across diverse regions, had to be constituted in a form that presented little immediate danger to the socio-cultural foundations of dominance. This was accomplished in two main ways: first, legislative institutions were embedded within a division of Union and State subjects that reserved powers for the states on most matters affecting the governance of the vast rural population, including agriculture, land tenures, and local government; and second, parliamentary government was conjoined to guaranteed Fundamental Rights, originally including property. Except under extraordinary conditions of a breakdown in the constitutional machinery of a particular state and a Proclamation of Emergency permitting President's Rule through the state Governors, the writ of the IAS did not run beyond the subjects on the Union or the Concurrent Lists. Under all circumstances, officers of the national administrative and police services did not occupy any position below the level of district administration.

The ruling Congress party, moreover, adopted a conciliatory approach to the privileged communities and classes that virtually ruled out any direct attempt to organize the lower castes and poorer classes for political action. As the movement credited with winning Independence for India, Congress continued to portray itself as the only secular party with a national constituency representing the interests of all social groups, including the poor and the minorities.

The party thereby retained its identity with Gandhi, and through him with 'Indian culture', subsequently transmuted into the accommodative politics of the 'Congress culture'. The poor were encouraged to look less to an individual, but more to the state, for improvement in their condition. The Constitution, the Parliament and the Congress party all made symbolic commitments to provide for the educational, social and economic advance of the poorest sections under the socialistic pattern of society.

During the Nehru years — the period in which the foundations of India's modern industrial economy were built — the Centre was greatly limited in what it could accomplish by way of institutional changes to help the poor in the vast rural sector. The Prime Minister and the score or so of committed officials appointed by him to the advisory Planning Commission enjoyed mainly the authority to set down general principles of policy. Powers of implementation rested with the state legislatures. The leaders of these state governments, although virtually all Congressmen until 1967, either belonged to or depended upon locally dominant landholding castes to mobilize the rural vote and win state and national elections. The names of these castes and even their ritual status — whether twice-born or *sat*-Shudra — varied from region to region, as did the configuration of the coalitions they put together, but the pattern was similar enough to make it recognizable as the one-party-dominant 'Congress system'. Within this system, the range of social groups represented in the ruling party was considered its most positive feature, making it possible for opposition parties to influence government policies by forging links with like-minded Congress factions. This whole process was represented as an example of restraint by the ruling party, which took the opposition seriously, and of the responsibility of the opposition parties, which functioned according to the norms of a loyal opposition. Along with these norms were associated practices of intra-party democracy; socially rooted party and political leaders at the state and district level, and honest and efficient administration.

Like all ideal types, this schematic picture of consensual politics under the one party dominant system abstracts from a much more complex reality, one which included very low levels of political awareness among the lower castes and poorer classes. It is, in fact, arguable that politics in the Nehru period as a whole is best understood as a continuum with the Raj. Whatever social configurations the Congress party confronted at the various states, its leader, like the British before them, did not attempt to change the social order but to adapt to it....

THE STRUGGLE FOR POLITICAL AND STATE POWER: RISE OF THE BACKWARD CLASSES

The politics of elite accommodation identified with the 'Congress culture' did not disappear all at once. At the states, where the level of political awareness remained relatively low, particularly in the former princely states like Rajasthan, or in backward areas like Orissa, or in Maharashtra with its unique pattern of social incorporation by the Marathas of the Kunbi peasantry, the model of elite pluralism prevailed into the 1980s. In a larger number of states, where politicization of the disadvantaged lower castes and poorer classes was further advanced, the competition for political and state power was carried out by social groups banded together into Backward Classes and Forward Castes in contours first shaped under the British Raj....

The political mobilization of the Backward Classes, whether pursued by regional or national political parties, rested on appeals to caste sentiments among cognate groups that cut across class differences to maintain the segmentation of the poor around distinctive social, ethnic and religious categories. The political divisiveness of this approach was least serious in the states of south India where the Forward Castes had themselves emerged from the landowning Shudra peasantry, and where backward Hindus demanded a share in the privileges of dominant groups without seeking to displace them. In Tamil Nadu, the sub-national Tamil cultural identity was associated with a community ideology that measured castes Hindu privileges mainly against the unprivilege of Scheduled Castes. Rising levels of reservations to 68 per cent of places (including 15 per cent for Scheduled Castes), and introduction of an additional category of 'most backward' by the late 1980s did little to disrupt the politics of accommodation. On the one hand, the DMKs provided significant new opportunities of social mobility for individuals from the lower castes, particularly in urban areas, who found employment in white collar jobs. On the other, the ruling parties quietly made more places for Brahmans and other upper castes excluded in the highly competitive 'merit' recruitment to government educational institutions, through the device of permitting privately founded engineering and medical colleges (sustained by high capitation fees) to affiliate with the degree granting state universities. These policies, in combination with the munificent social welfare programmes adopted by the state government stabilized popular support, without threatening the economic interests of the landed upper castes or business classes, who supported the DMKs while remaining outside formal political office....

On the whole, in south India, reservations for Backward Classes combined with high expenditures on social welfare programmes, sustained the politics of accommodation by enabling some small proportion of the disadvantaged castes to join the urban middle classes and find places in the political and public institutions for the state. By contrast, such policies in other regions, more rigidly structured around *varna* divisions, produced violent confrontations between Backward Classes and Forward Castes that made the institutions of the state into arenas of conflict and rendered them ineffective in defusing caste and class confrontation.

A complex example...was provided by Gujarat where the Patidars made an independent bid for political power by deserting the Congress in the 1975 election for the United Front (a forerunner of Janata). The Congress strategy of constructing the KHAM alliance of disadvantaged social groups (Koli-Kshatriya, Harijans, adivasis and Muslims), returned it to power in 1980. Yet, the attempt to shift the social base of political power from the Vanias, Brahmans and Patidars to the Kolis was resisted by the upper castes who felt superior in *varna* terms to these groups and also controlled much greater resources.

...By the early 1980s, the Vanias and Brahmans, worried about increasing levels of educated unemployment, already blamed their difficulties on implementation of the 21 per cent reservation for the Scheduled Castes and Scheduled Tribes. The Patidars, moreover, who claimed Kshatriya rank, were only roughly on par with the Scheduled Castes and artisan castes in college education. They did not benefit from the Janata state government's policy, in 1978, of providing 10 per cent reservations for the Socially and Educationally Backward Classes (SEBC). Resentment of the upper castes against all reservations had spilled over into violence against the Scheduled Castes during three months of sporadic rioting in 1981. Against this background, the decision of the state government, in 1985, to raise the quota for the SEBC to 28 per cent resulted in uncontrollable agitations, strikes and violence by high and middle caste students, government employees, doctors and the police, leaving only the Indian Army to restore order, and that after the higher quota was withdrawn. These events not only polarized Gujarat's society between the upper and lower castes, but perhaps more dangerous for social cohesion in larger areas of the country, led to communal riots between Hindus and Muslims.

In Bihar and Uttar Pradesh, the Backward Classes emerged as an important political force from the 1960s, in opposition to the Congress party, initially identifying with the Socialists, and then with Charan Singh's various coalition parties. In these states, the struggle was waged between more evenly balanced numbers, across *varna* lines of Shudra and twice-born, and for the purpose of replacing the upper castes as political leaders in the state legislatures, and, through reservations, diluting their virtual monopoly over senior posts in the state services. The confrontation also included a class dimension. Leaders of the Backward Classes attempted to expand their social base among the prosperous rich and middle peasantry by appealing to the poor peasantry's common resentment of the upper castes, who did not soil their hands with the menial tasks of cultivation historically assigned to the lower orders. An aggravating factor in both industrially backward states was that the towns offered few economic opportunities for the educated sections of the upper castes, except those in the enlarged civil services. Similarly, entry into these positions was perceived by the Backward Classes as the only avenue for overcoming the caste disabilities that prevented them from achieving equal dignity and power in society. The multiple strands of this conflict, which involved issues of ideology, status, class and power all at once, pulled against the whole fabric of the social order.

The first attempt by the short-lived Janata government, in 1978, to enforce a reservations policy in Bihar of 25 per cent for the Other Backward Classes triggered large-scale street fighting and polarized Backwards and Forwards in towns and villages throughout the state. The Forwards regained the upper hand after Janata split into the Lok Dal and the Bharatiya Janata Party, facilitating the Congress (I)'s return to national and state power in 1980. Nevertheless, the struggle continued unabated. The law and order machinery of the state appeared paralysed as political workers on both sides acquired weapons and sought the help of criminals in booth-capturing at election time. Although caste and community remained the primary identity for all groups, the Backwards began to forge alliances with poor peasants among the Rajputs, Scheduled Castes and Muslims. This coalition threw its support behind the Janata Dal (a combine of disillusioned ex-Congressmen, socialists and the Lok Dal who had earlier supported Janata), which ousted the Congress (I) at the national level in 1989, and displaced Congress (I) as the single largest party in Bihar in 1990.

Political developments in Uttar Pradesh during the same period, between 1977 and 1989, revealed some similar features. The Janata government's more modest reservation policy of 15 per cent for the Other Backward Classes had met with riots in the eastern districts. Subsequently, during the long interregnum of Congress (I) rule, the Backward Classes were outflanked by a Brahman and Thakur alignment with the Scheduled Castes. Nevertheless, the MAJGAR alliance (Muslims, Ahira, Jats, Gujars, Rajputs and other backward castes) pieced together by the Janata Dal in 1989 held together well enough to break up the Congress traditional vote bank, and to cost it control over both the Centre and the state government. Equally striking, the Janata Dal's victory was achieved with the electoral co-operation of the Bahujan Samaj, the first party led by a member of the Scheduled Castes to mobilize large numbers of these communities and the most backward castes on an anti-Brahman and anti-caste platform in the Aryan heartland.

Toward Restructuring of Dominance and State Power Relations

The victory of the Janata Dal under V.P. Singh at the Centre in 1989, and at several states in 1989 and 1990, indicated further the disintegration in north India of long established patterns of vertical mobilization, and placed in relief the outline for a new basis of horizontal co-operation of the disadvantaged social groups. Nevertheless, the coalition which defeated the Congress (I) had a contingent configuration formed out of shared ambitions and special antipathies.

The core of its support in north India came from an alignment between Rajputs (Thakurs) and the more prosperous sections of the Backward Classes, especially Yadavs, Jats, Kurmis and other middle castes. The co-operation between *thakurs* and the Backward Classes was itself a new social phenomenon in an area where memories were fresh of oppression by Thakur *zamindars* and *jagirdars* of Yadavs, Jats and other cultivating castes.

Beyond this, the support of Muslims, which was crucial to the Janata Dal victory, had represented an emotional repudiation of the Congress (I)'s Prime Minister Rajiv Gandhi. His transparent attempt to manipulate religious sentiments of both Hindus and Muslims by an ill-conceived election strategy for placating both sides in the long-standing dispute for control of the site in Ayodhya (Uttar Pradesh) of the Babri Mosque, believed by orthodox Hindus to be the birthplace of Ram (Ram *janmabhoomi*) alienated Muslims, and many Hindus alike, from Congress(I). Beyond this, the largest section of the Scheduled Castes and the smaller backward castes supporting the Bahujan Samaj, also turned away from Congress(I) to assert their antipathy to upper caste control whether of the secular leadership of the Congress(I) or the Hindu nationalist Bharatiya Janata Party (BJP).

The future of this alignment in 1990 was uncertain. The Backward Classes and *kisans* had supported the Janata Dal, as they had the Janata and the Lok Dal in earlier elections, perceiving it to be their own political vehicle for rising to power not only at the states but at the Centre. They placed the highest importance on promises of the party leadership to meet their social as well as economic demands as a new agrarian middle class, which had a dual origin in the low castes and cultivating peasantry. Among these promises were commitments by the national leadership to implement the recommendation of the (B.P. Mandal) Backward Classes Commission, first made in 1980, to provide 27 per cent reservations for the Backward Classes in the all-India services of the IAS and IPS. Above and beyond this, the Janata Dal promised to redirect plan priorities from the industrial to the rural sector, allocating more than 50 per cent of expenditure to agriculture, and waiving repayment of bank loans to agriculturists.

The outlook was also clouded by the minority position of the Janata Dal government, which was dependent on support in the Lok Sabha of ideologically opposed parties, the CPI(M) and the

CPI on one side, and the BJP on the other. Even as the Backward Classes savoured their first taste of political power at the Centre, their ability to establish an enduring social combination to displace the upper castes, remained in question. Day to day conflicts between the more affluent cultivating peasantry and landless labourers over both caste discrimination and economic rights, reflecting persistent caste and class divisions between Backward Classes and the Scheduled Castes, left the continuing support of the Bahujan Samaj for the Janata Dal uncertain. At the same time, the BJP's appeal to the 'Hindu identity' as an overarching basis of mobilization met with unexpected response in the states of Gujarat, Madhya Pradesh and Rajasthan.

The renewed salience of religion in politics in 1989 and 1990 brought the BJP to power in Madhya Pradesh and Himachal, and expanded its role in Rajasthan and Gujarat as a partner of the Janata Dal. It revealed yet again the almost inexhaustible possibilities in the Indian context for exploiting social and religious identities to divide and split the poor. This resurgence of religious sentiment,...first came into sharp focus in Punjab, as the Congress(I) secretly manipulated divisions between moderate and fundamentalist Sikhs as a means of defeating the Akali Dal. The same tactic was subtly employed by the Congress(I) in the 1984 national elections which appealed to anti-Sikh sentiments to buttress support from Hindu voters in northern and central India. Such subliminal religious appeals by the Congress(I) created a favourable climate for the better organized BJP, in an electoral alliance with the Janata Dal, to displace Congress(I) in several areas. This new climate was further charged by the rise of the Jammu and Kashmir Liberation Front which mounted a secessionist movement on the heels of the terrorist movement in Punjab, arousing renewed debate about the meaning of secularism under Indian conditions.

Although India's major political parties contrived to mobilize the poor on the basis of community rather than class, this did not mean that economic differentiation was unimportant in understanding the relationship between dominance and state power in the late 1980s.... Except in West Bengal and Kerala, the unorganized majority of the poor peasantry, agricultural labourers, artisanal classes and workers in the informal sector (including the forty per cent or so officially estimated to be living below the poverty line) were placed in the position of. dependents relative to the managerial state. Over the last twenty years, their situation has been ameliorated by financial resources provided through the central government to the districts for social welfare schemes administered by the bureaucracy; and by growing amounts of carefully monitored funds made available by foreign agencies to support activists working in grassroots voluntary groups. In areas where the numbers of agricultural labourers grew to a critical mass of relatively homogenous Scheduled Castes, such ameliorative measures...proved inadequate to prevent the outbreak of armed struggle. Over extensive areas of Bihar and Andhra Pradesh Naxalite peasant movements were treated as law and order problems to be repressed by police and para-military forces.

By contrast, the expanding urban middle classes, composed of the English educated upper and Forward castes, with infusions of individuals from backward communities benefited by reservations, constituted the core of the economically dominant classes in society. During 1984–9, when Prime Minister Rajiv Gandhi stepped up the pace of internal economic liberalization, the incorporation, expansion, growth and profits of private manufacturing companies, especially in TVs, telephones, scooters and electronic goods reached record levels. In the large cities, money (whatever its sources) and high official position (which made it easier to acquire wealth) began to override ritual rank, including in some cases 'untouchability' as the basis of social status. An estimated 40 millions enjoyed a standard of living comparable to their middle class counterparts in advanced industrial economies, and another 60 millions were on the threshold of comfortable middle class life. The urban middle classes, virtually cut off from the villages in the vast rural hinterlands, exercised influence primarily outside the electoral process, through their personal links to the senior bureaucrats in the IAS, the national technocracy inside and outside of government (constituted by graduates of the Indian Institutes of Technology (IITs), Indian Institutes of Management (IIMs) and universities abroad), and the executive officers of private corporations.

As India entered the 1990s, a discernible separation was taking shape between economic power and political power. In West Bengal...the propertied classes, whether village level *Jotedars* or Marwari capitalists in Calcutta, were generally excluded from governance, which was exercised by the disciplined CPI(M) allied with the lower and middle classes. In other states, and at the Centre, despite the lack of such effective political organization, the lower and middle classes of the backward castes were gaining ground in elected political institutions including state legislatures and the Lok Sabha. Still divided by region, community and caste, politicians from the Backward Classes and *kisans* were groping their way to the creation of a national farmers' class.

The decline of a homogeneous elite, rooted in status hierarchies erected upon devalued notions of purity and pollution, is likely to place even greater importance on access to the huge resources of the managerial state as a basis of rank and privilege in society. The battle for ascendance between the city and countryside, industry and agriculture, bureaucrats and politicians, the urban middle classes and peasantry, landowners and agricultural labourers, industrialists and workers, Forward Castes and Backward Classes, and even advocates of a Hindu state and those of a secular state, are all aspects of the social turmoil accompanying the collapse of the Brahmanical system as a source of legitimacy for the unequal social order. The downtrodden — Dalits, minorities and women — have begun to raise the question of which social forces are responsible for the persistence of grinding poverty. They have started to understand the benefits of organization in extracting from political parties tangible gains in return for their support.

The Indian political system may be reformed by adjusting relations between the Centre and the states to permit greater decentralization, but in themselves such changes cannot suffice to provide a new basis of legitimacy for the political community as a whole. Politicians in the states may still try to deflect attention from economic issues by blaming New Delhi for the niggardly flow of resources. The upper castes may blame reservations for educated unemployment. Muslims may be accused of extra-national loyalties sapping the strength of the Hindu nation. However, such tactics may be increasingly suspect by large sections of the unprivileged and become more and more costly to national cohesion.

Social change since the time of the Raj has been initiated by the political process which in 1989 empowered almost one-half billion people to vote. Now that they know how to use it, there is little reason to think that this process has run its course.

Crisis of Governability

ATUL KOHLI

Sooner or later all developing countries become difficult to govern and over the past two decades India has been moving in that direction. This trend contrasts with the situation during the 1950s and 1960s, when India was widely regarded as one of the few stable democracies in the non-Western world.

India is still, of course, a functioning democracy, but increasingly it is not well governed. The evidence of eroding political order is everywhere. Personal rule has replaced party rule at all levels — national, state, and district. Below the rulers, the entrenched civil and police services have been politicized. Various social groups have pressed new and ever more diverse political demands in demonstrations that often have led to violence. The omnipresent but feeble state, in turn, has vacillated; its responses have varied over a wide range: indifference, sporadic concessions, and repression. Such vacillation has fueled further opposition. The ineffectiveness of repression, moreover, has highlighted the breakdown of the civil machinery intended to enforce the law and maintain order. In order to protect themselves, citizens in some parts of the country have begun organizing private armies. The growing political violence has periodically brought the armed forces into India's political arena, whereas the armed forces once were considered apolitical.

Excerpted from Atul Kohli, *Democracy and Discontent*, Cambridge University Press, 1990, 3-32.

384 Atul Kohli

....Was this outcome inevitable? India had long been considered something of a political exception.... What happened? What went wrong?....

India's Problem of Governability

....The political arrangements in the early phase [of the post-independence era] were clearly dominated by an educated, nationalist elite. The business class was also politically influential, and the landed and caste elites were slowly brought into the ruling coalition. The new rulers enjoyed widely perceived legitimacy, in part because of the nationalist legacy and in part because the traditional patterns of authority in society, such as the caste structure in the villages, were still largely intact. The dominant political elites, moreover, practised a reconciliatory approach toward the competing elites, while professing the hope that they would be able to bring the poor and the oppressed masses into the mainstream of India's modernizing political economy. The legitimacy formula that the Congress Party had designed was clearly expressed in its proposed strategy for economic development: a marriage between nationalism and democratic socialism. The party's five-year plans accordingly stressed a mixed economy model of development that sought economic growth, self-sufficiency, and a modicum of wealth redistribution.

These were euphoric times in India, as new beginnings often are. Although many difficult problems confronted the new government, both leaders and followers had considerable confidence in the state's capacity to deal with these problems. The Indian state sought to guide development while standing above the society; it also simultaneously expressed the preferences of important social groups and thus was widely deemed legitimate. Over the past two decades, however, or since about 1967, much has changed. Most important, the state's capacity to govern (i.e., the capacity simultaneously to promote development and to accommodate diverse interests) has declined. Along with this decline, order and authority have been eroding. Since the mid-sixties the surface manifestation of this process has been widespread activism outside of the established political channels that often has led to violence, a problem compounded by the state's growing incapacity to deal with the pressing problems of law and order, corruption, and poverty. Below the surface lies an important cause of these political problems: disintegration of India's major political institutions, especially the decline of its premier political entity, the Congress Party....

....Below the established state elites, the vertical patterns of fealty in India's civil society have been eroding. Members of higher castes and other 'big men' have gradually lost their capacity to influence the political behavior of those below them in the socio-economic hierarchy. As a result, new social groups have entered the political arena and pressed new demands upon the state. Without a dominant party and other conflict-resolving institutions, democratic accommodation of such demands has been difficult. Without established law-and-order institutions, moreover, the agitation and violence that have resulted from these demands have been difficult to control. The result has been a dramatic increase in political violence in India. The state has had to increase its reliance on military and paramilitary forces. Thus, the current political situation features an outpouring of diverse new social demands, ad hoc and vacillating responses by the state, and a growing sense that order and authority — and perhaps even democracy — may be disintegrating in India....

The qualitative difference between political turmoil today and unstable rule in the past suggests that the political problems of today are, at least in part, the results of the 'developmental successes' of the past few decades. India's Congress Party was the midwife for the new nation-state. Having performed that crucial role, the party has now withered away. Other institutions came into being during that same time period: a functioning national market, national transportation and communication networks, an emerging but relatively strong indigenous capitalism, and moderately cohesive armed forces. These are the key rudiments of a nation-state that should ensure the existence of India as a viable political unit. Along with these developments, however, came another set of changes: an increased division of labour, the spread of commerce, and diffusion of both national and democratic values. These changes have reduced the isolation of one local community from another. Moreover, because the state has been heavily involved in all of these changes, the growing ineffectiveness of the state is likely to have wide repercussions.

The breakdown of political order in contemporary India puts

into question the future capacity of the Indian state to govern. The crucial questions related to the issue of eroding authority are these: How will India be ruled in the future — as a democracy, or by other means? If as a democracy, what type of democracy? Who within the state — which individuals, parties, and socio-economic groups — will exercise power? And finally, how effective is the state likely to be in solving India's pressing problems? The issue of governability in the contemporary context thus concerns the state's capacity simultaneously to accommodate disparate interests and promote development....

The irony of India's politico-economic situation is tragic: the state is highly centralized and omnipresent, but the leverage of its leaders to initiate meaningful change has diminished. The main reason for this development is that authority has seldom run deep, and the authority structures have in recent years fallen into disrepair. As a result, state authorities have little ability to persuade the people to support government initiatives — to build consensus. Coercion as a strategy of policy implementation is not in the cards, at least not at this time. Thus, major initiatives often face a dead end. It has become a vicious cycle: weakness in the authority structures makes it difficult to solve precisely those problems whose solutions could strengthen authority. The bulk of political energy is spent fighting one bushfire after another, guided by the central concern of how to hang on to power.

The roots of the decay in the national authority structures are to be found in a dilemma that consistently plagued Indira Gandhi: how to maintain her hold on power while either fending off or accommodating the growing demands of power blocs in the polity. Democratic incorporation of such diverse new demands often would have meant a downward transfer of power. Indira Gandhi perceived — not without some justification — that such moves would weaken the Centre and thus both national integrity and the state's capacity to steer economic development. As a consequence, she adopted a recalcitrant stance. Instead of accommodating power challengers, which might not have been easy in any case, she sought to block their access to power by undermining democratic institutions. Cancellations of elections within the Congress Party, appointment of loyal but weak chief ministers in the states, and personalization of general elections were all part of this ruling strategy.

The paradox is that the very strategy that enabled Indira Gandhi to hold on to power also undermined the possibility of using that power for constructive ends. Having reduced the significance of important institutions, she found that when she (and, later, her successor, Rajiv Gandhi) needed institutional support to implement desired goals, such support was not available. Personal control over a highly interventionist state has been maintained, but the interventionist arm of that state has gone limp; the trends towards centralization and powerlessness have run in tandem.

....During the first two decades after Independence, democratic institutions were introduced into India. With the advantage of hindsight, some have questioned the solidity of those early foundations. The view adopted here is rather that the beginnings of democracy were well founded and held out considerable promise. Over the past two decades, however, India's institutional capacity to deal with conflict and initiate solutions to pressing problems has declined. The issue now is, what factors can help explain this 'dependent variable', namely, the declining capacity to govern?

At a proximate level of causation, four interrelated factors can be identified as independent variables in the empirical analysis: the changing role of the political elite, weak and ineffective political organizations, mobilization of previously passive groups for electoral competition, and growing conflict between contending social groups, including the conflict between the haves and the have-nots. How each of these conditions can influence the problems of governability can now be briefly summarized.

As democratic factionalism and other types of power conflicts have multiplied within India, the leaders often have found their hold on power fiercely challenged. Many of them, including Indira and Rajiv Gandhi, characteristically have reacted in ways that have tended to preserve their power. One important method for preserving power has been populism: to establish direct contact between the leader and the masses and to undermine those impersonal rules and institutions designed to facilitate orderly challenges. Making direct promises that will affect as large a segment of the population as possible can enable a leader to mobilize broad electoral support. The destruction of institutional constraints will leave more matters to the leader's personal discretion, enabling the leader to promote those who are loyal, while shunting aside anyone who is a potential challenger with an independent political base.

This process has undermined the possibility of establishing a system of impersonal authority based on the procedural rationality of democracy. As traditional sources of authority have declined and the development of rational, legal bases of authority has been thwarted, personal rule has come to prevail. Personalization of power can, of course, be either a cause or a consequence of weak institutional rule. What is clear in the case of India over the last two decades is that, on balance, the nation's powerful leaders — especially Indira and Rajiv Gandhi, but also important regional leaders like M.G. Ramachandran and N.T. Rama Rao — have worked more to increase their personal power than to strengthen governmental institutions....

In addition to the detrimental role of its leaders, India's economic scarcities and heterogeneous social structure have made it difficult to strengthen political organizations. Whatever the causative factors...weak political organizations have also contributed significantly to the growing problems of governability. Weak political parties, for example, have ceased functioning as arenas for accommodation and resolution of conflict. In a social situation where most traditional modes of resolving conflicts are eroding and the political system allows, even encourages, association for the pursuit of group interests, which can lead to conflict, an absence of strong political parties leaves a serious authority vacuum. Unresolved conflicts often are fought out on the streets. Ineffectiveness of other institutions, such as the police force, further contributes to growing civil disorder. That is why the Indian state in recent years has increasingly resorted to its last line of defense — the armed forces.

Electoral competition has mobilized many formerly passive socio-economic groups and brought them into the political arena. On balance, this is a desirable outcome in a democracy. But given the state's limited capacities for redistribution of wealth and the intensity with which electoral support has been courted, these mobilized and dissatisfied groups have further contributed to the growing political turmoil. A major example of this phenomenon is the growing caste conflict between the 'backward' and the 'forward' castes. Leaders in state after state have utilized 'reservations' — the Indian version of affirmative action — as means to gain the electoral support of numerically significant backward castes. Higher castes, feeling that their interests are threatened, have resisted these moves. Once set in motion, however, those who have been mobilized have been difficult to satisfy or control. Conflict has often been the result.

A similar pattern has unfolded as competing elites have sought to mobilize ethnic groups who share language, religion, or race. The groups vary: the Maharashtrians in Belgaum; the Sikhs in Punjab; Hindu versus Moslems in various parts of the country; the Gurkhas in West Bengal. These mobilizations follow identifiable patterns. Leaders manipulate primordial attachments so as to gain access to the state. If they are accommodated, the conflict often recedes. Accommodation, however, is not always possible. Moreover, those in positions to make concessions sometimes have not made timely concessions, in order to protect their own political interests. Such recalcitrance has only further encouraged the leaders of ethnic and religious groups to use violence and agitation as means of accomplishing their political goals.

Quite independent of such mobilization aimed at influencing political competition, the general process of economic and social change has shaken people out of their traditional social niches. Changing roles have created a growing awareness of the individual's position in society. Long-established inequalities and beliefs about the legitimacy of these inequalities are thus increasingly under challenge. Members of lower socio-economic classes have begun associating themselves so as to challenge what they perceive to be unjust domination and exploitation. Privileged groups have also begun to counterorganize. Conflicts along traditional cleavages of caste and community have been around for quite some time, but what is new is the changing character and intensity of such conflicts. In states like Bihar, for example, one barely has to scratch the surface to discover that such group conflicts — often fought out by private armies — increasingly involve economic issues. Traditional conflict is thus evolving into new types of conflicts, and increasingly the theme is class conflict.

These four related variables — the changing role of the political elite, weak political organizations, the mobilization of new groups for electoral reasons, and growing social unrest, including class conflict — direct attention to the interactions between the state and social forces that help explain India's growing problems of governability. These variables are treated here as independent variables only insofar as one is not fully reducible to another. It will be clear to readers that these variables are fairly proximate to the phenomena being explained. Moreover, they 'feed into' each other in cause-and-effect relationships. In order to avoid circular reasoning, therefore, one must carefully analyse how, over time, they influence one another and how they affect the dependent variable of interest: India's growing problems of governability.

The overall picture of political change in India that these four variables help delineate is one in which ruling institutions have weakened and power challenges have multiplied. If we 'collapse' these four causal variables into broader analytical categories and move one step farther to a 'deeper' level of causation, it is eminently clear that in the general explanation developed here, political variables play roles as significant as those of socio-economic forces, if not more significant. Both the dislocative impact of economic development and growing class conflict have contributed to India's problems of governability. Neither of these socio-economic variables, however, has been decisive. The forces that also have been significant are best thought of collectively as political forces: the roles of leaders, the impact of weak political institutions, and, most important, mobilization of new groups for purposes of winning power and securing access to the state's resources. None of these political forces is fully reducible to explanation by the underlying socio-economic conditions. The explanation of the state's declining capacity to govern developed here is thus distinguished from both 'developmental' and 'Marxist' positions. While taking those positions into account, the explanation proposed here emphasizes the 'autonomous' significance of political structures and processes.

Numerous nuances and details of how political variables contribute to problems of governability will emerge in due course. So will the distinctive normative implications of this state-society focus. Suffice it to note at the outset that the additional emphasis on 'political causes' of 'political change' in a case like that of India should not be surprising. Only a part of this emphasis results from an analytical recasting of the available evidence. For the rest, the empirical materials are simply distinctive. In comparison with earlier historical cases of western European 'modernization', from which both developmental and Marxist arguments originate, the role of the state looms much larger in India's development. Thus, the significance of political forces often can be traced back to this dominant role of the state in socio-economic change.

In a situation like that of India, the state not only is the agent of political order but also is responsible for socio-economic development. India's highly interventionist state controls many of the 'free-floating' economic resources in a very poor society. Access to the power of the state is bitterly contested, not only for the political ends of exercising power and influencing policy but also as a source of livelihood and rapid upward mobility. The struggle for state power in these circumstances becomes simultaneously a struggle to influence people's life-chances. Thus, the conventional distinctions between the state and the market, or between the public and private spheres of activity, are not clear-cut in the case of India.

Moreover, because the state has been organized as an electoral democracy for nearly...[five] decades, the belief that the state is controllable has spread wide and deep. Competing political elites are willing to utilize any sets of appealing symbols and available means — including violent means — for political mobilization aimed at bolstering their electoral chances. Even before the arrival of democracy, the character of premodern Indian society had been highly fragmented, and an interventionist democratic state has facilitated rapid political mobilization of various castes, classes, and religious and language groups. Add to this the roles of powerful economic actors such as business groups and the landowning peasantry, who depend heavily on state resources and thus wish to block access by others, and a picture emerges of a state that is both centralized and interventionist but that finds it increasingly difficult to accommodate conflicting demands and thus to govern.

One unsettling conclusion of this study is that India's democracy has itself contributed to overpoliticization of the Indian polity. The prescription that follows this argument, however, definitely is not that democracy should be curtailed in India. This study is primarily analytical, aimed at exploring the causes of India's increasing political turmoil. To the extent that it has any clear normative and prescriptive implications, they are...fairly general: strengthening party organizations and bringing the state's capacities in line with its commitments are two crucial long-term actions needed for improving the quality of India's democratic government.

What aspects of India's political structure have made that country increasingly difficult to govern? The 'deeper structures' are often in the background in a process-oriented analysis. Without reference to them, however, important questions remain unanswered. Why should the Indian state attract so much attention from social groups? What enables a leader to play such a profound role in the Indian polity? Why should political mobilization result not in new organized political initiatives but in chaos? It is now important to move one level of causation deeper and focus sharply on the political structures that have conditioned political change in India.

The Indian state is highly interventionist, and whether one approves of this or deplores it, it is an important organizational feature in contemporary India that is not likely to change soon. An interventionist state at low levels of economic development, moreover, is a feature that India shares with many Third World countries, but in contrast with past experiments in capitalist economic development, especially those in the Anglo-American context. Two important political implications at that state-society macro-characteristic have been evident throughout this analysis, but have not always been recognized in the literature.

First, an interventionist state in the early stages of development has difficulty establishing a separation between the public and private spheres in social life. That has many consequences. The most important from the standpoint of a study of governability is that an interventionist state cannot claim that distributive problems are social and not political problems. The coexistence of political equality with considerable economic inequality facilitated the establishment of proto-democracies in parts of nineteenth-century Europe. The interventionist welfare state developed only under resource-abundant, mature capitalism. In an Indian type of situation, however, a highly interventionist state is inherent to the overall design of state-led development. That tends to politicize all forms of societal cleavages — old versus new, social, and economic. Thus, the accumulating distributive claims on the state partly reflect the state's attempt to penetrate and reorganize socio-economic life.

Second, an interventionist developing state typically controls a substantial proportion of a poor economy. Thus, many of the society's free-floating economic resources are controlled by politicians and bureaucrats. Who should have access to those resources? Unlike situations involving the products of private endeavor, the legitimacy of claims on public resources is not easy to establish. Given the scarcities in a poor economy, moreover, the competitive energies of the many individuals and groups seeking economic improvements tend to get focused on the state. Thus, competition over the state's resources often results in intense conflict, contributing to the problems of governability.

Another major characteristic of India's political structure is India's democracy. On balance, periodic elections and the existence of basic civil liberties are among India's most prized political possessions. Certain specific features of Indian democracy, however, have also contributed to India's growing problems of governability. India's democracy has been democracy from above. For most of its existence, it has been more of a gift from the elite to the masses than something the masses have secured for themselves. There is no doubt that the longer democracy is practiced, the more difficult it becomes for the elite to take away basic democratic rights. Nevertheless, a tremendous concentration of power in the hands of a few leaders is an undeniable feature of India's democracy. Leaders may not be able to turn democracy on and off, but Indira Gandhi came close.

That concentration of power cannot simply be wished away. It is part of the overall design by which the leaders have made democracy a gift to the society. One recurring consequence of that design is that whenever the ruling elite are threatened, further centralization of power is a readily available alternative. Because centralization of power in individuals nearly always emasculates fragile institutions — strong institutions do constrain the power of individuals — there is a built-in incentive in India for leaders to undertake periodic deinstitutionalization. As long as a democracy remains more a gift that a society's leaders give to its people and less an established framework that dwarfs the leaders, only exceptional leaders are likely to resist the tendency to maintain personal power at the expense of institutional development.

An elite-dominated democracy has also structured the patterns of political mobilization. Leaders have mobilized socioeconomic groups more as power resources in intraélite struggles and less to satisfy group aspirations. That pattern of elite-led mobilization is distinguishable from the more conventional concept of social mobilization that supposedly accompanies industrialization, urbanization, literacy, and so forth. Whereas social mobilization is generally produced by economic development and modernization, elite-led mobilization often reflects patterns of intra-elite conflict. Thus, Indira Gandhi discovered India's poor when she was pressed politically by other members of the Congress elite. Devraj Urs and Karpoori Thakur similarly discovered the backward castes when they desperately needed to establish new ruling coalitions. The Akalis began stressing issues of Sikh nationalism only when thrown out of power. The suggestion here is not that such patterns of mobilization are bad or wrong; they are the stuff of democracy. What is wrong here is the disregard for the consequences of such mobilizations....

Finally, the last important characteristic of India's political structure that needs to be noted is the weakness of India's political parties. The organizational viability of Congress has declined. Most other parties have failed to fill the organizational vacuum. Because party organization has been treated as an intermediate variable in this study, both the causes and the consequences of organizational weakness need to be spelled out briefly in general terms.

The diversity of India's social structure naturally militates against the development of cohesive national parties. Because regional parties have not done much better, however, one suspects that factors other than cultural diversity are also at work. One hypothesis that fits the Indian materials is that strong parties — parties with well-developed political identification, programmatic goals, and organization — develop mainly as vehicles for gaining power. Conversely, leaders who acquire power because of personal appeal have little incentive to encourage the development of parties from above; on the contrary, parties as institutions often constrain the individual discretion and personalistic power of charismatic leaders. Thus, well-developed parties often emerge from below rather than from above....

FURTHER READINGS

Although the idea of a crisis is widely used in the literature on Indian politics, the term is rarely closely defined or the theme systematically pursued. Consequently, there is a problem in identifying relevant literature. If state crisis is taken in its widest meaning of political turmoil, most of recent writing on Indian politics is about crisis. If, on the other hand, the idea is taken in a narrower sense, of a particularly intense difficulty of the reproduction of stable political relations, there is very little writing on this question. It is remarkable however that the sense of an imminent crisis of the state seems to have faded in the nineties. There is much greater discussion about the organizing principles on which the state was founded, especially, secularism and federalism, rather than the durability of the state itself. Two authors who address this question in very different ways, Frankel and Kohli, are included in the seclections.

Kothari, Rajni, *State Against Democracy*, Ajanta Publications, Delhi, 1988. Kothari's more recent work, collected in this volume, analyses the processes of state crisis in India from many different angles. It also tries to think about ways in which democracy is being stifled by formal institutions of the state, and what could be done to go beyond the conventional format of democratic politics.

Two works have sought to understand the *social* crisis in India (not a strictly political or state crisis):

Satish Saberwal, *India: The Roots of Crisis*, Oxford University Press, Delhi, 1986.

This short work argues that the crisis of Indian society is mainly due to its inability to develop a set of internally coherent social codes, and to devise rules of impersonal decisions required for an increase in social scale.

Bose, Arun, *India's Social Crisis*, Oxford University Press, Delhi, 1985. This work tries to combine an innovative reading of Marxist analysis with the caste sociology of Louis Dumont to produce an explanation of the social crisis in India.

Several papers have however sought to analyse the nature of the crisis of the state and political institutions. See, for example,

Sheth, D.L., 'Social Basis of Political Crisis', *Seminar*, January 1982.

Nandy, Ashis, 'The State of the State', *Seminar*, January 1982.

Kaviraj, Sudipta, 'The crisis of political institutions in India', *Contributions to Indian Sociology*, no. 2, 1984.

Manor, James, 'Anomie in Indian Politics', *Economic and Political Weekly*, no. 18, 1983.

Mitra, Subrata K., 'Crowds and power: democracy and the crisis of "governability" in India', in Baxi, U., and Parekh, (eds.), *Crisis and Change in Contemporary India*, Sage, Delhi, 1994.

Index